MW00604141

The Facilitator Era

The Facilitator Era

Beyond Pioneer Church Multiplication

TOM STEFFEN

Foreword by Sherwood G. Lingenfelter

WIPF & STOCK · Eugene, Oregon

THE FACILITATOR ERA
Beyond Pioneer Church Multiplication

Copyright © 2011 Tom Steffen. All rights reserved. Except for brief quotations in critical publications or reviews, no part of this book may be reproduced in any manner without prior written permission from the publisher. Write: Permissions, Wipf and Stock Publishers, 199 W. 8th Ave., Suite 3, Eugene, OR 97401.

All references to Scripture have been taken from the HOLY BIBLE, NEW INTERNATIONAL VERSION®. Copyright © 1973, 1978, 1984 Biblica. Used by permission of Zondervan. All rights reserved.
The "NIV" and "New International Version" trademarks are registered in the United States Patent and Trademark Office by Biblica. Use of either trademark requires the permission of Biblica.

Wipf & Stock
An Imprint of Wipf and Stock Publishers
199 W. 8th Ave., Suite 3
Eugene, OR 97401

www.wipfandstock.com

ISBN 13: 978-1-60899-537-0

Manufactured in the U.S.A.

This book is dedicated to our grandchildren—

Jailah,

Aaron,

Eden,

Aleksis,

Khristian,

Tristan,

Jaiden,

Gabriel,

Mateo,

Devan,

and Jackson—

who will have the opportunity

to influence the outcome of the Fourth Era of missions.

Contents

List of Figures

Foreword

I MET TOM STEFFEN in 1986 when he arrived at Biola University, a
veteran of fourteen years as a pioneer church planter among a tribal
group in the northern Philippines. Accepted into the Doctor of Ministry
program, Steffen began to write papers in my classes reflecting his experiences and his commitment to "phase out" church planting. It didn't
take long for me to learn about the disconnect between missionary
training and missionary practice, since he reported that he was one of
the first in his mission to turn the leadership of new churches over to national leaders. After completing his doctoral dissertation in 1990, Steffen
published a revised and expanded work, *Passing the Baton,* in 1993. In
that book, he provides details of his journey as a pioneer church planter,
challenging other church planters to think clearly, plan carefully, and act
intentionally to equip and release national leaders to carry on the ministries of evangelism and church planting. Since that time, Steffen has
continued his research and writing as a scholar and a teacher of church
planting.

Steffen the scholar has the same disciplines as Steffen the pioneer
church planter. He takes seriously what he has learned from others,
"steals" great ideas from those he respects as fellow workers in the journey, and fearlessly steps forward, taking theological and practical risks
that empower leadership in others. As church planter Steffen, he learned
the importance of the chronological teaching of Bible stories as a framework for evangelism and the mobilization of new believers to share the
gospel and plant churches in their national contexts. As Steffen matured
as a scholar, he researched the role of story in broader ministry contexts,
and in his next work, *Reconnecting God's Story to Ministry,* he concludes
that narratives are essential for equipping leaders and followers to develop sound theology and skills for ministry in most, if not all, church
planting contexts.

In this book, Steffen uses story as the medium for analyzing the history and current state of church planting. During a series of nine weekly
conversations, Bill and Bev Beaver, missionaries recently returned from

the Philippines, dialog with Dr. Nobley, a professor of missions, about a wide range of topics on the issues of where church planting has come from and where church planting is going. Using a creative conversational format, Steffen gives us an overview of protestant mission history from 1800 to 2000, reviews the literature on church planting, and then engages the reader in an assessment of the current state of evangelism and church planting in Western evangelical churches. Keying from Ralph Winter, Steffen suggests that the "Fourth Era" of protestant mission began in the year 2000.

For me, the delight and power of this work come through the narrative presentation of "Fourth Era" issues. The first issue Steffen addresses is the question of the role of the church planter, as pioneer or as facilitator. In their conversations, Nobley and the Beavers conclude that the role of facilitator is the critical role for church planting in the twenty-first century. Yet, Nobley argues that the role of the pioneer is not over, even if it is no longer central for cross-cultural church planting. Nobley also explores with the Beavers the role of megachurches and short-term mobilization, the ever-present but unspoken issue of mission and money, and the emergence of a completely new strategy—business as mission—as a key component of multiplication church planting. The conversations conclude with Professor Nobley making the argument that sacred stories and faithstories are crucial pieces for communicating the gospel in any cultural context.

Faithful to this philosophy, Steffen provides sixteen case studies in the book, true stories of both pioneer and facilitation church planters in the twenty-first century. Through the voice of Nobley and through his selection of case studies, Steffen sprinkles his reflections, gained from a decade of research, on the strengths and weaknesses of both pioneer and facilitator church planting, and he draws applications for creative cross-cultural church planting in the twenty-first century.

As is often the case, the former student has become the teacher. It has been my privilege to read this work and to commend it to others. Steffen has given us a story that will help us learn for ourselves how to navigate the challenges of multiplication church planting in the decades ahead.

Sherwood Lingenfelter
Provost and Senior Vice President and Professor of Anthropology
Fuller Theological Seminary 2010

Preface

IN *PASSING THE BATON: Church Planting That Empowers,*[1] I addressed Kingdom-based, holistic, pioneer church planting in cross-cultural contexts, driven by a phase-out oriented exit strategy. While using this text, among others, in courses on cross-cultural pioneer church multiplication at Biola University, I began to notice some not-so-subtle changes taking place from the mid- to late 1990s. More and more students were moving away from the pioneer role to a facilitative role in cross-cultural church planting. While *Passing the Baton* still remains relevant today for numerous parts of the world from both an expatriate and national perspective, a new area of investigation has emerged, begging for fresh research.

In *The Next Christendom,* Philip Jenkins identifies a key reason that twenty-first-century, Western, cross-cultural church planters should move beyond the pioneer role: "Whatever their image in popular culture, Christian missionaries of the colonial era succeeded remarkably."[2] Past decades of intense missionary work still bear fruit today, seemingly reducing the need for further pioneer efforts by Western expatriates, who (like their predecessors) continue to be successful overall. Churches birthed in every country of the world through expatriate efforts continue to mature and multiply on their own. This phenomenal growth led the Evangelical Missiological Society to adopt the theme, "Mission Initiatives from the Majority World Churches," for 2008. Does this mean that there are no longer roles for Western expatriates in cross-cultural church planting? Certainly not!

While some westerners will—and should—continue to enter pioneer church-planting roles in cross-cultural contexts, a growing majority will find other avenues to facilitate existing national church-planting movements in multiple ways. Some will facilitate the selection process of national church planters. Some will become involved in training na-

---

1. Steffen, *Passing the Baton.*
2. Jenkins, *Next Christendom,* 56.

tionals in theology, narrative, Bible translation, English, and missions. Others will facilitate the writing, production, and dissemination of Bible study curricula. Still others will use business as a means to facilitate and sustain church planting. This book will include a variety of case studies from around the world to highlight the multiple possibilities of facilitative ministries that enhance national church-planting movements. The Holy Spirit is very creative, not only for past generations of church planters, but for present generations as well.

The facilitative role in ministry is certainly not new, and God has been setting the stage for this change for some time. On the macro level in the Christian arena, World Evangelical Fellowship has called for cooperative partnerships in evangelism and church planting since the early 50s. The Lausanne movement, with its first major conference in 1974, has echoed this call. On the micro level, Wycliffe Bible Translators have used this role effectively in raising up competent national Bible translators around the globe. Community developers and church-planting strategists have modeled the same. The late Jim Montgomery, founding director of Discipling A Whole Nation (DAWN), advocated that national churches partner together around a local "John Knox" to reach their nation for Christ.[3] Saturation Church Planting (SCP), inspired by Dwight Smith and a host of others, stood upon the shoulders of the DAWN movement. Beginning in Eastern Europe, SCP encouraged churches to partner with others to develop saturated ministry in their own locale, and to strive to provide long-term facilitative team members for their host city, country, or region.

The words of the late Paul Hiebert are instructive regarding the facilitative era which is upon us:

> All missionaries now have a new role as *inbetweeners.* They are bridge-persons, culture brokers, who stand between worlds and help each to understand the other. They stand between the church and unreached people and between churches and missions in different lands. This calls for a new understanding of the psychological, social, and cultural nature of the missionaries of the future. They must truly be *bicultural* or *transcultural* people, living in different worlds but not fully at home in any of them.[4]

---

3. Montgomery further developed this philosophy in 1989 in *DAWN 2000: 7 Million Churches To Go.*

4. Hiebert, *Gospel in Human Contexts,* 120.

The Facilitator Era: Beyond Pioneer Church Multiplication attempts to cast a wider net than the models proposed and practiced by its predecessors, including DAWN, the five-manual Omega course of SCP, or other similar models. It seeks to step back and ask more preliminary and global questions: What is the history of the term *church planting*? Has it lost its meaning over time? Should the term be changed? What are the different types of church planting, and what assumptions drive them? Does the need for facilitators (in contrast to pioneers) raise questions about how successful former church planters really were? How does the profile of a cross-cultural, facilitative church planter differ from that of a cross-cultural, pioneering church planter? What makes a facilitator acceptable in a particular context? Which contexts are ripe for a facilitator-initiated church-planting movement? Should those in the facilitative role partner with (and thereby help perpetuate) legalistic national churches or those using imported church models? How do facilitative church planters assure that the national church movement progresses beyond monocultural church planting? Can a nation reach all the people groups within its borders? Should facilitative church planters have an exit strategy? Can one people group reach all the social strata groups within itself? Should cross-cultural pioneer church planting lead to facilitative church multiplication? How do dependence, independence, and interdependence relate to pioneer and facilitative church multiplication? What new models will the Holy Spirit inspire for facilitative church multiplication in the twenty-first century? Who will fund facilitative ministries?

Who should read *The Facilitator Era: Beyond Pioneer Church Multiplication?* If you feel comfortable with the current church-planting role and model that you are practicing, or if you have never had considerable ups and downs in application of the same, then this book is not for you. But if—deep down below the surface—a desire draws you to go deeper, challenge the familiar, slaughter sacred cows, and advance God's kingdom no matter what the personal or organizational cost, then this book is for you. I have written this book for cross-cultural church planters, trainers, national church planters, and those who support them. Church planters involved in monocultural settings, both in new plants and in training, should also find it instructive.

The Facilitator Era: Beyond Pioneer Church Multiplication will be presented as a story of two short-term missionaries who have just returned to the United States from two intense, yet rewarding, years of church-planting ministry in the Philippines. Should they return long-term in a pioneer church-planting role? Or should they return in another ministry role? Confused by the statement of a close national friend that expatriates should no longer become involved in pioneer church planting in the Philippines, the missionaries set up weekly meetings with a professor to discuss the issue and to explore options.

The British historian E. H. Carr offers a helpful insight: "The past is intelligible to us only in the light of the present; and we can fully understand the present only in the light of the past."[5] After providing the backstory for the young couple, the Beavers ("Meet the Beavers"), the book begins with a look at past key church-planting literature, identifying and categorizing the authors' salient areas of concern, emphases, and implications for twenty-first-century ministry (week 1).

Nothing happens in and of itself. Week 2 considers what is really happening out there that is causing changes. It reviews Ralph Winter's three eras, projects the fourth era, and investigates the pros and cons of dependence, independence, and interdependence. Week 3 tracks the development of the discipline's terminology over time, noting the significance of the changes. Using Acts 1:8 as a guide, it also begins to distinguish the pioneer role from that of the facilitator.

The fourth week differentiates a pioneer church-planter profile from that of a facilitator. Week 5 considers the megachurch's impact on global missions in unleashing the laity, particularly short-termers. Week 6 explores economic considerations related to facilitation, and Week 7 examines the role of narrative in facilitation.

The book then changes direction, first looking at sixteen facilitative church-multiplication case studies from around the world and then, in Week 8, debriefing them.

Week 9 addresses a controversial topic. Why still teach pioneer church planting if facilitation is king? The final week concludes with Bill and Bev Beaver summarizing all that they have *unlearned* through the weekly meetings with the professor, and all the possibilities that they may implement when they return to the Philippines.

---

5. Carr, *What Is History*, 69.

Acknowledgments

WHERE DO I BEGIN in trying to give tribute to all who have helped make this book become a reality? I'll start closest to home and work outwards. Special thanks go to my loving wife and partner, Darla, for allowing me to be married to a another for the past few years—my laptop computer—so that this project could be completed. Please take heart. The long honey-do list is next on the agenda.

Thanks also go to Dr. Douglas Pennoyer, Dean of the Cook School of Intercultural Studies at Biola University. I have deeply appreciated your encouragement over the years—and being kept off those many committees. *Maraming salamat po.*

Without the insightful help of my editor, Elizabeth Childs Drury, this book would not read as well or contain some of the insights that pepper its pages. Thanks, Liz, for your perceptiveness and hours of dedication. I also thank Elizabeth McCall for her hard work in providing a PowerPoint presentation for each of the main chapters of the book. I encourage the reader to take advantage of her stellar work available at https://sites.google.com/a/biola.edu/the-facilitator-era/.

I would also like to express my deep appreciation for all the Western missionaries who served and sacrificed around the globe through the first three eras of missions. They learned cultures and languages, contextualized the gospel, planted churches, and made mistakes, yet they improved the lives of many people in multiple ways, often under harsh conditions.

Last but certainly not least, I would like to extend a special thanks to those who contributed case studies for this book. Your ministries speak for themselves as to service, dedication, failures, lessons learned, and the role changes presently taking place for many westerners participating in global missions. You have been my teachers, and you will help instruct the next generation of pioneer and facilitative Christian workers serving in this fast-changing world.

The Backstory

Meet the Beavers

BILL AND BEV BEAVER have recently returned home to the United States after two intense but rewarding years of ministry in the Philippines. After graduating three years ago from a secular university with business degrees, they felt God leading them to the Philippines to become involved in a church-planting effort south of Manila on the main island of Luzon. Following a battery of tests and numerous interviews, Reach the Philippines through Church Planting (RPCP), an international, non-denominational agency, accepted them for service. With the blessing and financial support of their home church, the young couple headed to the Philippines.

The two-year term of service flew by. The Beavers believed before they left the field that they were prepared to make an intelligent decision about whether they should return long-term. But before making that decision, Bill and Bev need to complete a six-month home assignment.

✳   ✳   ✳

"It's so good to be home again," sighed Bev, "but I do miss all the friends we made. Adita, Jun, Sunny, Felix—"

"And the great food!" interrupted Bill, "*Lumpia, adobo, halo halo—*"

"Stop!" laughed Bev. "You're making me hungry."

Bill and Bev smiled at each other from across the bistro table in the coffee shop. Silently, they drifted into dreamy reflection, peacefully resting their chins in their hands, warmed by the afternoon sunshine streaming through the window, oblivious to the bustle and chatter around them.

"I've been thinking," said Bill.

"Uh, oh," chided Bev. "I've heard those words before."

"No, don't worry. This isn't a new idea," Bill reassured her. "We discussed it in the Philippines many times. Remember when we were learning Philippine culture and studying Tagalog?[1] It seemed like such a difficult language to learn. Remember when I ordered ice cream at a restaurant and we were served spaghetti?"

"Yes," answered Bev, smiling. "And I remember how surprised we were that even though the Filipinos dress a lot like Americans and enjoy the same types of music, they're still very different culturally from Americans. At the movies they always laughed when we didn't, and we laughed when they didn't."

"And they don't drive like Americans, at least most of them," reminisced Bill. "It's the biggest vehicle that dominates; it's the one who hesitates who gets stuck waiting; and it's the one who stops at a stop sign who gets rear-ended. Remember our first taxi ride? I thought we would literally be short-termers!

"Anyway," continued Bill, "getting back to my idea, I think we should try to further our understanding of cross-cultural church planting while we're at home. We learned a lot in the Philippines, but I think there is much that we have not been exposed to. What do you think?"

"We certainly had some great mentors, especially Dave and Donna," replied Bev. "Even though they had no formal studies in church planting, they learned it the hard way—on the job.

"Remember when we asked Filipinos to raise their hands if they wanted to accept Christ?" asked Bev. "And of course they all did. We were so happy with the results and could not wait to tell Dave and Donna of God's great moving in our Bible study. When we did, they graciously informed us that this response will happen almost every time because of the shame factor. Here we were, thinking Filipinos were coming to Christ, but the Filipinos thought they were just being polite to us Americans. Wow! What a disconnect."

"Dave and Donna taught us to be hungry, lifelong learners," added Bill. "'Don't just be critics; be contributors,' they would often say. What mentors!

"Maybe we could attend some seminars or audit some classes while we're home. That's one reason that I think we should study church planting during this six-month period. Another reason has to do with

1. Tagalog is the national language of the Philippines.   .

what our teammate Jun told us shortly before we left the Philippines. Remember when I asked him if expatriates should really be involved in pioneer church planting in the Philippines?"

"Not only do I remember the question," replied Bev, "but I will never forget his jaw-dropping answer. I was silenced—which is really something for this motor-mouth!—because what he said was so shocking. After all, he should know! He has pioneered more church plants in the RPCP agency than anyone else, expatriate and Filipino combined."

"That's for sure!" said Bill. "He demands respect for all that he's done, for his impeccable character, and for his spiritual depth. But why do you suppose he gave the answer he did? He said emphatically that *expatriates are no longer needed to go out on their own to pioneer church plants* in the Philippines—even among unreached people groups! Why would he say such a thing? Should we really be going back in that role? I'm confused."

"We both are," continued Bev as she nervously twisted her ponytail, "especially after I saw a crazy ad in a Christian journal the other day. It said, 'Thank you for staying home.' What's up with that?"

"And don't forget what that so-called 'missions expert' said at the missions society meeting yesterday," added Bill. "He claimed that the day of the career missionary is over, since God seems not to be calling North Americans for more than two- to six-week forays. He said that nationals can do it better, face less culture stress, live cheaper, and know how to suffer. Plus, he pointed out that they're more numerous and that they're ready to go.

"And I just read in Bob Robert's book, *Transformation*, that basically the day of the white man venturing out and starting churches is forever over. Could that be true?" Bill asked in exasperation. "The author seems to assume that all Americans are white men, by the way, but that's a topic for another discussion."

Bill and Bev sullenly sipped their iced coffees and stared out the windows with unseeing eyes.

"Bev, I still feel 'called' by God to cross-cultural pioneer church planting," Bill said with conviction. "I know you do, too—and not just for the short term! What's God trying to say to us?"

"I don't know, Bill, but I have an idea about how we could start exploring that question," Bev said, brightening. "Didn't our friend, Professor Nobley, transfer to the Christian university in town? He teaches church planting. Maybe we could talk with him about these concerns—about Jun's comment, for example."

"That's a great idea, Bev," said Bill. "Let's email him and see if he would spend some time with us while we're home."

Bev pulled her laptop computer out of her bag and quickly began an online search. "Here's his email address."

Three and a half hours later, they received a response:

```
FROM: CP Nobley <cpnobley@.....edu>
TO: The Beavers <eager2serve@.....org>
DATE: April 30, 10:02pm
SUBJECT: Re: former students seeking advice
_____

Hi, Bill and Bev! So good to hear
from you after all these years. Yes,
I'm teaching here at the university.
Since the semester is almost over,
would you like to meet during the
summer? I could probably work it out
so that we could meet on a weekly
basis. We could start in two weeks.
What do you think?

Cheering for you!
Dr. Nobley


----------------
C. P. Nobley, PhD,
Professor, Holistic Facilitative Church Multiplication
Department of Missiology
Great Christian University
```

Bill and Bev shot back an email. The first meeting was set up. Maybe they would receive some insights not only about cross-cultural pioneer church planting, but also about what legitimate roles Western church planters should play in the twenty-first century. They could hardly wait for their first get-together.

PART ONE

Facilitation in History and Theory

Week 1

What Do the Books Say?

"This is so disappointing," complained Bill glumly as he placed his laptop on the large, dark mahogany desk. "We finally get to meet with Dr. Nobley and he's called away for an emergency meeting. Sure hope he makes it back before we have to leave."

"Well, let's make the best of it," countered Bev as she walked toward the bookcases, ponytail swaying. "He said we could peruse the books on church planting. Here they are. Wow, two whole shelves of books on church planting! Where do we start, Mr. Organizer?"

For the next two hours, the couple surveyed the titles, read through the tables of contents, and began to stack the books according to emphasis. They made a separate stack for books that they were unsure how to categorize. As they were trying to figure out what to do with them, the door opened, and in walked Dr. Nobley, casually-dressed and carrying three cups of steaming coffee from their favorite shop.

"So sorry about that," apologized Dr. Nobley. "Maybe this coffee will help make up for it a little. Seems I can't get out of meetings even in the summer."

He set the coffees down on the table amid the neatly-organized stacks of books, which were marked with yellow sticky-notes. "Ah! I see you've created a number of different categories for the books on church planting. All those stacks look like the skyline of New York. What have you two discovered in my absence?"

* * *

"We've tried to categorize the books under various emphases, but we're not sure where some of them fit," replied Bill as he pointed to one stack. "This stack falls under cross-cultural urban church planting."

1. Harvie Conn's *Planting and Growing Urban Churches: From Dream to Reality*

2. Viv Gregg's *Cry of the Urban Poor*

3. Roger Greenway's *Cities: Missions' New Frontier*

4. Roger Greenway's *Discipling the City*

5. Ed Silvoso's *That None Should Perish: How to Reach Entire Cities for Christ Through Prayer Evangelism*

6. Keith Hinton's *Growing Churches Singapore Style: Ministry in an Urban Context*

7. John Fuder and Noel Castellanos's *A Heart for the Community: New Models for Urban and Suburban Ministry.*

"Well done," said Dr. Nobley. "Roger Greenway, who taught at Westminster Theological Seminary before he retired, has pioneered the field of urban church planting. Before the late 1970s, most church planting took place in peasant and tribal areas. Conn's book provides a valuable collection of signature articles formerly published in the now-defunct journal, *Urban Mission*. A great contribution! Hinton and Silvoso take a macro approach to reach a city for Christ, and Silvoso is open to the use of all the spiritual gifts to do it. Fuder and Castellanos consider appropriate ministries for those many city dwellers moving to the suburbs."

✳   ✳   ✳

Bev chimed in, "We found another grouping, too: planting churches through house churches and cell groups. Take a look at this pile."

1. Robert Banks's *Paul's Idea of Community: The Early House Churches in Their Historical Setting*

2. Robert and Julia Banks's *The Church Comes Home: A New Base for Community and Mission*

3. Ralph Neighbour's *Where Do We Go from Here? A Guidebook for the Cell Group Church*

4. Del Birkey's *The House Church: A Model for Renewing the Church*

5. Wolfgang Simson's *Houses That Change the World*

6. J. D. Payne's *Missional House Churches: Reaching Their Communities with the Gospel*

7. Paul Yonggi Cho's *Successful Home Cell Groups.*

"A very strong house church movement is happening today in the United States and abroad," contended Dr. Nobley as he sipped his coffee. "Some, like Neighbour, claim that the house church is God's *only* true biblical model for a community of faith, not the institutional church. Banks and Birkey provide a scholarly overview of the topic, and Payne will update you on the house church movement in the United States. Cho's book presents an Asian perspective from Korea, home to most of the biggest Protestant churches in the world, including Yoido Full Gospel Church, where he pastors. The house church seems to fare best in urban settings and, of necessity, in countries hostile to the gospel.

"And the next stack?" Professor Nobley asked.

※　　※　　※

"Actually we made another category—North American church planting—with two groupings: Anglo and multiethnic," continued Bev with a hand resting on each stack. "There may be some cross-cultural application. Here's what we included in the Anglo grouping."

1. Paul Becker and Mark Williams's *The Dynamic Daughter Church Planting Handbook*

2. Charles Chaney's *Church Planting at the End of the Twentieth Century*

3. Robert Logan and Neil Cole's *Beyond Church Planting* (a workbook with audio CDs)

4. Rick Warren's *The Purpose Driven Church*

5. Aubrey Malphurs's *Planting Growing Churches for the 21st Century: A Comprehensive Guide for New Churches and Those Desiring Renewal*

6. C. P. Wagner's *Church Planting for a Greater Harvest.*

"What a list!" remarked the professor as he scratched his head. "Logan and Cole, top church-planting consultants in the United States, give the practitioner a theologically sound, principle-based, well-thought-out, step-by-step approach to multiplying disciples, leaders, churches, and movements. They want you to plant a movement, not start a church. While some who tried their materials cross-culturally have not always found them applicable, avoid these books at your own peril.

"Warren's book has sold more copies than any other book in history in the area of church growth, and Wagner's book has one of the most quoted lines: 'Planting new churches is the most effective evangelistic methodology known under heaven.'"[1]

"One other collection we placed under the Anglo group were the books that focused on the missional church," added Bill. "Here they are."

1. Ed Stetzer's *Planting Missional Churches: Planting A Church That's Biblically Sound and Reaching People in Culture*

2. David Fitch's *The Great Giveaway: Reclaiming the Mission of the Church from Big Business, Parachurch Organizations, Psychotherapy, Consumer Capitalism, and Other Modern Maladies*

3. Bob Roberts's *The Multiplying Church: The New Math for Starting New Churches*

4. John Lukasse's *Churches with Roots: Planting Churches in Post-Christian Europe.*

"If the house church movement is a reaction to the traditional institutional church in the United States," interjected Dr. Nobley, "the missional church, with its strong ties to post-modernity, is a reaction to modernity's influence on the traditional church. Just look at the sub-title of Fitch's book: *Reclaiming the Mission of the Church from Big Business, Parachurch Organizations, Psychotherapy, Consumer Capitalism, and Other Modern Maladies.* You could add Alan Hirsch's *The Forgotten Ways: Reactivating the Missional Church* to the pile, but I don't have it here because someone borrowed it.

"Contextualization is at the center of the concerns of those within the missional movement, even though their critics would say that some—not all!—who emphasize contextualization have abandoned good theology in the process. Be careful in your own judgment," Professor Nobley warned. "The movement for contextualization is not monolithic, and it's a moving target methodologically and theologically.

"Anyway, what did you include in multiethnic church planting?"

---

1. Wagner, *Church Planting,* 11.

With coffee in hand, Bill made his way around the table to the multiethnic stack. "For multiethnic church planting," he resumed, "we have these."

1. Jerry Appleby's *The Church Is in a Stew: Developing Multicongregational Churches*

2. Manuel Ortiz's *One New People: Models for Developing a Multiethnic Church*

3. Francis Hozell's *Church Planting in the African-American Context*

4. Oscar Romo's *American Mosaic Church Planting in Ethnic America*

5. Mark DeYmaz's *Building A Healthy Multi-Ethnic Church: Mandate, Commitments, and Practices of a Diverse Congregation.*

"It's always good to have books that address specific peoples here at home and abroad," reflected the professor. "We need more of them. We should not forget that Paul and Barnabas were the first to plant multiethnic churches—that is, communities of faith composed of different ethnicities who worshiped together. Through their pioneer efforts, Jews and Gentiles learned to worship together.

"The Nazarenes have done a lot of excellent work pioneering multicongregational churches, which are what you get when a number of different ethnic groups worship separately at the same location, often in some old First Church in an urban center. The congregations coordinate the use of facilities and finances through joint-governance. And the North American Mission Board of the Southern Baptist Church has prioritized ethnic church planting in the States. DeYmaz even argues that McGavran's 'homogenous unit principle' will soon be replaced by strong multiethnic churches. Maybe we'll see more books on multiethnic church planting in the near future."

✳ ✳ ✳

"We found three books," interjected Bev as she tidied up the stacks, "that focused specifically on Muslim church planting."

1. Greg Livingston's *Planting Churches in Muslim Cities: A Team Approach*

2. Rick Love's *Muslims, Magic, and the Kingdom of God: Church*

Planting Among Folk Muslims

3. Daniel Sinclair's *A Vision of the Possible: Pioneer Church Planting in Teams.*

Picking up the three books, the professor scrutinized the covers, commenting, "On the Muslim side, Greg Livingston founded Frontiers, and Rick Love eventually succeeded him as CEO of the agency. Sinclair's book provides the agency's church-planting model, philosophy, and values. It's particularly helpful for audiences resistant to the gospel.

"What else do you have?"

Bev pointed to another stack. "Here are some that focus on different aspects of training."

1. George Patterson and Richard Scoggins's *Church Multiplication Guide: Helping Churches to Reproduce Locally and Abroad*

2. Trevor McIlwain's *Building on Firm Foundations: Guidelines for Evangelism and Teaching Believers* (Volumes 1–9)

3. The Alliance for Saturation Church Planting's *Omega Course* (Volumes 1–5)

4. Paul Gupta and Sherwood Lingenfelter's *Breaking Tradition to Accomplish Vision: Training Leaders for a Church-Planting Movement: A Case from India.*

"A strong collection on training!" Dr. Nobley confirmed with a broad smile of approval. "Patterson, a Conservative Baptist who planted elder-led churches among peasants in Honduras, and Scoggins, a church-planting coach for Frontiers with house church experience in the United States, emphasize the need for all disciples to obey Jesus' seven commands: repent, believe, and receive the Holy Spirit; be baptized; love God, family, fellow disciples, neighbor, and even enemies; celebrate the Lord's supper; pray; give; and make disciples. I think I got those right. Anyway, it has a strong New Testament focus.

"McIlwain's use of Bible stories told in chronological order, however, is based on biblical theology and calls for a much stronger Old Testament foundation. It takes seriously the interconnectedness of the two Testaments. He's the one who began the widely-used Chronological Bible Teaching model that evolved in the Philippines when he worked among the Palawanos with New Tribes Mission. I think it went public in 1981. Both McIlwain's works and Patterson and Scoggins's guide are essential reading and would integrate well in ministry.

"The Omega Course is used to train expatriate church planters for post-Communist Eurasia. These 'facilitation teams' train national followers of Christ in existing or emerging churches to start church-planting movements, often in the same or similar cultures. They like to start a lot of churches at the same time so that a movement ensues immediately.

"The Gupta–Lingenfelter book tells the story of the Hindustan Bible Institute—how it lost and regained its vision to train leaders to start church-planting movements throughout India. The book challenges the thinking of traditional Bible institutes, colleges, and seminaries.

"What else do you have there, Bill?"

✻ ✻ ✻

"We created another category for research," replied Bill. "We found only two books that seemed to deal more with research about individual churches."

1. Hakan Granberg's *Church Planting Commitment: New Church Development in Hong Kong During the Run-Up to 1997*

2. Christian Schwarz's *Natural Church Development: A Guide to Eight Essential Qualities of Healthy Churches.*

"Granberg conducted an empirical study of some 250 churches from 1989 until the Chinese returned in 1997," said Dr. Nobley. "He discovered three themes from the study: one, reproduce yourself; two, plant churches collectively; and three, commit to make it all happen. Much of the church planting was done within the same culture or similar cultures, or what could be classified CP-1 or CP-2.

"Remember Ralph Winter's three eras? E-1 is same culture to same culture evangelism. E-2 is evangelism conducted in similar cultures. E-3 is evangelism conducted in distant cultures. The abbreviation was changed to CP-1, CP-2, and CP-3 to go broader than just evangelism. We can discuss this further at a later time because now there's even another possible term.

"But back to Granberg. Running schools and social work were a natural result that followed the three themes, wedding spiritual and social ministries.

"Schwarz's book evaluates existing churches to assess eight areas of health: empowering leadership, gift-oriented ministry, passionate spirituality, functional structures, inspiring worship service, holistic small groups, need-oriented evangelism, and loving relationships. While some people question the basis of his research and the weak emphasis on church planting, it does help a church evaluate its spiritual and ministry vibrancy, and it helps explore possible corrections.

"Let's move on to another category. What do you have there, Bev?" Dr. Nobley asked.

❉   ❉   ❉

"We made this category a kind of catch-all that focuses on various church-planting models and strategies," Bev responded. "This is a big stack."

1. David Hesselgrave's *Planting Churches Cross-Culturally: North America and Beyond*

2. Paul Hiebert and Eloise Meneses's *Incarnational Ministry: Planting Churches in Band, Tribal, Peasant, and Urban Societies*

3. Tom Steffen's *Passing the Baton: Church Planting That Empowers*

4. David Shenk and Ervin Stutzman's *Creating Communities of the Kingdom: New Testament Models of Church Planting*

5. John Apeh's *Social Structure and Church Planting*

6. Gary Hipp's *Community Development and Discipleship: The Wedding of the Great Commandment and the Great Commission*

7. Jim Montgomery's *DAWN 2000: 7 Million Churches To Go*

8. David Garrison's *Church Planting Movements*

9. Ben Naja's *Releasing the Workers of the Eleventh Hour: The Global South and the Task Remaining*

10. Paul Nyquist's *There Is No Time*

11. J. D. Payne's *Discovering Church Planting: An Introduction to the Whats, Whys, and Hows of Global Church Planting*

12. Ott and Wilson's *Global Church Planting: Biblical Principles and Best Practices for Multiplication.*

"A collector's collection!" contended Dr. Nobley as he paced around the table with his hand under his jaw. "Let me offer a few comments. Hesselgrave served in Japan before teaching at Trinity, where he retired. He later founded the Evangelical Missiological Society. His book, which first came out in 1980, is considered by many a classic in the field. What he called the Pauline Cycle is anchored in Scripture and includes these phases: Missionaries Commissioned, Audience Contacted, Gospel Communicated, Hearers Converted, Believers Congregated, Faith Confirmed, Leadership Consecrated, Believers Commended, Relationship Continued, and Sending Churches Convened.[2]

"Hiebert and Meneses's book covers the bases in relation to types of societies. The authors—who, by the way, are father and daughter—acknowledge the blending and blurring of the four types of societies: band, tribal, peasant, and urban. They say that none of the four should be perceived as a stand-alone entity.

"Payne provides an updated introduction to church planting by investigating the past and present, identifying universal principles, and providing a firm scriptural foundation for evangelism that results in new churches.

"In *Global Church Planting,* two veteran church planters reflect on current trends and provide best practices for church multiplication, based on global research and empirical data. This comprehensive volume covers, among other topics, the role of short-term missions, partnerships, contextualization, church-planting movements (CPMs), and funding."

"Ott and Wilson's *Global Church Planting* and Payne's *Discovering Church Planting* both mention 'global' in the titles," observed Bev. "What's going on?"

"Excellent observation," noted the professor. "I think these two books reflect the current axiom that missions, or church planting, is everywhere. It's here, there, and everywhere in between. We live in an interconnected world that requires cross-cultural and missiological prowess."

"Thanks," nodded Bev.

"Apeh's emphasis on the need to identify the social structure is instructive. But whatever the social grouping, Steffen argues that a phase-

---

2. These stages constitute Hesselgrave's outline in *Planting Churches Cross-Culturally,* 47.

out oriented exit strategy should drive every aspect of a cross-cultural church-planting model. Steffen's is the only book that focuses specifically on exit strategy, The model begins with the end in mind and works backwards through each phase. This means role changes for nationals and expatriates, and he has identified what that involves. This would—"

The telephone rang, interrupting the conversation. Dr. Nobley shuffled his way to his cluttered desk, looked at the number on the phone, and let it continue to ring. Silence again filled the room, bringing noticeable relief to Bill and Bev. They did not want another interruption.

"Where was I?" asked the professor, mostly to himself. "Ah, yes. Let's start with DAWN.

"DAWN is an acronym for Discipling A Whole Nation. James Montgomery, the founder, calls for church planters of all stripes in a specific nation to pray, partner, plan, and plant churches throughout an entire nation—to saturate it with new churches.

"Remember the Omega Course? That's connected to Saturation Church Planting, or SCP, championed initially by Dwight Smith, former president of United World Mission. Their mission? 'To cooperate with the Holy Spirit in pivot nations around the world for the initiation and facilitation of indigenous saturation church planting movements.'[3]

"SCP took their cues from the DAWN movement, beginning in post-Communist Eurasia—first in Eastern Europe and then in Western Europe. I think I have a case study for you on this type of work or a similar one from Russia.

"Garrison's book on church-planting movements, which he defines as 'a rapid multiplication of indigenous churches planting churches that sweeps through a people group or population segment,'[4] stands on the shoulders of such missions statesmen as J. Waskom Pickett from the 1930s, and Donald McGavran and Alan Tippett from the 1970s.

"Terminology moved from 'mass movements' to 'people movements,' which would result in a 'homogeneous unit church.' But that's a topic for another day.

"In the short, easy-to-read book, *Releasing the Workers of the Eleventh Hour*, Naja puts his finger on the state of twenty-first-century missions. He identifies the people he considers to be the end-time work-

---

3. Saturation Church Planting International website, "SCPI Mission and Vision," para. 1.

4. Garrison, *Church Planting Movements*, 21.

ers of the Global South, suggests thirteen strategies for their ministry effectiveness, and considers a possible role for the Global North: serving as catalysts.

"Here's a rhetorical question for you. Was the book by Gary Hipp the only one you found that intentionally integrates the spiritual and the social in church planting?" Dr. Nobley asked.

After pausing dramatically and tossing his coffee cup into the trashcan, the professor answered his own question. "Yes, it's the only one. That doesn't mean that the other books are opposed to a holistic approach. It just means that the authors—like Granberg, for example—decided for some reason not to highlight the social part of the equation.

"The last book you placed in the stack, *There Is No Time,* is interesting in that it represents one of the oldest mission agencies in the United States. The author, the former CEO of Avant, believes that a changing world demands different approaches—approaches that don't require twenty-five to fifty years for planting a single church, as had been the practice.

"Instead of the old practice, Nyquist advocates short-cycle church planting, which aims for completion within around five years. I may have a case study on this team-based model that I can give you later. I'll see if I can find it."

The professor pointed to a medium-sized pile. "And what did you place in that stack, Bev?"

✳   ✳   ✳

"We found a number of recent books that tie business to church planting," she replied. "Some seemed more connected to church planting than others."

1. William Danker's *Profit for the Lord: Economic Activities in Moravian Mission and the Basel Mission Trading Company*

2. Tetsunao Yamamori and Kenneth Eldred's edited volume, *On Kingdom Business: Transforming Missions Through Entrepreneurial Strategies*

3. Steve Rundle and Tom Steffen's *Great Commission Companies: The Emerging Role of Business in Missions*

4. Patrick Lai's *Tentmaking: Business as Missions*

   5. Tom Steffen and Michael Barnett's edited book, *Business as Mission: From Impoverished to Empowered*

   6. Ken Eldred's *God Is at Work: Transforming People and Nations Through Business.*

"You've discovered a recent lay movement in missions," commented Dr. Nobley with a twinkle in his eye. "It's kind of like William Carey meets Adam Smith so that both companies and congregations can be created and multiplied. While it's a new movement now, it actually has strong ties to the past. Danker's book takes readers back to the Moravian lay missionaries who were first sent out around 1730 and the German Basel Mission in the early 1800s.

"*Great Commission Companies* calls for legitimate businesses on the macro level that not only make a profit but also have a ministry plan to multiply churches. The ministry plan is integrated with the business plan.

"Lai, a lay businessman, provides practical insights based on an empirical study of over 450 tentmakers working in the 10/40 window. The two edited volumes offer readers suggestions from mission history and a wide range of intriguing and insightful case studies.

"Eldred, founder and CEO of Living Stones Foundation, challenges capitalism, demonstrating how the spiritual transformation of people and nations can come through conducting 'kingdom business.' He calls it SST—spiritual and social transformation.

"You could also add an article called, 'Business as Mission,' which is Occasional Paper Number 59 on the website of the Lausanne Committee for World Evangelization. I access it on the web, and that's why it's not in my collection on the shelves.

"Oh, yes, I should point out, too, that Naja—remember *Releasing the Workers?*—argues that workers of the Global South should follow Paul's model and become tentmakers. This strategy would have many advantages, like solving the support issue.

"OK, Bill, what do you have in this stack, which is last but certainly not least?"

✻   ✻   ✻

Bill began to read off the titles for a category that emphasized the indigenous church.

1. Charles Brock's *Indigenous Church Planting: A Practical Journey*

2. Melvin Hodges's *The Indigenous Church.*

"We weren't sure what to do with John Nevius's *Planting and Development of Missionary Churches,* or Roland Allen's *Missionary Methods: St. Paul's or Ours?*" Bill said. "Maybe you could help us out here."

"I'm glad the indigenous church category came up last because in reality it has influenced many of the authors you've already mentioned," claimed the professor as he rubbed his right ear.

"These books go back to a missions theory promoted by Henry Venn and Rufus Anderson in the mid–1800s, an era of strong colonialism. Venn was a British Episcopalian with the Church Missionary Society of London, and Anderson was with the American Board of Commissioners for Foreign Missions. These two armchair missiologists, with little communication between them, came up with the theory separately but almost simultaneously.

"They called it the 'three-selfs.' Self-governing spoke to the political side. Self-supporting addressed economic sustainability. Self-propagating dealt with the spiritual side. Churches planted under their theory, they argued, would emerge as indigenous—that is, free from foreign funds, structures, leadership, liturgy, and even Western theology. Venn and Anderson wanted to see the 'euthanasia of the mission,' believing that after expatriate church planters leave a work they have established and all the foreign scaffolding disappears, the indigenous church is then truly able to emerge.

"The theory would take fifty to sixty years to take hold. Nevius, writing in the late 1800s, and the most influential practicing missiologist in the nineteenth century with missions experience in China and Korea, argued that the three-self theory works because it is *practical.*

"By the 1940s, Allen, an Anglican missionary statesman who had worked in North China and Kenya, argued that the three-self theory works not because it is practical, but because it is *biblical.* In fact, each self is Pauline-based!

"The three-self theory had no real rival through the 1950s, when Melvin Hodge, of the Assemblies of God, wrote his well-read and oft-referenced book. Brock's book, among others, serves as a more recent example.

"If I were to draw it, it would look something like this," continued Dr. Nobley as he stopped by his desk, picked up a black marker, headed for the whiteboard, and began to draw and talk.

"Colonialism influenced missions greatly during that era, producing many missionaries who saw themselves as superior in every area of life to those they sought to reach with the gospel," he began. "They tended to see civilization and Christianity as synonymous, a total package, a perfect package, and yes, a superior package! This message often created dependent recipients, relying on the outsider for everything.

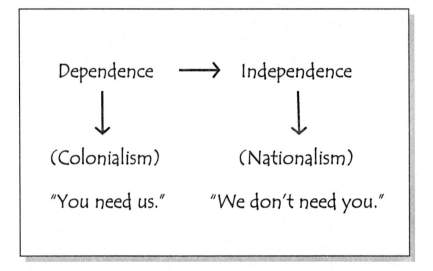

Dependence   ⟶   Independence

↓   ↓

(Colonialism)   (Nationalism)

"You need us."   "We don't need you."

"Enter the scene . . . the three-self way of thinking! This theory, advocates believed, would eliminate the dependency issue, replacing it with independence. Over time," continued the professor as he straightened some of the lines on the whiteboard with his index finger, "independent recipients began to replace dependent ones. But the theory also resulted in an unintended consequence."

"What was that?" asked Bev as she twisted her ponytail absentmindedly.

"It helped produce strong nationalism," answered Dr. Nobley, "which meant for some that the expatriate was no longer noble, needed, or necessary! The title of a book written by James Scherer in 1964 captured the feeling of some, certainly not all, of the independents: *Missionary Go Home!* Thankfully that attitude remains relatively rare today.

"This is grossly oversimplified, but hopefully you catch the drift," confessed the professor as he rubbed his ear again. "But it does raise another question. What follows independence? The answer to that question just may help answer *your* question about possible ministry roles for westerners in the twenty-first century!

"But for now, it's getting late," Dr. Nobley sighed. "I think we'd better save that one for the next time."

✻　✻　✻

"Before you go," he added, "I do have one last question for you. I like the way you categorized all those books on church planting during my untimely—but maybe Providential—absence. So tell me: what are the books saying to you?"

Always quick to respond, Bev chimed in. "Wow, there sure are a lot of books out there on church planting, and they cover a wide range of topics!"

"Most of them seem to focus on spiritual transformation rather than social transformation," added Bill. "Some of the recently published books seem more integrative, like Hipp's book and the business as mission books. And these seem more lay-oriented, while the earlier books tended to focus more on professionals."

"And they're more open to the use of all the spiritual gifts. Remember Silvoso's book," Bev reminded the two, nervously twisting her ponytail as she prepared to unleash a barrage of questions. "It seems to me that someone would have to continually ask a lot of questions. Who is this book written for? Anglos only, or others? A monocultural setting or a cross-cultural one? A multicultural mosaic? A rural setting or an urban center? Where no churches exist? Where national churches already exist? If you don't ask these questions, you may be trying to force US models and practices onto very different cultures."

"Or ticking off the Global South!" interjected Bill.

Bev continued with another series of questions, "Does everyone want to hear the gospel chronologically? Make individual decisions for Christ? Have individual devotions? Use their indigenous music? Meet in houses? Have a single pastor? Have only their spiritual needs met? Become an independent church? What if they prefer Western models and practices? Does the church planter have to be a professional, or will a practitioner do? Can the church planter pioneer in unchurched areas?

Become a facilitator in churched areas? Should pioneers eventually become partners?

"While some people claim to base their work solely on *biblical* principles, and thereby assume universal applicability, their principles just may be more culture-shaped and biased than they really know or acknowledge," Bev concluded. "Sorry, I'm getting carried away. This discussion is bringing back some memories from the Philippines."

Sensing her inner struggle and reliving some of the same experiences, Bill quickly jumped in, "No, those are great questions, Bev. They need to be asked and answered. A couple of other observations stood out to me. I think they will require further discussion. Maybe they can help set the agenda for our next meeting.

"The first is tied to what Bev mentioned. It seems that if an authentic church-planting movement is going to take place, it is imperative that the expatriates and the host participants be cognizant of the distinctives of CP-1, CP-2, and CP-3.

"Another observation. The terminology seems to be all over the place. Indigenous churches, healthy churches, missional churches, holistic churches, authentic churches—what's going on here?

"Also, Global South, Global North, Majority World. Does that mean we are the Minority World? We need to look at the terminology.

"My last observation is that the majority of the books focused on starting new churches or movements, including some of the business books. Only the Omega Course, which is tied to Saturation Church Planting, and two others—one of the missional books and Naja's *Releasing the Workers*—talked about working with existing churches.

"Pioneer and facilitator are two very different focuses. Is there a change in the wind? How strong is the wind blowing? How long has the wind been blowing? What are the implications?"

"Anything else?" asked Dr. Nobley as he looked into the eyes of each. The couple shook their heads *no.* "OK, I'll prepare something on these areas for our meeting next week. In the meantime, Bev, could you make a PowerPoint presentation summarizing our main points today?"

"I'd love to," responded Bev. "I could do it for all our weekly meetings."

"Excellent. One other thing," concluded the professor as he pulled together some manila folders.

"You've noted two different types of church planting, with one type being dominant. What metaphors capture each one? Think about it, and we'll add your metaphors to our discussion. See you next week."

Week 2

What's Happening Out There?

"**Y**OU'RE BOTH LOOKING CHIPPER today," commented the professor as he welcomed the young couple into his office. "Good to see you again."

After some small talk, the professor asked, "Bev, were you able to put together a PowerPoint presentation that reviews what we talked about last week?"

"I was!" beamed Bev. "Would you like to see it?"

"That sounds like a great place to start. Show us what you have," replied Dr. Nobley.

Bill dimmed the lights as Bev began the presentation.

"Great review," commented the professor when Bev finished. "I think a good start-point for us today would be to focus on one of the reflections that Bev included in her presentation: terminology. What is the Global South? The Global North? The Majority World? The Minority World? And if we have time, we can look at other terms as well, and possibly the different eras of missions.

"To answer the question about your future role in cross-cultural ministry, it is necessary to discern what's happening out there today. Last week we mentioned that colonialism helped produce dependency wherever Western Christianity spread—so much so that the 'three-selfs' advocated by Venn and Anderson required correction.

"Nevertheless, claims Philip Jenkins, missionaries during the colonial era did their job, and they and other nationals did it very successfully![1] Christianity spread globally and increased exponentially.

---

1. Jenkins, *Next Christendom*.

Bible translations were completed, as were grammars, dictionaries, and a host of other services, such as hospitals, orphanages, and schools."

Walking over to a wall map of the world, the professor began to point out locations as he talked. "Todd Johnson, who tracks the movement of Christianity, claims that the geographic center of Christianity has moved from Vienna in 1500 to Madrid in 1900 to Western Sahara in 1970 to somewhere around Timbuktu, Mali, today. The direction of Christianity is moving south and east."[2]

"What about the numbers? When did the balance of Christians tip from the North to the South?" inquired Bev.

"Two major shifts have taken place in Christianity in the last century," responded the professor. "The first happened in the early 1920s, when the North reached 50 percent of all Christians in the world.

"Somewhere around 1990, however, a second tipping point was reached as explosive growth took place in the South, and it continues today. Putting it into today's jargon, the Minority World became the Majority World, and the Global South Christians outnumbered their Global North brothers and sisters.

"According to Philip Jenkins, at the beginning of the twentieth century, 90 percent of Christians lived in the West or in the North, which together comprise what we call the Global North. The twenty-first century, however, finds 75 percent of Christians living in the East or South, which we call the Global South. Jenkins calls this the 'next Christendom.'"[3]

"How do Christians of the Global South differ from those of the Global North?" inquired Bill.

"Perceptive question," began Dr. Nobley.

"Spiritually, Global South Christians are much more charismatic, open to all the spiritual gifts of the Holy Spirit. So there are even theological differences, at least for some strands of Christianity. These Christians expect God to show up anytime and participate in their daily lives!

"Behaviorally, they're very conservative," continued the professor as he pulled nonchalantly on his ear. "Economically, they're poor and marginalized. Academically, they have little formal education. Relationally, they value community over individuality. Institutionally, little need or desire for expensive buildings. Socially, often perceived as provoca-

2. Johnson, "World Christian Trends." See also Hooper, "Heart of Christianity."

3. Jenkins, *Next Christendom.*

tive, dangerous, and divisive, thereby inviting persecution. Missionally, strong on sending out Christian workers. We can discuss where they send personnel at a later time."

"It seems we've entered a new era of missions," proposed Bev.

"Bingo!" concluded Bill. "Now things are becoming clearer; the fog is dissipating! We've been so involved in planting and developing churches in the Philippines that we couldn't see the forest for the trees. Even the Philippine churches have been sending out missionaries for years, and we know the Koreans, Indians, Brazilians, and Nigerians have been doing the same. It's definitely a different era!"

"A different era it is!" agreed the professor. "COMIBAM, a Spanish/Portuguese acronym for Ibero–American Missionary Cooperation, have some nine thousand missionaries out there, supporting them at the tune of almost four million dollars monthly.

"The Koreans have sent out around thirteen thousand long-term cross-cultural missionaries, second only to the United States. The Indian Mission Association have some forty thousand missionaries, most serving in India. More than 50 percent of the missionaries ministering today are neither white nor from the West. Formerly receiving countries have become sending countries. As Fareed Zakaria astutely noted, it's the 'rise of the rest.'[4] And they are going everywhere!

"In fact, almost every nation has become not only a receiving country *but also a sending country!* Missions is no longer the West to the rest, but multi-directional. From all nations to all nations. All nations feel empowered because there no longer remains one national power center for missions. The outreach power of the United States has been diffused. And the number of missionaries sent out from the Global South continues to skyrocket. It *is* a different era! We've never faced a world like this before! Lamin Sanneh believes that there has never been such a shake-up in the Western church since the Reformation.

"Maybe we should take some time to discuss this a little because it has direct impact on your question about what your role should be as North Americans in missions today."

"We'd love that," concurred Bev.

4. Zakaria, *Post-American World*, 52.

✳   ✳   ✳

"OK," replied the professor as he rummaged through a stack of folders. "We need to take a look at a chart designed by Ralph Winter. Ah, here it is."

Motioning to the couple to join him, he walked over to the dark mahogany table, wiped away a few cookie crumbs, and spread out the chart.

"Back in the mid–1960s, Dr. Winter identified three eras of Western Protestant missions that covered two hundred years of history, from 1800 to 2000. For each era, he identified the geographic focus, the influential player or players, the leaders, the participants, and how long they participated.[5] We'll add several new categories.

"Winter said that the First Era, 1800–1910, focused on the coast-lands of Africa and Asia. A young William Carey led the missions movement during that era. Young people, mostly men, streamed to the coastlands for a lifetime of service. Sickness, however, would claim the lives of many of these heroic volunteers within a couple of years.

"According to Winter, the Second Era, from around 1865 to 1980, saw missionaries moving from the coastlands to the inlands. This transi-tion would take a while because, as some voices would argue, why go inland when the work on the coastal areas remained incomplete?

"Hudson Taylor, another young man with short-term experience, would lead this era. Like William Carey, Taylor was an organizer and an analyzer of statistics and maps. He eventually started China Inland Mission, and successfully challenged others to start mission agencies.

"Did you notice the 'inland' in China Inland Mission?" asked the professor as he searched their eyes for validation.

"Heard of Africa Inland Mission and Sudan Inland Mission? Through Taylor's influence, over forty faith missions like them were formed, focusing on reaching the unreached—like the 'inland' agencies and Regions Beyond Missionary Union. As in the First Era, the youth of the Second Era surged overseas to minister for a lifetime, often buried in the coffins that carried their material goods to the far-flung fields of service."

---

5. The following description by Dr. Nobley of the first three eras is based on the historical overview provided in Dr. Ralph Winter's 1999 article, "Four Men, Three Eras, Two Transitions."

Dr. Nobley turned again to the chart, pointing to the Third Era. "The Third Era, which began sometime around 1935, continued to emphasize reaching the unreached. During that era a young man named Cameron Townsend recognized a linguistic barrier. A question from a tribal person helped him zero in on the issue: 'If your God is so smart, why can't he speak our language?'[6]

"Noting the need for tribal people in Guatemala to hear God's word in their own language, rather than in the national language, which was Spanish, Townsend founded Wycliffe Bible Translators. It's called the Summer Institute of Linguistics, or SIL, overseas. And you have SIL offices in the Philippines."

"We've visited the one in Manila," interjected Bev as a broad smile filled her face. "And that reminds me: right down the street is a great place—the Magnolia ice cream parlor! The SIL missionaries used to take us there."

"Uh, oh," teased Bill. "Bev is getting distracted by memories of excellent ice cream."

The professor laughed. "But back to the Third Era," he continued, "there was another barrier that needed to be broken—a social barrier. Ministering among people living in a caste system in India, Donald McGavran, the father of the Church Growth movement in the 1970s, soon realized that social structure played a significant role in the spread of Christianity.

"McGavran alerted the mission world to the 'homogeneous unit principle,' or HUP. This principle focused on how families are connected socially. Following these natural 'bridges of God,' McGavran said, the Christian worker would help ensure that entire 'people groups' were reached for Christ. Otherwise, extended family units within the castes would be fragmented.[7]

"McGavran believed the homogeneous unit was a necessary starting point. He also believed it was not the end point. Homogeneous churches could and should eventually become more heterogeneous.

"McGavran helped move our thinking from reaching geographic areas to reaching people groups, or ethnic groups, particularly those

---

6. Ibid., 260.

7. McGavran, *Bridges of God*.

'unreached.' As in the former two eras, youth played a major role in supplying workers for long-term service.[8]

"This leads us to the twenty-first century. How would you two define the Fourth Era?" challenged the professor, throwing the ball back into the couple's court.

"Not having given this any thought," acknowledged Bev without missing a beat, "it would seem to me that a Fourth Era would have some residue of all the former eras sticking to it."

"Excellent observation, Bev," responded the pleased professor. "And what may be some of that residue?"

"Well, one part would be the focus on unreached people groups," responded Bev as she twisted her ponytail.

"Another part would be geographical," continued Bev, "including both the coastlands and inlands, depending on where the unreached people groups reside. Many of these may live in large cities and may not be rural, tribal, or peasant peoples. But," she said uncertainly, "this doesn't seem to receive any attention in the chart."

Nodding affirmation, the professor turned to the bookcase and pulled out two journals that focused on reaching the unreached, *The International Journal of Frontier Missions* and *Mission Frontiers*. "Both of these are published through the US Center for World Mission in Pasadena, California," he said as he handed them to Bev.

The professor then turned to Bill. "What about you, Bill?"

"I, like Bev, have not really thought about it," confessed Bill. "As I reflect on the schema, it is definitely addressing the role of Western missionaries: where they should go, whom they should reach, how long they should stay. While earlier eras focused on geography—coastlands and inlands—McGavran challenged and changed the conversation, focusing on the ethnicity of an unreached people group. So the direction is social rather than geographical; it's reaching people groups rather than conquering territory.

"When I reflect on our church-planting ministry in the Philippines," Bill continued, "I can see that there were some differences between what we did and the approaches in the three eras. We were pioneering—that

8. Winter, "Four Men."

First Era From 1800	Second Era From Mid-1800s	Third Era From Early-1900s	Fourth Era From Late-1990s
Coastland	Inland	Unreached Peoples	Reached to Unreached
William Carey	Hudson Taylor	Cameron Townsend Donald McGavran	Rick Warren
Youth surge overseas long-term	Youth surge overseas long-term	Youth surge overseas long-term	Youth & adults surge overseas short-term
Spiritual →Social	Spiritual →Social	Spiritual →Social	Spiritual ←→Social
Pioneer	Pioneer	Pioneer	Facilitator

is, planting churches where there were none—but we were doing it with Christians who were Filipinos, Australians, and Germans. Westerners and easterners teamed up to plant new communities of faith among an unreached people group."

"And we were planting and developing churches in a major city," interjected Bev.

"Yes, and there's something else. The westerners on the multinational team were not just young people, and they were not all there just for the short term."

"Were they professional ministers, or were they lay people?" inquired Dr. Nobley.

"Some of both," answered Bev. "Some were retired, bringing with them life experience in multiple disciplines and using it. Some were using their vacations to be there. Others had little life experience and had never planted a church before. Most of the expatriate team had little cross-cultural training, which created a lot of interesting strategy meetings," noted Bev as a wry smile radiated across her face.

"You've made some excellent observations," observed the professor as he made his way to the whiteboard. "If you two are looking for a school to do a master's degree in missions or intercultural studies, I know a good one you could attend—and a prof who might write you a great support letter!" He picked up some colored markers and began to draw.

"I know that Dr. Winter developed a Fourth Era," continued the professor as a broad smile broke over his wrinkled face, "but his direction is slightly different from what I'm proposing. So I'll depart from Dr. Winter at this point and give you the 'Nobley Version' of the Fourth Era.

"This era probably began in the late 1980s or early 1990s," proposed the professor. "I'd chart it like this. See if you see any of your comments reflected in it. You should.

"Now, remember that I'm speaking in broad brush-strokes here, and that there will always be exceptions," said Dr Nobley, "but I think one of the major differences in the Fourth Era is the shift from unreached to reached peoples. The majority of Western missionaries used to go directly to unreached people groups, but they have begun going primarily to the *already* reached. They go to the discipled rather than to the undiscipled, and then they *partner* with them in a multitude of ways to reach unreached people groups.

"Some work side-by-side with already-discipled believers in the trenches. Some provide technological assistance. Some provide training in cultural analysis and adaptation, language acquisition, church multiplication, curriculum development, community development, or member care.

"Some establish financial support structures such as Great Commission companies.[9] Some serve as networkers to make or restore relationships between nationals, mission agencies, governments, NGOs, and other churches. Some . . . well, there are so many options, you can fill in the blank.

"That's not to say that there won't be, or shouldn't be, any westerners going directly to the unreached in a pioneer role. Pioneering is part of the first three eras that will continue, as Bev has perceptively pointed out."

"But don't the majority of today's missionaries already work with national churches?" asked Bill. "I thought that I heard somewhere that around 80 percent of missionaries already work where national Christians reside."

"That's true," conceded Dr. Nobley. "But for our current discussion, I am focusing strictly on Western missionaries who plant churches cross-culturally. I'm not talking about those who concentrate just on evangelism, or just on discipleship, or leadership development, or curriculum development, or ethnotheology, or sports, or drama, or member care, or any other necessary aspect of holistic ministries. I'm not trying to minimize any of these. I'm just trying to bring focus to our discussion.

"In former eras church planters *pioneered* among unreached peoples," noted the professor as he pointed to the bottom line on the chart. "I am proposing that in this Fourth Era, they *facilitate*, whether they are mission agency personnel, independents, or those sent out by local churches. Next week we'll delve into this deeper.

"There's another subtle change that's happening in the Fourth Era. While each previous era ministered holistically, the soul tended to be seen as priority. Social activity—like medical care, food assistance, or community development—were often seen as a means to reach the soul, but not as something of ministry significance in and of itself.

9. See Rundle and Steffen, *Great Commission Companies.*

"The Fourth Era challenges that bifurcation, arguing for ultimacy rather than primacy.[10] Basically, what this means is that this generation wants to avoid an either/or mentality when it comes to ministering to physical and spiritual needs. They don't like primacy, or an exclusive focus on one to the neglect of the other—a weakness they have seen in both the 'soul only' Bible Institute mentality and the Social Gospel focus of the 1920s liberal movement. Instead, they're all for ultimacy, seeking to wed the Great Commission from Matthew 28 with the Great Commandment of Matthew 22. They want to offer what is necessary at the time without settling for either/or. Ultimacy is this seeking of *both/ and*—both Great Commission and Great Commandment, both conversation and compassion. It sees redemption and restoration as two sides of the same coin."

"Whom do you see as the major players in the Fourth Era?" inquired Bev. "The youth were predominant in the former three eras."

"You're correct, Bev," responded the professor. "The youth were predominant in the earlier eras, often influenced by the Student Volunteer Movement founded in the late 1800s. A major difference in the Fourth Era is that it includes not only youth—and lots of them—but also a sea of adults. And this group wants to accomplish missions through partnerships with national churches! Many of these will be lay Christians with professional experience in some secular career.

"Another difference is the length of service to which these individuals are willing to commit. In the former eras, long-term service reigned. Some took their material goods to the field in a coffin. Today, short-term rules, but both are present. In relation to short-termers, some even take their vacation time to serve abroad. While we can argue the pros and cons of short-term service, it is a strong reality in the Fourth Era.

"Maybe a better question would be, how can long-termers and short-termers complement each other's ministries?" the professor reflected. "But that's a discussion for another time."

"Who do you think are the most influential people promoting Fourth Era distinctives today?" inquired Bill as he stroked his goatee. "Or put a different way, who replaces McGavran and Townsend?"

10. For a thorough discussion of primacy and ultimacy, see Wright, *Mission of God.*

"Well, it's still early in the Fourth Era, so I'm definitely guessing here," answered the professor. "Only time will tell the accuracy of my projection." He erased the whiteboard and picked up a black marker.

"A couple of pioneers who have had, or still have, global influence in relation to the facilitative role are the late Jim Montgomery and Phill Butler," surmised the professor as he wrote their names in the middle of the whiteboard.

"Jim Montgomery founded DAWN, Discipling A Whole Nation, as we discussed in the first week. The Philippines became the first nation in 1974 to use his facilitative model. There he helped Filipinos partner with expats to plant fifty thousand churches by 2000.

"Others, such as Dwight Smith, built on this movement to saturate areas with new churches. Remember Saturation Church Planting?" he asked rhetorically. "Smith also helped mobilize US churches and para-church organizations to participate in these national church-planting movements.

"Phill Butler—who first headed up Intercristo, then Interdev, and presently VisionSynergy—pioneered the partnership movement. This ministry facilitates the formation of networks and partnerships composed of westerners and nationals from churches and mission agencies. VisionSynergy's goal is to leverage God's resources through effective kingdom collaboration.

"This facilitative ministry has impacted somewhere around a hundred unreached people groups, addressing a host of needs: HIV/AIDS, microenterprise, refugees, children at risk, specialized training. VisionSynergy provides facilitation on multiple levels, from local to national, rural to urban, novice to professional.

"You can get a good feel for Butler's heart and philosophy in his book, *Well Connected: Releasing Power and Restoring Hope.* I also find his course, "Cause Collaboration: A Better Way to Change the World," to be very helpful. You'll find the VisionSynergy website at

www.visionsynergy.net.

"While Montgomery and Butler laid a strong foundation for the westerner's facilitative role and definitely deserve honorable mention, I think there is another person who will eclipse not their hearts but their global impact and visibility," said the professor, with pen poised at the whiteboard and eyebrows raised. "Ready?"

The couple shifted in their seats, waiting with baited breath.

"The person who most personifies the Fourth Era today for me is Rick Warren, senior pastor of Saddleback Church," offered the professor, writing the pastor's name on the whiteboard above Montgomery's and Butler's. "He stands on the shoulders of a lot of people, including these two pioneer facilitators, Montgomery and Butler.

"Warren has a degree in missions, served short-term in Japan during college, and was on the Lausanne III Advisory Council.

"Warren has championed what he calls the PEACE Plan, challenging *every* member to participate and urging those in other churches to join him. PEACE is an acronym. The *P* stands for promoting reconciliation—and by the way, 'promoting reconciliation' replaced 'planting churches' when the plan was redesigned in 2007. The first *E* equals equipping servant leaders, *A* is for assisting the poor, *C* means caring for the sick, and *E* stands for educating the next generation.

"Warren believes that the local church, God's plan A, has abdicated her role and has given it to mission agencies and professionals, God's plan B. God's plan B represents only one percent of God's workforce, while God's plan A represents 99 percent!

"By the way, in the late 1800s, Roland Allen opposed the creation of a professional class of missionaries because he believed that it would slow the spontaneous expansion of the church. Anyway, back to Warren.

"Warren argues that there are no more excuses for the 99 percent! No longer should the laity abdicate her role to professionals, God's plan B! Interestingly, nowadays, the majority of local churches don't seem to want to offer excuses; rather, they want to go, participate, serve.

"While the authors of the PEACE Plan are on a steep learning curve in urging hundreds of amateurs to minister abroad with little cross-cultural training or experience, the plan does represent the Fourth Era: local church, lay driven, youth and adults, holistic, little cross-cultural experience, partnership with the national church, mostly short-term forays.

"A quick aside. I find it interesting that this movement tends to bypass the agencies on the fields in order to work directly with national churches, many of which were birthed through the tedious labor and tireless efforts of church planters within those agencies. I've not figured that one out yet!

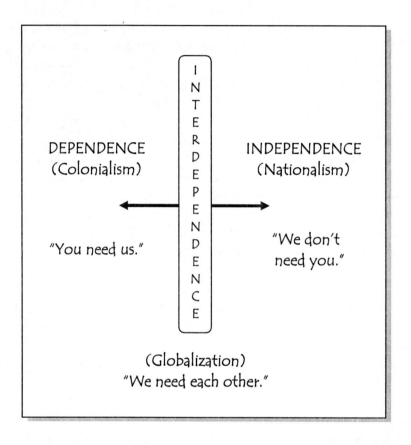

DEPENDENCE
(Colonialism)

INDEPENDENCE
(Nationalism)

INTERDEPENDENCE

"You need us."

"We don't need you."

(Globalization)
"We need each other."

"And we should note," added the professor, "that agencies have not rolled over and died. Most do not consider themselves God's plan B, but rather, God's plan A. Convinced of their legitimate scriptural role from such passages as Acts 13, these organizations provide services to the national churches to expedite the Great Commission and the Great Commandment.

"While Rick Warren may personify the assembly side of the Fourth Era," continued Dr. Nobley as he slowly rubbed his jaw, "I'm not sure who will emerge on the agency or academic sides. We'll have to keep our eyes open for these individuals."

"Last week we talked about dependence and independence," recalled Bill. Raising a question more than stating a fact, he continued thoughtfully, "It seems that in the Fourth Era, those two are now challenged."

"Very insightful, Bill," noted the professor. "Let's build on last week. Last week we noted how Christian workers in the First Era, influenced by colonialism, believed that Christianizing and civilizing were both necessary parts of missions. This, however, often resulted in strong national dependence on the expatriates.

"Henry Venn and Rufus Anderson later challenged this philosophy through the three-self idea. This eventually resulted in independence for the nationals. It moved from expatriates thinking, 'you need us,' to the nationals saying, 'we don't need you.' It didn't take long to learn, however, that nationalism could prove as devastating to Christianity as colonialism.

"As you have observed *and* experienced, Bill and Bev, there is a strong push for partnerships in the twenty-first century. A significant socio-cultural reason for this is globalization. Global economics and technology have shrunk the world, resulting in everyone competing for everything. Remember, nothing happens in a vacuum.

"Today there's no need for anyone to fly overseas to meet different people, eat their food, or enjoy their products. Just walk across the street. Globalization has been the great leveler, providing unprecedented opportunity for international exchange of human, technological, and material resources. The twenty-first-century world is interdependent!

"Every generation of Christian workers absorbs, often unintentionally and unknowingly, some cultural biases. First Era Christian workers were influenced by colonialism that resulted in, according to Bosch, 'patronizing charity.'[11]

"Our generation has been influenced by globalization. We, therefore, must be cognizant of its strengths and weaknesses. We must know the scriptural principles that challenge and support all aspects of globalization. And we must take advantage of this new paradigm. Globalization generates unparalleled opportunity for the global reign of Christ."

Walking over to the whiteboard, Dr. Nobley picked up a few markers and began to draw. "If I were to draw how missions interacts in the twenty-first century, it would look something like this—minus, of course, my artistic inabilities.

11. Bosch, *Transforming Mission*, 290.

"I'd keep what I drew last week but add interdependence in the center. Globalization and, of course, Scripture pull us toward the center. In the midst of the pushes and pulls from colonialism and nationalism, interdependence argues that we need each other. It calls for partnerships and networks, rather than dependency or isolation."

"That's so true!" exclaimed Bev. "We often saw this need for interdependence in our multinational team in the Philippines. We also felt the implications of different economic levels. Maybe we could address that some time?"

"I'd be glad to," replied the professor. "Economics plays a major role not only in funding missions, but also in destroying it. You can't talk about missions without talking about economics. Or at least you shouldn't. I'll try to get to this topic one of these weeks.

❋   ❋   ❋

"It would seem from Scripture," continued the professor, "that you as a Western couple have a legitimate role in fulfilling the Great Commission, including participation through pioneer *or* facilitative efforts. The Holy Spirit has *not* negated the Great Commission, nor will he!"

"That's encouraging!" said the couple in unison.

"It would seem from the interdependence perspective," added the professor, "that you as a Western couple also have a legitimate role in participation through partnerships. Global challenges require global cooperation. But partnership raises a central question, one that your Filipino church planter may have had in mind."

"Oh, you mean our partner, Jun," interjected Bev. "What central question might he have had in mind?" she asked, brow furrowed in anticipation.

"Well, any partner would want to know what role you will play. Will you serve as a pioneer or a facilitator?" quizzed the professor.

"What do you mean by 'pioneer' and 'facilitator?'" asked Bill as the three walked back to the large dark mahogany table and sat down.

"Let me set out a broader context before answering your question," countered Dr. Nobley. "Over the years I've identified four roles that individuals play in multiplying churches at home and abroad: pioneers, or some call them apostles; founder–pastors; renewers; and facilitators.

"I'll start with the middle two because they really don't impact your situation. Founder–pastors, or some call them planter–pastors, start the churches that they will eventually pastor and multiply. These individuals possess spiritual gifts and skills not only to start churches but also to maintain and multiply them. For the most part, these multi-gifted individuals accomplish this among people of their own culture and language.

"Renewers enter broken churches, attempt to pick up the pieces, and start anew. They just may face one of the most difficult ministries in the world, in that bitterness and deep wounds are par for the course. Renewers concern themselves not just with the renewal of a church but also with its multiplication, so that a movement results. You'll find these individuals serving in places like England, Ireland, France, and the United States.

"The other two typese do impact you as a couple: pioneers and facilitators. Pioneers may be church planters (PCPs) or church multipliers (PCMs). I prefer the PCM role, but we'll talk more about that next week.

"In the meantime, let me just say that PCPs possess spiritual authority and model godly character as they endeavor to plant, develop, multiply, and oversee geographical movements of holistic communities of faith. Their ambition is 'to preach the gospel where Christ was not known' and to call people to faith and obedience, as Paul wrote in Romans 1 and 15.[12] PCPs often do this in cross-cultural contexts, sometimes on their own, sometimes in teams.

"A possible metaphor for a PCP could be a Conestoga wagon—a vehicle that heads into an unknown area to establish a new frontier community that can not only sustain itself but also multiply.

"Facilitative church multipliers, or FCMs, serve existing national churches as a 'supporting ligament,' using Paul's phrase from Ephesians 4:16. They provide encouragement and specific training and services in multiple ways to encourage a sustainable national church-planting movement, often a holistic one. A possible metaphor for a FCM could be a toolbox full of the essential tools for making such a movement become a sustainable reality.

"If I were contrasting the two," continued the professor, "PCM is leading from the front while FCM is more about leading from multiple positions. Sometimes it's from beside, sometimes from behind, some-

---

12. Rom 1:5; 15:20. All scriptural references are to the *Holy Bible: New International Version*.

times from the front. It all depends on the need. Both types are necessary, but they're different. And there is a right time and place for each.

"In the Fourth Era, we have moved from pioneering to partnering. And, as Bev has pointed out in her review of last week's discussion, today's bibliography is much stronger on the pioneer church planting side than on the facilitative."

"Why do you think Jun, our Filipino partner, was not in favor of us doing PCP?" inquired Bev. "Do you think it's nationalism? Or does he fear we would head out on our own to some unreached people group without Filipinos on the team? Or start a Western organization that may become competitive with our Philippine-based agency, RPCP, drawing away some of its quality personnel?"

"I really can't answer those questions, Bev, as I am not familiar with the specific situation," responded the professor.

"It may be a combination of all," suggested Bill, hesitantly. "I don't really know. Sometimes you hear the catchphrase, 'Asia is by Asians!' But I can say this. Jun does have a legitimate fear, since there is a long history of expats doing their own thing in the Philippines and drawing away effective workers through higher wages. Not all expats see their 'little brown brothers' as equal spiritual partners—nor can indigenous movements compete economically with US agencies."

"The challenges of partnership raise other interesting questions," began Bev. "When we return to the Philippines, we will be ministering to a different people group. Chances are very strong that if we partner with Filipinos, we'll be assigned to an ethnic group that has already been reached, but which still has unreached pockets that require further church planting.

"One of the things we have observed—and I would appreciate your input here, Dr. Nobley—is that there is a strong tendency for nationals to work among the already reached and among those of the same culture and language. So here are my questions. How do you define 'unreached'? And, should the ministry focus be cross-cultural or same culture?"

"Those are interesting and complex questions, Bev," responded the professor. "I think we'd better save them for next week. Until then, what stood out to you today?"

✻   ✻   ✻

"For me," offered Bev without hesitation, "it was the four eras. I found it extremely helpful to differentiate between the eras, particularly between the third and fourth—that is, the *reaching the unreached* focus of the Third Era, and the *reaching the reached to reach the unreached* focus of the Fourth Era. That distinction helped put our situation into focus.

"Also helpful to our situation was the chart on dependence, independence, and interdependence. 'We need each other' is where it is today," she said.

"I also like the distinction between PCP and FCM," added Bill. "But I think this idea needs more development. Hopefully you can discuss it further next week because it also ties to Bev's question about the definition of the unreached."

"That we can do," responded the professor, "That we can do. See you next week."

Week 3

Why Mess with Good Terminology?

"A NOTHER EXCELLENT POWERPOINT REVIEW, Bev," remarked the professor as he jotted down a few notes.

"Ah, where do we start today? Last week we ended with your question about the definition of *unreached*. I think that before I attempt to answer that question, we'll dig a little deeper into some of the terminology. We need to look at some of the terms that we often use but know very little about. We need to get back to Voltaire."

"Voltaire?" inquired Bill. "What does Voltaire know about the Global South, the Majority World, church planting, interdependence, or the Fourth Era?"

"Well, probably not a lot," acknowledged the professor. "But he did raise a significant point when he said, 'If you wish to confer with me, please define your terms.'[1] So we'll start with some more definitions, and then we'll tie them to your question, Bev. Is that OK?"

"Go for it!" responded Bev enthusiastically, as she passed steaming coffee around to all.

✱　　✱　　✱

"Let's begin with the term *church planting*, a household term beyond the missions world," continued the professor.

"*Church planting* is used extensively in the missions world overseas, as well as in domestic circles. Its meaning, however, has become quite elastic, from playing basketball for Christ in China, to community development, to creating a movement of new communities of faith, to flying an airplane in Alaska. Where did the term originate? Who were the major players who helped canonize the term? How has it changed over time?

---

1. Anderson, "Define your terms," para. 1.

"I'll begin with various proposed viewpoints. Then we'll work backwards through history to seek its origin. Finally, we'll consider its future, and you'll be able to see how it relates to pioneer ministries, facilitative ministries, and efforts to reach the unreached.

"Some feel that the term has a relatively short history. For instance, Stephen Timmis advances that the term *church planting* was most likely used in the first instance in the 1960s.[2]

"But others take the opposite view, arguing for a long history. Hakan Granberg believes it goes back to the Roman Catholic theologian, Thomas Aquinas. That puts it in the thirteenth century. He describes how Frank Retief takes it even further back by redefining the term altogether, saying that it is just another word for evangelism, that it's the life-blood of the church, and, therefore, that it goes all the way back to New Testament times![3]

"Well, did the term start in the 1960s, or does it date back to the New Testament? Let's walk through time, stopping at significant landmarks along the journey to trace the term's illustrious past."

The professor walked over to his library and pulled out a book.

"Donald McGavran's magnum opus, *Understanding Church Growth,* which was first published in 1970, used the term *church planting* numerous times. But McGavran did not stop with planting churches. He wanted to see the *multiplication* of churches, and he wanted them to address social needs as well as evangelism. For him, church growth meant a holistic effort not just to plant churches, but to plant multiplying churches—to start a movement. So he frequently used the term *church multiplication*, as we'll see in a little while. He prioritized evangelism without neglecting the social."

Dr. Nobley opened the book, thumbed through well-worn and marked pages, and read McGavran's definition of church planting. "Church planting is the 'proclamation of the gospel by word and deed, resulting in conversions and a banding together of converts into congregations.'[4] McGavran would add that one task is paramount: 'the effective multiplication of churches.'[5]

---

2. Timmis, *Multiplying Churches.*

3. Granberg, *Church Planting Commitment.*

4. McGavran, *Understanding Church Growth,* 354.

5. Ibid., 41.

"Melvin Hodge, writing back in the 1950s, assumes, like most others during that era, that a missionary is primarily a planter of churches.[6] In the late 1940s, Alexander Rattray Hay wrote about church planting and church planters.[7] Roland Allen used the terms in 1912, when he wrote about churches *planted* by Paul. He also noted *established* churches and *founded* churches.[8]

"Although Henry Venn, who died I think in 1873, never used the term *church planting*, he did talk about *founding* churches.

"The Protestant Dutch missiologist Gisbertus Voetius, who died in 1676, fired a shot across the bow in his inaugural lectures at the University of Utrecht, entitled 'On Church Planting.' His threefold vision of missions, which would eventually permeate the university curricula, included the conversion of the heathen, planting the church, and the glorification and manifestation of the divine grace.[9]

"From this brief survey," summarized the professor, "you can see that the term *church planting* has had a long and storied history. But like any useful term, its meaning continues to change over time. Let's consider some of those changes.

✠ ✠ ✠

"While he was ministering in India, McGavran quickly discerned that the true meaning of the term *evangelism* had been lost. Some missionaries had redefined evangelism as a class for church membership, or as baptism of children and adults, or even as training for nationals in becoming westernized before becoming Christianized. Social activities clouded the true meaning of evangelism, and energy-draining institutions allowed little time for proclamation.

"To correct the matter, McGavran reasoned that the output of evangelism should result in the growth of the church. In other words, the term *church growth* could salvage the biblical concept of evangelism. And the best way to accomplish church growth, thus fulfilling the Great Commission, would be through the planting of new churches.[10]

6. Hodges, *Indigenous Church.*
7. Hay, *New Testament Order.*
8. Allen, *Missionary Methods.*
9. Neely, "Missiology."
10. McGavran, *Understanding Church Growth.*

"Still with me?" inquired Dr. Nobley as he looked at Bill and Bev intently. "This can get a little nuanced, a little deep in the weeds."

"Yes, we're with you," responded the couple in unison.

"As church growth courses entered the American seminaries in the early 1970s, the meaning of terms changed again. Many teachers, and eventually their students, redefined *church growth* to mean the principles and methodologies for growing churches larger and stronger. Bob Logan critiqued this mischaracterization of McGavran by calling for a return to the goal of church planting in his book *Beyond Church Growth*. Not everyone appreciated that book!

"It's interesting to note that shortly before Donald McGavran went to be with the Lord in 1990, and after completing his last book entitled *Effective Evangelism*, he remained sensitive to the changing meanings of key terms. McGavran told Jim Montgomery to drop the term *church growth*! The Father of the Church Growth Movement now preferred *church multiplication*.

"But that's not the end of terminology changes," continued the professor as he walked to the whiteboard, picked up a red marker, and began to write.

"In *The Healthy Church*, C. P. Wagner offered another substitute term for *church growth*. He argued that healthy churches are foundational to true church growth, so he recommended that the term *healthy churches* replace the term *church growth*.

Instead of Church Planting . . .

"Church Growth"   —1970

"Healthy Church"   —1996

"Missional Church"   —2000

"But proponents of *church growth* countered that the focus on internal renewal does not necessarily guarantee numerical growth or multiplication. Too much concern with health, they argued, could easily result in an 'I–focused' mentality that appeals to our current North American culture.

"Well, sometime in the mid to late 1990s, until the early 2000s, the term *missional church* became vogue. Such churches have a strong outward focus in both word and deed. They believe that *every member* is a missionary sent forth to minister in word and deed in his or her specific context. And that context can be monocultural or cross-cultural—which is a slight change from the traditional missions focus that is only cross-cultural.

"What has happened to the term *church growth* has also happened to *church planting*. Some hear the term and immediately ask, 'What about follow-up? What about leadership development? What about followership development?' And they give the opening of Russia as a troubling example. So they have tried to improve the term by adding to it, calling it *church planting and development*. But that's a little cumbersome.

"Others argue that church planting overlooks social concerns, that it fails to take seriously the Great Commandment or kingdom theology. They seek a more integrative ministry that doesn't ignore kingdom theology and that addresses structural sins as well as personal and corporate sins. I've seen terms like *kingdom-based church multiplication*, *holistic church multiplication*, and *church cultivation* as attempts to address this tension.

"Still others believe that the term *church planting* fails to move beyond planting a single church. They want to see multiplication take place. They want to see a movement result. That's one reason McGavran and a host of others, including myself, prefer *church multiplication* or CM. I also like *holistic church multiplication*, or HCM.

"More recently, David Garrison has popularized the term *church-planting movement*. Like Roland Allen, Christian Keysser, J. Waskom Pickett, Donald McGavran, James Montgomery, Dwight Smith, Tom Steffen, and others, Garrison advocates the rapid multiplication of churches. For this to happen, the multiplication DNA must be present in the first church planted. The danger is that sometimes, if we're not careful, the holistic side of the equation gets lost in this definition—or an authentic movement gets lost to one that is just sustainable. But that topic will have to wait until we discuss why I still teach pioneer church planting," smiled Dr. Nobley as he sipped his coffee. He then continued.

"Instead of *church planting*, some people are now advocating what they call 'gospel movements' or 'insider movements.' Ministering among Muslims, they argue that church planting implies the interjection of a foreign structure, rather than the support of a more-natural, indigenous one. They prefer to work through indigenous social networks, and some seem to assume that all expatiates are incapable of working within an indigenous system without contaminating it culturally. Maybe *church multiplication social networks* are needed.

"So now I have some questions for both of you," continued the professor with a gleam in his eyes as he set down his steaming coffee and headed for the whiteboard.

"Last week, we talked a little about pioneer and facilitative church planters in relation to the four eras, and we said we'd develop it further this week. I'd like to do that now. Let's do some deeper drilling.

	Pioneer	Facilitator
Monocultural focus	✓	✓
Cross-cultural focus	✓	✓
Short-term service		✓
Long-term service	✓	
Modeling of ministry to new believers	✓	
Engagement with existing believers		✓
Team orientation	✓	✓

Recognizing that there are always exceptions," he said as he continued to diagram, "where would you place check marks under the categories I've drawn on the board?"

As Dr. Nobley refreshed his coffee, the couple walked up to the whiteboard, had a short discussion about the chart before them, and entered their checkmarks. They admitted to the professor that they had guessed on several of them.

"Excellent!" responded the professor enthusiastically, surveying their work. "Talk me through your answers."

"Both roles can be done monoculturally or cross-culturally," Bev said.

"And facilitators tend to be more short-term than pioneers, who tend to stay longer on location," Bill added. "Of course, staying longer provides pioneers more opportunity to model a variety of the aspects of ministry to the new believers, rather than just having to explain them and leave."

With her finger on the fifth column, Bev said, "Usually, pioneers go where few or no believers exist, but facilitators minister among believers."

"Right," said Dr. Nobley. "And remember that typically, the goal for both pioneers and facilitators is to see maturation and multiplication."

"We assumed that both sometimes minister in teams," Bill mused, pointing to the last column.

"Yes," the professor affirmed, "but pioneer teams tend to be more predominant, especially today in the States. Long ago, US pioneer church planters tended to go out as lone rangers. Not so today. Working as a team allows for a variety of personnel, making holistic ministry a possibility."

The three studied their chart for a few moments in thoughtful silence.

✵ ✵ ✵

"Let's take it a step further," said Dr. Nobley as he set his coffee down beside the whiteboard. He picked up the eraser, wiped away the diagram, and began drawing a new one.

"I'll use Acts 1:8 as an outline to help discern the levels of complexity in planting new churches: 'But you will receive power when the Holy

Spirit comes on you; and you will be my witnesses in Jerusalem and in all Judea and Samaria, and to the ends of the earth.'

"I'll make a concession to the familiar and use *church planting* rather than my preference, which is *church multiplication*. But I'll probably use them interchangeably during our times together.

"In Acts 1:8, Jerusalem represents church multiplication conducted among a people of the same culture and language as the missionary—for example, Jew to Jew. Possibilities for miscommunication are minimal. Judea and Samaria represent church multiplication conducted among people with similar—but not the same—culture and language as the missionary. This type of focus would be Jews reaching Samaritans, for example. The cultural distinctions intensify somewhat from Jerusalem to Judea and Samaria, increasing the possibilities for miscommunication.

"The 'ends of the earth' represent languages and cultures with large distances between them and the expatriate church planters—for example, US Americans ministering to Filipinos. Possibilities for miscommunication increase exponentially, as your time in the Philippines could illustrate," said the professor, wincing empathetically.

"We'll call these three degrees of distance CP-1, CP-2, and CP-3. CP-1 is monocultural; CP-2 is intra-cultural; and CP-3 is cross-cultural."

Jerusalem	Judea & Samaria	Ends of the Earth
CP-1	CP-2	CP-3
Same Culture	Similar Culture	Distant Culture
Same Language	Similar Language	Distant Language

The professor continued, "I have another question for you, based on this diagram. When Pauline teams went out to plant churches in Acts, which two types of church planting were they engaged in the most: CP-1, CP-2, or CP-3? I'll give you a little time to think this through. But relax," commented the professor as he smiled and took another sip of coffee. "You can only miss one out of three."

The couple stared at the diagram as they dialogued back and forth about the Acts account. Three minutes later, they were ready but divided about their answer.

"Bev, if you're ready, go ahead and circle the two correct ones," challenged the professor, who was definitely enjoying the moment.

Twisting her ponytail, Bev quickly made her way to the whiteboard and circled CP-2 and CP-3.

Hoping to get immediate feedback, she noticed that the stoic professor was giving nothing away through facial expressions. Instead of responding to Bev, he asked, "What about you, Bill?"

"Bev and I disagreed on this one," Bill began as he slowly made his way to the whiteboard, never taking his eyes off the diagram. "I think the two predominant types of church planting conducted by Pauline teams in Acts were CP-1 and CP-3," he said confidently, circling the two.

"Well, you both can't be right," observed Dr. Nobley gleefully. "Let's unpack this a little. Bill, why did you choose CP-1?"

"I circled CP-1 because every time a Pauline team went into a city for the first time, they went straight to the Jewish synagogue—that is, if there was one," Bill said, awaiting affirmation from the prof.

But Dr. Nobley only asked, "Bev, why did you circle CP-2?"

"Well, a lot of the people where the Pauline teams went spoke Greek, so the teams could communicate through Greek even if the cultures were somewhat different," she answered. "Kind of like English in certain parts of the Philippines today."

Again, no affirmation.

"It's your turn, Dr. Nobley," insisted Bev. "Which two are they?"

"OK, OK," sighed the reluctant professor. "The correct two are . . . ," he said, hesitating in order to build on the teachable moment, "CP-1 and CP-2."

The couple considered the professor's omission of CP-3 with furrowed brows.

"Bill correctly pointed out why CP-1 must be included. Pauline teams were so at-home in their efforts to share the Gospel with fellow Jews that we could even call them synagogue splitters rather than church planters!" chuckled the professor.

"But CP-3, where culture and language are very different and distant, are actually rare in Acts! That's counter to what many believe about the book of Acts. In fact, there are only three really clear cases of CP-3 ministry that I can find in Acts, and their circumstances and outcomes lead me to doubt that Paul focused primarily on CP-3. I'll show you what I mean."

"First, take Athens. Persecution had driven Paul from Thessalonica, so he found himself in Athens waiting for teammates. Receiving an invitation to speak at the Areopagus, Paul laid out a case for Jesus Christ to the philosophers and other foreigners living in the area. A few became followers, including Dionysius and Damaris. We know that Damaris was one of the foreigners because no Greek women of polite society would have had the opportunity to hear Paul in public. This was all clearly CP-3.

"A second example comes from Malta. Do you remember that the ship Paul was sailing in had sunk because of a storm, and that they all ended up on the island of Malta? Like Athens, that stop was serendipitous, not planned. And also, just as in the Athens example, we're not really sure what happened in relation to a church being planted. Although we know that healings took place in this CP-3 experience, Luke gives us no church growth report.

"My favorite, and strongest, example of CP-3 is the Lystran one found in chapter 14. This example suggests the unexpected difficulties of CP-3 evangelism, even for the apostle Paul. Remember when Paul and Barnabas showed up and the Lystrans mistook them for Zeus and Hermes? Out came the bulls and garlands for worshiping the guests! Being good Jews determined not to commit blasphemy, Paul and Barnabas reacted out of their own cultural backgrounds like we all do—a natural response when things get messy—and began tearing their clothes.

"Think about it from the Lystran perspective. You're trying to worship these guys, and they began tearing their clothes! '*What on earth are they doing?*' you'd wonder. Talk about miscommunication! Like ships passing in the night. This case captures the complexity of CP-3.

"What Paul and Barnabas did not realize was that the Lystrans believed that Zeus and Hermes had come to their town years before. According to Lystran legend, when only one couple responded positively to these mythological gods, that couple's home became an honored temple—and the rest of the Lystrans were drowned!

"Determined not to repeat history by shunning or insulting the visiting gods, the Lystrans offered to Paul and Barnabas what they thought would appease Zeus and Hermes, only to have their gracious offerings rejected. And they couldn't understand why these visitors were tearing their clothes.

"Now the Lystrans were as confused as Paul and Barnabas, who seemed unaware of the myth that drove the Lystrans' behavior. That's the complexity of ministering in a CP-3 environment. Miscommunication in such foreign contexts is a given. Count on it!"

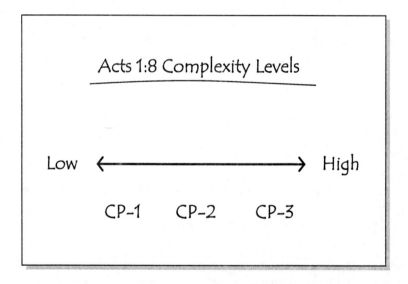

"Got it!" responded Bev. "The further down the line a church-planting team goes, the more complex the task of starting a sustainable movement becomes, and the more likely misunderstandings become. The further down the Acts 1:8 continuum—from Jerusalem, to Judea and Samaria, to the ends of the earth—the more cultural and linguistic sophistication is required of the church planters."

"Precisely," said the professor as he moved to the whiteboard and began to draw.

"And," he said pointedly, with a sympathetic smile, "the people you worked among in the Philippines, and those you hope to work among when you return, are located in CP-3! This is the most complex ministry environment of all—and it's more complex than the majority of church plants found in Acts!"

Approximate Timeframes for Pauline CP Teams:

Antioch	4 years
Corinth	4 years
Ephesus	3 years
Caesarea	2-3 years
Rome	2-3 years

Bill and Bev let out a sigh.

"Now I have another question for you," continued the professor as a broad smile flashed across his face. "There may be other CP-3 cases in the New Testament—Ephesus, for example. But if my premise is correct that most church planting by Pauline teams in Acts was predominantly CP-1 and CP-2, then humor me now by thinking about this: What were Paul's timeframes for planting these churches?"

"Several years, maybe even three?" offered Bill.

The professor moved again to the whiteboard and began to write.

"Remember, these timeframes are approximate. And we must not forget that Pauline teams tended to come and go rather than stay for protracted periods of time, like many do today.

"Here's your next question, which has application particularly to pioneer church planting but also to the facilitative side. If the time-frames for CP-1 and CP-2 took two to four years for itinerant apostles, what should we expect the timeframe to be for CP-3 in present-day contexts?"

"It's going to be much longer," answered Bev without hesitation.

"Exactly," responded the professor. "This is an important reminder to pioneers like you who are doing CP-3. It will take longer! It may take five years, eight years, ten years, or more, depending on Bible translation, social unrest, and so forth.

"And this factor says to facilitators, be careful! Worldviews are distant and distinct at this level. Do your homework *before* making your contribution so that you don't experience what Paul and Barnabas did in Lystra!

"If we had time, we would investigate other related questions. How does the personnel profile of team members change from CP-1 to CP-2 to CP-3? How should training differ for each of the three? How will the emergence of local leadership—such as what happened in the New Testament with people like Timothy, Titus, Silas, Apollos, Priscilla, Phoebe, Tryphaena, and Euodia—change the ministry role of expatriates?

"And if we had time for some wild hypothetical thinking, we could explore some fun questions. If Paul would have made it to Spain, as he had hoped, would he have heard Latin being spoken there? Would he have reached out through the common language and similar cultural experience that he shared with the people in Spain of living within the Roman empire, vast and diverse though it was? And I wonder if maybe these CP-2 bridges were what made him want to establish a new mission base in Rome . . . ?" Dr. Nobley stared vaguely into the distance as he tugged thoughtfully at his ear. "And think about Thomas, too. What CP level would he have faced in India? He would have been way out there both linguistically and culturally. . . . Ah, these are interesting rabbit trails, indeed," he said, shaking his head. "But we must move on."

The professor erased the whiteboard and glanced at the clock.

※ ※ ※

"Since we're just about out of time, let's tie this back to your question last week about the unreached, Bev," suggested the professor.

"Excellent," responded Bev.

"Bev, you mentioned last week that nationals often have a tendency to reach their own people, CP-1, or peoples of related cultures and languages, CP-2. The question arises: Should the national ministry focus on the same culture, similar cultures, or distant cultures?

"The answer to this question takes us right back to Acts 1:8—reaching one's Jerusalem, one's Judea–Samaria, and the distant parts of the world. It's true that there is some confusion in the Majority World about what constitutes cross-cultural church planting and about whether people involved in CP-1 should be counted as missionaries or evangelists. But at least these believers are zealous about making disciples, congregating them, and multiplying them.

"One of the things that nationals, not to mention expats, should consider in relation to the unreached is the people flow. Why? Because the gospel tends to follow people flow."

"What do you mean by 'people flow?'" inquired Bev.

"People flow has to do with communal connectivity," responded the professor. "In the first century, the places where communities connected with others were the Ignatian highway and the Mediterranean Sea. People flow is so important because the gospel tends to follow it.

"A present day example of this factor's importance can be found in the social ties that exist between West Africa and the East Caribbean. Years ago, the Gambia River served as a major conduit of slave trade to the east. Today, Caribbean people are welcomed back as brothers and sisters in Gambia. This flow of people can be of great benefit in missions.

"In the twenty-first century, people flow happens not only on highways or seaways, but also on train-ways, fly-ways, and cyber-ways. Where do the nationals naturally walk, ride, drive, fly, or Skype? Such thoroughfares are natural places where relationships already exist and continue to be cultivated. These are places where ideas get exchanged and challenged—natural locations for starting sustainable, holistic church-planting movements.

"In case you didn't notice, I've just extended McGavran's 'bridges of God' concept beyond bloodlines to include other types of relationships, such as friendships through business, education, government, tourism, technology, and so forth.

"So when nationals are involved in CP-1 and CP-2, that's great! Of course, their mission boards, churches, and agencies should be careful not to count nationals involved in CP-1 as *missionaries*, because this skews the data, and at a certain point, it becomes a stretch to call such ministry cross-cultural. But nationals participating in these two types of church planting are involved much like the Pauline church-planting teams were in the first century—predominantly in their own Jerusalem and among those of close cultural and linguistic proximity, the Judea–Samaria types.

"Some travelers, business or otherwise, will involve themselves intentionally in CP-3. This requires some specificity not necessarily found in CP-1 and CP-2. What is the overlap between the first two types and CP-3? What are the differences? What training will be necessary for these church planters to be effective in very different cultures and languages in a CP-3 environment?"

"Maybe next week we could discuss this topic," suggested Bill.

"Sounds good," confirmed the professor as he jotted down a note. "It's on the agenda for week 4. For now, there's one other thing that should be said about the penchant to plant churches in CP-1 and CP-2," continued Dr. Nobley. "Wherever the first church is planted, it must be successful. What happens there will set a model positively or negatively for the fledgling church and the movement. Statistically, CP-1 and CP-2 offer more opportunity for a successful first attempt than does CP-3.

"I would also add that I think *every* church should eventually attempt all three levels. Success will require careful planning and preparation because many churches find themselves presently in a survival mode. They don't even think about evangelistic outreach, much less starting new churches; their thinking focuses on just surviving another week. This is where partnerships could prove helpful.

"Well, what did you learn this week?" inquired the professor as he looked at his watch, walked back to his desk, sat down, and searched the faces of his pupils.

"For me, it was helpful to review the long history of the term *church planting*," began Bev. "I was totally unaware of the history. I think I agree with you that *church multiplication* is a more inclusive term, although some will misinterpret the term to mean that the holistic side has been overlooked.

"Maybe we need HPCM—holistic pioneer church multiplication. Or maybe HFCM—holistic facilitative church multiplication," she proposed with a smile. "For sure, we must be careful not to become too romantically involved with any term; the concepts must never take a back seat to the nomenclature, which always has a shelf-life."

"Wise observations, Bev!" applauded the professor. "What about you, Bill?"

"I've never known what to do with kingdom theology," admitted Bill. "For instance, I've always been befuddled at the eight mentions of *kingdom* in Acts. Today, I think I may have found a legitimate place for it.

"I've been uncomfortable with the dichotomies between the soul and the social, the verbal and the visual, redemption and restoration— thinking it's more a part of our Western culture than sound biblical theology. I want to think more about what you said about primacy versus ultimacy."

"Check out Christopher Wright's *The Mission of God* for a good discussion on the topic of primacy versus ultimacy," interjected Dr. Nobley.[11]

"It's also good to know a little of the history so that we don't naively repeat the mistakes of our predecessors," Dr. Nobley continued.

"In the early twentieth century, the Conciliar movement, and even the Missio Dei movement, emphasized the Social Gospel to the exclusion of the soul gospel. Primacy went to the social aspects of ministry.

"The Bible Institute movement, and later the Church Growth movement under Donald McGavran, challenged both social- and soul-focused movements to restore evangelism to its rightful role, giving primacy to winning people to Christ.

"Interestingly, the missional movement of today is challenging the excesses of the Church Growth movement. Balance seems hard to find in church and missions history.

"I should also add that today, the Social Gospel goes under the rubric of social justice and has expanded its categories somewhat. Proponents of the social justice movement address concerns such as HIV/AIDS, racial reconciliation, humanitarian disasters (like the 2004 Indian Ocean tsunami or the 2010 Haiti earthquake), police abuse, poverty and disenfranchisement, illegal detention, the environment, illegal land seizures, human trafficking, health concerns, unemployment, genocide, and the list goes on.

---

11. Wright, *Mission of God*, 265–323.

"There is a contrast, however, between the theologies of the early twentieth-century Social Gospel movement and today's social justice movement. Former theology deemphasized Scripture, hell, and the divinity of Jesus, preferring the Kingdom of God and a post-millennial eschatology that would hasten the return of the King to a just world made possible through human efforts. Primacy went to social activism.

"Present social justice theology, in contrast, tends to argue that fulfilling God's numerous commands to help others and care for the creation legitimizes the believers' faith before themselves, others, and God. Though this theology approaches balance and holism, primacy again too often goes to social activism."

"Why do we have such a hard time bringing balance to ministry?" asked Bev, perplexed.

"I hear you," responded the professor. "A one-wing airplane is destined to crash. We need an airplane that flies with two wings. Kingdom theology says we need both wings: the Great Commission and the Great Commandment, proclamation and presence, loving God and loving our neighbor. I like the way Bryant Myers captures it: 'Only kingdom people view the world as a seamless material–spiritual whole.'[12]

"Hopefully we've learned some lessons from the past's overemphasis on presence so that proclamation will not get lost—again! We must remain diligent so that history doesn't repeat itself. As my friend Ed Stetzer would say, 'Today's evangelicals are tomorrow's mainliners.'

"The choice of where to begin—social focus or spiritual focus—should be determined by the ministry context. Starting points should differ, just as they did in Jesus' and Paul's ministries. Sometimes proclamation preceded social ministries and included miracles. Other times, social ministries preceded proclamation.

"That's ultimacy: doing what is needed at the time, with the expectation that ultimately, holistic ministry must develop. Ultimacy trumps primacy because it demands both the social and the spiritual while at the same time recognizing that start-points differ.

"Well, there you have it," Dr. Nobley concluded, leaning back. "That's the Fourth Era. Remember the social and spiritual emphasis in our chart from last week? The Fourth Era will emphasize ultimacy over primacy—or at least I hope so. Time will tell. Balance will be a chief

---

12. Myers, *Walking with the Poor*, 164.

challenge for twenty-first-century Christian workers in the Fourth Era. They'll determine the outcome of this fifty-plus-year-old debate."

"That's a very helpful overview, Dr. Nobley," said Bill. "I will take a look at Wright's book. I also really appreciate the diagram that you drew that distinguishes pioneer church planting from facilitative church planting. I had not made such delineations between the two. Separating these roles out has tremendous implications both for the selection and training of team personnel, and for the models and strategies they implement. And it looks like we need more literature on facilitation."

"I liked the Acts 1:8 diagram showing CP-1, CP-2, and CP-3," added Bev. "It's so simple, yet so profound. If we can make these three distinctions, maybe we won't be talking over each other so much about what constitutes cross-cultural ministry, or about when nationals should—or shouldn't—be counted as missionaries. And we can be more realistic about the timeframes for completing work in each of the three contexts as we recognize their different complexity levels."

"You've also helped me see the importance of CP-1 and CP-2 for people who are just beginning church-planting ministries," acknowledged Bill. "I think I may have been too hard on nationals who focus on those two." Bev nodded.

"We must also never forget the ultimate goal," Bill continued, "whether through a pioneer role or a facilitator role. We must see, with the help of the Holy Spirit and the Word of God, a holistic movement that continues to mature spiritually and to multiply numerically. And we must start to think about *churching* areas, rather than just evangelizing them. I don't remember if you said that or not, Dr. Nobley, but that's one of the conclusions I drew from your discussion on church-planting terms."

"Excellent!" responded the professor. "Excellent!"

The students soaked in the affirmation, and Dr. Nobley beamed.

"Bev," he asked, "can you apply your creativity to a PowerPoint review for this week?"

"I certainly can," responded Bev cheerfully.

"Next week we'll take a look at the differences in the profiles for pioneers and facilitators, and we'll consider some of the ramifications," concluded the professor. "Have a great week!"

WEEK 4

What's in a Profile?

"GREAT DIAGRAMS ON THE roles of pioneer and facilitator church planters, Acts 1:8, and the timeframes for Pauline teams, Bev," approved a smiling professor. "Very well done. Keep up the good work on those weekly PowerPoint summaries.

"This week I thought we would continue to unpack the differences between pioneer and facilitator church planters. From there we can build profiles that will show both definite overlap and some clear distinctives.

✳   ✳   ✳

"Maybe we should begin by identifying what effective pioneer and facilitator church planters must know, do, and be," suggested the professor as he headed for the whiteboard, coffee cup in hand.

"From there we can do some 'backward mapping,' an education phrase, and create some profiles that will suggest role distinctions. What do you think?"

"Sounds good to us," said Bill. Bev nodded.

"OK," replied the professor as he wrote *pioneer* and *facilitator* at the top of the board and *know, do, be* down the left column. "What do a pioneer and a facilitator have to *know* to be effective? I'll write down your suggestions under the appropriate categories and maybe throw in a few myself along the way.

"We'll begin with *know* and work our way down the list. If you jump ahead some, that's OK, too."

"Well, they will have to know the Bible, the main cultures found in the Bible, the host culture or cultures, and their own culture," offered Bev without wasting a moment. "It's definitely knowing more than the Bible. How many people really know their own culture? I really didn't begin to understand my own culture until I lived in the Philippines. It was involvement in a different culture, painful as some of it was, that helped open my eyes to my own cultural blind spots and changed some of my theological assumptions."

"But some facilitators may not have to know the culture of the host audience," challenged Bill. "They will, however, need to become very familiar with the organizational cultures of all who want to work within the host culture."

"If that's true," suggested Bev, "facilitators have to be individuals who can see the big picture and be able to integrate a team of people from various backgrounds and disciplines to make it work. They can identify intersections, like matching people with the case. They can spot them and unite them no matter what their theological or ideological differences are.

"You know," she continued, "as I think of it, I guess *both* have to be big picture people and be able to put a team together. Pioneers have to be able to conceptualize a church-planting movement and find the personnel, expats, and nationals to make it happen. Facilitators have to be able to visualize the big picture and know which people and organizations, when brought together, can implement the vision."

"Very perceptive, Bev!" noted Dr. Nobley as he thoughtfully pulled his earlobe. "Very perceptive! I'm impressed. What about language acquisition?"

"For sure it would benefit both," offered Bev. "A pioneer church planter who did not learn the language would find it difficult to build deep relationships, since that's the first human step in seeing a church-planting movement begin. Pioneers must learn the language.

"A facilitator, if I'm beginning to understand this role correctly, may be able to get away without it if a good translator is available. But it seems to me that anyone who knows the language will benefit greatly in a multitude of ways.

"And don't forget that language and cultural understanding go hand-in-hand. Pioneers and facilitators should strive to gain both. I suppose people from bi-cultural backgrounds could get by without learning both, especially when you consider that many of the key players that God chose in Scripture were bi-cultural: Moses, Esther, Daniel, and Paul, for example."

Bill chimed in, "Both will also have to know cross-cultural church planting. They will need to know various models and strategies for evangelism, church planting, leadership development, followership development, curriculum development, ethnotheology, and ethnodoxology, just to name a few. And they will need to know which models and strategies will work in which contexts. They must be able to contextualize."

"Seems church planting bleeds over to the *do* column as well," suggested Bev. "How effective can a pioneer, or especially a facilitator, be if he or she has no experience in a church-planting movement?"

"Good question," responded Bill. "But maybe more importantly, they must know that this is what God wants them to do. Some people label this a 'call' from God. A call is about one's spiritual commitment. It will help keep you from leaving during the inevitable hard times, of which we've sure had our share."

"Both must have a vision that drives what they do," added Bev. "The content will vary, but the concept is necessary for both. They must not only know that God wants them there—a clear call—but also the specifics of what is to be done while they are there.

"While I think of it," she said, second-guessing herself, "the pioneer will have to cast a vision, but a facilitator may encourage the fulfillment of a vision already in place."

"Excellent observation," noted the professor. "That would fit well in the *do* category. Let's move to that category now.

✳   ✳   ✳

"What do pioneers and facilitators *do*?" asked Dr. Nobley.

"Here's a possible difference between the two," offered Bill. "Pioneers usually live among the people they are reaching, and it will usually require years of service to see a movement take place.

"Facilitators, on the other hand, usually parachute in for short periods of time—a seminar or conference or a consultation—and then return home. There are no doubt exceptions, like those who are permanent. But it seems to me that unlike pioneers, facilitators are much more transient; they come and go."

"Or," interrupted Bev, "maybe we have three classes of facilitators: parachute facilitators, semi-permanent facilitators, and permanent facilitators. By semi-permanent I mean extended stays, which could be several years. Permanent may be four years or more. There seems to be not only room but also necessity for all three. I'd draw it like this," she said as she headed to the whiteboard.

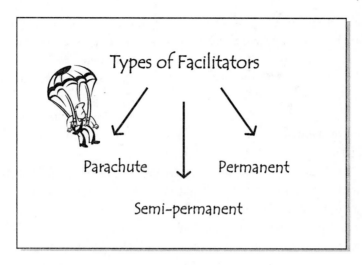

"This one will make the PowerPoint slides!" she said with a twinkle in her eye.

"I can buy your savvy suggestion," continued Bill, engaged, "and I would also add that pioneers *model* ministry rather than just *teach* about it. This modeling would include evangelism, leadership development, followership development, organizing the church, multiplying the church, curriculum development, compiling a songbook, establishing training institutions. . . . What have I missed? Oh, yes, it would also include any holistic ministries covered under the vision statement. Commitment to community involvement of some kind would be present for many pioneers, though probably not as much for the facilitators unless it's their specific ministry focus. The context would determine the type and amount of social involvement.

"Instead of modeling the ministry long-term, many facilitators coordinate or train others for ministry in multiple ways. They help people think through issues and get past problems. They cultivate the environment and connect existing dots, and they offer encouragement, expertise, challenge, critique, stimulation, guidance, and so forth. Rather than initiate, facilitators enhance. Rather than *do* the job, they aid and champion its completion.

"And neither the pioneer nor the facilitator should be in a hurry! I think that's a Western curse. Some things just take time. Some people and places just move slower. We must learn to relax and let God work in his own time. Fatigue and burnout are real. I've seen friends burn out, and it's not pretty," said Bill.

"Love your comments," said the professor. "It's obvious that you two have spent some time cross-culturally. What else should I add to the *do* list?"

"An issue we discussed constantly in the Philippines pertained to the transfer of power from the expatriates to the nationals, or from nationals to nationals," reflected Bev. "Some expats thought it was way too early to transfer power—for example, in evangelism or worship. Others thought the baton should have been passed a long time ago. There was always a tension that centered around the use, or some would say *abuse*, of power. Some held on to power far too long, while others gave it away too freely. Both paths can endanger the infant churches.

"That's why a pioneer church planter must be a good listener," Bev continued. "I'd think this would also be true for effective facilitators. The ear should precede the tongue. That way, *their* questions get answered rather than just those of the pioneers or facilitators."

"That's why Jacob Loewen talks about scratching where it itches," interjected the professor.[1]

"I like that," smiled Bev. "It seems to me that to be a good practical communicator—one who communicates with simplicity but not oversimplification—you have to be a good listener. That's true of both pioneers and facilitators, whether in formal, non-formal, or informal settings. Communication skills are a must if either wants to see true transformation happen."

"Building and maintaining close relationships will be central for pioneers or facilitators," added Bill. "Both will have to be good at developing long-term friendships. That's especially essential in relational-oriented societies such as the Philippines. For pioneers, that includes relationships with pre-Christians. Lots of them! Both must be effective social networkers."

"Building and maintaining relationships also means interpersonal health on the team," interjected Bev. "It takes a lot of prayer, talk, tears, and sweat to keep good relationships maintained among team members,

1. Loewen, *Culture and Human Values*, 3–26.

especially on a multinational team. Every cultural group—like every individual—has its own values and traditions, and inwardly, each believes that its own way is right," she quipped with a wink.

⁕   ⁕   ⁕

"What about *be*, the last category?" inquired the professor as he glanced at his watch.

"Several things come to mind," commented Bill. "Both pioneers and facilitators have to be flexible, able to roll with the punches. And they must be optimistic in spite of Satanic and human attacks! I remember when a bunch of us visited the mosque in Manila. Some of the younger women didn't want to wear a head covering or long sleeves. That resistance led to a long and heated discussion—and finally, thank God, openness to Muslim culture. At the time and under the circumstances, that issue turned out to be minor, despite the ruffled feathers on the team. But in another place and time, it could have become a much bigger issue, not just for the team but for national believers as well, and I'm not sure how well I would have rolled with the punches then."

"That leads to the obvious," noted Bev as she mentally tied the dots together. "Godly character is the most important part of the profile for both pioneers and facilitators; it's the backbone. Godly character requires all types of spiritual disciplines practiced in solitude, in community, and in service so that everyone—Christians and non-Christians—can see God in us. Godly character paves the way for true transformation.

"Godly character also has close ties to spousal and family support. Even though the standards are sometimes difficult to live up to, we must try our best in our marriages and families through the power of the Holy Spirit. If we don't, Satan will attack the weakest link in hopes of destroying the entire family. And he's pretty effective at that. Both pioneers and facilitators need to know how to pray, and they need to be open about areas of weakness. They also need to have *lots* of people praying regularly for them."

"Singles face somewhat different issues than families but nevertheless must live above reproach," Dr. Nobley said.

"One last thing I would add," said Bill. "Both pioneers and facilitators need to expect God to intervene on a daily basis. They should be looking for serendipitous supernatural intervention. I learned that from some of my Assemblies of God friends."

	PIONEER	FACILITATOR
KNOW . . .	Bible	Bible
	Cultures	Cultures
	Language	Language?
	Big picture	Big picture
	How to unite & integrate a team	How to unite & Integrate a team
	Church-planting models & strategies	Church-planting models & strategies
	Your Call	Your Call
	Commitment to holistic ministry	Commitment to holistic ministry
DO . . .	Cast vision	Encourage vision
	Reside there	Visit
	Model ministry	Train for ministry
	Listen	Listen
	Communicate practically	Communicate practically
	Network socially	Network socially
BE . . .	Flexible	Flexible
	Optimistic	Optimistic
	Godly in character	Godly in character
	Healthy at home	Healthy at home
	Open to spiritual intervention	Open to spiritual intervention

✳ ✳ ✳

"You two have done some good thinking!" said the professor with a sense of pride. "OK, here's what I've written so far."

"As you continue to think about the differences between pioneers and facilitators, let me make a few observations," continued the professor. "Four areas of concern are obvious from the chart: competencies, commitment, culture, and character. And all apply to both pioneers and facilitators, even as there are degrees of specification.

"The chart also reflects the life and ministry of the apostle Paul. His character was impeccable. He was totally committed to Christ. He had a foot in the Jewish cultural world as well as a foot in the Gentile cultural world, and he could walk knowledgeably in either. And he had the spiritual gifts and human skills to do the work of an apostle.

"Often overlooked in the area of competencies is that Paul was much more than a systematic theologian, if he ever was that. Walt Russell, a professor at Talbot School of Theology at Biola University, rightly calls Paul an 'incidental theologian.'[2]

"Paul was first and foremost a great pioneer missionary strategist and practitioner in both word and deed. That would fall under 'church planting models and strategies' in the chart," Dr. Nobley said, as he pointed it out on the whiteboard. "Missionary activities led by Pauline teams and others advanced the gospel from Jerusalem to Spain. From these recently planted churches evolved detailed theologies documented in the Epistles that addressed the specific needs of these new communities of faith.

"Now *that's* a model for us to follow! It will help cross-cultural church planters guard against just transferring their theology indiscriminately to another culture, overlooking critical theological issues in the host culture, or missing the contextualization process entirely. Contextualization, as Bill noted earlier, also falls under church planting.

"It would also demand the critical side of contextualization. Theology must not only be contextual; it must also challenge all aspects of culture that run counter to Scripture. Paul Hiebert called this 'critical contextualization.'[3] Practical communicators know not only how to

2. Russell, "An Alternative Suggestion," 179.
3. Hiebert, "Critical Contextualization," 287.

keep things simple, but also how to contextualize biblical truth without compromising it.

"I think another way that Paul serves as a model for church planters in the area of competencies is the emphasis given in his writings to missions. His writings are truly missional in nature, something often overlooked by Bible commentators. But I'm getting off course."

"We don't mind," tempted Bev.

"OK, OK, OK," agreed the professor, obviously happy for the opportunity. "Rabbit trails are fun to go down once in a while.

"If the missional nature of Scripture is missed, theology becomes just that: theology—cold doctrine without an inner missionary spark to keep it alive and burning. 'Making disciples that congregate together and multiply into movements? Well if it happens, great. If it doesn't, well, too bad.' That becomes the attitude.

"I'm amazed at how many Bible commentators miss the missional nature of Scripture, including Paul's writings. For example, in almost sixty chapters that span some thirteen hundred pages, Wayne Grudem's *Systematic Theology* fails to include key terms such as *missio Dei, mission, justice, missions,* or *the kingdom of God* in the chapter titles.

"Herman Ridderbos's *Paul: An Outline of His Theology* outlines Paul's theology in almost six hundred pages without a single mention of the mission of the church in eighty separate headings!

"Romans becomes a theological textbook on justification by faith for guilt-oriented individuals *rather than* God's message of holistic salvation communicated to honor-oriented communities so that they can bless others. It challenges the divided Roman church composed of Jews and Gentiles to become the next unified mission base of operation—mirroring God's universal blessing—so that global expansion can continue to Spain. Sadly, many Bible commentators miss the missional nature of justification by faith described in Romans. The Roman Christians were blessed through this doctrine so that they could bless others, including those living in Spain.

"Back in the very early 1700s, 1 Timothy, 2 Timothy, and Titus became popularly called 'Pastoral Epistles' even though they were written to apostles who were establishing churches. While the three documents have definite pastoral application, they would more accurately be called 'Apostolic Epistles.'

"The missional nature of Scripture is the basis of the Great Commandment and the Great Commission. This is part of knowing the Bible that we placed in the *know* column. Pioneers and facilitators must know experientially God's missional nature from Genesis through Revelation so that they can live it and teach it. That knowledge will help ensure a church-planting movement.

"The missional nature of Scripture is also the biblical foundation for giving our lives as co-laborers to start holistic church-planting movements around the world. We can't ever afford to lose or minimize this aspect of Scripture, even if some of the great Bible commentators do. Paul must remain our model and become the endeared model of those we are privileged to teach. That will help keep the movement alive.

"That rabbit trail does raise an interesting question. Should another competency for pioneers and for facilitators be the ability to teach and write curricula that are missional in nature?"

The professor sighed, smiling. "OK, now you've heard one of my hobby horses. It's time to return to the profiles.

✳   ✳   ✳

"When you look over the two profiles, what significant differences stand out to you between pioneer and facilitator church planters?" asked the professor.

After a short pause, Bev proposed, "There certainly is a lot of overlap between the two. I see two items, language acquisition and power transfer, that are definite distinctions. Both, however, seem to relate to how long the individuals remain on site, which I guess is a third difference.

"Facilitators tend to parachute in for short stays and then leave because a work is completed. Pioneers, on the other hand, tend to be more permanent—maybe four to ten years—because they start a movement from scratch. That's why language acquisition is much more important for pioneers than for facilitators."

"True," countered Bill, "but it seems to me that permanent, semi-permanent, and parachute facilitators—notice I used your terms, Bev—could all be much more effective if they were fluent in the language. This would allow all of them to be much more contextual, not to mention more comfortable, knowing what's going on all around them. I'm with you on language acquisition for pioneers.

"But I do need clarification on something that you talked about, Bev," he continued. "You mentioned power transfer. Do both pioneers and facilitators transfer power, and if so, how?"

"In our pioneer church planting in the Philippines, we transferred power often and immediately as Filipinos became effective in evangelism, leadership, and so on," responded Bev. "Bill, you were a great advocate of this practice, even when some team members fought you on it. Maybe Dr. Nobley could address the facilitator side, since I'm not too familiar with it."

"Be glad to," responded the professor. "Facilitators also transfer power, but in a different way. Let me backtrack a little to explain this.

"Every social encounter within a family, with friends, with co-workers, or with strangers becomes a political encounter. Why? Because every social relationship is unequal, creating power differences and distances.

"In other words, the baton is always in someone's hand first, including the facilitator's. This is true because a hierarchy always exists in any social structure, even in egalitarian societies. Mere presence automatically creates hierarchy.

"Teachers carry very high prestige in the Asian world, as you well know. When national Christians invite expatriates to consult or teach in relation to some aspect of church multiplication, they believe that the baton is in the expatriate's hand and that by the time the seminar, or conference, or meeting is over, the baton will be in their hands.

"Knowledge exchange becomes opportunity for shared power. Experience exchange becomes opportunity for shared power. Responsibility exchange becomes opportunity for shared power. Even a funding exchange becomes opportunity for shared power.

"Why? Because power is always on loan, and genuine facilitators want to give it away. They understand that within the spiritual domain, shared power results in multiplied power, expanding God's kingdom.

"Facilitators, who tend to be specialists, give away power in their specific area or areas of expertise while pioneers have to cover everything from forming a team to starting a movement. That's why pioneers often work in teams, because few, if any, individuals have all the gifts and skills necessary to cover every aspect of holistic, pioneer church multiplication."

"Thanks, Dr. Nobley. That was helpful," confirmed Bill.

"I'd add a fourth distinctive," Bill continued. "It too is related to time on-site. It's *modeling* ministry versus talking about it. That's a big difference. One is cognitive, cerebral, while the other is practical. Paul liked to demonstrate Christianity to his teams, not just teach them cognitively. Seems Paul had a lot to say about modeling."

"He sure did," affirmed the professor as he reached for his Bible, opened it, flipped through the texts, and began to read. "'In everything I did, I showed you.'[4] 'You became imitators of us and the Lord.'[5] 'Follow my example, as I follow the example of Christ.'[6] "We did this . . . in order to make ourselves a model for you to follow.'"[7]

"Ah, I almost forgot," remembered Bev. "Pioneers and facilitators also differ in what they do with vision. Pioneers cast vision and work it, while facilitators encourage fulfillment of a pre-established vision."

Dr. Nobley returned to the whiteboard and began to write down the distinctives between pioneers and facilitators.

"Anything we missed?" he asked.

Major Distinctions Between Pioneers & Facilitators

—Language acquisition
—Power transfer
—Time on-site
—Modeling
—Role of vision

---

4. Acts 20:35
5. I Thess 1:6
6. I Cor 11:1
7. 2 Thess 3:9

"What about community involvement?" continued Bev. "It seems to me that pioneers become much more involved in community needs than do facilitators."

"Possibly true," countered Bill. "But what if the facilitator's role *is* community development?"

"OK, I withdraw that one," conceded Bev. "Seems a development focus would require a totally separate profile. The same would be true for other emphases as well, like business or ethnomusicology or Bible translation, for example."

"Nothing else comes to mind, Dr. Nobley," said Bill.

"I'll have a case study on community development for you later, as well as one on Bible translation," Dr. Nobley said. "And you are correct, Bev. Multiple profiles are needed. It's getting late. What stood out to you this week?"

"I think for me it's the time factor," offered Bill. "While some facilitators, maybe the majority, will parachute in, others may be there for the long-term. At least those who parachute in will not have to worry about creating dependency! I wonder if anyone has gathered any stats on that," he wondered aloud, talking more to himself than to the others.

"I think modeling is key," Bill continued. "While there is a time and place for lectures and dialogue, nothing beats seeing it being done in person. The apprenticeship model has great merit.

"It scares me to think about facilitators who have never planted a church but who go overseas to teach nationals how to do it," he complained. "We saw some of that in the Philippines. I think facilitators should have ministry experience in the area or areas that they teach nationals. That should be a given. And they need cross-cultural experience. So many of them come over with their pet models and strategies, expecting that they'll work there as well as they did at home."

"That raises another interesting question," mused Bev. "What makes a facilitator acceptable in a foreign context? Experience? Education? Money? Gender? Gray hair?"

"That's a great question, Bev," said the proud professor. "Very few people ever ask that question."

"I've been thinking," pondered Bill as he stroked his goatee. "I wonder. . . . If we were to return to the Philippines as facilitators rather than as pioneers, would we feel that we were violating our role as missionaries? Would we be able to learn that working in the background as encouragers and mentors is okay? Would we be able to appreciate the fact that churches are getting planted, even if we don't physically plant them?"

"We really need to think about that," responded Bev. "It seems to me that pioneers and facilitators both facilitate but do it differently. Pioneers begin with pre-Christians, win them to Christ, and try to see Second Timothy 2:2 become a reality: that is, to see multiple generations continue, creating a movement. Pioneers not only teach but also model, passing the baton as soon as possible in every area of ministry and service.

"Facilitators begin with Christians, often working from behind the scenes. They, like pioneers, pass the baton of knowledge, experience, finances, technology, and so forth.

"The starting and ending points also differ," added Bev. "Nothing happens if the pioneer doesn't show up and get it started. Pioneers focus on starting a movement, but facilitators come in at various points of the journey to stimulate certain initiatives. The time of stay is, therefore, also different. Pioneers stay for the entire process; facilitators stay for parts of it."

✻　✻　✻

"Excellent observations," concluded the professor. "Creating a profile is very helpful in discerning the differences between pioneers and facilitators. It also is helpful to churches and mission agencies in the areas of promotion, selection, job descriptions, and training.

"In that the Fourth Era sends out people of many ages, from youth to senior citizens, it might be good to look at the megachurch movement's role in facilitation. What are its strengths and weaknesses? How well do those sent out as facilitators by megachurches match the profile we developed today?" asked the professor as he pointed towards the whiteboard.

"This, of course, has connections to the short-term missions movement as well. Using Ralph Winter's term, does the Fourth Era represent the *amateurization* of missions?[8] What do you think?"

"Can't wait to explore that," said Bill. "See you next week."

8. Winter, "Re-Amateurization of Missions."

Week 5

Who Unleashed the Megachurch?

"WELL, I SEE YOU were able to include your slide on the multiple timeframes for facilitators," commented a smiling Dr. Nobley after the PowerPoint review. "I like the little guy with the parachute!"

"Thanks," said Bev. "Where do we go in our lesson today?"

"Megachurches," Bill reminded her enthusiastically.

"That's right," said Dr. Nobley, "but where do we start? The topic is as big as the churches it represents. Maybe a step back will be helpful before we forge ahead on megachurches. Anyway, there's a lot of interconnectedness."

※　※　※

Rearranging a stack of manila folders and books on his desk and brushing off some remaining cookie crumbs, the professor headed for the large table with steaming coffee in one hand and notes in the other.

"In the last three or four decades," he began, "a number of movements have taken place that have exponentially expanded the roster of players in global missions. We've moved from the professionals being the dominant Western players to the laity becoming prominent, from the few to the many, from the highly trained to the minimally trained."

Grabbing a piece of paper from one of the folders, the professor continued, "Consider some of the stats. From 2001 to 2005, the number of full-time and non-resident missionaries dropped from 42,787 to 41,329. That's a loss of 1,458 workers. That's the bad news.

"The good news is that the number of full-time tentmakers—including staff and associates—grew from 25,424 to 39,446. You do the math. Do we have a shift in mission personnel taking place here or what?

"At least three current populist movements have fueled this new growth. The first is short-term missions, which sent out some 2.2 million in 2006, a third of whom went to Mexico. The other two are business as mission and megachurches. And, yes, they are interconnected.

"Many Christians in the West today want to make a difference in the world. And they want to do it not just by writing a check, but through participation in some capacity, preferably in their area of expertise. We talked a little bit about this in the second week, if I remember correctly."

"I remember," concurred Bev. "We talked some about the PEACE Plan."

"Did you know that half of the seminary students in the United States have taken short-term trips abroad?" continued Dr. Nobley. "Did you know that since 2000, 12 percent of active churchgoing teenagers have gone out short-term? Did you know that approximately one third of all US churches send out short-term teams that average around eighteen people annually?

"Some of this desire to make a difference internationally is definitely generational. Younger generations, such as the Millennials or Gen Y-ers, have a penchant for travel, especially abroad. They like openness, as is evidenced in MySpace and Facebook. They want networking, teamwork, green stewardship, institutions, and family. They're optimists: they're the ones who received trophies whether they won or lost when they were kids. And they're charged up about community service. All of these characteristics feed right into the short-term missions movement.

"John Zogby calls them the 'First Globals' for their cross-border perspective, arms-wide-open acceptance of other people and their ideas, and their nomadic attitude toward work and life.[1] Joel Dylhoff says that this group thinks of the world as their job market and that their most permanent address is their present email address."[2]

"I can relate to that!" laughed Bev.

"In the evangelical world," continued the professor, "this translates into a generation that is actively participating in ministries, often short-term—that is, a week to two years. This hands-on generation favors addressing poverty, justice issues, creation care, HIV/AIDS, and related social topics, as we discussed a couple of weeks ago when I mentioned the PEACE Plan.

1. Zogby, *Way We'll Be*, 107.
2. Dylhoff, "Gen X," 448.

"While I have a few cautions, some of which I noted last week, I personally welcome this change," continued the confident professor. "It opens up unprecedented opportunities for service for all generations and both genders at home and abroad. Volunteerism, teamwork, and philanthropic opportunities abound! It means more followers of Christ are literally following his footprints around the globe!

"This 'army of amateurs' often comes back from short-term trips excited about what God has done. They've seen deep spiritual hunger, abject poverty, malnourished children, child soldiers, AIDS victims, demonic darkness and activity, answered prayer, and a national church composed of strong and weak members, just like at home. They feel frustrated that so much social injustice prevails. They reevaluate life's priorities. They take initiative in building relationships with those of different ethnicities. They volunteer for evangelistic and/or social activities. Some make other short-term trips. Others generously fund upcoming trips for friends. A few become career missionaries.

"While it's true that a few go just for the adventure, most want to see God in action. And that's what they often find. It's also true that good intentions birthed abroad often soon evaporate in the midst of daily realities once they return home.

"But even as it affords tremendous opportunities, it also brings mind-boggling challenges, *at least to the practiced eye*. Effective cross-cultural ministry is not a walk in the park. It requires incredible missiological insight, endurance, flexibility, and the ability to laugh at oneself. Sounds a little like our profile from last week, huh?"

"That it does," agreed Bill.

"STM, an abbreviation for short-term mission, has received a lot of poor press," proposed the professor. "Some of it is deserved—going to find a new girlfriend or boyfriend, or to help 'those poor, pitiful people' over there, etcetera. But some of the negative opinion is based on misunderstanding.

"You both were short-termers, and have been around them. What have you heard, read, or experienced?" asked the professor as he made his way to the whiteboard with black marker in hand. "We'll begin with the poor press and then move to the positive press."

"I think many who go have completely oversimplified the complexity of cross-cultural ministry," responded Bill. "They should review Bev's chart on CP-1, CP-2, and CP-3 that we covered two weeks ago to catch the complexity levels and the timeframes related to each. I would hope that they could gain appreciation for the complexity of communicating the gospel cross-culturally without becoming so paralyzed that they do nothing. They should also make some pre-field attempt to learn key phrases of the language and vital parts of the host culture. Really, this much should be required."

Bev added, "I think some go just as spiritual tourists or as if they're on some kind of a spiritual pilgrimage. They want to have a good time, hang with friends, see exotic sights, taste foreign cuisine, and visit some national Christians. This often takes valuable ministry time away from career missionaries, who pick them up at the airport and shuttle them from place to place. As one of my friends working in Africa said, 'I have become a tour guide.'"

"And don't forget to mention all the career funding that now goes to short-termers," added Bill.

"STM does eat up lots of funds that normally would have gone to career missionaries," continued Bev, "making it difficult to maintain sufficient annual support—and making it even tougher for new career missionaries to raise funds. Bill and I are experiencing that challenge right now.

"In fact, the STM trend could bankrupt long-term missions. And it causes some career missionaries to consider going short-term, particularly those who have high school or college-age kids, or who work in countries that are expensive to live in. I just heard the other day that over sixty career missionaries have left Japan this year due to the recession and lack of financial support. I wonder if recessions also slow down fundraising for STM."

"Some short-termers seem averse to any missions training," added Bill, "seeing it as a total waste of time and finances. They consider theological training not only sufficient but superior to any other studies. After all, the Word of God is for all peoples and will not return void. They seem to forget that their Western background does influence how they perceive Scripture, as you noted in one of our previous sessions, Dr. Nobley.

"Some see themselves as visiting heroes riding in on white stallions, ready to rescue the damsels in distress rather than become servant-learners. They go to give and help the less fortunate, not to receive or learn from such needy people."

"Missiologists call this type of attitude and cultural captivity *ethno-centrism*," interjected Dr. Nobley. "It's sometimes a subtle, condescending attitude; at other times it's just blatantly cold contempt, much like some Jews had for Gentiles during New Testament times."

Bill shook his head and said, "The team leaders of STM groups often lack legitimacy in the eyes of nationals. One reason is that the leaders are sometimes very young. Many societies respect age and life experience over youth and inexperience."

"Even though some teams go with high ministry expectations of what they can accomplish on a short trip, wise nationals know differently," noted Bev. "And being goal focused in event-oriented societies brings its own set of challenges, at least to the host culture. Some short-termers even mock the missionaries for taking years to get the same ministry results that they supposedly accomplished in just a couple of weeks. We've seen some of these 'cultural conversions'—nationals whom short-termers claim to have led to Christ because they prayed the prayer or raised a hand. Many dried up before the expatriates landed on home soil ready to tell their friends how receptive the nationals were to the gospel."

"Some nationals see short-termers as cash cows," noted Bill. "They keep coming, loaded with money for pet projects. This often creates jealousy because some nationals receive these benefits while others don't.

"And there's also another side," Bill continued. "Short-termers sometimes undermine the local infrastructure by using raised funds to construct buildings, wells, and so forth," said Bill. "The Thai government, for example, wants to know why such funds are not used to hire Thai workers to do the construction. They want jobs to go to Thais, not expats. While the short-termers assume they are doing good for the community, the Thai government sees them as undermining the local economy."

"I'm afraid that STM often benefits personnel from the sending churches more than the national churches," added Bev. "Long-term ministry impact among host communities may not be as long as most short-termers assume, especially if there are no protracted follow-up visits over the years. It may be more like 'missions lite' in lightening time!

Poor Press for STM

1. Naïve missiologically
2. Can't do much because don't know language or culture
3. Spiritual tourist on vacation
4. Take time away from career missionaries
5. Career missionaries lose funding
6. Career missionaries tempted to STM
7. Anti missions education
8. Ethnocentric
9. Unrealistic ministry expectations
10. Come as heroes rather than learners
11. Leaders lack legitimacy
12. Many cultures don't appreciate youth
13. Goal-focused in event-oriented societies
14. Mock missionaries
15. Take jobs away from nationals
16. Assume doing good
17. Benefit sending church rather than field
18. Little long-term ministry impact
19. "Missions lite"
20. Colonizers of Christian culture

"One other thing comes to mind. Some short-termers believe that they know how 'true' Christians should respond to cultural issues, even though they have no clue about the nuances of that culture. You *can't* drink alcohol, or you *can* drink; you can wear *these* clothes and listen to *this* type of music, but not *these*; and so forth. They're like Christian culture colonizers."

"Wow, that's some poor press alright!" noted the professor as he finished the category and created a new one on the whiteboard. "Every movement, however, has some positive press as well. What positive press have you noted about STM?"

※   ※   ※

Playing with her ponytail, Bev began. "One of the great things about STM is that it provides a legitimate means to enter restricted countries. Teams can enter because they offer desired projects.

"I think STM teams today have the opportunity to receive a lot of helpful training, from pre-entry to reentry," she continued. "Trainers challenge them to learn some culture and language, go as learners, build long-lasting relationships, serve those they meet, and so forth. When the short-termers return, they have opportunity to reflect on their experience, making any future trips that much more effective. The debriefings also provide trainers ideas on how to improve training. It's cyclical."

"STM also provides a safe means to ascertain possible future career moves," offered Bill. "People can test the waters in a secure environment to see what it's like to discover or practice their profession in a cross-cultural setting. As I think of it, it's probably good to separate youth from those who have a work history, whether mid-career or finishers. Each group goes with a different set of objectives and interests."

"I'd call the career people 'professional amateurs,'" suggested Bev. "They are professionals in their respective fields but amateurs missiologically, even if they don't know it. They will have to learn to do their work in a culturally sensitive way to really advance the Kingdom of God."

"I like that," agreed Bill. "It is so true. And I think it would be advantageous if short-termers could receive an invitation to do something that enhances the ministry vision of career missionaries rather than just show up. They need to mesh their vision with the long-term vision of the career missionaries on the field. This type of partnership will provide the team immediate legitimacy with the nationals while furthering the field's long-term ministry objectives. This sure beats hit-and-miss forays."

"It will also help build long-lasting relationships between short-termers, their home churches, the national believers, mission agencies, and career missionaries," added Bev.

"We've also seen entire families come to the Philippines on their vacation," she continued. "It's great for the nationals to see a family unit functioning and ministering together."

"STM expands the participants' understanding in many ways," said Bill. "They gain a greater understanding of God's passion for the world. Their understanding of missions broadens as they see the various ministries required to reach a people spiritually and socially. Their assumed theology also often receives challenges. For example, some of the Filipinos we worked with relied on dreams to tell them what to do. No short-termers we've ever met have had a theology of dreams before they arrived, including us!"

"And they had to rethink some of their accepted worldview assumptions," noted Bev. "Filipinos tend to make group decisions rather than individual decisions. This challenged those doing evangelism as they insisted that the Filipinos make an individual decision for Christ. They also found it difficult to see, as did we, that praying the 'sinner's prayer' was perceived by many as just another ritual to control the spiritual powers that impact their daily lives.

"We also noted that the short-termers deeply appreciated their time working in partnership with career missionaries. Those willing to learn did gain a lot of knowledge about living and ministering cross-culturally, all the while experiencing the synergy of partnerships."

"So STM provides people the opportunity to grow missionally and missiologically," Bill summarized.

"And they grow spiritually!" interjected Bev excitedly. "Following the example of national followers of Christ, they learn to pray, trust God, and wait for an answer. And they also learn more about genuine worship! Involvement in missions on all levels creates a desire to worship the God behind missions. They begin to realize that they don't go to the field for themselves, their churches, or the nationals—they go to glorify God."

"Action tends to follow worship," concluded Bill. "Returning short-termers often become strong advocates for missions. They help raise

Positive Press for STM

1. Opens restricted countries
2. Pre-entry and re-entry provision
3. Safe means to test for career possibilities
4. Professional amateurs
5. Enhances ministry of career missionaries
6. Builds networking relationships
7. Gives vacation a purpose
8. Serve as a family
9. Expands understanding of God's passion
10. Expands understanding of missions
11. Expands understanding of theology
12. Expands understanding of evangelism
13. Experience partnership
14. Grow missionally
15. Grow missiologically
16. Grow spiritually
17. Worship God (big view of God)
18. Become a missions advocate

funds, pray, promote, join Missions Committees, take other short-term trips, or do whatever they can to promote missions."

"Excellent summary," commended Dr. Nobley. "It's obvious you've been there, done that! Here's what I've summarized from your comments."

Dr. Nobley walked back toward the young couple. "If I were to summarize the key points out of the 'positive press' for STM, here are four that I would include. First, a 'God-listening heart,' what Solomon requested in 1 Kings 3. Second, sanctified professionalism; the story of Bezalel's Spirit-driven skills in Exodus 35 is helpful here. Third, missiological astuteness, something Peter continued to learn slowly in his dealings with Gentiles as shown in Acts 10:34. And fourth, worship of the King, something we've seen expressed with Noah after the flood in Genesis, through the scene in Revelation 7:9 when a 'great multitude' worships the Lamb."

The professor continued, "Let's build off of the STM movement and show its relationship to missional megachurches. I think we should realize that this populist, church-based movement of short-term teams will impact global missions for decades to come. Mission agencies, career missionaries, and national churches will find themselves interacting with short-termers whether they like it or not.

"Megachurches—such as Saddleback in Orange County, Redeemer in New York City, Perimeter in Atlanta, Church of Brook Hills in Birmingham, and NorthWood and NorthWood Church in Dallas—will play a major role in this STM movement as they continue to place more boots on the ground. Megachurches will be 'shape-shifters' in global missions strategy.

"I think we'll need a separate session for BAM, business as mission. Maybe we can discuss that next week, if that's OK?"

"Can't wait," responded Bev.

"Excellent," Dr. Nobley said. "Let's move on to megachurches."

"Interestingly," began the professor, "the twenty largest megachurches in the world are found outside the United States, in countries such as South Korea, India, Argentina, and Cote d'Ivoire. Of those twenty, half are found in the Southern Hemisphere, where church growth presently far exceeds that in the Northern Hemisphere. For our purposes, we'll focus on the Northern Hemisphere.

"Out of the approximate 335,000 churches in the United States, more than 1250 of them qualify as megachurches. Scott Thumma and Dave Travis define a megachurch as a congregation that has at least two thousand people attending weekend services. Most of these megachurches have emerged late in the twentieth century.[3]

---

3. Thumma and Travis, *Beyond Megachurch Myths*.

"These authors expect megachurches to increase by around fifty per year, and note that there are no typical ones. Megachurch activities move far beyond evangelism and church planting to include other ministries that address physical, educational, and economic needs.

"Scott Thumma and Warren Bird released the results of a survey in June of 2009 of almost 25,000 people from twelve megachurches in the United States. They found that two-thirds had attended five years or less; 45 percent never volunteer for anything at the church; they give less financially than those attending small churches; worship style is the biggest attracter, followed by the senior pastor; and they prefer spiritually-oriented small groups over all others.[4]

"A growing number of megachurches in the United States and Canada have, or will have, plans to unleash 'an army of missionaries sitting in the pews' to engage the world locally and globally.[5] They want *all* their laity to become missional—that is, to become totally committed Christians who reach the lost wherever they find themselves. We talked a little about this in the third week, if I remember correctly.

"Anyway," continued Dr. Nobley as he searched for a website on his laptop.[6] "I want you to be sure to look up this informative website sometime this week.

www.rickwarrennews.com/peace_plan.htm

Rick Warren, senior pastor of Saddleback Church puts it this way: 'Ordinary people empowered by God making a difference together.'[7]

"And send out they do. Saddleback Church, the second largest church in the United States, has sent out some four hundred volunteer teams—close to eight thousand people—to sixty-nine countries to help in hospitals, clinics, schools, orphanages, and refugee camps. They are presently staging their first countrywide initiative in Rwanda."

"Do they send mostly to reached areas of the world, following your Fourth Era theory?" asked Bill.

---

4. Thumma and Bird, "Not Who You Think."

5. Bob Roberts, interviewed in Galli, "Glocal Church Ministry," 45.

6. Warren, "PEACE Plan."

7. Ibid., para. 3.

"For the most part, yes," answered the professor. "That's because. . . . Well, I'll get to that a little later when we discuss which theology drives Saddleback.

"I applaud such a volunteer amateur movement at Saddleback and many other missional megachurches, like NorthWood Church in Dallas, where Bob Roberts is the senior pastor. He has authored *Transformation* and *Glocalization,* both dealing with mobilizing the laity within the megachurch for short-term missions, or STM. These churches are so New Testament in many ways. I hope they continue their pursuit and multiply. May their tribes increase!

"But along with celebration, I also have some deep concerns," the professor said. "As I discuss missional megachurches here at home and in Canada, please see my heart." His bright blue eyes focused intensely first on Bill and then on Bev.

"Anything I say that may sound like criticism is not meant to condemn, but rather to challenge, to bring clarity, to be constructive. It's meant to improve something I consider a relatively new, yet legitimate, movement of God. I want it to succeed! With fewer than 20 percent of the US churches engaged globally, we need all the missional megachurches we can get.

"But I would like to see the STM movement modified by megachurches. I'd like to see them stand on the shoulders of effective missionary predecessors so that they don't reinvent the wheel and make the same mistakes of former generations. Sadly this has already happened on far too many occasions. We must become better stewards of limited resources."

"Examples?" asked an inquisitive Bill, stroking his goatee.

"A recent example on the STM side would be Bruce Wilkinson's Dream for Africa, or DFA. It began in Swaziland in 2002 when he moved his family to Africa, and ended abruptly in 2005. Author of the *Prayer of Jabez* and *The Dream Giver,* Wilkinson set out to rescue a million orphans, thousands of whom lived in Swaziland. Many of these children were products of the AIDS epidemic. He sought land from the government to create a center that would include a large orphanage and other capital ventures, one being a game reserve.

"A quick aside. Some of our university students and staff went over for a summer to work with DFA. I asked one student why he would be teaching the Swazis how to plant gardens when they have been doing this for centuries. Didn't get a response," the professor shrugged and then continued.

"Anyway, altruism, entrepreneurialism, enthusiasm, compassion, spontaneity, spiritual vision, spiritual passion, and even living among the people were all insufficient to counter Swazi culture. Government officials were not about to be pushed by deadlines or give land to a modern-day moneyed colonizer. Nor did they appreciate their extended-family kinship system being misunderstood or modified. It was the extended family who became responsible to care for family members with HIV/AIDS.

"We must learn from this well-intentioned, but misguided, experiment. We must take the time to learn the host culture's history and the political, economic, religious, and social structures, among other things.

"Going it alone is not appreciated in most contexts. We need to learn to listen long to the locals and to the expatriates who also serve there. I just hope making Rwanda the first Purpose Driven Nation does not repeat history. It doesn't have to, but it certainly could if ethnocentrism prevails. We must be wary of the McDonaldization of so-called proven programs.

"I should also note that what is happening on the ground level of a country is of utmost importance for consideration by expatriates. Paul Kagame, authoritarian President of Rwanda, provides strong leadership that does not look outward to foreign aid for rebuilding the country, but inward to its own people. For Kagame, aid must do things that wean people off of it, not make them dependent upon it.

"So you see," said the professor, "There's lots to consider when one decides to reach a nation holistically.

"Another example can be found in a major difference between the first PEACE Plan and the PEACE 2.0 instituted in 2007. They've dropped 'Church-in-a-Box,' which included Saddleback music, sermons, books, including the *Purpose Driven Church,* and so forth. There were other boxes, too—or at least consideration of such: Leadership-Training-in-a-Box, Business-in-a-Box, Clinic-in-a-Box, School-in-a-Box."

"I could have told them these would not work," interjected Bill. "I wonder what people in Orange County, California, would think if a mainland Chinese missionary showed up with a Chinese-Church-in-a-Box!"

"No doubt," responded the professor. "That's because you are missiologically astute. Saddleback eventually began to realize that prepackaged Western programs, however relevant for Saddleback Sam and Sally, have limited cross-cultural relevance at home or abroad. If they remain learners, expect more revisions of the PEACE Plan down the road. I suspect we will see more.

"Here are a few questions that demand answers if the missional megachurch is to be successful at ministering cross-culturally," noted the professor as he reached for his coffee.

"How effective can short-term amateurs—or using Bev's term, 'professional amateurs'—really be in cross-cultural contexts?

"What strengths do they bring to the table? Limitations?

"Should everyone go? Should there be a profile for such volunteers?

"Should they work with the existing national churches? Career missionaries in mission agencies?"

"Or," interjected Bev, "should the megachurches send career missionaries as well as short-termers? We must not forget that Jesus did ask some to 'leave their nets' to change professions permanently!"

"Excellent," responded the professor as he continued to raise questions. "Should they visit the same place annually or springboard from one country to another? How do they handle the language and cultural barriers? Should there be pre-field qualifications that must be met before they can go?

"What type of training should they receive for the first trip? The second? The third? Is theological training alone sufficient?

"How well do prepackaged programs really work long-term?

"We'll touch on some of these questions and probably add others along the way. Buckle up. Here we go. We may go overtime today!"

※   ※   ※

Quickly finishing a chocolate chip cookie and taking another sip of coffee, the professor continued. "Megachurches have the personnel, the finances, and the time to impact global cross-cultural ministry tremendously.

"The STM movement within the megachurches has begun and will continue. As Thomas Friedman would say, 'Later is over.'[8]

"The central questions remain: How effective will such engagements be for long-term kingdom growth? Will the megachurches repeat the errors of their missionary predecessors? Will they be inquisitive? Servant learners with 'God-listening hearts'?

"That's one thing I appreciate about Rick Warren," continued the professor as he searched through a file. "He stated early in the evolution of the PEACE Plan that his team would be humble learners, open to any feedback or comment.

"Why? Because Warren recognizes that he needs all the help he can get for such an ambitious endeavor. Warren likens the PEACE Plan to building an airplane while you're flying it. He'd say we're making this up as we go along because nobody has done this before—which may be a slight overstatement.

"He tells his leadership team to *learn to fail faster* so that others don't have to repeat the same mistakes. Even so, he believes that this volunteer amateur movement will be successful.

"Maybe the best place to start to answer these questions is to reflect on the foundational underpinnings of the PEACE Plan," proposed the professor as he refilled his coffee cup and headed to the whiteboard.

"Here's what I perceive them to be," said the professor as he began writing. "Let's take a brief look at each of them, recognizing that overlap exists."

"What's the goal of the PEACE Plan?" the professor asked. "Get 100 percent of Saddleback members involved in some capacity—not just the 14 percent of committed Christians who are typically active in the average church. That's no easy task! Remember the stat that 45 percent of attendees in megachurches don't volunteer for anything? The Saddleback church faces the same challenge. Members may love Rick and the PEACE Plan, but that doesn't mean that they have plans to participate. They consider that type of work to be for paid professionals.

"Nevertheless, the Saddleback PEACE leadership team does all it can to mobilize the laity. . . . Here's the quote," said Dr. Nobley as he stopped thumbing through Bob Roberts' book entitled *Glocalization*. "Roberts shows one way they try to mobilize members. Listen to this."

8. Friedman, "(No) Drill, Baby Drill," para. 11.

Underpinnings of the PEACE Plan

—Unleash the laity
—Mobilize through strength
—Prioritize ecclesiology
—Pastors focus on mobilization
—Train from the laity out
—Make reproducible & sustainable

> For the kingdom to spread virally means that it will of necessity not be a 'religious movement,' but a 'human movement' tied to people and vocations. . . . How do we make the chief and primary 'missionary' the person in the pew? Here's a good place to start. What do they know best? Their job! Why not let them do what they do best and use it to bring about transformation?[9]

"They mobilize through strength, through their job! Think of the numbers that could go abroad, or are already there, compared to the total number of professional missionaries. There's no comparison!" Dr. Nobley exclaimed. "Ingenious!"

"That means they go as professionals," insisted Bev. "And while they may go as experts in their professions, they need to remember that most go as amateurs as cross-cultural workers. *Being missional is one thing; being missiologically astute is quite another!*"

"Very perceptive, Bev!" responded a nodding professor. "This mobilization model assumes that people not only love their jobs, but also are good at them. It also assumes that the said profession is needed over there. But it is about more than the job. It's about ecclesiology.

---

9. Roberts, *Glocalization*, 82.

"Warren seems to believe that missions is the rightful role of the church, not of mission agencies, nor of NGOs, nor of any other institutions, such as colleges, universities, or seminaries. Missions belongs exclusively to the church; the church is the missionary. It's the church's turn now. It's time for another reformation. He feels that agencies have had their chance and have not done a great job. That's for sure in some cases but certainly not all.

"But more importantly, Scripture places the mantle of missions exclusively on the shoulders of the church. That makes every member a potential missionary. And that means looking for other churches at home to partner with, and national churches abroad for the partnership to serve. They call the first 'Local PEACE' and the latter 'Global PEACE.'

"Bill, does that answer your earlier question about where megachurches send the majority of their personnel?" inquired the professor.

"Yes, it does. To the unreached," responded Bill. "Thank you, Dr. Nobley."

The professor continued with a rhetorical question: "And why do they send personnel to build partnerships with national churches? Because ecclesiology, the centrality of the church, drives their practice. Yes, the missional megachurch is not only a prime example of ministry models found in the Fourth Era; it is also a major player."

"I have read dissertations," noted Bill, "that eloquently argue for the validity of both positions, the church and the para-church. And both think they are correct biblically. This has led me to question whether the church is the *center* of God's mission or *central* to it. At this point in my spiritual journey, I see the church not as the *center* but rather as *central* to God's mission.

"And this raises an interesting question. Which theology drives our missional practice? Bibliology? Christology? Pneumatology? Ecclesiology? Kingdom theology?"

"Wish we had time to explore that," commented Dr. Nobley as he glanced at his watch, "but that will have to wait for another time."

Bev could not contain herself, even though she knew time was of the essence. "Interaction with our friends working in Pakistan has shown us that partnering with the national churches sometimes calls for renewal because of existing deep-seated challenges on both sides. And those renewal relationships have not always worked out well.

"The same could be said for national churches in other parts of the world that are steeped in legalism or some other 'ism.' Some expats have chosen to by-pass the local national churches completely to avoid being stigmatized with 'inferior' brands of Christianity. Working with the national church is not always as easy as it may sound."

"Thanks for that insight, Bev," said a pleased professor, "That's where the rubber meets the road.

"Another underpinning of the PEACE Plan is the major role of the missional pastor in mobilizing the masses. The pastor challenges people in the pews to become active, missional participants—to move from 'Sunday Christians' to 'everyday missionaries' in their daily routines and hopefully, to reach out cross-culturally, too.

"I commend that aspect," said the professor. "I should also note that the PEACE leadership team is not trying to turn their pastor into an apostle."

"I commend that, too—that is, seeing the pastor as mobilizer," responded Bev energetically. "But if the pastors stop at mobilization, we have a definite problem: *missiological naiveté!* Those who go will just think that how they did their job or ministry at home is how they can do it abroad. Such thinking is ethnocentric, disrespecting the vast creativity of the Creator."

"I would concur," said Bill, nodding approvingly. "Loosing the laity for missions calls for more than a pastor mobilizing a talented pool of educators, business people, plumbers, doctors, lawyers, Sunday School teachers, children's workers, and counselors. Just as these individuals were trained for their various professions, which took some time and financial sacrifice, moving them cross-culturally will require additional training and financing, *if* a high level of competency is to result. Otherwise, this Holy Spirit-driven movement is prone to repeat the errors of missions past."

"Some of the errors we've seen," noted Bev, "include the total financing of buildings and the offering of non-contextualized testimonies, evangelism models, discipleship models, Bible curricula, worship music, counseling, and business models, just to name a few. A little collegiality and cooperation could mitigate a lot of this."

"That point leads us to the next assumption: training from the laity out," continued the professor. "What does that mean? Probably just the opposite of the way you were trained. Allow me to unpack this statement.

"First, most pastors are not trained missiologically, even though they may live in multicultural settings. So, you can expect senior pastors to remain mobilizers rather than trainers. Trainers will have to come from elsewhere. And that's OK. That's the body of Christ at work.

"There are a lot of effective cross-cultural workers out there who would be more than willing to help train another generation of workers. I should add, too, that those who do the training should be those who have cross-cultural experience. Because they've done it, they can speak from experience. Nothing like authenticity, especially for this generation!

"It should also be noted that Saddleback is not focused on field impact like the career missionaries are. Rather, the church is focused on laity impact. This focus is problematic in that any mobilization automatically bleeds into long-term field strategy, impacting it positively or negatively.

"Do field impact and laity impact have to be mutually exclusive? Certainly not! Is the focus on laity impact rather than field impact just a modern-day version of colonial paternalism?" Dr. Nobley asked. "Could be!"

"Ouch!" winced Bev.

Bill frowned.

"Another reality is that most Christians who do volunteer for STM within the megachurch do not want to spend four hours in training, much less eight or twenty-eight. Consequently, the PEACE leadership team must begin with crawl-steps, which to you two would seem embarrassingly simple, if not hopeless. Then it is on to walk-steps and run-steps. Mobilizers and trainers have to boil things down to the simplest components possible. Hence, 'PEACE' and 'five global giants,' like the Four Spiritual Laws, are concise and memorable."

"Five global giants?" asked Bev.

"Yes," explained Dr. Nobley. "These giants are five worldwide problems in the church that Warren's PEACE Plan was designed to correct: spiritual emptiness, corruption, poverty, disease, and illiteracy. You can see how these needs fit with the PEACE Plan's aims to 'promote reconciliation, empower servant leaders, assist the poor, care for the sick, and educate the next generation.'" [10]

"OK, that makes sense," said Bev, appreciatively.

"Anyway," continued Dr. Nobley where he had left off, "the aversion to lengthy training, of course, results in minimally trained personnel being sent out cross-culturally to be involved strategically with possible long-term consequences. It's what Dr. Winter called the amateurization of missions. In some cases, there's almost a glorification of zeal without knowledge. One author goes so far as to promote such a short-term worker as 'ignorance on fire.'[11]

"I did a little research on the topic," said Dr. Nobley as he fumbled through some folders. "This amateurization thing has been an issue in missions for some time.

"William Danker wrote about how the early Moravians felt about it. 'When the latter [amateurs] dabble in it, they often bring harm to both the mission and economic activities.'[12]

"J. I. Packer puts it this way when referencing business as mission: 'The blunderings of sanctified amateurism, impervious to the need to get qualified in the area where one hopes to function, are neither good Christianity nor good business.'"[13]

Smiling, Bill added, "We saw a lot of expatriates who were frequently wrong but never in doubt. Simplicity is a good starting point, but it sure should not be the final destination."

"Very true," agreed Dr. Nobley. "Add to amateurism the shallow relationships produced by short stays, and the challenges mount for any effective long-term field-ministry strategy.

"Short-termers often go as tourists, use interpreters, and have brief encounters with nationals. Long-termers tend to live among the people, participate in daily activities, and build long-term relationships. Let me write up these generalizations," said the professor as he headed to the whiteboard.

"So how do we help short-term amateurs become more effective 'professional professionals?'" inquired Bev.

---

10. Warren, "PEACE Plan," para. 2.
11. Roberts, *Transformation*, 143.
12. Danker, *Profit for the Lord*, 137.
13. J. I. Packer, "Christian's Purpose," 24.

Long Term	Short Term
Participant Observer	Interpreter
Incarnation	Tourist
Relationships	Encounters

"I thought you'd never ask," beamed Dr. Nobley. "Let me paraphrase one of Clint Eastwood's memorable movie lines from *Magnum Force.* 'A short-termer's got to know his [or her] limitations.'[14]

"But not only must they recognize their limitations, they must also learn to *minimize them!* Here are a few ways megachurches, not just Saddleback, can minimize these limitations.

"First, NGO personnel and missionaries often serve as gateways into communities. Megachurches should create partnerships not only with national believers, but also with expatriates when appropriate. Some of these people may have helped birth the very churches with whom the short-termers now wish to partner. These pioneers—who have often sacrificed much over many years—deserve deep respect from megachurch personnel. Megachurches should have the short-termers work alongside these individuals and see them in action, particularly the missionaries. It amazes me how many short-termers never meet, much less see, a missionary in action while on the field."

"So true," commented Bill, "and so sad. One student in a missions class Bev and I are teaching was shocked to find out that there was more than STM! He was not familiar with long-term missions. If all they see modeled is STM, will this not become the expected norm?"

"Another way to minimize limitations," continued the professor as he picked up a book from the table, "is to make relationship building part of the field assignment. In other words, one of the main reasons to

14. Post, *Magnum Force.*

go abroad is to build relationships as deep as possible in the time you have.

"Not all would agree. Listen to this: 'In relational evangelism, you take time to build relationships with others—some call it "earning the right to be heard." . . . [This] is a mistake because it takes time to build those relationships.'[15]

"I would prefer that relationship building be an intentional part of the overall strategy, no matter how long it takes. Pre-field, discuss how people in the host country build and maintain relationships. On-field, build deep relationships by collecting stories. Maybe we can discuss the whole area of story one of these weeks. Post-field, have some kind of accountability structure set up during debriefing.

"As Jim Lo astutely said, 'It is hard to be influenced by strangers.'[16] Remember when Paul said good-bye to the Ephesian elders at Miletus in Acts 20? Departure was difficult because bonds had been forged deeply over time. Their grip on Paul was like that of a mother clutching her baby as someone tries to rip it from her arms. They didn't want Paul to leave. That type of departure usually requires some time to move beyond being a stranger.

"But we must go deeper," Dr. Nobley continued. "Megachurches would do well to require—yes, I said *require*—appropriate levels of pre-field training. This training should be graduated: for example, longer trips and repeated participation would call for further in-depth, integrated training. The Willingdon Church, a megachurch in Burnaby, British Columbia, does an excellent job of trip-appropriate training for those from junior high through college. They require the training for all who want to go short-term. No exceptions!

"Some possible non-formal training models beyond the high-school level could include the Kairos Course, a nine-session course on world Christian missions designed for the local church and special interest groups, such as business people. Kairos considers a variety of adult learning styles in investigating the four main areas of missions: the biblical, the historical, the strategic, and the cultural.

"Meg Crossman's five-week PathLight or her twelve-week PathWays will provide two levels of depth.[17] Either of these could be followed by

15. Nyquist, *There Is No Time*, 72.

16. In Guthrie, *Missions in the Third Millennium*, 88.

17. See Pathways to Global Understanding website, "Resources," http://www.pathways2.org/index.php?id=73

the fifteen-week Perspectives course that uses *Perspectives on the World Christian Movement* as a textbook.[18] For those headed for Muslim contexts, *Encountering the World of Islam,* a twelve-week program, will prove helpful.[19] Lots of practical options out there today.

"Megachurches should not feel guilty for making such realistic requirements for short-termers. Why?" asked Dr. Nobley rhetorically. "Because if these individuals were to launch out into some new hobby, they would be surfing the internet, reading books, buying magazines, joining small groups, attending seminars, and so forth. It should be no different for prospective short-termers. Requiring minimal preparation for each level of participation will pay great long-term benefits for the short-termer, the megachurch, career missionaries, *and* the nationals.

"While there is disagreement on this point, another way to minimize limitations is to focus like a shot from a rifle rather than scattering random pellets like the blast of a shotgun. Focusing on a few locations around the globe allows deep relationships to develop over time so that the departures become like that of the Ephesian elders and Paul.

"Focus also brings long-term continuity to the ministry, thereby allowing depth to occur. Remember how Pauline teams returned to the churches they planted in order to see how things were going? This approach allows for long-term strategic planning rather than just parachuting in and exiting quickly. It also allows time for short-termers to go as learner-contributors rather than just as contributors to 'those poor, needy people over there.'

"Those doing evangelism would first learn how the host culture defines all the components of the gospel—Bible, God, Satan, sin, Jesus Christ, free gift, cross, faith, heaven, hell, and so forth—so that they can anticipate how the host culture will understand the message. The bridges and barriers to the gospel could then be identified and addressed intentionally when presenting the gospel. This is worldview-based evangelism at its best, providing opportunity for deep-level transformation.

"For those involved in marriage counseling, they would first learn how the host culture defines a good marriage. The same would apply to

18. See Perspectives on the World Christian Movement website, http://www.perspectives.org/site/pp.aspx?c=eqLLIoOFKrF&b=2806295

19. See Encountering the World of Islam website, http://www.encounteringislam.org/

business, worship, community development, leadership development, children's ministries, and any other type of ministry."

"What a great model that would be for the host people when it's their turn to go minister cross-culturally!" posited Bev.

"So true!" replied Dr. Nobley. "And so rare! Our short-termers are often so busy giving that they forget that they could learn something as well. One reason for this oversight is that they often assume that a global culture exists. Big mistake! There's little room for cultural naiveté among short-termers *or* long-termers. Otherwise, you'll have—using your term, Bev—'missiological naiveté' followed by questionable outcomes.

"A further way to minimize limitations is for the megachurch not only to mobilize, but also to manage those who have been mobilized. They should tell some, 'No, you can't go to Afghanistan!' 'No, you can't go to Libya!' Not all should go to places like these. I'll tell you a couple of recent cautionary tales.

"In 2006, hundreds of well-intentioned Koreans descended on Afghanistan to travel the country and pray for its peoples. Warned by many not to do this, including long-term Koreans residing there, they came anyway. The government eventually caught them and expelled them. But the damage was done—damage that would immediately impact Afghani believers and long-term expatriate workers for years to come.

"A year later, twenty-three Koreans from Bandung's Saemmul Presbyterian Church near Seoul went on a ten-day aid trip to Afghanistan. Failing to take certain prescribed precautions, they were kidnapped by Taliban militants as they traveled by bus in the dark of night.

"The Taliban demanded that the government release twenty-three prisoners in exchange for the Koreans. The government refused. In retaliation, the Taliban executed Pastor Bae Hyung-kyu on his forty-second birthday, and Shim Sung-min, who was twenty-nine.

"The Taliban also demanded that the Korean government remove its troops from the country, which they agreed to do. The Korean government also promised not to allow other missionaries to enter Afghanistan. Some believe a twenty-million-dollar ransom was paid to the Taliban for the team's release.

"So what can we learn from this disaster?

"Needless to say, those mobilizing and those participating in STM must be, as Matthew 10:16 states, 'shrewd as snakes and as innocent as doves' because their actions, no matter how well intended, no matter how noble, no matter how sacrificial, have much broader implications than just the mobilizers and team in question.

"This disaster also has long-term implications for local and global Christianity. Sometimes, 'No' is the right answer to give. Mobilization requires management!"

Dr. Nobley leaned back against his chair and continued. "One more way to minimize limitations—and I'll stop here since we're past time—is having an exit strategy that is driven by reproducibility and sustainability. The megachurch should measure success not by the number of members who go, but by the reproducibility and sustainability of what's left behind.

"That will put focus where it should be: on field impact rather than laity impact. Reproducibility and sustainability would include such factors as finances, technology, and other materials. Product is a measure of the process.

"A few weeks ago I asked a prominent US mission mobilizer speaking in my Introduction to World Missions class if he thought the PEACE Plan would be successful. His response? 'Very little will change in the mission world!'

"'Why?' I asked.

"'Because it transfers models rather than transforms them,' he told me.

"He continued kind of like this, and I'm paraphrasing:

> Do the models match the moment? What if the host culture focuses on a sixth giant rather than the proposed five?
>
> The PEACE Plan lacks incarnation—that is, living among the people for prolonged periods of time as Jesus did.
>
> It tends to offer strong, church-based, Western theological training, training that is missiologically weak. It should study and present indigenous case studies rather than provide yawning, Western lectures.
>
> Across the pond, the PEACE Plan should provide lay training in a church context. Part of this non-formal education should include learning their questions rather than answering ours. The training should also develop ways to move the nationals beyond indoctrination to reflection. Lastly, it should attempt to develop indigenous theological writers.

"To say the least," Dr. Nobley concluded, shaking his head, "this mission mobilizer was *not* optimistic about the outcomes of the megachurch's unleashing of the laity. He feels there are *no* shortcuts in missions, and that they are taking too many of them.

"Let me close with a quote from Steffen and McKinney-Douglas," said the professor as he flipped through the pages of *Encountering Missionary Life and Times.*

> Participation in missions by amateurs is healthy, but it does have its limitations. We think it was Mary Wong who wisely pointed out that the 'best witness is professionalism.' Will amateurs do all they can through networks and partnerships with the experienced to demonstrate professionalism in their specific field? When practitioners and professionals fulfill their roles responsibly, short-term or long-term, God is glorified and his kingdom is expanded.[20]

"If short-termers can minimize their limitations through networks or partnerships with long-termers and become servant learners before contributors, our colleague may be incorrect about his dire prediction of the effectiveness of missional megachurches.

"But if megachurches choose to bypass these talented individuals, and go as contributors rather than servant learners, his prognosis just may be dead-on. I suspect we'll see some of both.

"Sorry we went so long," concluded the professor as he collected books and folders and shut down his laptop. "Look forward to your review, Bev, so I can see what I said. I don't think we've done justice to the topic.

"Next week we'll take a look at the financial side. Who pays for what, and how?"

---

20. Steffen and McKinney-Douglas, *Encountering*, 353.

Week 6

Who Pays for What, and How?

"So that's what I covered on the megachurches and short-term-ers," reflected a smiling Dr. Nobley after viewing Bev's PowerPoint review. "Not too shabby for an old duffer!" Bev, Bill, and the professor all laughed.

"The role that the megachurches will play in missions by unleashing short-termers abroad will be phenomenal in the coming decade," Dr. Nobley affirmed, starting to count on his fingers. "I just hope they'll remember some of the things we have learned.

1. Take the missiological side of the equation seriously.

2. Learn to build long-term relationships with the nationals.

3. Become humble learners.

4. Learn to transform models rather than just transferring them.

5. Learn to co-create curricula rather than creating or transferring them.

6. Partner with expatriates and nationals alike.

7. Measure the results by what happens in the host culture, not by how many short-termers go.

8. Decide not to feel guilty or superior for bringing something new to the host culture.

9. Know when and how to leave graciously.

Those nine corrections will help offset some of the limitations of STM, which should make long-term ministry much more effective.

"There's one thing I would add to our discussion from last week. Bill, do you remember when you mentioned the student in your class who thought that missions was only conducted short term?" asked the professor.

Bill nodded, and Dr. Nobley continued. "Well, that assumption, though inaccurate, does reflect a real trend toward short-term missions. But there's another contemporary aspect of missions that will likely become a common perception, one quite distinct from that of the first three eras. That is, many monocultural or cross-cultural ministry workers from the West will define missions as going to the 'reached' rather than to the 'unreached.' This shift to people who have already been reached with the gospel will be another indicator that we have entered the Fourth Era.

"How this shift meshes with the Great Commission passages found in Scripture demands some dialogue. Just as your classmate thought that all missions was short term, so others will begin to comprehend missions as going to the already reached, locally or globally. They may also begin to interpret support raising as something you do to go on a short-term trip rather than to fund a possible career.

"Maybe we can address this change in a future week. Right now we need to get to this week's topic, finances, so we don't go overtime like we did last week," proposed Dr. Nobley cheerfully.

✳   ✳   ✳

"How Christians view the funding of missions varies greatly. It ranges from being a boring topic to being a source of constant conflict, an investment, unspiritual, central, contentious, a necessary evil, embarrassing, or a competitive challenge, just to identify a few.

"As you two well know, whatever your perception, missions and money go together. Whether raising funds for personal support or projects, *money matters!*

"If you plan to reach a nation—by, say, attempting to make Rwanda a Purpose Driven Nation—or a people group, or an affinity group within or across people groups, failure to address the economic side will cause you to be ineffective!

"Even the gospel is encapsulated in economics. Is it not a free gift? How does the communicator of the 'free gift' understand the concept? The audience? What does it mean to reject a free gift?

"Money motivates and moves holistic missions on both sides of the pond either positively or negatively. Sadly, most short-termers—or long-termers, for that matter—never investigate economics.

"Interestingly, probably one of the weakest areas of training that cross-cultural Christian workers receive is in the area of economics, particularly global economics. Just as interesting is that many if not most of the conflicts on the field find their roots wrapped deeply and securely around economics. The conflicts surround questions such as who pays for what? How? How much? For how long?

"What about you two?" inquired Dr. Nobley. "Did you ever receive any training in global economics in relation to missions?"

"Never heard the topic ever mentioned," responded Bill.

"But I do remember some challenges we experienced in the Philippines that had to do with financial expectations," said Bev. "Some national team members felt that we should contribute more to projects because we were rich Americans. If they only knew what we lived on!"

"You're right," Bill agreed, shrugging. "We also saw some ministry teams come to the Philippines and pay for the construction of an entire new church. Sadly, the recipients were thankful but never felt it was their responsibility to take care of it. And what's more, the expatriate churches that provided the funding felt they could now send short-termers there anytime. Kind of a long-term kickback for their one-time generosity.

"And remember what our friend from Pakistan told us about church attendance and baptisms?" Bill asked his wife. "The full-time paid national evangelist *pays* participants to attend church and get baptized so that his numbers will look good on reports submitted to his expatriate donors!"

"We definitely didn't expect that financial twist," Bev jumped in. "A missionary friend of ours in India told us about a paid Christian worker who switches denominational name signs on church buildings, depending on which US or Canadian supporting group is visiting at the moment. The individual donor's numbers may not be as large as he or she thinks they are—because each visiting group counts the *same* people!

"And some of these guys, not just in India, think nothing about switching from one denomination to another depending on who is paying the highest salaries. Remember that guy in the Philippines who swindled expatriate funds designated for the construction of a church building? Said he 'only' took a small portion of the lump sum."

"And," Bill added, "I remember how a generous church in the United States decided to pay a national Christian worker's salary for a whole year. After all, they reasoned, it was only seventy US dollars a month.

Well, that unexamined generosity effectively killed local giving. Now leaders in this group visit the United States and Europe to raise funds, rather than promoting generosity among their own people. What's sad is that local followers of Christ have lost the opportunity to experience the thrill of giving back to the Lord financially."

"Wow. Lots of war stories out there," said Dr. Nobley, shaking his head in chagrin. "Raising funds or giving money away always impacts missions. Good intentions not based on best practices sometimes end with shadow effects, as you have just noted."

"I have another illustration," interjected Bev, unable to restrain herself. "We've seen generous groups come to the Philippines, give a guitar or a motorbike to an individual, or provide finances for a family member to get an education. It was great for the recipients of the goodies, but it created jealousy and animosity between individuals and families."

"As I said," repeated Dr. Nobley, "there are lots of war stories out there. Money is a two-edged sword. It can be used intentionally or unintentionally for good or for evil; it can foster ministry or obstruct it. It can produce worship or greed, celebration or jealousy."

"But problems with how we raise and use funds don't just emerge overseas," added Bill. "We sometimes don't view the process constructively on the home front, either.

"I overheard some students on campus the other day discussing raising support as career missionaries. Both of them were adamant. They were looking for an organization to go out under that did not require that they raise their own support. Their reason was simple. *They said they did not want to be humiliated by going around 'begging for money'!*

"Can you guess how many contacts they had with potential donors outside of the two churches they were presently attending? Virtually none."

"Yes, Bill," said Dr. Nobley. "That conversation should serve as a reminder that our thoughts about support-raising can be poorly-developed. There are a lot of resources out there to guide thinking about support-raising. You should check out this website and look under financing."

www.missionaryresources.org

"Any good books out there that address the overseas dynamics of sharing missions resources?" asked Bill.

"There certainly are," responded the professor. "Check out these titles sometime." He took pen and paper from his desk and began to write:

1. Jonathan Bonk's *Missions and Money: Affluence as a Missionary Problem;*

2. Glenn Schwartz's *When Charity Destroys Dignity: Overcoming Unhealthy Dependency in the Christian Movement;*

3. Steve Corbett and Brian Fikkert's *When Helping Hurts: How to Alleviate Poverty Without Hurting the Poor and Yourself.*

"Thanks," responded Bill. "We'll take a look at them."

"One more thing," continued Dr. Nobley. "Corbett and Fikkert discuss the North Americans' and Europeans' largely unconscious 'god-complex.'[1] They believe that the god-complex drives us to help the poor materially and/or immaterially, but often in an unhealthy way for all parties involved. The authors offer concrete suggestions to stop different kinds of harmful paternalism—managerial, labor, knowledge, and spiritual.

"I believe C. K. Prahalad has something to teach us about our perception of the 'poor.' Where is that book?" Dr. Nobley ran his fingers along the edge of a heavily-laden bookshelf. "Ah, here it is. Listen to this jewel. 'If we stop thinking of the poor as victims or as a burden and start recognizing them as resilient and creative entrepreneurs and value-conscious consumers, a whole new world of opportunity will open up.'[2] Pahalad's perspective should challenge our god-complex that often produces more harm then help for the locals. We must learn to cultivate a listening lifestyle." He squeezed the book into its snug slot on the shelf.

"OK, back to our discussion." he insisted. "Lets begin by looking at some of the fundamentals, move to some basic economic theories, and then consider another contemporary movement: business as mission. Economics is a big topic, so we can only scratch the surface today. More study will be necessary to begin truly to grasp the topic. And there are a lot of different viewpoints out there! Bev, I'm glad you requested we discuss the economic side of missions back in week two.

1. Corbett and Fikkert, *When Helping Hurts*, 69.
2. Prahalad, *Bottom of the Pyramid*, 1.

"But let me digress a little. We'll begin with something that egalitarian westerners working cross-culturally tend to overlook, but that has major implications for building and maintaining relationships. And yes, it does have ties to economics.

※　※　※

"Something oft overlooked is that when two people meet, a power review takes place. Both parties attempt to define their status and role based on cultural perceptions of power. Terminology kicks in: sir, ma'am, uncle, father, sister, auntie, rabbi, president, pastor, professor, doctor, farmer, and so forth.

"Actions differ as well. Someone should go first, take the best seat, have the last word, be the first to eat, pay the bill, be the first to arrive, be the last to leave, be the driver, be the rider, give the smallest gift, receive the largest gift, bow, bow lower, and on and on.

"Social differences and distances are part of everyday life at home or abroad. All leadership, all followership, is a political activity. Every social encounter is political because every social relationship is imbalanced."

"It sure is in the Philippines," interjected Bev. "It's a very hierarchical society, with appropriate terms used at the appropriate times. Terms like *kuya* (older brother), *ate* (older sister), *oho* (sir/ma'am), and so forth."

"Hierachical societies are often difficult for people from egalitarian societies like the United States to comprehend," continued the professor. "After all, are we not all created equal?" The professor watched Bev and Bill with raised eyebrows.

"Well, not exactly!" he quipped, answering his own question. "You see, hierarchies are alive and well in every country—just more so in certain countries. It's the *datu* (hierarchical leadership) system found in the Philippines that assumes that you as 'rich Americans' should expect to contribute more, even if you consider yourselves to be living at the poverty level."

"So *that's* what was going on!" exclaimed Bill. "Now I get it. They must have thought we were really stingy."

"Live and learn," offered the professor with a twinkle in his eye. "That's the name of the game.

"When a short-term team, or any cross-cultural worker for that matter, shows up to work in a certain country, a new hierarchy is created. Presence in and of itself automatically creates that hierarchy, including all work relationships. And many of these relationships are driven by economics.

"This reality, of course, impacts ministry strategy. As Bolman and Deal would say, 'No strategy will work without a power base.'[3] The question thus arises: Whose power base will become the standard?"

"But do there have to be winners and losers?" inquired Bev. "Can't kingdom ministry result in both sides being winners?"

"Definitely possible," responded the professor. "All depends on the attitude of both parties.

"It would seem to me that both sides come with batons to pass to the other: material goods, ideas, time, finances, hospitality, and so forth. How will the exchange take place? Will both sides be genuinely and graciously open to receiving batons from the other?

"Even if both sides exchange batons, the economic value of the batons given and received may differ tremendously. Nevertheless, if both parties feel that the stated goal is being reached, both will feel comfortable with the partnership.

"In a hierarchy, equality is not necessary in order for exchanges to be successful or effective. In fact, in most cases, exchanges in a hierarchy can't and shouldn't be equal. That's where the body principle and stewardship kick in. Each person in the body of Christ contributes what he or she has to offer: time, talent, treasure. This shared effort demonstrates admirable stewardship of all the spiritual and material resources that God has loaned his people to accomplish his will globally.

✳   ✳   ✳

"Let's take a quick look at some economic theories and their implications for missions strategy," suggested the professor. "The first is what I was just describing: the unequal exchange.

"One type of power exchange is the patron-client relationship. The patron provides supplies and assistance, and the client provides loyalty and service. The relationship, though unequal economically, is interdependent, relying upon reciprocity. It's bi-directional because both need each other in order to succeed.

---

3. Bolman and Deal, *Reframing Organizations*, 184.

"The relationship is legitimized when healthy exchanges are made with tangible and intangible objects. What do cross-cultural workers bring to the table? What does the host culture bring to the table?

"Your story about salaried evangelists in Pakistan who pay people to attend church and get baptized represents unhealthy patron-client exchanges on multiple levels. These exchanges involve at one level, the expatriate donors (patrons) and the receivers of their gifts (clients), and at another level, the national evangelists (patrons) and the people they pay (clients). The system tends to perpetuate itself either positively or negatively, with patrons offering something valuable and clients accepting it with 'payments' of loyalty. Still with me?" inquired the professor.

Bill and Bev both nodded affirmatively.

"Looking from a broader perspective," continued Dr. Nobley, "two main economic theories compete for validity in the production, distribution, and consumption of goods and services. They are collectivism (which some call socialism) and capitalism. Both have a wide continuum of variations. Consider these contrasts between the preferences or tendencies of each:

- little power in the hands of the individual, versus little confidence in centralized power;

- top-down initiatives, versus bottom-up initiatives;

- redistribution of wealth, versus encouragement of the production of goods and services through entrepreneurism and a free-market system;

- government planning and ownership calling for cooperation and sacrifice, versus individual competition and freedom;

- promotion of institutional entitlements, versus calls for personal charity;

- stoking the system, versus encouraging innovation;

- emphasizing equality, versus seeking opportunity;

- institutionalized greed, versus institutionalized envy; and

- turning a blind eye to centralized irresponsibility, versus overlooking private irresponsibility.

Both collectivism and capitalism constantly change, have some common elements, and easily overlook the spiritual dimension."

"Hmm," mused Bev. "I think I'm beginning to see how these economic theories relate to missions. For example, the three-selfs reflect the values of capitalism, correct?"

"Correct," responded the professor. "One of the weaknesses of the three-self theory, if you recall from one of our previous discussions, is that it failed to lead to interdependence. This weakness all too often led to the assumption that the Western patron who paid the bills would also call the day-to-day operational shots, including what theology would be considered appropriate. That's too bad.

"On the flip side, there are those who would argue that the missionaries in China implemented the three-selfs successfully. Some sixty years after missionaries were kicked out of China in 1951, the Chinese churches have grown from a million believers to hundreds of millions without expatriates present!

"So," Dr. Nobley continued, "we face some interesting questions. Who should give? Are all resources to be found in the harvest? Should they be?

"Some would argue an emphatic 'Yes!' to the last two questions. There should be no need for external materials or outside specialists. Expat involvement only creates dependency and paternalism.

"Others would argue just as emphatically, 'No!' Westerners have funds. Nationals need funds. Give the nationals whatever they need. God gave us this extra money for a reason. Give it to them. Keep the blessing going.

"Still others, like Ben Naja, call for scaled attenuation. He believes in providing an economic jumpstart—but one that should eventually end!

"Rather than seeing funding driven by nationals or expatriates, some prefer it to be driven by the body of Christ from *all* nations to *all* nations.

"Still others encourage bivocationalism for the Christian worker. They believe that it provides a much more realistic role model for new believers in Christ to emulate. It's reproducible."

"So how much funding should be given? And for how long?" inquired Bill.

"Some argue that funding should be sporadic," responded the professor. "Others say, no, it should be continuous. Still others believe in sustainability. They want to see national Christian workers eventually make it on their own, enjoying the privilege of giving back to God their time, talent, and treasure.

Funding Considerations

—Throw money at it, or make it sustainable?
—No support, full support, or partial support?
—Project only, or perpetual?
—Full funding, or bivocationalism?
—Cut all funds, or scaled attenuation?
—STM or Career?
—Traditional approach, or Business as Mission?

"If outside funding has already been ongoing, some believe it should be stopped immediately. Others prefer it stop over time.

"Bill, why don't you summarize our discussion about funding principles?" nudged the professor. "Feel free to add to it. Bev, help him out."

Bill and Bev headed to the whiteboard. After the two interacted together for a few minutes, Bill wrote the summary onto the whiteboard.

"Excellent work," praised the professor. "What do you have in mind with 'STM vs. Career'? That seems a little different than those noted above it."

"I heard the other day," responded Bill, "that one third of all missions giving from the United States is now channeled to support short-term missions. I wonder if the STM phenomenon will be what drops the final curtain on career missionaries from the United States and Canada.

"I wonder because Bev and I have noticed that donors now tend to want to support short-termers and one-time projects rather than making long-term financial commitments to career missionaries. What do you think?"

"Or," countered Dr. Nobley, "will God raise up new ways to support his long-term workers from the United States and Canada? Is business as mission one of those ways? Will the present system change rather than become the final curtain dropped on career missionaries?

"Your question presents a great segue to business as mission, Bill. But before we get into that topic, I'd like to throw a couple more economic theories onto the table. I do so to show how complicated and confusing the economic issue can be. Cross-cultural Christian workers must take the time to learn how the host culture defines generosity, charity, gift-giving, reciprocity, patron-client exchanges, trade, and so forth.

"I'll begin on the macro level with Paul Collier's book, *The Bottom Billion*. Collier is Professor of Economics and Director of the Center for the Study of African Economies at Oxford University, and former director of Development Research at the World Bank. In his book he argues that one billion, representing fifty-eight countries, of the six billion people on earth continue to fall further behind economically, and that 70 percent of the one billion reside in Africa.

"Do you think Rwanda might be among the 70 percent?" inquired the professor as a sly smile stretched across his weathered face. "That's a rhetorical question. Check it out later.

"Collier believes that if genuine change is to come, it must come primarily from *within*. What will impede positive change from within? Four big traps.

"The first trap is conflict—such as civil war—and includes 73 percent of those in the bottom billion.

"The second trap is natural resource riches, like diamonds or oil. Ever hear the phrase 'Diamonds are a guerrilla's best friend?' Governments with natural resources do not have to require taxes, which means that leaders have no accountability. Certain constituencies therefore win big time through fixed elections, continuing their ruthless rule.[4]

"The third trap is being land-locked and surrounded by bad neighbors. That trap catches around 30 percent of Africa. This trap impedes trade.

"The last trap is bad governance, of which there seems to be no scarcity. Does the name Mugabe ring any bells?

4. Malaquias, "Diamonds Are a Guerrilla's Best Friend."

"So what can the five billion do to help rescue the one billion at the bottom? Not too much, contends Collier.

"Aid can help, but only up to a point. When it reaches 16 percent of the GDP, it basically becomes meaningless. Sadly, however, around 40 percent of Africa's military funding finds its source through financial aid!

"Collier also calls for outside military interventions, such as what was done successfully in Kuwait. After the battle of Mogadishu in Somalia where eighteen US soldiers were killed in 1993, that's unlikely to happen.

"It certainly didn't happen in Rwanda in 1994 when mobs of Hutus, many of whom claimed to be Christians, slaughtered eight hundred thousand Tutsis. That was one tenth of the entire population! Nor did it happen in Darfur."

"Collier proposes other interventions: laws and charters. How about global laws that require banks to report deposits? Laws that protect countries from exploitation of natural resources? Laws that demand fair trade? Great ideas, but it all sure sounds utopian. But they could help inspire reformers from within a country.

"Allow me to introduce a second perspective. C. K. Prahalad, whom I just quoted, is professor of corporate strategy at the University of Michigan's Ross School of Business. He takes a different approach to solving the economic woes of 80 percent of humanity in his book *Bottom of the Pyramid: Eradicating Poverty Through Profits.*

"Prahalad believes that the most enduring contributions that the private sector can make are to build self-esteem and entrepreneurial drive among the poor. Providing jobs, products, and services at affordable prices for the world's four to five billion poor who live off of less than two dollars a day, and have little if any access to regional or global markets, will help make this happen.

"Prahalad believes that the fastest growing and largest market share in the world today is at the bottom of the pyramid, not at the top. He calls this 'BOP,' for *bottom of the pyramid.*

"Businesses that set up infrastructures within communities at the BOP will provide the poor not only a means to make and spend money, but also to restore personal dignity. He provides captivating case studies from India to Mexico that demonstrate his theory on the micro economic level.

"Prahalad goes beyond Collier by involving the private sector. While he is not opposed to development or aid agencies, or working with local governments, Prahalad refuses to stop at river's edge."

✳   ✳   ✳

"Well, let's address your last topic on the chart, business as mission, or what is now called BAM," continued Dr. Nobley. "I'll build on Prahalad's perspective of private enterprise.

"Among other things, BAM can provide one way to keep the curtain up for career missionaries. But it can go beyond that as well: it can facilitate holistic church-planting movements."

"In the last decade BAM has received a lot of press. Books continue to roll off the presses—over two thousand of them if you count those addressing work! Websites proliferate. One of my favorites is:

www.businessasmissionnetwork.com.

It will give you great articles, list the top twenty-five BAM books and businesses, provide dates and locations of upcoming conferences, and more.

"New courses abound on the formal and non-formal levels. Conferences and seminars multiply at home and abroad. Nomenclature is becoming more precise. A movement is underway that can provide Christian businesspeople with opportunity for personal involvement in business that integrates missions on the micro and macro levels. We'll look at it from the macro level.

"BAM comes in many terms. What are some of the terms you two have heard?" asked the professor.

"Besides tentmakers and business as mission, I've heard of Great Commission companies, kingdom business, and marketplace ministries," responded Bill.

"I can only add one more," said Bev, "and that's holistic entrepreneurs."

"Excellent," responded the professor. "I see you two have been doing some investigation on the topic."

"That we have," responded Bev. "We've even asked ourselves if we should become involved in BAM when we return to the Philippines, since we both hold degrees in business."

"You would not be the first, nor the last," noted the professor. "Continue to pray about the possibility. If we still have some time today, maybe I can give you a few pointers."

"We'd like that," responded Bev.

"BAM is certainly not new," continued the professor. "Paul made tents when he needed funds to help support himself and his team, hence the term *tentmaker*. Why did Paul know how to make tents? Because all rabbis at that time were encouraged also to have a trade. How do you think missions would change if all missionaries had secular job skills as well as ministry skills?" The professor winked and said, "That's rhetorical, too.

"And don't forget Aquilla and Priscilla. They were also tentmakers, intentionally planting three house churches in three cities: Corinth, Ephesus, and Rome. These three helped pioneer the BAM of the New Testament.

"In the classic *Profit for the Lord,* author William Danker argues that the early Moravian church is unrivaled when it comes to illustrating the total apostolate. Nor should we forget that the Moravians sent out over half of all the missionaries in the eighteenth century. The Moravians integrated faith and for-profit business as they established self-supporting communities around the world. For them the workday was as holy as Sunday. They believed that making Christians was equal to making bricks.

"The Moravians considered every believer a missionary who witnessed daily through his or her vocation. That's why they were careful not to send out amateurs who could easily damage such enterprises. The Moravians integrated church, community, company, and missions.

"William Carey continued the tradition, mixing business with ministry in multiple ways. One way he did this was to wed business structures with mission agency structures.

"By the twentieth century, a new focus on tentmaking began. Brother Andrew helped bring attention to the resurging movement by carrying hidden Bibles into restricted countries. *God's Smuggler* documents his heroic exploits. J. Christy Wilson recognized that some 80 percent of the world restricted access to Christianity, and decided— unlike Brother Andrew—to reside in the resistant country. He became involved in education in Afghanistan for over twenty years. You'll want to read his book, *Today's Tentmakers.* Ted Yamamori's *God's New Envoys:*

A Bold Strategy for Penetrating Closed Countries continued the journey, and so did the first tentmaker organization, which was started by Ruth Siemens. Check out this website:

www.globalopps.org.

"Today, growing numbers of people want to participate in and/ or facilitate missions through their vocational calling." Searching for a book, the professor said, "Remember the quotation from Bob Roberts that I mentioned last week? It bears repeating in this discussion of economics:

> For the kingdom to spread virally means that it will of necessity not be a 'religious movement,' but a 'human movement' tied to people and vocations. . . . How do we make the chief and primary 'missionary' the person in the pew? Here's a good place to start. What do they know best? Their job! Why not let them do what they do best and use it to bring about transformation?[5]

"Many of these people come from the field of business. Like the Moravians of long ago, these Christian entrepreneurs desire to integrate their professions with missions. These don't want to do business *and* mission; they want to do business *as* mission, hence the acronym *BAM*. They want to marry worship with work at home and abroad.

"They want to create businesses that not only support missions at home and abroad but that also serve as missions on the frontiers of unreached peoples. They want to start church-planting movements as well as make a profit. They want to help develop a middle-class, something often missing in many countries but that Thomas Barnett argues is necessary for the rise of civil liberties.[6] Barnett also believes that BAM helps liberate women through providing economic opportunities that can initiate social change.[7] But there is a problem, a *big* problem!

"The problem is this. Many theologians, and hence pastors, view businesspeople negatively, or at best, find them confusing. Pastors like the financial contributions they bring but not necessarily their business practices or personalities.

5. Roberts, *Glocalization*, 82.
6. Barnett, *Great Powers*, 67–68.
7. Ibid., 47.

"Listen to these quotes," said the professor as he fumbled through a packed folder. "Here they are. Neil Johnson says, 'For people in the pews, business can be both a calling and a ministry, but for people in the pulpits, business is often a mystery, and for some, even an anathema.'[8] David Miller continues, 'Most clergy don't know how to help those parishioners, and they often show benign neglect, or even outright hostility, toward the marketplace.'[9]

"That's sad and should not be. It reminds me of a story I heard the other day of a business in India, a Great Commission company, or GCC, that started a church among the Indian business community. As the numbers grew, the company hired a pastor. Sadly, the pastor was unable to relate to this profession and left after just a year and two months. He was willing to visit attendees in hospitals and homes, but not in their places of business, the location where business believers log many hours weekly and interact with those outside of the faith.

"If the BAM movement is to advance to its full potential, it will require the backing of pastors. But most seminaries do not validate the business profession. That's one reason that author Ken Eldred, in *God Is at Work,* calls for all seminary graduates to have a desire to mobilize the many business professionals in the pews. Eldred is correct."

"How can we make that validation and mobilization happen?" inquired Bill.

"Here's what we need," responded the professor. "We need a macro 'theology of work' and a micro 'theology of business.' Is there such a thing as righteous riches? Are people divinely called to professions outside of ministry? Does God give some the ability to produce wealth as Moses argues in Deuteronomy 8:18?

Dr. Nobley strolled to his desk, found his Bible, opened it to Deuteronomy 8:18, and read: "'But remember the LORD your God, for it is he who gives you the ability to produce wealth.'

"We need commissioning services for those entering the workplace, just like the ones we have for those entering professional ministry, so that we formally recognize different divine callings. We need visits by pastors to the workplace as well as to hospitals and homes. We need sermons and books that address the 40-hour work week, providing comfort and challenges. We need the challenge of John Mackey to move towards

8. Johnson, "The Mission of Business," 28.

9. Miller, "Scripture and the *Wall Street Journal,*" 33.

'conscious capitalism'[10] so that success is defined as a social return—with a unified team, partnerships with suppliers, satisfied customers, motivated investors, and environmental responsiveness—as well as a financial return. Why? Because there is a shadow side of the business world with its Arthur Andersens and Bernie Madoffs. But remember: there are also the Bill Gateses and Warren Buffets."

An idea hit Bev. "We need a new position in churches entitled something like 'Workplace Ministries at Home and Abroad.' Seminaries could help make this become a reality. Why should the Devil have all the good businesses?"

"Excellent point," responded the professor. "And a great question. Let me move the conversation briefly to the 'abroad' side of the equation, to Asia.

"A major deterrent for Asian Christians to enter missions is that their parents see it as an automatic track to poverty. While parents may have a heart for missions, they do not like to see their children take on this family stigma. BAM cuts the feet right out from under this argument. It offers the opportunity for ministry without the stigma of poverty."

"That is, as long as the business remains solvent," quipped Bill.

"Very true," responded a smiling Dr. Nobley. "Let me move to Latin America.

"Two of the major reasons for the premature return of Latino missionaries to the homeland are one, inconsistent or dropped financial support, and two, loneliness and homesickness. What if . . . just what if Latin churches would send out a number of members of the *same* family, including family members experienced in business? This model would also help address the loneliness issue because it would avoid total separation from family."

❋   ❋   ❋

Looking at his watch, Dr. Nobley noted, "Well, our time is about up for today. Since you two are considering BAM possibilities in the Philippines, let me lay out a few preliminary steps you may want to consider."

"I was hoping we would have some time for this," said Bev enthusiastically as she unthinkingly flipped her ponytail.

"OK, here we go," said the professor. "I'm going to borrow strongly from Rundle and Steffen's *Great Commission Companies* on this matter,

10. Mackey, "Conscious Capitalism," para. 1.

and then I'll add some thoughts of my own. I'll begin with some steps to start up.

"You begin by evaluating the business opportunities in the country of interest. According to Rundle and Steffen, some questions you two would want to ask yourselves are

1. 'How large is the market?'

2. 'What makes the business unique?' and

3. 'Is the idea financially viable?'[11]

"Then it's time to investigate the missions opportunity. Key questions here would include these:

4. 'What location or people group will benefit the most from this type of company?'

5. 'What can this company do that other Christian companies in the area cannot?'

6. 'Where will the resources for ministry-related activities come from?'[12]

"Then it's time to assemble a management team and an advisory network. Make sure your team members have a strong missional heart, are trained missiologically, and have business savvy. There are far too many non-business missionaries out there trying to do business—just as there are business people trying to minister cross-culturally without missions training. And both are lacking something!

"Assemble an advisory board that will not be afraid to ask the tough questions. These individuals should come from multiple backgrounds, both in business and ministry.

"Still with me?" inquired the professor.

"Keep going," said Bill as he looked up from his laptop.

"Now comes the fun part," continued the professor as he pulled together some papers. "It's time for a plan—actually *two* plans: a business plan, and a Great Commission plan.

"What should be considered in the business plan? Four things: the people, the opportunity, the context, and the risk and reward. *People* refers to those involved in starting and maintaining the business, and outsiders who will interact with the management team. *Opportunity*

11. Rundle and Steffen, *Great Commission Companies*, 78.

12. Ibid., 82.

refers to a profile of an attractive and sustainable business model: what is sold, to whom, rate of growth, cost factors, and possible obstructions. The *context* considers the favorability levels of government regulations and the economic environments. *Risk and reward* refers to an assessment of everything that can go right and wrong.[13]

"What do you think would be the categories to consider for a Great Commission plan?" asked Dr. Nobley.

"The same four," responded Bill without missing a beat. "Both require the same type of scrutiny for the simple reason that both are plans. Good stewardship will demand nothing less."

"I'm impressed!" said the professor. "You must have read the book."

"It's on the reading list," responded Bev.

"Let's consider the four categories for a Great Commission plan," continued Dr. Nobley. "*People* refers to kingdom professionals who make church planting an equal priority with the business, or find outside-insiders who can handle ministry. *Opportunity* refers to clear and achievable business and ministry goals that are reproducible by the host community. The *context* considers the worldview of host culture and the role of the churches within the community. *Risk and reward* refers to the level of freedom to express Christianity in the community, and its implications for the business.[14]

"A good GCC management team will not only have a well-thought-out business plan and Great Commission plan; they will also know how to integrate the two," noted the professor. "And they should never forget that God gave them the GCC, and now he's waiting to see if the team will give it back to him.

"Now that I've described Rundle and Steffen's suggestions, I'll add one of my own," continued the professor as he glanced at his watch. "Any good GCC will attempt to balance three aspects of the company: the business, apostolic activities, and deaconal services.[15]

"On the business side, the goal is for the company to make a profit, but following John Mackey's 'conscious capitalism' that I mentioned earlier, the company must do it in such a way that success has a social return as well as a financial one. Apostolic activities refer to evangelism,

---

13. Ibid., 92.
14. Ibid., 93.
15. Steffen, "Making God the Hero-King."

discipleship, leadership and followership development, curriculum development, and the multiplying of new communities of faith. Deaconal services refer to meeting the social needs of the workers, their families, and the community.

"GCC management teams recognize that tensions always exist between the three, with one point of the triangle always vying for supremacy. At certain times in the lifecycle of the company, it will be necessary for one side of the triangle to dominate the other two. For example, when starting a GCC, the management team will of necessity focus the most effort on the business side. Once the business begins to stabilize, attention can focus on something else. It's the role of the management team and the advisory board to keep a keen eye on the situation so that balance ultimately results over time. The high probability for imbalance should drive the managers of GCCs to rely constantly on the Holy Spirit in their day-to-day activities. Here's how I would draw it up.[16]

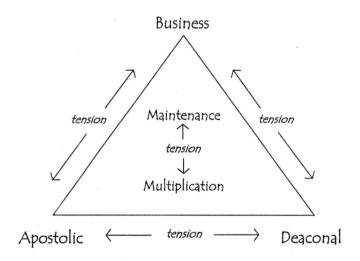

Maintaining Balance in the Great Commission Company

Business

tension

Maintenance

tension

tension

Multiplication

tension

Apostolic ← *tension* → Deaconal

"GCCs *create* jobs rather than *take* them or *fake* them. They offer fair wages, making it possible for the employees to have a better life, to see Christianity lived in the workplace, and to hear about the God of all gods. Once churches emerge, a GCC makes it possible for truly

16. Figure originally published in Steffen, "Making God the Hero-King," 16.

indigenous churches to emerge. As Danker would say, 'Non-Western churches will never become truly indigenous until they are economically supported from within their own lands.'[17] Hope these few tidbits help you as you consider BAM possibilities in the Philippines.

"Well, we're past time—again," noted the professor with great satisfaction in his eyes. "You two must stop talking so much," he chided.

"Well, next week we'll take a look at narrative. What's narrative have to do with the Fourth Era? Well, just about everything. But that's for next week. See you then."

17. Danker, *Profit for the Lord,* 140.

WEEK 7

What's Story Have to Do with It?

"A NOTHER EXCELLENT SUMMARY, BEV," praised the professor. "The topic of money and mission deserves much more thought than it's normally given. Long-termers and short-termers coming from wealthy countries like the United States and Canada must be cognizant of their economic philosophies and those of the host culture. Part of that understanding of the host culture must include the implications of gift-giving because gifts definitely affect how people understand the gospel.

"How do people with money use it in missions so that it furthers rather than impedes the kingdom of God? No easy answers here, as we saw last week. Whether philanthropy or BAM or micro-enterprise, cross-cultural Christian workers should think through the short and long-term ramifications of their individual and corporate economic actions. The benefactors and losers certainly will. Money matters in missions.

"This week I want to discuss another important topic for the Fourth Era: narrative, or as some prefer, story. I'll use the terms interchangeably. During the week, I pulled together some pertinent information on the topic," said the professor as he pointed to a bulging folder. "As you may know, I have undergone a major paradigm shift, moving from laws and propositions to story. And as we'll see, story has played a prominent role in all the earlier eras for some players, and it just may play its most dominant role in the Fourth Era. Let's begin with a little history from the first three eras.

※　※　※

"Not sure how I missed this in my own ministry," said Dr. Nobley as he scratched his head. "Guess I was just too busy *doing* ministry to take time to reflect on mission history. Anyway, I'll highlight a few of the individuals from the first three eras who considered the use of story to

121

be an excellent way to evangelize and see church-planting movements come into existence.[1] As I do, take note of what each proponent adds that may be appropriate for Fourth Era evangelism and holistic church multiplication. I'll begin with Father Francis Blanchet, who represents the First Era.

"Working out of one of the Hudson Bay Company's outposts, Father Francis Blanchet began the first Catholic mission outpost in Washington in 1839. The Nisqually Indians who came in from the surrounding areas continually requested to be instructed in Christianity. Not knowing their culture or language, Blanchet carved ladders—long flat sticks not unlike totem poles—to teach the Catholic faith. He placed dots and bars on the ladders to represent time, along with drawings to note key Bible events and characters. Father Blanchet presented the 'Catholic Ladders' to the chiefs among the Northwest Indians as gifts, promising to send black-robed priests someday to tell them the stories behind the symbols in their own language.

"Later, in the 1860s, representing the Second Era, Johannes Gustav Warneck documented the power of Bible stories among people groups in Sumatra, Nias, Borneo, and New Guinea. He argued that the best way to communicate the gospel message is not through lectures on God, but by proclaiming the deeds of God through Old and New Testament stories that speak to the specific needs of the people. You'll want to check out his book, *The Living Christ and Dying Heathenism.*

"We now move to the Third Era. Hans-Ruedi Weber worked in Central Celebes, Indonesia, arriving in 1950. He was tasked with providing some thirty thousand Christians in Luwuk-Banggai the basics of Scripture. Most had only three years of education and little Bible knowledge. Weber soon realized that if these people were to learn the Scriptures, they must first be liberated 'from the abstract ideas of our catechisms and doctrines. . . . We must proclaim picturesquely and dramatically rather than intellectually and verbally.'[2]

"In his *Communicating the Gospel to Illiterates*, Weber describes his views of the Bible as God's picture book that includes great drama and great symbol. He advocates tribal evangelism that incorporates storytelling accompanied with simple drawings. He calls this 'chalk and talk.'[3] Weber

---

1. Steffen and Terry, "Sweeping Story."
2. Weber, *Communicating the Gospel*, 19.
3. Ibid., 67.

would draw simple pictures, tell the stories behind them, and contrast them with traditional legends. He concludes, 'The most exciting discovery of that time, however, was a new Bible: the Bible as the story and oral tradition of God's great acts, the Bible as God's picture-book, the Bible pointing to the symbols by which God both conceals and reveals himself.'[4]

"Weber makes another cogent point when he argues that 'this Bible as a manuscript and as a liturgical drama (including the cycle of feasts in the ecclesiastical year) forms a whole.'[5] To understand Scripture as an unfolding story that has a beginning, middle, and end, both the written and the liturgical are necessary. Weber also believes that Bible stories and symbols should be contrasted with traditional stories and symbols. These rivals will challenge and help convince the audience, offering eternal hope.

"Also during the 1950s, Donald McGavran, the father of the modern church growth movement, and one of two people representing the Third Era, generally used eight stories to evangelize the Satnami people of India. Of the eight stories, only one came from the Old Testament, the story of creation and the fall. The remainder of the stories were from the New Testament.

"During the 1950s and 1960s, Jacob Loewen used Bible stories in Central America. In a provocative chapter entitled 'Bible Stories: Message and Matrix,' Loewen describes a growing understanding of the use of a sweeping sacred story in ministry. His thesis: 'Narrative, because of its extensive use in so many (if not all) cultures, its flexibility for emphasis, dramatization, and personal style, and because of its holding power over even a very heterogeneous audience, is a form par excellence for a beginning witness of the Good News.'[6]

"But all did not go well. A first attempt that used isolated stories with no introductory story or transitions between stories resulted in confusion and misunderstanding. Loewen and his colleagues concluded 'that the sequence was as important as the truths contained in the stories. So we began to tell the Old and New Testament stories in a chronological sequence over a period lasting many months.' This approach worked satisfactorily for regular attenders, but was found to be 'seriously flawed for new additions or the erratic attenders.'[7]

4. Ibid., 4.

5. Ibid., 29.

6. Loewen, "Bible Stories," 370.

7. Ibid., 373.

"While I could add to the list of players, let me conclude with one more from the 1980s."

"Let me guess," said Bill. "Trevor McIlwain? Chronological Bible Teaching, or CBT?"

"Right on," answered the professor. "You should know him, since he and his family served in the Philippines among the Palawanos for many years. Have you read his *Building on Firm Foundations* series?" inquired the professor.

"All ten volumes," answered Bev.

"Here are some of the major assumptions of CBT, or what is now called Foundational Bible Teaching, or FBT.

1. The Bible is one story.

2. The Bible not only records God's words but also presents the progressive, historical, revelatory acts of God.

3. A firm foundation for the gospel is necessary; therefore, the Old Testament (particularly the law) must not be overlooked or minimized.

4. Doctrines can only be correctly understood if taught from their historical development in Scripture.

5. A chronological presentation corrects doctrinal errors related to salvation.

6. Evangelism and follow-up should be connected as a single sweeping story from Genesis to Revelation.

7. While the content of Scripture is important, so is the way it was delivered: predominantly through narrative.

8. The way God's Word was delivered to the human race provides a model to communicate his message to the rest of world.

9. God prepared the Bible as his message for all cultures, therefore no outside redemptive analogies are necessary.[8]

"McIlwain then designed a multi-phased model that covers Genesis through Revelation in a relatively short time, with the first phase— Genesis through the ascension—designed primarily for evangelism. The remaining six phases were designed for the new followers of Christ.

---

8. Paraphrased from McIlwain, with Brendle, *Chronological Approach.*

Recognizing the story nature of Scripture, the model connects evangelism seamlessly with ongoing discipleship. This approach contrasts with most other approaches that use one model for evangelism and another for discipleship, hoping that the recipient will eventually be able to connect the two. McIlwain designed CBT for long-term church planting.

"Soon the Southern Baptists in the Philippines picked it up, renaming it Chronological Bible Storying, or CBS. I actually like that term better than CBT. Anyway, many others have since spread various versions of the model throughout the world in both urban and rural settings. I recently heard that a third model is forthcoming that focuses on worldview transformation: Expositional Storying. Anyway, a large cottage industry of curricula and paraphernalia has evolved. And don't forget to check out the International Orality Network. Will post-modern North America be next? If you want a great resource website, check out this one." Dr. Nobley uncapped his marker and wrote on the whiteboard:[9]

www.wsaresourcesite.org/Topics/storying.htm

Fourth Era Narrative Nuggets

Consider Scripture as a sacred drama.

Cover the big picture of Scripture.

Provide an Old Testament foundation for the New Testament.

Teach the Bible chronologically.

Focus on Bible characters rather than propositions.

Keep symbols and stories together.

Remember that CBT takes time!

---

9. See International Mission Board, "Chronological Bible Storying."

"OK," he continued. "What values or practices have you picked out so far that should continue in the Fourth Era? See if you can write them on the whiteboard."

As the couple made their way to the board, the professor could hear them talking. Bev began to write.

"Excellent summary," responded the professor. "Were you able to implement any of these in the Philippines?"

"We tried to use CBS, but our teammates were not too excited about our endeavors," responded Bev. "They said that stories are for kids, too open to multiple interpretations, not sophisticated enough to communicate theology, and take far too long in presenting the gospel. Never mind that Filipinos are great storytellers, love soap operas, go to movies every chance they get, and are avid readers of comic books," Bev vented, flailing her arms in exasperation. "To say the least, we didn't get a lot of support."

"Certainly not an atypical response," consoled the professor as a smile softened his face. "Maybe if they took my narrative course, they would think differently! Anyway, let me make a few comments about my own narrative journey. My thinking wasn't much different than that of your teammates! Let me begin with how people view the Bible."

✳   ✳   ✳

"As a young Christian growing up in a very conservative church in the mid-western United States, I never dreamed that different people could perceive the Bible in different ways. I had no idea that some see the Bible as a *Sacred Encyclopedia,* full of important facts, or that others see it as a *Sacred Self-Help* book that can meet emotional needs, whatever they may be. I hadn't ever thought about differences among people I knew—like how my grandmother seemed to consider the Bible as a *Sacred Private Devotional* for inspiration and encouragement, or how a professor I knew perceived it to be a *Sacred System* composed of propositions placed in coherent and comprehensive categories, or how the youth pastor preached as if it were a *Sacred Rule Book* demanding certain behavior.

"Well, I guess the youth pastor rubbed off on me, because to me, the Bible became a *Sacred Rule Book.* Several years later, during my formal studies at a Bible institute and a Bible college, the Bible became a textbook for me—albeit a *Sacred Textbook.* It took me a long time to realize that both of these views, like all of the others, come with a major shortcoming: they all result in a fragmented understanding of the message of Scripture. Something was missing from all of them.

"Fieldwork in Central Asia changed me, and I discovered as an adult another type of Bible that totally took me by surprise. Unimpressed with my propositional presentation of the gospel, the people of my host culture demanded a new approach. So I—probably not unlike your colleagues in the Philippines—went kicking and screaming into the exploration of the use of narrative. And to my great surprise, the people loved it! And they retold the stories with accuracy! God used tribal people to reintroduce me to the importance of story.

"That began a life-long journey of exploration on the nature of narrative for understanding Scripture, building relationships, conducting research, evangelizing, discipling, leadership and followership development, community development, and Bible translation, among other things. Here's what I learned about the Bible.

"Rather than seeing the Bible as a Sacred Rule Book or a Sacred Textbook, I began to see it as a Sacred Storybook. I saw it as a string of stories that constructed a meta-narrative. I saw it as a kaleidoscope of events that culminated in the meta-event of Jesus Christ. I saw it as an assortment of small struggles within and between the material, human, and spiritual worlds that found their roots all embedded in the meta-struggle between Good and Evil. I saw it as a *Sacred Storybook* that was able to move beyond bare-boned and boring propositions to a sacred text that incorporated not just the facts, but also the emotions and the imagination."

"That's quite a journey, Dr. Nobley," said Bill. "I can't help thinking, though, that some of our Philippine teammates would say that calling the Bible a *Sacred Storybook* is lowering its value. Stories, they would say, are perceived as fictional and for fun, not for capturing and communicating the sacred. How would you respond to them?"

"For starters," answered the professor, "Jesus would probably totally disagree with them. He was *the* master storyteller of all time, as we well know. And OK, if they don't like the word storybook, call it a drama. Call it a Sacred Drama. I like the way Dorothy Sayers expresses it. She calls the Bible 'the greatest drama ever staged,'[10] and 'a terrifying drama

10. Sayers, *Creed or Chaos*, para. 1.

of which God is the victim and the hero."[11] A dynamic drama can give life to dull dogma by placing it into events surrounded by interacting characters. Dynamic drama will captivate most audiences."

"OK, I see," said Bev. "But our friends would also say that propositions are more precise than story, and much more economical because of brevity."

"There's a misconception out there, Bev, and it is this," responded Dr. Nobley. "While some feel that propositions, or systematic theology, are superior to narrative, they overlook something of significance. You really can't have one without the other. They are integrated; both need each other to be the best they can be. Propositions require narrative foundations for context and life; narrative requires propositions for focus and clarification. It's not an either/or but a both/and.

"Think about the concepts of superiority and sequence. The proposition 'Jesus is Lord' is obviously centrally important in a new believer's understanding of the Bible. You could say that grasping this proposition is superior in importance than, say, understanding any isolated story. Yet, despite its *superiority* in effecting a heart change, this proposition alone is hard to appreciate apart from the plot line, the long story *sequence*, that leads up to it. This clearly superior concept means little without Old Testament prophecies and the stories of Jesus' healings, exorcisms, turning water into wine, walking on water, taking on the money changers, forgiving sins, and resurrection. The first task to delve into, then, is not that of superiority but rather of sequence. Propositions normally evolve from stories, not vice-versa.

"Just a little aside. Sequence is a pedagogical preference. We come with a Western perspective, which often biases systematic theology—linear thinking, sequence, categories, propositions, axioms. In reality, this is the West's ethnotheology. An oft-overlooked question that begs for an answer is whether the host culture has the same pedagogical preference.

"Anyway, this is one reason that it is so important for evangelism to include the story of the sweep of Scripture. Jesus' story is embedded in many former stories, like Israel's, Abraham's, and Adam and Eve's. The New Testament required a firm foundation—and that was the Old Testament. The same is true of Jesus, who required a forerunner, John the Baptist. And the same should be true for evangelism. Wise cross-

11. Ibid., para. 7.

cultural witnesses will provide as much of the Old Testament backstory as necessary so that the Jesus story has a legitimate context. The New Testament was never intended to *introduce* Jesus to the world.

"But many who witness cross-culturally fail to provide the big picture of Scripture, often because they have never been trained to do so and, consequently, don't know the story or how to present it. In that we tend to teach as we were taught, this omission of most of the story just may make the Bible one of the worst taught religious books in the world!

"But this deficiency can change if we begin to see the Bible as a Sacred Storybook or a Sacred Drama that has a beginning, a middle, and an end—an important sequence. We must never forget, as Scot McKnight reminds us, that 'Jesus' birth came in the midst of a story with a beginning, a problem, and a lengthy history.'[12] Every story begins in the middle of some other story. Here are two rhetorical questions for you. Why do we tend to amputate the story's beginning, the Old Testament, and give the New Testament most-favored nation status? Why does the North American church tend to understand the usefulness of the OT as being solely for the education of children?"

"Including the big-picture sweep of Scripture would seem to have major implications for the JESUS film," noted Bill. "I know that a seven or eight minute Old Testament overview has been added for the Muslim world, but that seems more of an admission of the problem rather than a solution."

"Foundation, foundation, foundation!" exclaimed the professor. "It should be neither neglected nor minimized in evangelism.[13] To do so is to minimize the story nature of Scripture, making evangelism—and yes, ongoing discipleship of new followers of Christ—more difficult. The yet-to-follow and the follower of Christ will have a more difficult time understanding how their stories connect with the meta-narrative of the Bible and with Jesus' story.

"While some see spending time laying a foundation for the gospel as a waste of time, I see it as follow-up in advance. That's not a waste of time; it's a necessary plank for an authentic church-planting movement. We would be wise to follow the late radio commentator Paul Harvey, and give them 'The Rest of the Story.' Evangelism that includes promi-

12. McKnight, "Eight Marks," 38.

13. See Steffen, "Don't Show the Jesus Film," for fuller discussion.

nent parts of both Old and New Testaments provides listeners with framework and accountability expectations for a faith-allegiance change and a Christian worldview. It will help move people beyond professing a system of beliefs to practicing a way of life.

"Let's move to the oral world, which comprises probably more than 50 percent of the world's population, depending upon whose definition of literacy you use. Oral cultures, along with the postmodern world, bias story over propositions. Just as the Enlightenment denarrativized the Bible, so postmodernism depropositionalized it, bowing to the altar of any and all stories. Wise cross-cultural witnesses will follow the post-modernists' lead in the use of stories, but will recognize the superiority of the Jesus story over any and all other stories. They will not be content to overlook propositions. In that the Sacred Storybook biases both story and proposition, they will seek to embed abstract ideas into concrete contexts. As Kevin Vanhoozer argues, 'Concepts have contexts.'"[14]

"It's sequence over superiority," noted Bev as she played with her ponytail.

"Correct," responded the professor. "One more quick point, and we must move on. A major benefit for teaching the sweep of the Sacred Storybook is the opportunity for the listener to gain a necessary un-derstanding of the various roles of members of the Trinity. The North American church's penchant for emphasizing the New Testament (the last third of the story) to the exclusion of the Old Testament (two-thirds of the story) actually jeopardizes an adequate understanding of God the Father. Nowhere in Scripture is the awe of God, which is the beginning of wisdom,[15] more dominant than in the Old Testament. Perhaps this New Testament tunnel vision is one reason that Christianity in North America remains so nominal. Here," Dr. Nobley said as he started to draw on the whiteboard, "is how I would illustrate this problem.[16]

"In our efforts to understand the Trinity, we should consider the en-tire biblical story, not just any particular part. While the Old Testament focuses primarily on revealing the holiness of God the Father, it also shines a slightly dimmer light on two other members of the Trinity, illu-minating their roles. The powerful manifestations of the Holy Spirit are evident not only in Acts, but in the Genesis creation story as well. The

14. Vanhoozer, *Drama of Doctrine,* 90.

15. Prov 9:10

16. Figure adapted from Steffen, "Pedagogical Conversions," 154.

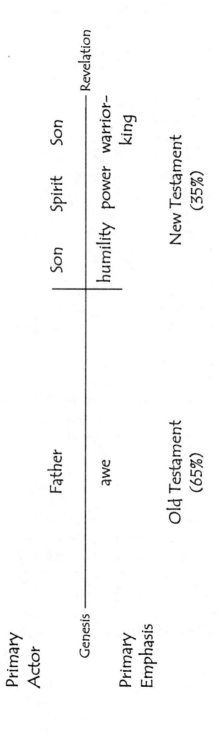

Role of the Trinity Throughout Scripture

same could be said of Jesus: 'Let *us* make man in our image.'[17] Within the New Testament, the bookends—the Gospels and Revelation—provide two very different, yet distinct, pictures of Jesus Christ. The first bookend reveals an incarnate Jesus. We see a loving, humble human being who experienced birth, death, resurrection, and ascension, demonstrating vulnerability. Evangelism from this perspective presents Jesus as a lovable, tender lamb.

"The last bookend, Revelation, reveals a warrior-king ready to set things right justly through deadly and decisive warfare. Jesus returns as Judge. Evangelism from this perspective reveals Jesus as a righteous judge. But one bookend without the other depreciates the total personage and message of Jesus Christ—the Lamb and the Lion."

"That reminds me of one of my favorite images from C. S. Lewis's classic stories," noted Bill. "It's captured well in the movie *The Chronicles of Narnia: The Lion, the Witch, and the Wardrobe.*[18] Mr. Tumnus, the fawn, describes Aslan to Lucy, saying, 'He's not a tame lion.' Lucy responds, 'But he's good!' That truth corresponds to what you just said. Mr. Tumnus and Lucy understand the differences between the two New Testament bookends. Both the Lion and the Lamb must be understood if a correct picture of Jesus is to emerge."

"Right on, Bill!" responded Dr. Nobley. "Foregoing any major aspect of the whole will of God will result in an inadequate understanding of members of the Trinity. This mistake will harm understanding of the gospel rather than guard it,[19] crippling the possibilities for a transformed worldview.

✳   ✳   ✳

"If you mess up the message, you mess up the movement," continued Dr. Nobley. "I was about to mess up the message big time in the beginning of our ministry. Let me unpack this. After months of culture and language acquisition, medical work, and literacy teaching, I was finally ready to present the gospel verbally to the people with whom we had laughed, cried, eaten, sweated, and even *shivered* from December through February. They invited us into their lives, providing us with multiple op-

17. Gen 1:26
18. Adamson, *Chronicles of Narnia.*
19. 1 Tim 6:20

portunities to serve them in word, deeds, and signs.[20] As Haji Ali would put it, 'Here (in Pakistan and Afghanistan), we drink three cups of tea to do business; the first you are a stranger, the second you become a friend, and the third, you join our family, and for our family we are prepared to do anything—even die.'[21] We had shared three cups of, well, not tea, but heavily-sweetened coffee! We were family. And they would die for us. We were ready to conduct business.

"I began as I was taught: start with the authoritative source of the message, the Bible. Then cover God and Satan, contrasting the attributes of each, something missed in most evangelism models. From there, address the creation of the world, animal life, and people; then address the fall and its resulting consequences: broken relationships with the human, material, and spiritual worlds, leaving all in desperate need of restoration. When the hearers understand these concepts, present the solution to the dilemma—the Restorer, Jesus Christ.

"To make sure they understood each lesson, I reviewed it through a series of questions that were designed to capture the central points. Rather than relying on the oft-accepted evangelism ritual of 'pray this prayer,' I looked for transformed behavior that included a faith-allegiance change, a desire for the Word, reordered relationships, change in the use of resources—time and finances—and the desire for baptism.[22] Authentic followers of Christ change beliefs and behaviors. Christ's Christianity has no place for deedless words.

"In my mind, the logic of this evangelism model flowed freely and purposefully from point to point—Word, God, Satan, humanity, sin, judgment, Jesus Christ. The concepts built to a climax as they moved through the topical sequence from innocence to separation to solution. The model presented the Bible as the source of Truth, contrasted the protagonist—creator, initiator, love, sovereign, just—with the antagonist—conniver, deceiver, jealous, liar—and covered the concepts in order—the creation, fall, and solution.

"To my great surprise, however, the narrative logic of the audience did not perceive this approach to be as free flowing or intuitively sequential as I did. In fact, they found it extremely boring, difficult to follow, and hard to replicate to others. They wanted stories; I gave them systematic

20. Luke 4:16–19; 19:9–11

21. Mortenson and Relin, *Three Cups of Tea,* back cover.

22. Steffen, *Passing the Baton,* 146.

theology. They wanted relationships; I gave them reasons. They wanted a cast of characters; I gave them categories of convenience. Instead of events, I gave them explanations. Instead of experiential apologetics, I gave them evidential apologetics. That's how you mess up the message and a church-planting movement.

"Perplexed but not paralyzed, I began to rethink the failed evangelism model, considering more contextual models that would move beyond my preferred propositions but still guard the gospel. Then it hit me. I needed to be reminded of what Thomas Boomershine perceptively points out: 'The Church now tends to think of the gospel as a set of abstract ideas . . . divorced from story. The gospel has lost its original character as a living storytelling tradition.'[23]

"It was time to leave behind my categories of convenience and enter the messy nature of narrative, messy at least to me. So I added illustrative stories to go along with the propositions. After completing a back translation of the first evangelism curriculum, it was time for publication. It was then that I serendipitously met McIlwain. After perusing the English back translation, he unceremoniously informed me that there was a much better way to conduct evangelism than this illustrative story-proposition approach. Not a little shocked, I asked him what he meant. In the next hour, McIlwain introduced me to the curriculum he had been developing over a number of years while ministering among the Palawanos. As you noted earlier, Bill, it would later be called Chronological Bible Teaching.

"That discussion made me ask some questions that would change my ministry forever. What would happen in evangelism if I would begin to think of the gospel as a story rather than a set of laws or propositions? How would the presentation differ if I asked these questions about the gospel? Who is the major protagonist? Antagonist? What is the plot—always driven by conflict—of the cosmic drama? How is the plot resolved? What are the choices and consequences?

"Paul Hiebert captures some of those changes:

> We no longer have to be God's lawyers, proving to people the truth of the gospel. We can be bold witnesses to what we have experienced and know. The gospel we bring is not abstract propositional truth; it is a living relationship with Jesus the Christ that involves our whole being: cognitive, affective, and moral.

23. Boomershine, *Story Journey*, 17.

> We no longer come with a sense of arrogance and superiority, as those who have found the whole truth. We invite people to follow Christ and the church and to let him transform their cultures.[24]

"Not only had the Bible become a story for me; so now had the gospel message. So I did some necessary revisions. I focused on Bible stories, making them the message rather than just illustrations of the propositions. I also modified the review questions so that the answers would focus more on themes and characters within the stories, rather than on minutia and factual details. The response was phenomenal. I was hooked, as was my audience. But there were still some more messes to clean up.

"I soon discovered that teaching a series of Bible stories does not necessarily tie the individual stories to the meta-narrative of Scripture. To illustrate, what if each lesson were a piece of clothing being handed to listeners to carry? Pretty soon, as separate stories accumulated, the listeners would be dropping clothes all over the place. They wouldn't be able to organize the whole load or to appreciate each item. But a clothesline could easily remedy the situation! Metaphorically, the clothesline is the meta-narrative of the Sacred Storybook. Offering listeners a clothesline—or a big-picture view of the Bible—provides a place for them to hang the individual pieces in their rightful order so that they can make sense of the whole. But what's really cool is that it also helps them to examine, understand, and define—more readily and in a more informed manner—each individual piece. Not a perfect analogy," Dr. Nobley admitted lightheartedly, "but you get my drift.

"My audience in Central Asia preferred to learn whole-to-part rather than through my pedagogical preference, which was part-to-whole. They wanted to hear a brief meta-narrative presented up front and then to see how the individual stories played into it. I, on the other hand, wanted mystery, so I tried to force them to let the meta-narrative emerge over time. Eventually, I learned to work with their style and ended up with a whole-part-whole approach. I first gave an overview of the big story from creation to ascension to glorification, then tied individual stories into it, and continually reinforced the big story all along. According to my analogy, I hung the clothesline, added each garment, and then pointed to the clothesline again. My audience enjoyed

---

24. Hiebert, "Anthropology, Missions, and Epistemological Shifts," 22.

the mystery of seeing how the parts made up the whole—but only when I presented it within previously outlined, though fuzzy, boundaries.

"There was another potential mess that I had to keep an eye on continually. If evangelism resulted only in changes of external behavior, the movement was in trouble. If it resulted in internal transformation, the movement would be authentic. Changes in external behavior are easy. Demonstrating worldview transformation is much more difficult in that it calls for the deconstruction of one's worldview. The gospel story is driven by conflict and therefore creates conflict. For internal transformation to happen in my situation, I needed to know the host culture's worldview—and how the selected Bible stories related to that worldview.

"Cross-cultural narrative evangelism that results in transformed worldview is much more than just telling Bible stories. It requires a worldview approach that demands that the communicator know the inside's core assumptions and values, and how these play out in observable behavior on the outside.[25] The gospel Paul presented demanded worldview transformation from within. We can present no less. We must continually ask, what type of faith does our evangelism produce? Faulty? Fickle? False? Fragmented? Firm? There's an Asian proverb that goes like this: 'If the water is dirty downstream, it is dirty upstream.' If our evangelism results in nominalism, legalism, syncretism, denominationalism, or any other 'ism,' we need to take another look upstream—at our evangelism."

"Example?" queried Bill with one eyebrow raised.

"How about three," responded the professor with a smile. "I once had a guest speaker in my narrative class who made this statement to the students, most of whom were missionaries working on their PhDs in intercultural education. I'm paraphrasing, but it's close: 'You cannot choose a wrong Bible story. You do not have to study their worldview before selecting a story. God did his worldview study before he gave the Bible. He knew all the *isms*.'

"Well, many of the students *had* picked the wrong Bible story a few times in their missions experience, and/or had told stories with insufficient understanding of the host culture's worldview."

Dr. Nobley read uncertainty on Bev's and Bill's faces. "Think about this," he offered. "One student in the class had worked in Africa, and she

25. Strauss and Steffen, "Change the Worldview."

described what happened when she told the story of Joseph. Her audience thought that the main point was not that God had worked though evil circumstances to bring about good,[26] but that Joseph never forgot his family. She said she couldn't understand their interpretation until she finally realized how they defined family. Their social structure demanded care for the entire extended family, even if feuds existed among family members. She was trying to get them to catch God's ability to bring about his purposes in any situation, but they came down on faithfulness to family.

"What's more, another student in the class said that if you taught that same story in certain places in Thailand, the people would interpret it to mean that Joseph—the client—had remained loyal to Potiphar—his patron. And when the Joseph–Potiphar part of the story is taught in the United States, listeners talk about how he didn't fall into sexual sin with Potiphar's wife.

"So, in that class, I just sat back and watched the feathers fly as the students, speaking out of their cross-cultural experiences from around the globe, challenged the statement. It was a rough evening for the guest speaker. Even with the evidence mounting, I don't think the class persuaded the guest.

"Bible story selection is important in any curriculum. And worldview study is, too. The two should be integrated or you, the outsider, just may be the last to know the misunderstandings that have arisen. So much for an authentic church-planting movement!

"After several years of studying the host culture, I was able to summarize their worldview into unifying and opposing themes.[27] I found it helpful to keep this list posted before me when selecting Bible stories for designing a teaching series. Of course not all Bible stories connected with their worldview, but the list helped enable me to be intentional to include the appropriate stories that did. It also alerted me to possible cultural bridges and/or barriers within the stories.

"A second thing I did was to create a list of all the components that comprised the gospel message. For example, the Bible, God, Jesus, the Holy Spirit, Satan, demons, sin, judgment, gift-giving, substitution, cross, forgiveness, faith, heaven, and hell, to name a few. Then I asked myself how the host culture understood each component. I found this

26. Gen 50:19–21

27. Steffen, *Passing the Baton*, 260.

exercise extremely helpful when I was telling Bible stories because it helped me to anticipate how they would interpret them, and to make clarifications and challenges as warranted.

"While it is the Holy Spirit's role and responsibility to prosper the message of Jesus Christ, it is the communicator's role and responsibility to connect relationally and to bring as much clarity to the message as possible. This is just good stewardship. Twenty-first-century redemptive analogies are as appropriate today as those used by the Holy Spirit during Bible times. Does the communicator know which redemptive analogies will work? Every Bible story whispers the name of God, the hero of the story, in some way. Does the communicator know in which way or ways? How often can the communicator rely on the Holy Spirit to compensate for his or her cultural mistakes?[28] *Just telling Bible stories does not guarantee Bible meaning.*

"Number three. A worldview approach to narrative evangelism demands that we also be cognizant of the ways in which *our own* culture has influenced our understanding of the gospel. One of these ways is how we seal the deal. From Charles Finney's walking the aisle during the Second Great Awakening to more contemporary symbolic acts like raising a hand or 'praying this prayer,' westerners have sought tangible ways—rituals if you will—to signify when a person has crossed the line from Satan's family to God's.

"It's interesting to note how different this is from Jesus' teaching model. He loved to cast a little truth out there, step back, and watch the audience grapple with it. He often preferred to tease people into Truth through parabolic stories rather than just to give them the answer to their question. This model, however, required process time.

"Not so with many of our current Western evangelism models. Our time orientation does not permit such processing. We have to get bang for our buck, and fast. Reports need to be written; donors need to be satisfied. Sadly, this approach flies in the face of the majority of the world, who are event oriented. Major happenings in their lives are associated with particular events, not times or dates. They need process time to talk with the appropriate people, challenge the rival story, understand its implications to their worldview, social relationships, and economic status, and make a decision as to how to respond to it.

28. See Steffen, "Flawed Evangelism and Church Planting," for discussion on this topic.

"You'll notice also that this processing usually happens in the context of a group, just as it does in Acts: through extended families—like those of Cornelius, Lydia, and the jailer—and in villages and occupational groups. Multi-person decisions were made. Such a communal process, rather than a private one, helps assure that a true faith-allegiance change has taken place, making worldview transformation a strong possibility."

"It would not be hard to get a group of Filipinos to raise their hands to accept Christ," interjected Bev. "But because of their strong family ties, I've often wondered how sincere they really are."

"In cultures of courtesy where shame reigns, like in the Philippines, asking someone to 'pray this prayer' will usually receive a positive response," responded Dr. Nobley. "While the evangelist thinks the individual has entered God's kingdom through this action, all too many who say the prayer believe that they have merely avoided shaming the person of importance who made the request. And shame-oriented cultures normally like to make decisions in community, not individually or in private.

"Or there may be other reasons for agreeing to the request," said the professor as he retrieved a paper from the folder. "Listen to this disturbing conversation recounted by Steve Saint."

> A friend of mine opened my eyes to the reality of this when he described what happens in the area where he works in Mexico. 'Short-term mission trips from the United States have been coming here for years,' he pointed out, 'and the results have been amazing! Entire neighborhoods have gone forward to accept Christ at evangelistic events.' There is obviously nothing wrong with that, but my friend continued, 'One day I happened to be with several of the local people when they had a special meeting to decide who would go forward at the next foreign missionary's altar call. I couldn't believe my ears! They wanted the gifts (often a bag with pencils and Bible literature) and wanted the missionaries to come back again. I asked one of the leaders how many times he had gone forward to receive Christ, and he said, "About a dozen times." Then he added, "If we all go up, the missionaries won't believe it. We have learned that half or two-thirds is a good number to keep them coming back."'[29]

---

29. Saint, *Great Omission*, 43–44.

"Lesslie Newbigin is correct when he says that, 'there can never be a culture-free gospel.'[30] There are no shortcuts when it comes to effective cross-cultural narrative evangelism that results in an authentic church-planting movement. A worldview approach to narrative evangelism demands we know not only *their* culture but also *our* culture. We could also add to this list the Bible cultures, but that's a topic for another day.

"We must also never forget that a Bible story comes out of a cultural context. Not to know that context, or how our culture interprets the Bible story's context, or how the host culture interprets it, is to open the floodgates to possible misinterpretation. Remember Don Richardson's story in *Peace Child* about how the Sawi considered Judas Iscariot to be the hero of the story, the super-Sawi? Talk about a cross-cultural inter-pretation problem!

"A worldview approach to internal transformation is no guarantee, but it's certainly a better way to begin the journey. Colossians 2: 6–7 re-minds us that discipleship that produces internal transformation starts from and stays with the grace-based gospel. The gospel is the founda-tion, middle, and culmination of authentic discipleship. Discipleship is rooted in the gospel, not a separate post-gospel program. Here are two rhetorical questions for you. How much of the gospel—and how much discipleship—can be understood apart from the Old Testament?"

"Very helpful cautions about considering worldview, Dr. Nobley," commented Bill. "I have a couple of other questions related to CBS; ac-tually three. Our teammates believe that CBS takes way too long, as I mentioned earlier. What do you think about its length? They don't like being tied down to following a strictly chronological order to tell Bible stories. Second, how valid is a chronological approach? My third ques-tion is why do you think stories are so powerful? Maybe you could com-ment on these."

"Be glad to," began the professor. "Let's start with your last ques-tion. Bible stories are powerful witnesses of God and his holistic plan of reconciliation for the world in multiple ways. They're powerful because, as Gabriel Fackre notes, 'narrative speaks in the idiom of the earth.'[31] They're powerful because the extraordinary enters the ordinary.[32] They're

30. Newbigin, *Foolishness to the Greeks,* 4.

31. Fackre, "Narrative Theology," 345.

32. Ibid., 346.

powerful because they make 'the ordinary strange again.'[33] This quality is particularly important for a cynical, secular, postmodern audience. Narratives are powerful because they create dialogue. They're powerful because they evoke emotions, a key 'to learning . . . to imprinting. The stronger the emotion, the more clearly the experience is learned.'[34] They're powerful because they help us identify ourselves—and others— in the characters, and they sometimes help us identify ways to transform our own lives.

"Meaning-making finds its roots in a narrative process. And this process can take time, as one attendee said at a *Simply the Story* workshop: 'This is a lifetime way of knowing God.'[35] That's the power of story.

"To answer your question, Bill, about length, I'll focus on the evangelism phase. McIlwain was fortunate because he could meet with the Palawanos for two to three hours daily, seven days a week. That time-expectation certainly did not work with my people group, nor will it work in most urban settings. This reality should take us back to culture. How often do the people you are trying to reach meet for religious activities? For how long? How much material can they realistically assimilate in one setting?

"Answers to these questions will help determine the appropriate length of the evangelism phase, and the appropriate content load for each lesson. There's nothing sacred about the sixty-eight lessons that McIlwain selected; we don't now have sixty-eight spiritual laws. The number of lessons in a phase, and the depth of the content within an individual lesson, should be determined by the host culture, not by a pre-canned program. Otherwise, it's model-centralism.

"Let's say we can meet for eight weeks. What eight stories would you choose that would take you from creation to the ascension? Some of the audience will love the stories and want to continue the study. Now you can add to the stories presented, providing more depth to the meta-narrative of Scripture and the Jesus story embedded within it. Some long-termers, and many short-termers, will need expandable mini-tracks.

---

33. Bruner, *Culture of Education*, 140.

34. Rapaille, *Culture Code*, 17.

35. From promotional brochure for *Simply the Story* workshops; see website http://www.gods-story.org/sts/

"As for your question about the validity of teaching chronologically, your teammate's concern has some merit. McIlwain reminds us that it was God who chose the order of Scripture. But even McIlwain's CBT does not follow Scripture chronologically.[36] For example, the author placed the fall of Lucifer in the initial CBT lessons, even though it is not mentioned in Genesis. The author took this literary license so that the story would make sense. We must do the same. Start-points matter! And they are multiple. But to start in a constructive way for the audience, we must again go back to culture.

"The best place to start is where the host culture presently finds itself. If the people are into proverbs, for example, start in the book of Proverbs. Have you ever considered that proverbs are like dehydrated stories? Once told, they draw fuller stories to hearers' minds. For cultural groups that really value sayings and maxims, you can use proverbs as the clothespins to hang stories on the line.

"What if proverbs aren't that exciting to your group? If they're really into discovering their origins, like my villagers were, then start there. Gumangan, a believer, suggested an evangelism start-point for me that was much better than what I had in mind. He recommended that I start with the flood, where their history begins, since they had no creation story, and then to backtrack to Adam through the genealogies, which lend credibility in their culture to any story. Next, cover creation, move quickly though the Old Testament, and finally tell the Jesus story.

"Gumangan preferred seeing things together—themes, rather than one-thing-after-another chronology. Historicity trumped chronology. An event-line trumped a timeline. Metaphorically, a pond full of lily pads captures his model: begin where they are, and jump from one story to another thematically-related one until you finally get to the Jesus story. Here's another rhetorical question for you. Did God present his Word in chronological fashion or through thematic events, or some combination of the two?"

Dr. Nobley winked and then continued. "I was at a missionary candidate school where someone asked, 'Don't we need to teach people to think linearly so that they can understand Scripture?' Definitely not! There are multiple start-points in evangelism, even though eventually the communicator must get back to Genesis. This need to be flexible calls for *transformed* narrative evangelism models rather than *trans-*

36. McIlwain and Everson, *Firm Foundations.*

ferred models. Adaptable models should assist in genuine worldview transformation. Flashbacks and foreshadowing in the evangelism curriculum should be a given; but so should the clothesline, even if that clothesline doesn't always go straight. It may even run zigzag or look like an octagon—the configurations are innumerable!—depending upon the needs and expectations of the audience.

"Since we're talking about narrative evangelism models, let me chase a rabbit here. There are basically three models available: global, glocal, and local. Global narrative evangelism models are imported; it's one curriculum fits all, one for all the world. Glocal narrative evangelism models assume that one curriculum fits *some*. Designers develop several generic models that target a wide, but specific, audience—say Buddhists, Muslims, Hindus, animists, secularists, atheists. The last, local narrative evangelism models, refers to curricula designed specifically for a particular audience, like what we did for our people group. It's one fits one. So we have one for all, one for some, and one for one.

"Global narrative evangelism models assume that everyone thinks the same and comes from the same worldview grid. It's cheap to reproduce and doesn't take much time. Glocal narrative evangelism models recognize that religious differences exist, and they try to provide a generic-specific model for each group. This takes more time to produce and consequently is more expensive. Local narrative evangelism models are designed for a specific audience. This takes a lot of time and is therefore very expensive. Another rhetorical question: which of the three do you think has the best chance of facilitating genuine transformation of worldview? Here I'm reminded of a statement made to Leighton Ford by Howard Hendricks: 'My greatest fear for you is not that you will fail but that you will succeed in doing the wrong thing.'[37] We must certainly make haste in evangelism, but—and this is important—we must not forget that foundations are forever. In other words," Dr. Nobley said, smiling for an emphatic pause, "we must *make haste slowly*."

✻   ✻   ✻

The professor refilled everyone's cups with steaming coffee and offered some homemade chocolate chip cookies. "Lets talk now about the most powerful evangelism tool that exists: your faithstory. By *faithstory* I

37. Howard Hendricks quoted in Ford, *Transforming Leadership*, 79.

mean how you came to Christ and what has happened since. Just as stories form and organize our identity and worldview, so faithstories form and organize our Christian identity and worldview.[38] They announce the core assumptions and values of a particular brand of Christianity, including code words and symbols that separate insiders from outsiders. Most of us, however, have never received any training to make this most powerful tool a sharper instrument for spiritual growth or warfare. And this in an era when short-termers hit the four corners of the world annually in record numbers!

"As Kouzes and Posner perceptively point out, 'Each of us will become at some point a character in someone's story. . . . The obvious question is, What will they say?'[39] There's no better way to become such a character than intentionally to tell your faithstory. And there is no better way to offer a rival redemptive story than through your faithstory. Not only do stories play a key role in *forming* us; they also play a key role in *transforming* us. Stories of changed lives change lives. Becoming a character in someone else's story opens the door for the hearer to make restoration with God. Restoration is, in reality, what I like to call *re-story-ation*,"

The professor opened his Bible and began to read:

- "'Go home to your family and tell them how much the Lord has done for you, and how he has had mercy on you.'[40]

- 'Those who had seen it told the people how the demon-possessed man had been cured.'[41]

- 'Return home and tell how much God has done for you.'[42]

- 'Many of the Samaritans from that town believed in him because of the woman's testimony, "He told me everything I ever did."'[43]

- 'Because of his words many more became believers.'[44]

38. Steffen, "Foundational Roles."

39. Kouzes and Posner, *Leader's Legacy*, 25.

40. Mark 5:19

41. Luke 8:36

42. Luke 8:39

43. John 4:39

44. John 4:41

"These individuals became characters in the stories of others, making Jesus—the Giver of Grace—the hero of the story. As a consequence, through the power of the Holy Spirit, they facilitated the expansion of the kingdom of God. Telling faithstories spawns faithstories that transform core beliefs and behavior, making an authentic church-planting movement possible. They do this because, as Slack and Terry correctly note, 'Stories are the last frontier in a fight between worldviews.'[45] And all this is done through experiential apologetics rather than evidential apologetics!

"But we must take it further as we're talking about telling faithstories to peoples of different cultures. Paul's three—somewhat different—testimonies in Acts provide instruction: adapt your faithstory to your audience. This takes us back to culture. How must we adapt our faithstory so that it rings true to the host audience? I'll not take the time to work through how this can be done but rather suggest you take a look at Steffen's *Reconnecting God's Story to Ministry*. It has a chapter on how to contextualize your faithstory, along with examples from Kurdistan, Estonia, and Bulgaria.

"Let me close our time on faithstories with a comment made by a Kenyan woman studying here for her doctorate. She grew up around missionaries who had led her family to Christ. She told her classmates that she had never heard a missionary's testimony. She asked, 'Why don't they tell stories? Don't they have a story to tell?'

"Needless to say, that last question sobered and silenced the class. You could have heard a pin drop. The missionaries whom she knew had failed to tell her the most important personal thing that had ever happened to them. By denying her their faithstories, they had made it difficult for her, and certainly others, to participate in a relationship. Faithstories provide opportunities to participate in a relationship. They offer not only the gift of friendship, but also the gift of all gifts, Jesus Christ."

✳   ✳   ✳

"Wow, today went fast," observed the professor as he checked his watch and rearranged a stack of papers. "Let me conclude with a little blue-skying. Every era has seen the use of Bible stories in multiple ways. What

45. Slack and Terry, *Chronological Bible Storying*, 34.

might this look like in the Fourth Era? What will follow Chronological Bible Storying? Of McIlwain's seven phases, few people have done anything beyond the first four, which provide a quick sweep from Genesis to Revelation, to address the needs of unbelievers and believers in a unified way. Even McIlwain says that the missionary could leave before teaching the fifth phase.[46] So where do we go from here? What follows CBS?

"Listen to what one student wrote in an interaction assignment.

> Raised a Roman Catholic, I had never really read the Bible, and when I began to read all the way through, I was astonished at the stories and the entertainment afforded: power struggles, personal crises, character development, sex, betrayal, anger, love, and each story seemed to have a positive moral implied.

"What intrigued this young woman about the Bible was the drama, the mystery. It rang true! So lifelike, so her, so those she knew. She discovered that 'stories do not convince by argument; they surprise by identification.'[47] Do you know how rare this discovery is, especially in an era when theologians constantly lament Bible illiteracy and lack of interest in doctrine within the North American church?[48] People need to be invited to discover the big picture drama of the Bible!

"Do you think we could make theology and doctrine just as enticing? Just as mysterious? Just as connected to life? I do. But it will demand some paradigm shifts. Major paradigm shifts!

"One reason for this boredom with doctrine may be more related to pedagogy and hermeneutics than to outright disinterest. Discussion of a doctrine, such as justification by faith, even by an articulate theologian or pastor, can be a real sleep inducer! Hannah Arendt famously said that 'storytelling reveals meaning without committing the error of defining it,'[49] but the same cannot be said for the way most doctrines are taught. Why? Because we too often separate doctrine, the text, from the story context that defines it. When Bible teachers make such separation, eyelids become heavy. No curiosity created here. When they focus on characteristics rather than Bible characters, what else can we expect?

---

46. McIlwain, *Chronological Approach*, 49.

47. Shaw, *Storytelling in Religious Education*, 61.

48. Wells, *No Place for Truth*.

49. Hannah Arendt quotation from *The Quotations Page* website, "Hannah Arendt," www.quotationspage.com/quote/4861.html

"Could character theology be what follows and integrates CBS? Does Paul provide a model by using the lives of Abraham and David in Romans 4 to help define the abstract doctrine of justification by faith? Does the author of Hebrews do the same in chapter eleven? What if Bible storytellers would take every major Bible doctrine, identify at least one Bible character that could help define it, and then use the life of that character to teach the doctrine? Could the face of God be more clearly drawn—making genuine worldview transformation stronger—by beginning with characters found in the Bible rather than with abstract doctrines?

"From the almost three-thousand characters present in the Sacred Storybook, Bible storytellers have all kinds of personalities to choose from to teach doctrines: sages, crooks, kings, the poor, the privileged, tax collectors, prostitutes, the faithful, politicians, the pious, priests, prophets, missionaries, teachers, fence-sitters, murderers, the haughty, the generous, the humble, prodigals, the self-righteous, the righteous, slaves, freedmen, farmers, enviers, business people, liars, hoarders, thieves, and

---

Old Testament Character Theology

1. Adam - sin / fall / promise for humans and material world

2. Noah - hope for all creation

3. Abraham - justification by faith

4. Moses - law and grace

5. Job - God's sovereignty over Satan and circumstances

6. David - kingdom rule

7. Jonah - God initiates grace for the undeserving

8. ? . . .

so forth. Would not these personalities provide a much more earthy way to make friends with the Bible, the Trinity, and its doctrines? Could the same be done to teach God-honoring morals and ethics pertinent to the host culture?

"This doesn't mean that Bible storytellers would never discuss abstract doctrines; it just means that character studies would precede and follow the abstract concept. The sequence would begin with the concrete (the character), shift to the abstract (the doctrine), and then return to the concrete (the character). It's a both/and, not an either/or, but with a definite sequence. And neither is superior to the other. And remember, we're talking about long-term church-planting movements, so most of this will be new to the hearers.

"One more caveat. To protect the hearers from a fragmented understanding of the Bible, storytellers will intentionally place the character that defines the doctrine within the meta-narrative of Scripture, that is, within its historical context—Pentateuch, Prophets, Gospels, Acts, Epistles, Revelation. Bible storytellers will attempt to hang the character in the correct spot on the clothesline so that listeners have some sense of the order of individual stories. Moses, for example, comes after Adam but before Jesus.

"Each character helps expand understanding of the meta-narrative. And the meta-narrative influences understanding of each character. We have to study not only the spiders, or the Bible characters; it is equally important to study the web, or the meta-narrative.[50] Just as the web provides food for the spider—and catches more insects in its broad expanse than the spider could on its own—the meta-narrative gives individual character studies what they need to be complete. No one can fully understand Moses, for example, without also apprehending God's bigger plan and where Moses fits into it. And no one can follow the plot line of the big story without considering God's keeping of His promises through Moses. Maybe I'm stretching the analogy a bit," Dr. Nobley chuckled, "but no spiders, no web—and vice-versa—because God has chosen to weave His grand story with the smaller stories of particular people.

"For CBS we could ask, how many Bible *stories* should be known by the host culture before the expatriates—pioneers or facilitators—leave? For character theology we could ask, how many Bible *characters* should be known by the host culture before the expatriates leave? Just as CBS

50. Robert, *Christian Mission*, 177.

provides a great way to start an authentic church-planting movement, so character theology provides a great way to promote worldview transformation that leads to genuine Christian maturity within that movement.

"Let me flesh this out a little in relation to evangelism. Jurgen Moltmann notes that a 'sacred thread' interweaves its way 'through the biblical testimonies.'[51] Here are a few Old Testament characters, biblical testimonies if you will, that could be used in evangelism," Dr. Nobley suggested as he erased the whiteboard and began to write.

"Concrete characters that personify abstract concepts should dominate the landscape of evangelism models because narratives author and sort ideas. The same should be true for teaching new followers of Christ. For example, Sarah and Abraham, Rachel and Jacob, Hannah and Elkanah, Elizabeth and Zechariah, and the Shunammite woman address barrenness.[52] A cast of characters for Christmas, Easter, Communion, giving, leadership development, followership development, and so forth should be commonplace in the mental libraries of Bible storytellers. Richard Losch's *All the People in the Bible* can be helpful here.

"Character theology moves from the concrete (Adam), to the abstract (sin), and back to the concrete (Adam), a process which should work well with much of the Majority World, not to mention the Minority World. Each character, however, should make God the hero of the story. Charles Koller expresses it this way: 'The Bible was not given to reveal the lives of Abraham, Isaac, and Jacob, but to reveal the hand of God in the lives of Abraham, Isaac, and Jacob; not as a revelation of Mary and Martha and Lazarus, but as a revelation of the *Savior* of Mary and Martha and Lazarus.[53] The Adam story, for example, should take the listener beyond Adam and Genesis to the second Adam, the King of Kings. The Sacred Storybook is the story about how God restores broken relationships on multiple levels.

"Will character theology take the world by surprise in the Fourth Era just as CBS has in the Third Era? I hope so—because story is so important. A. Steven Evans tells us that 'it is not until the role of story in worldview and culture is firmly grasped that one can fully compre-

51. Moltmann, *Trinity and Kingdom*, 95.

52. See Wilson, "Blessed Are the Barren," 22–28.

53. Koller, *Sermons Preached Without Notes*, 51.

hend the necessity of story in worldview change and in life and cultural transformation."[54]

"I'll wait for your emails and Tweets and Facebook updates from the Philippines to let me know how it goes," Dr. Nobley said with satisfaction, leaning back in his chair and running his hand through his silver hair. "So what's story have to do with it? Just about everything!"

"Yeah, I see now how true that statement is," sighed Bev. "It could make a big difference in our evangelism and discipleship effectiveness—and even in our own thinking about the Bible."

"I agree," asserted Bill, "though it will take some time for me to get a feel for this new approach."

"Not new, Bill," Bev chided, "but different. Sounds like teaching and learning through story are approaches that have been around awhile!"

"True," Bill laughed in agreement. "You've given us so much to think about over these past weeks, Dr. Nobley. I sure would love to be able to see some of these concepts in action—especially facilitation. Most of what I have experienced until now has been rooted in a pioneering perspective."

"Well, that reminds me! Ask and ye shall receive!" exclaimed professor Nobley as he turned and shuffled toward a pile of disarrayed manila folders. "Before you leave, I want to give you some case studies that focus on facilitation.

"It's one thing to talk about abstract concepts like we've been doing over the past few weeks, but it's a whole different ballgame when we hear from those in the trenches dodging real bullets. Read these sixteen true case studies, and we'll discuss them next week. Think about how you would like to categorize them for our discussion."

"Sixteen?" gaped Bev as she thumbed through the case studies. "Amazing. Where did you get these?"

"I've been collecting facilitation models over the years from students, practitioners, and colleagues," replied the professor. "But keep this in mind. The examples that I'm giving you were not necessarily chosen because of their great numerical results, or because they have a long or proven track record. Rather, they were chosen to show a variety of ways in which God is using his Western global co-laborers to reach today's lost world.

---

54. Evans, "Matters of the Heart," 192.

"These case studies, for the most part, represent the small giants, not just large, successful ministries. Hopefully they will help us better discern possible ministry roles for westerners in the twenty-first century, as well as stimulate new ideas for creative ministry models.

"As you work your way through the case studies, keep these questions in mind. What are the role shifts that God is orchestrating in today's mission world? How does each case study inform the requisite role for North Americans, or for those in the Global South? What challenges face North Americans? The Global South? What would you say are the best practices that promote authentic, long-term, sustainable church-planting movements? How do these case studies instruct your own future ministry plans?

"I hope the cases satisfy your desire to see the concepts in action," Dr, Nobley beamed. "Have fun reading them. See you next week."

PART TWO

Facilitation in Practice

Case Study 1

The Amazon and Lowland Tribal Empowerment Coalition[1]

IN JANUARY OF 2004, a group of select people from fourteen major mission organizations that work in the Amazon Basin in South America were sitting around a table at the Pioneers Guest House in Orlando, Florida. Paul Johnson, the CEO of Amazon Focus, who had tirelessly initiated the gathering, had one goal in mind: discuss how they might network together to better use their respective resources to complete the daunting task of making the gospel available and planting churches in each of the more than 200 people groups that remain unreached in that vast region of the world.

The task in the Amazon is enormous. The river, its tributaries, and the jungle that shades it cover 2,200,000 square miles—more than a billion acres—an area roughly the size of the continental United States. Saving the rainforest in the Amazon is one thing. Facilitating church-planting movements among those who live under those trees is quite another.

More than four hundred people groups call the Amazon home. Only about half of those groups have heard the gospel in their heart language. Ninety or more of the remaining groups have had no contact with the outside world. Nor can they be listed because they are not known.

While mission work began in the Amazon more than a century ago, the task remains unfinished. And it will not be finished until an initiative is taken that makes better use of available resources.

I moderated the meeting. After introducing myself, I had all participants do the same, including the organization they represented. All did so, highlighting their respective visions and goals.

---

1. My deep appreciation goes to my longtime friend Jay Jackson (jjackson4@charter.net) for providing this case study. Jay is presently the CEO of Alteco.

Their passion was obvious: they wanted to see the light of the gospel dispel the darkness of the Amazon. The last to speak, however, was an older gentleman who had an established reputation for being careful and conservative. I wondered how he would respond to such an eclectic group. He began his introduction with an ominous tone.

"I have been in mission work a long time," he said, "and I am preconditioned to mistrust some of you here at the table just because of the organizations you represent. But, as I have sat here and listened to your introductions, I have heard the desires of my own heart repeated over and over. I realize now that you want what I want: to see the church grow where it has never gone before. I'm thankful to have the privilege of being here this morning."

I breathed a deep sigh of relief. By now half of the morning was gone, and it was time for a break. "Before we take a break," I said to the group, "I want to ask you a few questions.

"You have just heard a group of leaders introduce the organizations they represent. Did it occur to you how much we all have in common, how much we all have to offer one another? What if there were a way for us to get together on a regular basis to share questions and answers, needs and resources? What if we had a forum to discuss strategies for getting the job done?" I asked them to think about those questions before they reconvened after coffee.

As I was getting some coffee, one of the participants approached and said, "I see what you're trying to do here. You're trying to get us to work together. But it isn't going to work. Missions have been going on in the Amazon for more than a century, and we haven't been able to work together in all that time. If it's going to work this time, we'll need a grade A, class one, parting-of-the-Red-Sea miracle from God Himself."

"From your lips to God's ears," I responded. "Let's ask Him for a miracle."

The meeting ended four days later with a half-completed strategy statement. Seven leaders from seven organizations were commissioned to finish the document and submit it for approval within three months. God *had* worked a miracle. The stage was set to partner together, but at that time, none of us really understood what God was planning. We had not really anticipated what "together" would come to mean.

THREE WAVES

While we were busy breaking new ground—or so we thought—the churches in Brazil were busy as well. They already had in place what the expatriates were hoping to form: a forum where leaders of the Brazilian national churches were meeting with leaders of the existing tribal churches in the region.

The Brazilians were discussing what Ronaldo Lindorio has frequently called the three waves into the Amazon. The first wave represented the North American and European missionaries who invaded the Amazon in the twentieth century. They had made their way as deep into the jungle as they could. Some had traveled three weeks upriver to reach their destinations, but that still left the interior of the Amazon untouched.

The second wave had hit with the awakening of the Brazilian national church. Brazilians from all walks of life had left home, family, and careers to take the gospel into the jungle that formed their own backyard, their Samaria. Now, the third wave is beginning to build. The tribal churches on the rim of the Amazon are taking up the challenge to carry the gospel deeper into the Amazon. The baton is being passed, but there is a problem.

LIFE OR LIVELIHOOD OR BOTH?

The mission organizations that made up the first wave have historically divided into two camps: life organizations and livelihood organizations. Life organizations focused on the spiritual aspects of church planting, such as preaching the gospel, teaching the church, discipling believers, mentoring leadership, generating an oral scripture, writing and publishing curricula, and translating the Word into the heart language.

Livelihood organizations focused on the physical or social aspects of church planting, such as community development (food, water, and shelter), medical and dental facilities and training, economic stimulation and business enterprise, education, and the ability to emerge successfully into the surrounding culture and society.

Both of the camps worked very hard to establish Christianity in the people group in which they worked, and both worked from a scriptural mandate. Christ came to redeem not only the individual, but the community as well. Integration of the Great Commission and the Great Commandment, however, was difficult to find.

It seems to me that the newly established churches require both life and livelihood. In order for the church to *exist*, it requires life; in order for the church to *survive*, it needs livelihood.

A church that is spiritually equipped to train missionaries but lacks the funds and resources to send them out will have no missions outreach. A church that is growing in numbers but lacks the funds and resources to build a facility will not expand. A church whose leaders have the capacity and calling to step into full-time ministry but which lacks the funds and resources to support them will not thrive. A church that cannot meet the medical and dental needs of the community, cannot help the poor, cannot minister to orphans, and cannot feed the hungry, clothe the naked, give water to the thirsty, and provide shelter for the homeless is an incomplete church.

Of course, the converse is true for all of these points as well. If we offer the church a means to support itself but fail to present a clear gospel or train the believers in godliness, our efforts ultimately vanish.

Providing life and livelihood to new church plants will require churches and mission agencies to rethink their goals and strategies. The skills required to establish and sustain an economy within a people group are quite different from those needed to plant a church. Even so, the long-term survival of the church and, in fact, the people group itself, is dependent as much upon creating renewable financial resources as it is upon imparting spiritual resources.

Church planters who do not have the skill set to help implement the livelihood side should partner with those who do. Organizations that give life should not be required to retool so that they can provide livelihood; rather, they should partner with organizations that have the skills to provide livelihood. Both groups must learn to depend on one another, to work together, to need each other, and to pass this same attitude along to the people reached.

When the group first met in Orlando in 2004, we had only a general understanding of the implications of what working "together" might mean for North American and European organizations. As time passed we began to perceive the expansiveness of the task. It soon became obvious that no single organization had all of the assets necessary to get the job done; that no single nationality had all the resources, material or human, required to finish the job.

The pursuit to reach the peoples of the Amazon would require a broad partnership of players. This partnership would have to include those involved in all three waves: foreigners, nationals, and indigenous tribal peoples.

The faith journey brought other realizations. If a group bought into the partnership proposal, present philosophy and strategies would be deeply impacted. For some, this would mean no longer doing things *to* or *for* indigenous people, but *with* them. Interdependency would be the final goal so that each player is able to fully play the role that God has designed.

THE TRANS-AMAZONIAN NETWORK FORMED

In November of 2008, another historical meeting took place in Shell, Ecuador. Indigenous representatives arrived from seven of the ten countries that share the Amazon basin. These highly capable leaders, who had proven themselves not only among their own people but in their regions as well, had met for four days to write a strategy statement to form the Trans-Amazonian Network. The indigenous people covenanted together to reach the remaining unreached people groups in the Amazon, groups that range in size from the dozens—among the nomadic tribes—to the tens of thousands.

After writing the strategy statement, the group took a break to tour a factory where Ecuadorian nationals and tribal people make airplanes to sell in North America. Steve Saint, the CEO of ITec, had started the business as a livelihood project for the people of Shell Mera and the Waodani tribe and just two days before had shipped two RV–10 airplanes to their new owners in the United States.

There was another group touring the factory at the same time, a group from a church in Missouri that had raised the funds to make it possible for the Trans-Amazonian Network to meet! Serendipitously, North Americans, Ecuadorian nationals, and tribal people from across the Amazon had all converged in the same room, on the same day, at the same time. As they mingled with one another, speaking through interpreters, it was obvious that one of God's whispered dreams was being fulfilled: all three waves found themselves together on the sandy shore at the same time.

But there would be another remarkable event that day. The day before, the company had sent an airplane deep into Woadani territory to bring out one more tribal man, Dyui, to the meeting. Dyui is one of the five men who killed Nate Saint, Jim Elliot, and their three friends back in 1957.

As Dyui mingled with the group, the other tribal men did not know who he was. I called for the group's attention, made some announcements, and then introduced Dyui, telling what he had done on Palm Beach long ago. Not expecting such an emotional response, I was stunned to see the tears in the eyes of many of the tribal men.

One of them stepped forward and began to speak. "This is a very important moment," he said. "We're standing here all together. There are representatives from the people who brought the gospel to the Waodani and paid the highest price. There are national believers here. Dyui is here, the link to our past, and other tribal representatives are here.

"As a tribal man myself," he continued, "I want to invite you, all of you, to work together with us to reach those who are still waiting to be reached in the Amazon."

When I heard that, I could not help but smile. Networking was happening right before my eyes. Even so, I wondered if the speaker knew how sharply he was cutting across the North American mindset by suggesting that we join with *them,* that we work together with *them.* Wasn't he supposed to be asking for the privilege to work with *us?*

Instead, he had turned the tables; he had invited us to join them. This was a prophetic moment. These tribal Christian leaders had picked up a baton that should have been passed to them years ago. In some cases, they were forced to wrestle it out of the hands of expatriates. More often they have found the baton lying on the ground where expatriates had dropped it.

Whatever the past experience, the tribal leaders had retrieved the baton and begun to run the race, and now they were asking expatriates to run with them. I'm convinced that if we do not join them in this race, they will run it alone.

WHAT DO THEY REALLY WANT?

If we do join the race with the indigenous leaders, what can we provide that the indigenous leaders really need? During many hours of countless discussions with tribal church leaders, I have heard the same three themes repeated consistently: one, communication; two, transportation; and three, a sustainable economy.

Tribal church leaders need a way to communicate with one another. Smoke signals and jungle drums are the stuff of Hollywood lore. In the Amazon jungle it takes days to send a message from one place to another, and by the time it arrives, it is old news. All too often the event has already taken place.

The internet and radio could meet this need but will require equipment and training to use and maintain them. This will require finances to buy the equipment and personnel to do the training. Even so, this may prove to be the single best investment expatriates could make to advance the church in the Amazon.

The second need pertains to transportation. It is not unusual to see tribal missionaries spend three weeks on the river in dugout canoes taking the gospel to some remote place deep in the interior. Mission aircraft could change this by offering reasonable rates, as could powered parachutes.

ITec, for example, has developed a flying car that can reach speeds of sixty-five miles per hour on the road and then stop and raise a parachute wing to fly past the point where the road ends. Tribal people can live a long time in places where most North Americans would experience great difficulty; they just need to find better ways of getting in and out.

A sustainable economy is the third need. Rich land and a conducive climate makes the Amazon replete with natural resources: bamboo, hardwood, pepper, coffee, chocolate, cinnamon, vanilla, cloves, ginger, sugarcane, metabolites, medicinal plants, fruit, fish, cattle, and a long list of other things.

Indigenous people groups will require guidance in producing some of these, transporting them out of the jungle, and marketing them. If the Christian business community, national and/or international, were to take an interest in tribal economies, it could be profitable for both parties. Great Commission companies initiated from the outside that practice fair market trade are needed.

PARTNERSHIP GROWTH

The group of fourteen mission organizations that met in 2004 has grown and incorporated. The Amazon and Lowland Tribal Empowerment

Coalition (Alteco) incorporated in 2006 as a 501(c)(3) with the steering committee becoming the board of directors. Our present board includes Terry Lassiter, an Affinity Group Leader from IMB; Doug Baughman, an Associate Director for Wycliffe; Paul Johnson, the Director of Amazon Focus; Phil Goddard, a Colorado businessman; Tom Khazoyan, a media producer from 10x Productions; Steve Saint, the director of ITec; and myself.

Alteco continues to serve as a networker to bring mission organizations, North American churches, national and tribal churches from the Amazon, and the Christian business community to one table. We have had five annual consultations so far in Orlando; the last was attended by almost 120 people representing seventy organizations. We continue to build a network of individuals and organizations that are focused on the Amazon and committed to empowerment. We have all agreed to work together to empower indigenous tribal churches to live out God's dream for them.

Alteco also provides training during the consultation on key issues such as worldview, storying, and establishing sustainable economies in tribal settings. We understand that it is no longer enough to provide those we teach with the qualities that produce life; we must also provide them with the capabilities that produce livelihood. Our marching orders are echoed in our vision statement: We envision an indigenous community of healthy, reproducing churches providing life and livelihood for all the peoples of the Amazon Region.

The North American churches that send out missionaries understand the principles of life and livelihood. They choose pastors and recompense them for their ministry. They train missionaries and support them as they go. They have the physical and financial resources to accomplish what God lays on their hearts.

The churches we plant among indigenous people should be just as capable. We must help them to emerge as joint partners in reaching the unreached, partners who no longer stand facing us, waiting for a handout, but who stand shoulder to shoulder with us, gazing into the distance and envisioning how we can get the job done *together*.

WORKING TOGETHER

Alteco is finding new ways to work together. Dr. Paul Seale, from the Mercer School of Medicine, made a presentation of his ministry at the annual consultation in 2006. He spoke about his work with alcoholism, a very pressing problem among tribal people around the world.

During the question and answer time after his presentation, one of the tribal leaders stood up and spoke through an interpreter. "We have been discussing your presentation and your ministry, and we would like to invite you to come to our country next year to work with us in helping tribes to recover from alcoholism."

With the help of his tribal coworkers, Dr. Seale developed a culturally relevant curriculum and not only taught that curriculum, but also taught tribal leaders to teach it. He has made numerous trips to South America and is empowering the people of the Amazon to deal with this problem that has almost destroyed them.

Alteco also works together to equip tribal church leaders. In September of 2007, the Trans-Amazonian Network met in a large, round, thatched-roof building in Iquitos, Peru. There was another group meeting in the smaller building nearby at the same time. Two dentists from North America were training five tribal men in the basics of dentistry, passing on in four days what had taken them years to learn.

The Trans-Amazonian Network meetings and the dental training ended at the same time with a remarkable demonstration of skill. The newly trained dentists worked in our midst on some of the delegates—diagnosing, giving anesthesia, and then filling some teeth while pulling others.

These jungle dentists left the gathering with solar-powered dental chairs strapped to their backs. IDent, a division of ITec, had developed and built the chairs to fold into a backpack and sold them to the tribal representatives at a reduced price. As the men left with the chairs strapped to their backs, it occurred to me that six organizations had worked together with two tribal groups to make that moment possible.

In November of 2008, representatives from Alteco took a side trip to look at a Christian camp not far outside the little jungle town of Shell, Ecuador. Buildings on the property include four dorms, a chapel, a kitchen, and a dining area. Crops and livestock could be raised on the many acres. It would be perfect for use as an empowerment center—a place where life truths and livelihood skills could be taught together.

It would be very simple and quite efficient just to push ahead right now with our plans and do something *for* the tribal people, but the last five years have taught us that that would be unwise. The Trans-

Amazonian Network tribal leaders have made it clear to us that they want to hold a stake in everything that is done.

The tribal leaders want to play a part in deciding how the property is developed, how the decision is made as to who attends the training, and how it will be paid for. They even want a part in developing the curriculum so that it is culturally relevant. And they want to employ oral learning methods rather than literate ones. I am convinced that they will own the future of this project if we will make a commitment to work *together*.

THE FUTURE

The business world is catching on to the idea that the world is flat—that the global marketplace has changed. The distinctions between the East, the West, and the third world have faded; the boundaries have blurred.

We can, of course, choose to be threatened by the idea that others will build on the foundations we have laid, or we can choose to remember that we all build on the foundations laid by others. We must show caution just as Paul warned those who were building on the foundation he had laid in 1 Corinthians 3:10, "Each one should be careful how he builds."

But we can still choose to take pleasure in the way the edifice around us is taking shape:

1. *We do not have to be territorial.* No single organization has all the resources needed to finish the job in any people group. We can work together and offer jointly what none of us can offer alone.

2. *We do not have to be exclusive.* God is calling and equipping the people of other places, other cultures, and other generations to ministry. If we plan to be displaced, we will not have to be replaced.

3. *We do not have to be overburdened.* There is a second and third generation ready to carry the gospel and help finish the task.

4. *We do not have to be protective.* We can stop making decisions based on what is best for our organizations and start making decisions based on what is best for God's glory among the nations.

5. *We do not have to minister alone.* Seeds that fall into the ground

and die reproduce and bear fruit. That has been Christ's plan for his Church for two millennia, and we can only accomplish *his* goals by sharing *his* objectives.

It seems that God has birthed Alteco for such a time as this, not just for the Amazon, but for other parts of the world as well. Facilitation through genuine partnerships is the name of the game for the twenty-first century.

Case Study 2

Ibero–America's COMIBAM International[1]

IN FEBRUARY 2004 IN Colorado Springs, Dr. Omar Gava visited Paul Lere, the President of International Training Partners, which provides the Sharpening Your Interpersonal Skills (SYIS) training worldwide. Gava directs the missionary training network in Ibero–America for COMIBAM International (Cooperación Misionera Iberoamericana),[2] which has a strong passion to reach Muslims. Ministries that prepared him for this vital role include forty years of church planting and another decade of involvement in a missionary training center in Cordoba, Argentina.

While in Colorado Springs, Lere suggested that Gava meet George Walker to hear about Worldview Resource Group (WRG). Lere knew about WRG through his friendship with Walker, the Vice-President, because they attended the same church.

WRG provides equipping, training, and consulting in cross-cultural church planting methodologies with a particular focus on a worldview approach.[3] WRG believes that the degree to which the worldview of the host society is brought to tension and is transformed by a biblical worldview is the degree to which the church plant will be successful. Besides worldview, WRG provides training on animism, narrative, Chronological Bible Teaching, and church multiplication that is proven, identifiable, doable, and measurable. Omar was intrigued.

---

1. Thanks go to Robert Strauss for supplying much of this case study. Dr. Strauss is President and CEO of Worldview Resource Group based in Colorado Springs, Colorado.

2. More information about COMIBAM is available at www.comibam.org

3. For more information about World Resource Group, see www.wrg3.org

COMIBAM COMES CALLING: A DIVINE ENCOUNTER

Early one evening that February, Lere and Gava knocked on Walker's front door, and Gava and Walker were introduced. For two hours the two talked and viewed more than sixty slides of a PowerPoint presentation.

Gava told Walker that he had not seen or heard anyone talk about worldview and narrative like this and that these components were missing in the Ibero–America mission movement, now approaching forty years of age. He invited Walker to come to Argentina to facilitate a seminar on the subject of worldview. The seminar would be offered for masters-level credit through the extension program of the South America Theological Seminary in Londrina, Brazil.

The front door had hardly closed as Lere and Gava left Walker's house, and Walker was on the phone with Dr. Robert Strauss, President of WRG. "God has answered our prayers," he told Strauss excitedly. Some background is necessary to understand the significance of this Divine encounter.

Robert Strauss, George Walker, and Mark Zook founded WRG in late 2001 with a vision to impact the global mission enterprise through an emphasis on worldview, narrative, and church multiplication. Rather than create new platforms of ministry abroad, they strategized to work within large-scale networks and platforms that God had already established. So the first step was to look for what God was already doing in missions, particularly in Majority World countries attempting global missions, one of which would be Latin America.

COMIBAM International is a network in Latin America with more than ten thousand missionaries sent out from local churches to reach unreached peoples through some four hundred sending agencies. In that much of the mission movement emerging from Ibero–America, representing some seventy thousand evangelicals, takes place within the network of COMIBAM International, WRG began to pray that God would connect the two. And the rest is history.

Through a Divine encounter God brought Gava, representing the COMIBAM connection, to Colorado Springs to meet Walker. In faith WRG launched its new ministry to multiply key leaders in the region of Ibero–America.

RELATIONSHIPS RESULT IN REWARDS

One of the first questions Gava asked Strauss was whether he was in this relationship for the short-term or for a lifetime, indicating preference for the latter. Strauss answered for a lifetime. What started as an introduction in a living room in Colorado Springs developed into a full partnership of ministry with the creation of a branch affiliate in Argentina called *Recursos Estrategicos Globales* (REG).

WRG relies on relationships. They consider making friends as the first and foremost priority. This takes time. So they pray for each other; they communicate regularly through email, Skype, and in person; they open their lives to each other. When Strauss and associates go to Villa Carlos Paz, Argentina, they stay in the Gava's home. They eat Argentine *asados* and drink *vino tino* together. They know all of Gava's children and have become friends with them. Strauss spoke at the dedication of Gava's grandson.

Gava has been known to take Strauss on a drive into the mountains of Cordoba Province for the day to talk, laugh, pray, and plan. One time when Strauss and Walker were in Cordoba, Omar and his wife Stella paid their way to go to Buenos Aires to enjoy a weekend in the capital city, to see the great soccer stadiums, and to be exposed to the Argentine tango. The couple has been extremely generous to WRG with time, talent, and treasure.

The relationship between WRG and REG is *not* one way. It is a partnership of mutuality and of reciprocity, in which each learns from and serves the other. WRG personnel provide new insights into worldview and narrative in relation to church multiplication, while Latino personnel, who have now become close friends, teach and model for WRG personnel family closeness, community, sacrificial living, how to convert the abstract into the concrete, holism, how to network, how to truly put relationships before work, and what it means to be wholly committed to the Lord Jesus Christ with passion, purpose, and possessions.

WRG carries out its ministry in Ibero–America under the auspices of REG. Gava serves as the Executive Director of REG and continues in his role of COMIBAM International Director of Missionary Training.

REG has a staff of approximately nine people: administrators, board members, translators, and trainers. The REG staff is bilingual and has masters and/or doctoral degrees in missiology and other disciplines, and their life in ministry is inimitable. Each activity, all the programs, and every initiative come from the leaders of the movement. WRG is there by invitation only.

Today, REG oversees five MA/DMiss programs throughout Ibero–America in Chile, Argentina, Paraguay, Mexico, and Cuba. From the students in these programs, all of whom are already in ministry as missionaries, directors of training centers, pastors of local churches, or leaders in mission organizations, WRG/REG envision a network of one hundred facilitators/consultants over the next ten years. These individuals will be capable of teaching worldview and narrative-driven church multiplication throughout the Ibero–America mission movement.

THE HOLY SPIRIT MOVES

The first seminar in Cordoba was a seminal event. Half-way through the seminar, Gava stopped Walker and called the participants to a time of repentance. Gava reflected that core premises of WRG material were new. As far as he could discern, the strategies and methodologies that Walker had presented so far in the first half of the seminar were not how the Latinos had been executing their ministries in Latin America, Spain, Morocco, Turkey, India, and a host of other countries. They were not thinking about worldview, but merely addressing issues at a surface level—outward behaviors and social institutions.

The men and women at that first seminar got on their knees and spent time in prayers of repentance and in expressions of commitment to change the way that ministry would be done from that day forward. Practices were changed. For example, Marenrri and Yoamirka Duboy, Cuban missionaries working in the Patagonia of Chile, changed their strategy and methods of church planting after they attended that first seminar. Some of these changes included using concentric circles to look underneath behavior to discover the values and assumptions that drive it, and Chronological Bible Teaching.

Several seminars later, promptings from the Holy Spirit and more feedback from Gava resulted in some restructuring of the curriculum for a concrete relational setting.

- Begin with unrushed personal testimonies (include family).

- Provide a coursepak, including a glossary of terms and helpful sources.

- Use PowerPoint with minimal text and/or the whiteboard.

- Review previous day's lessons and/or preview present day (whole to part).

- Start all lessons with a story and move to reflection.

- Have limited points per lesson.

- Chunk points into meaningful sections.

- Repeat key points frequently and creatively.

- Illustrate everything with authentic, concrete examples (geographic locations, real names, dates, and earthy details).

- Transition smoothly from lesson to lesson.

- Always summarize the day, tying it back to the overarching story.

- Conclude with a discussion after each day.

- Call for reflections on the discussion: What was missed? What can I learn from you?

- Evaluate and adapt at the end of the seminar.

BACKWARD MAPPING

Through the able work of Dr. Jonathan Lewis (World Evangelical Alliance), the Latin movement has been better equipped to design and deliver intentional and integral training that is based on competency models. In 1991, he facilitated the development of a profile for an entry-level Latino missionary that is used in training centers like *Centro de Capacitación Misionera Transcultural* (CCMT, Cross-Cultural Missionary Training Center) in Cordoba, Argentina. The profile is used as a starting point for determining the curriculum content of the training program.

In April 2005, COMIBAM International convened a consultation in Villa Carlos Paz, Argentina, to profile a Latino missionary trainer and training center administrator. Jonathan Lewis, Rob Brynjolfson, Omar Gava, and Robert Strauss facilitated the three-day workshop. Stakeholders who participated in the workshop came from as far as Spain. The profile focused on character qualities and ministry capabilities. Rather than create this profile in isolation, the group also looked at several of the profiles created by New Tribes Mission and the World Evangelical Alliance.

From the Latino trainer profile, the group began to identify the types of courses that could be offered to equip trainers and administrators. Ultimately, this profile served as the foundation for the curriculum offered by REG in a three-track masters program and a Doctor of Missiology program accredited through the South America Theological Seminary (Facultade Teologica Sur America) in Londrina, Brazil. The three tracks include trainer in missiology, administration of a training center, and general intercultural studies.

WRITTEN RESOURCES MULTIPLY

Because of limited print resources in missiology, three books have been translated into Spanish for student use: *Strategic Alliances* by Daniel Rickets, *Passing the Baton: Church Planting That Empowers* by Tom Steffen, and *Understanding Folk Religion* by Paul Hiebert, Daniel Shaw, and Tite Tienou. The REG translation department has just completed translating a *Narrative Reader* into Spanish and will soon complete a *Worldview Reader*.[4]

All of WRG's training courses have been translated into Spanish. Gava and Strauss have edited a missionary training manual, commissioned by COMIBAM International, that provides explanations about all facets of missionary training design and delivery, along with extensive lists of available resources. Yamina Gava Rudaz, a professor in the National University of Cordoba, oversees the translation department of REG.

TRAINERS MULTIPLY

David Szostak, a pastor outside of Asuncion, Paraguay, who also directs a missionary training program, personifies one of the goals of the partnership between REG and WRG. He participated in the workshop that profiled a Latino trainer and has co-facilitated a course with Brynjolfson that addresses the design of intentional and integral training. He will accompany Greg Melendes from WRG to Puebla, Mexico, to co-facilitate the worldview seminar that will be offered in that location through the REG masters program. Szostak is one of many who will make up the

---

4. Translated versions available at the REG website, http://www.reg.org.ar/q_s .html

network of facilitators and consultants that will equip the Latin mission movement for the future.

FUNDING THE PARTNERSHIP

Funding for this partnership comes from varied sources in that a structure of support (comparable to USA/Canada) is not in place. WRG uses funds that come from large grants from Christian foundations in the USA and personal savings.

REG personnel also give of their own moneys and form a business venture, a Great Commission company that is burgeoning in Villa Carlos Paz, a tourist village near Cordoba, Argentina.

Gava is also a chiropractor who practices with the activator, one of three people in the whole nation of Argentina to use such a technique of adjustment. Omar is training two assistants with the vision that the moneys from the medical practice, another Great Commission company, will fund the ministry of REG. These creative responses to raise funds challenge a long-held cultural value that "We can't do that!"

This strategic partnership exemplifies God at work in bringing together the North and the South to improve Latino workers for his kingdom. It shows the necessity and reward of sharing resources and of building deep relationships with the entire family. We continue to learn together so that we can continue to work together in this God-ordained journey.

Case Study 3

Training Latin Americans for Missions Among Muslims[1]

LATIN AMERICANS ARE TAKING their place on the frontlines of the world mission movement. This in itself does not come as news to missiologists, who have tracked their rapidly growing numbers over the past two generations. Increasingly, however, Latin Americans are demonstrating that they add more than numbers to the ranks of international mission. God is using them in strategic ministries that are making a difference among some of the most neglected and unreached peoples in the world, particularly Muslim peoples.

For more than a decade, my wife (Angie) and I have had the privilege of participating at the request of Brazilian mission leaders in training missionaries for cross-cultural service. While most of these missions candidates have been Brazilians, a significant number have been from Spanish-speaking countries in Central and South America. More than half of those trained have prepared for service in the Muslim world. Most of our experience in training both Brazilian and Hispanic missionaries for service among Muslims has been under the auspices of the Brazilian Baptist World Mission Board, and it is this experience that I describe here.

I begin with a true success story about how God has used Latin American missionaries in just one Muslim village. All the names given

1. Don Finley and his wife, Angie, are missionaries with Converge Worldwide/ Baptist General Conference and have served twenty-two years in Brazil and Central Asia. They have worked with the Brazilian Baptist World Mission Board for over ten years in missionary training, where Don served as Coordinator of Training from 2007 to 2009. They are now seconded to The Mission Society to work with IMFORM, the Methodist Institute of Missionary Formation, in Teresópolis, Brazil, where Don is the Academic Coordinator for missionary training. He has a PhD in Intercultural Studies from the E. Stanley Jones School of World Mission & Evangelism at Asbury Theological Seminary in Wilmore, KY. He may be contacted at rioworldreach@gmail.com.

are fictitious. Although similar stories could be told of other teams in other places, not all ministry stories have had such positive outcomes. For this reason, following the story, I describe details of our approach that have helped produce such success.

FIELDS WHITE FOR HARVEST

After extensive training, the time had finally arrived for a brand new Brazilian team to be taken to the unreached Mediterranean village where they would eventually introduce the Gospel. This first Volunteers Without Borders (*Voluntários Sem Fronteiras*, or VSF) team was escorted by Alex and Lúcia, career missionaries who had been ministering in the area for fifteen years. In that time, the couple had established good relationships with people throughout the region, but there had been little response to the gospel message.

The first days were consumed with the task of settling in, beginning to learn the tribal language, learning how to take care of their rice field, and becoming familiar with the mundane tasks needed for survival. Soon Fernanda, who had done a course in physical therapy before entering the VSF program, noticed that the chief's mother was bedridden. Fernanda began visiting her, giving her massages, and helping the elderly woman exercise her atrophied muscles. Before long, she was walking again, and the team experienced new levels of acceptance and friendship in the village.

As they learned the language and observed the conduct of children in the village, the team began gathering outside their hut after a day of work. João, the team leader, was a gifted musician, and he made up songs for the children around themes encouraging good behavior. Pretty soon older brothers and sisters, and then parents, were coming to the Brazilians' veranda every day for the sing-along. Finally the village elders came by with a question. "You are teaching our children songs about values that are important to us. But you aren't from here. Where did you learn these things?" The team answered that they learned them in the Bible. Their credibility continued to grow.

A linguistics team translating the Bible into the tribal language using Arabic script visited the village with a copy of the first eight chapters of Romans. Marisa, one of the girls on the team, studied the pages and felt something click. She announced to her team, "I think I can read this." Nobody believed her, because she had been speaking the tribal language for just a few months and had never studied Arabic a day in her life. So Marisa started reading—and nailed it. The linguistics team left the scripture portion with her, and asked her to get some feedback in the village.

One afternoon, Marisa was leaving a session where she had been reading to a group of women in a fairly unproductive effort to get some feedback. As she came out the door, she saw the village chief sitting with his brother on the veranda of a house across the road. "Marisa," he called, "what are you doing?" Fearful she might be getting her team kicked out of the village, Marisa replied truthfully, "I'm reading part of the Injil." The chief told her, "Come read it to us."

Marisa read the first half of Romans 1 and stopped. The chief protested, "No, this is interesting. Keep going." At the end of the first chapter, the chief and his brother stopped to discuss what they had heard. As a young woman, Marisa could not participate in the conversation between the two men. But as she listened, she was astonished by their depth of comprehension. The pattern continued throughout the first eight chapters of Romans, Marisa reading and then hearing these two Muslim leaders discuss the passage with understanding. "All my life," she told us later, "I had heard that the word of God is sharper than a two-edged sword. That day I lived it, as I saw the truth of God penetrate the hearts of these two men."

When they had finished reading and discussing, the chief told Marisa, "You have to get us more of this. This is the most beautiful and profound truth I have ever heard."

Not long after this, Alex visited the village to check on the team. It was the month of Ramadan, and he was invited to preach in the mosque, where he had forty-five minutes to go "from Genesis to Jesus." When he finished speaking, a man from the village rose to speak. "We have heard the teacher speak truth today. We know it is true because we have seen this truth lived out by the Brazilian young people among us. We need to learn this truth, and we can learn from the teacher and the Brazilians. But my brother has been learning from them, and he has become a follower of Jesus. He has learned a lot, and he can teach us also." So, a respected adult male in the village was recognized as a follower of Jesus in the mosque and, rather than suffering persecution or ostracism, was seen as someone who could help the entire village learn God's truth. After this, the village chief appointed ten men whose primary work from that time would be to learn the Bible and pass on what they learned to the rest of the village.

The VSF team spent their two years in the village working alongside the people there. They developed projects like an elementary school, a health clinic, and a soccer program for children in response to needs that they encountered. The team saw a few people accept Jesus openly and perceived that many more were becoming increasingly interested. When they left after their two years were completed, the village wept.

Years after the first VSF team left, Alex was visiting with the village chief when he heard a remarkable story that had been passed down in the chief's family. The chief, now an elderly man, told Alex that the village had been founded generations ago by his grandfather, during the time of French colonialism. Shortly after the village was established, the founding chief had a dream that one day, foreigners would come to live in the village, work alongside them, and share their food. These foreigners, he dreamed, would teach his people the ways of God. The chief looked at Alex and said with conviction, "The spot my grandfather indicated as the place where these foreigners would live is the exact spot where the Brazilians have their house. I believe that God sent these young people as a fulfillment of the promise God made to my grandfather. I believe also that Jesus is the Son of God, and that he died on the cross to save us from our sins."

Today, the church is being born in that village, and in other villages in the same area. Alex tells us that there is a regional openness to the gospel that he never saw before, and he attributes it to the influence of the VSF teams. Here and in other Muslim villages scattered around Africa, the church is being born, and the instruments God has chosen are young South American Christians committed to a radically incarnational lifestyle among people they have come to love in Jesus' name.

FACILITATING SUCCESSFUL OUTCOMES
THROUGH TRAINING

We celebrate successes like that of the preceding story, and we also recognize that not all stories have such happy endings. One of the weak spots in Latin American missions during the early years, identified both by Latin American missiologists and international mission leaders, has been a lack of pre-field training. Among the identified consequences of this lack of training have been inadequate cultural adaptation, triumphalism, relationship difficulties, and a high rate of missionary attrition. In response, a number of Brazilian mission organizations have made significant commitments to provide adequate pre-field training for their missionaries—and have at times invited expatriates like Angie and me to help. I will now document the small role we played as expatriate facilitators in helping restructure the training programs.

The Context of Training

The Agency

The Brazilian Baptist World Mission Board, or *Junta de Missões Mundiais* (JMM), was established in 1907 at the same meeting that inaugurated the Brazilian Baptist Convention. With over a century of existence, it is among the oldest cross-cultural sending agencies in Central and South America. Today, approximately six hundred missionaries serve under its umbrella. Half are Brazilians or spouses of Brazilians. The other half are indigenous missionaries serving in their native countries within their national leadership structure, but in situations where the church is small and often persecuted.

In the 1990s, JMM experienced rapid growth. Its traditional focus on South America, the Iberian peninsula, and the former Portuguese colonies of Africa expanded to include a new focus on unreached peoples. Eventually, this focus on unreached peoples became the central, but not the sole, focus of JMM. At the same time, under the leadership of Executive Director Waldimiro Tymchak, JMM was becoming concerned with the need for better pre-field training of its missionaries. The roughly simultaneous developments of an increasing focus on unreached peoples, a rapidly expanding number of missionaries, and a growing realization of the need to make pre-field training a priority, were consistent with what was happening in other cutting-edge mission movements in Brazil during these years.

The Programs

In February of 2003, JMM launched a new mission endeavor for young people, creating a new category of service called the Radical Africa Project. This project was modeled after the Radical Program of Missões Horizontes of Brazil and adapted to the needs of JMM. Though the official name of the project has been changed to Volunteers Without

Borders (*Voluntários Sem Fronteiras*, or VSF), the young people in the project continue to refer to themselves as Radicals. Through VSF, young adults volunteer for four years of mission service. The first year is spent in intensive, 24/7 training. After a period of support-raising, the group departs for six months of French study and cultural adaptation at a base in an African Muslim country.

From there, the group is divided into teams of four or five people, and they travel to the field where they will spend the next two years, usually in a remote Muslim village. All live from a common purse and make decisions regarding both ministry and daily life together, under the direction of one team member who is designated as the leader. All teams work under the direction of a career missionary who lives within a few hours' drive. The career missionary maintains periodic contact to monitor the work and well-being of the team, and is available in the event of an emergency. The missiological approach of the teams is to live a radically incarnational lifestyle. They learn the tribal language, labor alongside Africans in sharing the work of the village, serve the village by starting ministries that meet the felt needs of the people, and walk through doors of opportunity opened by their lifestyle, character, and service, to share a verbal witness about Jesus. As a result, people are coming to faith in Christ, and churches are being born.

Upon successful completion of their VSF term of service, the overwhelming majority of participants come back to Brazil with a commitment to return to the field as career missionaries. Before his death in 2007, JMM Executive Director Waldimiro Tymchack was committed to find a way to give these young people additional training that would qualify them for career appointment more quickly than a traditional four-year seminary course. Consequently, we developed a one-year, highly intensive course of biblical and missiological studies. Combined with their pre-field training and practical experience, this course was accepted as adequate alternative preparation for career service. While many returning VSF missionaries opted to enroll in university or seminary courses in areas such as medicine, nursing, physical therapy, computer science, anthropology, linguistics, education, and theology, eighteen students completed the one-year biblical/missiological course that JMM offered. Most are now back on the field as career missionaries.

The Setting

In the nineties, JMM began holding an annual two- to four-week training session for career missionaries at a simple bed-and-breakfast vacation site in the countryside near its headquarters in the city of Rio de Janeiro. This training was basically an orientation to the agency, with an introduction to a few missiological topics included in the program. In the late nineties, due to my new role as professor of missions at the South Brazil Baptist Seminary in Rio, I received my first invitation to participate in this training.

While beneficial, this relatively short training experience did not completely meet the needs of JMM or its missionaries. So, in 2000, a work group to plan a new missionary training center was formed. I was invited to participate. As a result of our deliberations, Brazilian Baptists launched in 2002 the Integrated Center for Education and Missions (CIEM) as a partnership between the World Mission Board and the Women's Missionary Union. The first students began their courses of study in August of 2002. Options included a three-year undergraduate course in missiology and a one-year post-graduate course, designed for the pre-field training needs of JMM career missionaries. Newly appointed JMM career missionaries were enrolled in that course, which accepted independent students as well.

In 2007, all JMM pre-field training was transferred to the campus of the South Brazil Baptist Seminary, also located in Rio de Janeiro, with all programs directed by JMM itself. JMM leadership asked me to serve as coordinator of that training.

The Candidates

Participants in the career pre-field training program are new missionaries already appointed by JMM, or candidates invited by JMM to participate. They are Brazilians or spouses of Brazilians, and members of Baptist churches. Typically, their ages range from thirty to forty-five. The most common educational preparation for mission service is a seminary degree in theology or religious education. For career appointment, candidates must have two years of full-time experience in the kind of work they plan to do on the field.

Increasingly, candidates with secular degrees and professions are being appointed for service, particularly among Muslim peoples. The most common professions include an area of health care or a background in sports—especially soccer, a field that opens many doors for Brazilians. Credentialed Brazilian soccer coaches are in such demand that Muslim governments sometimes invite Brazilian mission agencies to supply coaches, and even provide housing and salary for them.

Experience has shown that for professionals with no background in seminary or full-time vocational ministry, pre-field training is especially important. On the field, they have several adjustments to make at once: adapting to the local culture, adjusting to being in full-time ministry even as they continue to exercise their profession, and learning to be a Christian witness in a Muslim context. Training offers invaluable tools that help in the process of cultural adaptation and inculturation. In addition, training offers a period of time to make mental and emotional adjustments to the new realities of vocational ministry in the environment of a supportive Christian community.

Career missionaries are supported by Brazilian churches and individuals, and missionaries must raise their full support before departing for the field. During training, they receive agency-owned housing on campus and a stipend rather than a full salary. They may come for training before they have full support in place, and they often travel on weekends to speak in potential supporting churches.

VSF accepts unmarried volunteers between the ages of eighteen and thirty-five with at least a high-school diploma and the recommendation of their local Baptist church. Most come for training right after high school. Because a number of volunteers are under the age of twenty-one, signed parental consent is required as well. This requirement is maintained for older volunteers, understanding that the expression of parental support serves as an encouragement to them. It also reflects the Brazilian cultural understanding that sons and daughters are part of the parents' nuclear family until they are married, regardless of age.

Everything in VSF for volunteers is done in teams, including the sharing of finances. Each person on a team receives ten US dollars per month for discretionary personal spending. All other ministry and living expenses are shared and administered by teams. Hence, in keeping with the project philosophy, everything that is needed to complete the support package of a group is done through group presentations of the ministry and the financial needs in churches. No one goes to the field until everyone is fully supported. Support-raising is an intense, pressure-packed experience, and it is used as a new phase of training with a focus on personal spiritual formation and group development.

All of the native Spanish-speakers have suffered culture shock in the early stages of the training and have benefited from some special attention and support. With one exception, all have overcome language and cultural differences, and integrated well with Brazilians on their team. They have made significant contributions to the work and successfully completed their terms of service. We have observed that while cultural differences certainly exist between Brazilians and other South Americans, enough cultural similarities exist that the training program designed with Brazilians in mind has been suitable for Hispanic volunteers. If anything, the cross-cultural dynamic within the group has contributed to the overall effectiveness of the training.

Two additional observations are needed to complete a generic profile of the VSF volunteers. One is that there have always been more female volunteers than male, a trend that has grown more acute over the past few years. This imbalance is problematic because it is culturally necessary to include on every team at least one male who can, in the minds of African villagers, serve as the authority of the team and deal with village leaders (even if JMM appoints one of the females as team leader for the internal working of the group).

Secondly, it is important to note that many of the VSF volunteers are first- or second-generation Christians. Backgrounds in dysfunctional families and familial involvement in spiritism are common, leaving scars and unresolved issues that must be discovered, unpacked, and dealt with before volunteers are spiritually and emotionally ready to go to the field. This reality reinforces the priority of spiritual formation and sets part of the agenda for training.

How the Training Works

The Trainers

Ideally, professors in a pre-field training program will meet two basic qualifications: extensive and successful cross-cultural experience; and solid missiological studies. A third desirable element would be for the majority of trainers to be nationals from the same country, or countries, as those who are being trained.

Sometimes, the ideal must give way to the possible. There are multitudes of Brazilian missionaries who are very effective on the field. Some of them have completed advanced missiology courses, making them great candidates to serve as trainers. However, most of the Brazilian missionaries with solid missiological studies and a history of effective service are staying on the field and are not ready to return to Brazil. There exists a mid-term shortage of trainers that needs to be filled by missionaries to Brazil, or by Brazilians lacking one (or both) elements of the ideal profile (field experience and advanced missiological studies).

This reality was reflected over the seven years of training described here, especially at the point of the makeup of the leadership team. Being located in Rio de Janeiro, near the agency headquarters, we were able to enlist mission agency executives, as well as retired and furloughing missionaries, to serve as professors of specific courses. Students benefited from consistent contact with knowledgeable and experienced Brazilian professors. The leadership team itself consisted of coordinators of specific academic areas (including Angie and me), leaders of the pastoral care ministry (another North American couple), and two young women (a Brazilian and a Spaniard) who had leadership roles in VFS. They had been VSF missionaries, and both had bachelor's degrees, but neither had theological or missiological studies. As overall coordinator of training, I worked under the supervision of the Missions Director of JMM, ensuring effective Brazilian leadership of the training program.

The Training: Philosophy and Implementation

The philosophy underpinning the pre-field preparation of missionaries in our program reflects a commitment to holistic training, incorporating formal, non-formal, and informal elements. This reflects the predominant approach advocated within the Brazilian Association of Missions Professors.

Formal training refers to the kind of learning that occurs in a highly structured academic setting. Its primary concern is to transmit content, which is often theoretical in nature. It is characterized by the lecture method and does not necessarily require personal interaction between the professor and the student. The most common model for this kind of training is the university.

In all of our training programs, the formal element has been valued as an essential part of missionary preparation. Required courses in pre-field training include basic biblical and theological studies, anthropological studies on culture and mission, studies in Islam, research on particular countries and regions, and classes designed to support the work of spiritual formation. Some courses in the above list are for all missionaries and missionary candidates, regardless of their category (career or VSF) or their anticipated place of service. Other courses are program- or region-specific.

Believing that good missionary practice is informed by good theology and good missiological theory, JMM training took the formal element seriously. However, we differed from the university model used in the West at several points. We recognized that Brazil, like most of Hispanic Latin America, is a high-context, oral culture. One implication of this fact is that the preferred learning style for most missionaries in pre-field training is interactive and experiential. A variety of pedagogical styles to engage students in the classroom is helpful. Lectures are an important element, but they are used in a way that invites and stimulates dialogue. Individual reading assignments are necessary, but we mixed in group reading assignments that led to creative class presentations.

Many of our students did not intuitively make the connections between theological truth or missiological theory on the one hand, and practical applications of these truths on the other. Teachers and trainers needed to be intentional to help students bridge the gap between theory and practice. For that to happen, we needed teachers who had put theory into practice themselves. That's why we selected professors with missions experience. Furthermore, we promoted personal interaction between teachers and students through sharing life in community.

Non-formal training focuses on practical ministry skills and personal development through planned but non-classroom activity. While experience and competency in ministry can be assumed in the case of career missionaries, they still receive training in some practical ministries, such as literacy and sports ministries. VSF volunteers also receive this training; in addition, they do chaplaincy work in a local hospital, take a mission trip, and develop ministries in the *favelas*, or slums, of Rio that last most of their year in training. All of this activity is done with experienced supervisors. Also, all missionaries in training participate weekly in a small group with a mentor who has had cross-cultural experience.

Regular worship, Bible study, and prayer times in community are scheduled. This happens daily in the case of the VSF volunteers, who live, study, and work constantly in the context of their group. Career missionaries live in two houses with common living and kitchen areas but separate apartments. A weekly highlight of our life in community is the missions forum, which includes a meal, prayer, worship, and discussion of a missiological subject. It serves as a time when professors, career appointees, and VSF volunteers can come together to catch up on what is happening in each other's lives, learn from one another, and grow together.

A final non-formal element in the preparation of VSF volunteers is survival training, led by Christians in the Brazilian military. Students learn to hike overland using a map and compass, identify plants with nutritional or medicinal value, cross a river with the aid of a rope, repel, and survive a physically demanding rustic survival camp. In the process, they learn to trust one another, work together toward common goals, overcome fears, live with minimal resources, test their physical and emotional limits, and depend on God.

Informal training happens through the normal ebb and flow of life, including the everyday exchanges that occur among students and between students and professors outside the programmed calendar of formal and non-formal learning. It involves spontaneous community events like parties, teachers inviting their students into their homes for meals, or conversations stimulated by studies in other settings.

We implicitly recognized that spiritual and ministry formation ultimately are not something that can be taught in a program. Discipleship is not something that is learned in a classroom or by filling out a notebook, but through sharing life together. And the most important moments often are not the times when everything is going great, but when things go wrong, when people are tired and irritable, or when conflict arises in the group.

It is interesting that years ago when I interviewed experienced Brazilian missionaries working with unreached peoples for my doctoral research, almost all of them affirmed that they would rather work on a team than alone. Then, in almost the same breath, most would say that their own experience in a team was difficult, and that they knew few, if any, teams that were healthy.

While JMM career missionaries frequently work in teams, all VSF missionaries do so, and with a much greater degree of proximity and intimacy. For them, building healthy teams must be a priority. Living in isolated Muslim villages, VSF missionaries will need to depend on each other for mutual support and accountability to an extraordinary degree. Conflict within a team is inevitable, and they need to learn during training how to deal with it, precisely because they need each other so much. They are taught to confront problems early and directly, to have the humility to seek and offer forgiveness, and to keep a clean slate in their relationships.

CONCLUSION

We rejoice in what God has done among Muslims through people like Alex, Lúcia, Fernanda, João, Marisa, and their teammates. We thank God for visionaries like Waldimiro Tymchack, who recognized the need for providing Latin American missionaries with better pre-field training and who worked diligently to make it happen. And we thank the Latin Americans for inviting us to participate in facilitating these changes.

Case Study 4

Facilitative Church Planting in Japan[1]

ASIAN ACCESS, AN INTERDENOMINATIONAL evangelical organization, has a policy that calls for partnering with national church leaders to start a church-multiplication movement in their respective countries. As the group's name implies, the ministry focuses on Asia.

Currently, Asian Access missionaries work in Japan and seven other Asian countries. Plans are in place to open cooperative works in all twenty Asian countries by 2012. The vision driving this process is "to see a vibrant community of servant leaders with vision, character, and competence leading the church across Asia."[2]

The foundation of this vision was the evangelistic work of the Language Institute for Evangelism Ministries (LIFE) started in 1967 by Kenneth Wendling. Meeting the felt need of many Japanese to learn conversational English, LIFE missionaries taught English in partnership with a Japanese chaplain or pastor who presented the gospel during chapel time. Even though LIFE had been a very fruitful ministry for decades, society began to change with the bursting of the Japanese bubble economy in the 1990s.

A new pervasive competitiveness prevailed. Several commercial English-teaching schools sprang up seemingly overnight, quickly developing into school chains. LIFE's church-based classes with their primary objective of friendship evangelism no longer looked as professional as the schools that focused on helping people get high-paying, English-

1. Appreciation goes to my friend Mike Wilson (mwilson@asianaccess.org) for providing the information used in this case study. Mike, his wife Mary Jo, and their two children serve as missionaries in Japan. They have been involved in facilitative church development in Tokyo and Okinawa for nearly fifteen years.

2. From Asian Access website, "Our Vision," para. 1, http://www.asianaccess.org/about/vision.html

requisite jobs. Sensing the closing of one door of opportunity from the Lord even as another was opening, LIFE's vision gradually shifted to a focus on church multiplication—planting churches that reproduce themselves.

From the start, LIFE's two-pronged approach to church multiplication involved developing Japanese church leaders in order to multiply churches. The Japan Church Growth Institute (JCGI) division of LIFE Ministries has trained over three hundred of the top pastors in Japan, inculcating the vision and competence to play their role in developing a church-multiplication movement that will encompass the entire nation of Japan. Success in Japan, the Institute believed, will flow over to other Asian countries.

As the leadership development work eventually expanded from Japan into other Asian countries, the name of the group had to be changed due to politically-sensitive reasons. Asian Access became the new name, continuing to work to develop the vision, competence, and character for long-term involvement in church multiplication.

Only in Japan does Asian Access deploy missionaries on the ground to partner with Japanese pastors and congregations that desire to develop new reproducing churches. These expatriate partners in the church multiplication cooperative relationship engage in evangelistic outreach in a variety of ways and participate in some of the planning for the new church.

Missionary involvement in outreach has two goals in addition to the obvious one of evangelism. First, their evangelistic activities are to provide a model for members of the mother church, and to engage Japanese lay Christians in the cooperative evangelistic activity in order to recruit any whom God would call for the church development team. Second, their input and encouragement in the prayer and planning process is meant to synergize creative involvement by participating lay Christians.

As LIFE Ministries/Asian Access transitioned into a church multiplication ministry focus in 1996, a number of expatriate families went to Japan to become part of this exciting new work. One of them, the Wilsons, was assigned to work with a church in Tokyo after a year in full-time Japanese language school. This assignment was unique in that the Wilsons would work with an individual church to plant another church. Normally, one missionary unit is assigned for each church participating in a network.

As the pace of the movement has picked up, the number of Japanese churches wanting to participate in a church-multiplication network has greatly surpassed the number of available missionaries. The result has been the formation of some missionary-less networks, networks with two missionaries serving five churches, and other combinations. The networks without missionaries on site receive coaching support from JCGI National Director Rev. Hiroshi Kawasaki and other national leaders.

This evolving process has resulted in a fluid job description for Asian Access missionaries working in a church-multiplication role. The agency assigns some to an individual church in a network to model evangelism while recruiting a church-planting team from among the church membership. The more experienced may serve in several churches to model evangelism and coach national church planters.

Returning to the fledgling days of the movement in 1996, the Wilson family was assigned to work with Nerima Grace Chapel in Tokyo. Mike had just completed a year of full-time language school. Mary Jo, his wife, who already spoke intermediate Japanese from her previous ministry experience as a single in Japan, cared for their small children aged five and two. Their daughter and son attended a Japanese pre-school/kindergarten (*yochien*), providing Mary Jo opportunity to reach out to other preschool (*yochien*) moms.

During the initial work at Nerima Grace Chapel, which was planning to birth a new church, Mike engaged in outreach through teaching some English classes, an English Bible class, and an evangelistic Bible study entitled "God's Love Letter." At least one Nerima Grace Chapel member teamed up with Mike in each evangelistic work. Another opportunity for outreach came when a student from nearby Musashi University visited the church office and asked if anyone could help him start a Christian English club on campus if he procured a charter for such a club.

As time went on and Mike became more fluent in Japanese, Nerima Grace Chapel's Pastor Ogasawara asked him to preach on a number of occasions. At these times, a woman in the church would help Mike craft his sermon in Japanese.

Mike had a habit of asking the housewives in the church about their husbands' work, hobbies, and interests. Seeing so many housewives attending church alone burdened him. The average ratio of women to men in the Church in Japan is approximately 70 percent female to 30 percent male.

His language helper told him that her husband used to play tennis before he became so busy at work, and that his doctor had recently told him to take up tennis again to maintain his health. Mike arranged to go to his language helper's family residence at a time when he could meet her husband, ostensibly for help on a sermon.

Mike met his helper's husband, Toshi. As the two talked, Mike mentioned that he was looking for a tennis partner to get some exercise. Toshi agreed to join him. A close friendship quickly formed.

One day as they were playing tennis, the two friends finished a set and were walking to exchange sides when Mike thought he heard the Holy Spirit tell him to tell Toshi about the little spat he had had earlier in the week with his daughter. So Mike shared the conflict with him, and added that conflicts with his wife or children were usually quickly resolved through application of biblical principles and prayer.

Toshi stopped in mid-stride, asking to hear more. What Mike did not know at the time was that Toshi and his high-school-age daughter were in the middle of a serious conflict. Toshi was at his wit's end trying to find resolution and reconciliation. Mike told his friend he was forming a men's small group to learn together and encourage each other as men, husbands, and fathers. Toshi's response: "I can't wait!"

The men's group, composed of Toshi, Hiroshi, another newcomer, and four church members, began with Mike leading the meetings using the four W's: Warm-up, Worship, Word, Work. Warm-up questions were gleaned from a number of sources. At first worship began with singing a familiar song like "Amazing Grace" a cappella. But after a short time it became known that Toshi had been a rock guitarist and that he still had six guitars at home gathering dust. So this seeker became the leader of the group in praise songs using an acoustic guitar.

For the Word portion, Mike led the men in an inductive study of John using a translated text from Precept Ministries. This fit Mike's advanced beginner's Japanese language level, and it engaged the men, providing insights they had never before perceived. Toshi and Hiroshi remarked that they had heard of the name of Jesus but had not known that he was the Creator of everything or that he had become the sacrifice for sinful humans. With every meeting the two newcomers to

Christianity were drawn closer to Christ by the testimonies, inductive study of the Word, and the warm fellowship.

One cell member had cerebral palsy and had never experienced acceptance or love, even from family members. The men's cell group changed all that. Some of the work projects included service projects for Tsuyoshi and some of his friends with physical handicaps.

Toshi and Hiroshi were deeply touched by the active compassion shown by the group as they participated in service opportunities. All the cell members were strongly impressed and grew to love God and each other more as they saw Tsuyoshi transformed by their active love and compassion extended to the community.

About the same time, two of Mike's English students accepted Christ, and then the two of them led both of their husbands to Christ. It was harvest time at the mother church; Mike and the church member partners were rejoicing daily. Most of the church members had never been involved in leading anyone to Christ before. The new experience lit a fire in them.

After about a year of the Wilson's partnership with Nerima Grace Chapel, the pastor and church elders arranged for a number of meetings to be held in a rented room on the sixth floor of a bank building in the nearby community of Kiyose. The Wilsons and cell group leaders would attend to discuss and dream together what God might want to do to establish a new church through them.

During the discussions the group eventually developed a plan to plant churches at approximately thirty-minute intervals up and down the Seibu-Ikebukuro train line located near Nerima Grace Chapel in northwest Tokyo. The pastor would commission five cell groups based in the Kiyose area to plant the first new church.

Initial outreach efforts focused on the cell group members' friends and families (*oikos*) in the Kiyose area, just over thirty minutes north of the Nerima Grace Chapel location in Tokyo. Mike made some advertising flyers for English classes and English Bible classes and had them distributed through members. They discovered that word-of-mouth referrals were much more effective than just distributing the flyers to strangers.

Mike taught a dozen classes—some three times a week, some twice a week, some only once a week—all around the Kiyose area. He went to class carrying his books and materials on a bicycle. This proved to be somewhat challenging in the winter when a wet snow sometimes falls.

During this phase, outreaches included a celebrity Christmas concert in a rented hall, a concert in the lobby of the city hall, home parties, barbeques, the ever-present English classes, cooking classes, kids' clubs, and many cell group initiated activities designed to provide fishing-pool opportunities for members. It was very gratifying for Mike to see his old friends Toshi, Hiroshi, Setsuko, Megumi, and others, leading outreach events targeting their friends and families, the next generation of believers.

As time went on, Mike realized this type of disciple multiplication was not that common in the Japanese churches to which he had been exposed during his six years of ministry in the hierarchical "Land of the Rising Sun." Rather, believers tended to compartmentalize their faith. Often they did not even let their faith be known in the workplace. Most church members left evangelism to the professional pastor or missionary. In addition, many believing housewives were forced to continue ancestor veneration rituals in order to keep their marriages and families intact.

One question increasingly challenged Mike: How could these dear Christian brothers and sisters be freed from the cultural "prison of disobedience"[3] that kept them from multiplying disciples generation after generation so that they could reach their loved ones with the good news of Jesus Christ?

From the beginning the vibrant spiritual DNA of the Kiyose Grace Chapel plant had a stimulating effect on her mother, the Nerima Grace Chapel. The core of the new church consisted of twenty-five members from the Chapel. The friendship evangelism and resulting multiplication of new Christians became an item for study by teams of elders who came periodically to learn more about what God was doing in the Kiyose location.

A number of Nerima church members were mobilized for evangelism like never before, in part through exposure to the multiplication that was occurring at the church plant. It was almost as if a holy envy took over at Nerima Grace Chapel, spurring certain members to try new things, including a round of home parties and barbeques. A number of conversions resulted.

3. Lingenfelter, *Transforming Culture*, 19.

A monthly combined worship service brought members from both churches together. This initiated mutual stimulation and encouragement, resulting in increased fruitfulness at both locations.

As the final year of the Wilsons' stay began, it became obvious that no one on the church-planting team seemed ready to take the reins of the new work and become the pastor. The Wilsons prayed long and hard about who would be the right pastor to take the fledgling Kiyose church to the next level in extending Christ's reign in the Kanto, the region around Tokyo.

As noted earlier, the mother church and daughter church had maintained a close relationship, which included financial support. As the offerings increased at Kiyose, financial support from the Nerima church ceased.

Because of the close contact between the two churches, the Wilsons were aware of the personal development of Katsuhiro Sugaya, Pastor Ogasawara's right hand man at Nerima Grace Chapel. Sugaya led worship, managed the office, and had become a zone pastor for about half of the Chapel's cell groups. In addition, he was exposed to a lot of innovative thinking about church by his visionary pastor as well as by the many guest speakers who came to the church to consult with Pastor Ogasawara.

Early on, Mike and Mary Jo had considered Sugaya for the pastoral role of the new church, but he was so busy and could not join the church-planting team, even though his wife did. In addition, he was not involved in evangelism.

As the new church core grew at Kiyose, Sugaya developed a cell group back at Nerima, and multiplied it twice through evangelism. Some of the new Christians were emotionally troubled so Sugaya developed compassionate competence in pastoral counseling as well as evangelism. The Wilsons noted the new developments and prayed for an opportunity to talk with Pastor Ogasawara about releasing his key number two leader to become pastor of the new church.

The opportunity eventually came for the Wilsons to meet with Pastor Ogasawara and share their conviction that God might be calling Sugaya to pastor the new church in Kiyose. They noted that by releasing the ultra-efficient Sugaya, opportunity would be given to two or three other leaders to emerge in the church who would otherwise likely stay undiscovered.

Pastor Ogasawara, a man of exceptional faith and vision, agreed that Sugaya seemed to be God's man for the new church and began to make arrangements to release. The timing would coincide with the Wilson's departure.

As a kind of final crescendo for the Wilson's service with the Nerima and Kiyose churches, the leaders agreed that taking a combined summer mission team overseas would be a good way to jump start discipleship with several new believers and younger long-term believers at the mother church. They agreed that Sugaya and Mike Wilson would co-lead the combined mission team.

Assuming Mike was an expert in cross-cultural missions because of his missionary tenure, the Nerima Grace Chapel leadership asked him to lead the training for the combined short-term mission team. He led team members in intercessory prayer, testimony preparation, and asking the "prior question of trust" (PQT): Is what I'm saying, doing, or thinking building or undermining trust?[4]

Taiwan, like many Asian countries, still has many citizens who resent Japan's aggression of more than sixty years ago. The language difference provides multiple opportunities for misunderstanding and breaking trust. Building trust is an essential element of incarnational evangelism anywhere, but particularly in Asia.

The original plan had been to take the team to work with a cooperative of churches in India, but just at that time, India and Pakistan were challenging each other with the use of nuclear missiles. So the Nerima Grace Chapel elders decided that the team would do better—and be safer—in Taiwan.

From the time their feet hit the ground in Taichung, Taiwan, the Tokyo short-termers were amazed at how God had prepared the way and was working through them. Another team from mainland China met up with them. The unity and cooperative spirit on both sides were inspiring to behold. Every morning began with a 5:00 a.m. prayer meeting and then a quick breakfast of noodles and tea or juice before heading off to do park evangelism with a translator.

A number of the older folks doing tai chi chuan exercises in the park were touched by the team's unity and joyful spirit. In the morning team members invited the youth they met to attend afternoon evangelistic events. In the evening there were rallies where someone translated

4. Mayers, *Christianity Confronts Culture*, 7.

Mike's preaching. When all the outreach activities were over, the leaders would meet to debrief the day and plan for the next. Finally, the exhausted but joyful team leaders went to bed around 1:00 a.m. most nights.

The Lord opened up an amazing opportunity to go to the largest hospital in Taichung and share the gospel with individuals from the top floor to the bottom. Many came to Christ in moments of crisis or as the Lord healed them in answer to the short-termers' prayers.

There were several other special outreach events that featured cooperative efforts with the Japanese, Taiwanese, and Chinese Christians effectively working together. In ten days, seventy-two people made decisions to follow Christ, but that was only part of what the Lord had planned for the short-term mission team from Japan.

About halfway through the ten-day trip, some of the Japanese team members noticed that the Taiwanese pastor was uncomfortable around them. Though the Taiwanese expressed unambiguous hospitality in multiple ways, the pastor would often leave the room when the Japanese arrived. Sugaya eventually told Mike about the situation, and what a Taiwanese church elder had told him—that the pastor's grandparents were tortured and killed by the Japanese during WWII.

The mainland Chinese team leader and Sugaya decided to have a foot washing ceremony to attempt reconciliation by employing identificational repentance. They asked Mike, the only American, to represent the American people who suffered. The Chinese team leader represented the mainland Chinese who suffered. One of the Taiwanese grandmothers who had personally suffered terribly at the hands of the Japanese represented the Taiwanese people.

At the start of the ceremony, the entire Japanese contingent crawled into the room on their faces, many weeping uncontrollably. They washed Mike's feet first, and there were a few sniffles in the crowd. Then they washed the feet of the Chinese team leader. More sniffles. When they washed the feet of the Taiwanese grandmother, there was not a dry eye left in the gathering of about four hundred.

From that time on, the pastor often embraced his newly reconciled Japanese brothers and sisters. A cooperative relationship between the Taichung, Taiwan, church and the Tokyo, Japan, church was initiated. God's special surprise capped a trip that was transformational for everyone involved.

At this writing the Kiyose Grace Chapel is preparing to partici-pate in the North Kanto Church Multiplication Network scheduled for April 1, 2009. The church plans to plant a granddaughter church for their parent church, Nerima Grace Chapel. By the time the Wilsons had left the Kiyose church for their next assignment, it had grown to forty members.

The Kiyose church has since grown to ninety strong. And as it con-tributes members and funds to birth a new church, God will no doubt infuse it with a renewed passion to reach souls for Christ, and again increase its numbers. In addition, the process will provide a catalytic effect for members to grow into all that God wills for them.

Case Study 5

A Chinese Missionary Training Center to Reach Muslims[1]

THOUGH I HAVE NEVER lived there, I have been traveling to China regularly for the past thirty-five years. I have a special burden to help believers who are being persecuted for their faith in Jesus Christ. That burden was planted deep in my heart in the mid-1970s when my wife and I spent a good part of a year in an African country that experienced a communist takeover. The resulting brutal regime left our Christian friends raped, imprisoned, killed, or scattered to the four winds. That vivid experience has driven me to spend much of my life training, encouraging, mentoring, and coaching young believers cross-culturally, especially in difficult and restricted-access settings.

AN UNUSUAL CANDIDATE TRAINING SCHOOL

At present I am lying prone in the back of a small van in a major city in China. I cannot see a thing because I'm covered by a dingy tarp to hide my presence from locals who might glance into the vehicle. It is midnight. Soon the driver pulls into an open garage on the ground level of a multi-story apartment complex in a quiet neighborhood away from the downtown sector. The van engine stops, the garage door is pulled closed, the van door is opened, and I'm encouraged to come out of hiding.

We quickly leave the garage through an inside exit, climb many flights of dark stairs, and quietly enter a seventh-floor apartment. Our underground school has lookouts posted on each floor up the stairwell, and they smile and greet me in hushed tones as I ascend. We listen intently a long time. No one has followed us up the stairwell.

---

1. Thanks for this case study go to Dr. Monroe Brewer, International Director for the Center for Church Based Training in Richardson, Texas (www.ccbt.org). Dr. Brewer is also on staff with CrossGlobal Link, located in Wheaton, Illinois (www.crossglob-allink.org).

We enter a dark room on the top floor, lock the door behind us, and breathe a sigh of relief. Now we have to wait, as others—one by one and family by family—make the same life-changing journey over the next twenty-four hours, ascending hallowed steps that lead from traditional Chinese life to the surreal world of an illegal training program preparing Chinese nationals to be sent as missionaries to the Muslim world. As their American uncle, I know that this week promises to be transformational for me, too.

Selecting School Locations

Finding an appropriate location for an unregistered underground school is no easy task. I work with five large Chinese house church networks. Each network has full-time workers that do nothing else but scour and scout out neighborhoods of their adopted cities to find the kind of properties to lease that best serve their school's training needs. For security purposes, at this leadership level, no one can serve in the city in which he or she grew up.

Chinese landlords are overly thrifty, so most apartment complexes in China are only seven stories high. Chinese law requires any building having eight stories or more to have an elevator—something a landlord does not want to pay for. The best properties for underground schools are located on the seventh, sixth, and fifth floors of seven-story apartment complexes, especially in the extreme "outside" flats. The outside flats have neighbors on only one side, and the other three sides buttress up against the stairwell or the outside walls of a building. The fewer neighbors a school is exposed to, the less likely it will be reported to the authorities by nosy or suspicious tenants. Also, tenants in complexes without elevators want to live on lower floors for obvious physical reasons, so some high-level flats stay unoccupied. For our school, though, this is the best location to be: "staying high up, to stay under the radar."

Various Kinds of Schools

Over the years, I have worked in various kinds of schools. Every school is run by one house church network: things get too complicated for schools to be joint ventures among two to four different movements. Some schools turn over their students every month, some every six months, some every year, and some every two or three years.

For security concerns, promotion of school programs and schedules is by word of mouth within a movement, and a few one-month schools even have a one-year waiting list. One-month and three-month schools in particular offer only one specific course at a time for lay leaders wanting an ordered learning experience. The longer-running schools provide multiple offerings that run simultaneously. The content of most schools is biblical and theological in nature, but some one-year and three-year schools are missiological in scope and for advanced students.

The school in which I am presently teaching is a three-year missions training school. This is the first week—a "candidate school" of sorts—of a long, intense training path for lower-level cadre leaders from our rural house church network. Most schools have two to three house church leaders assigned as the official teachers, one usually being a woman because at least half the students are female. Ours is no exception.

Selecting Students

Our particular school is big—in fact, too big. We have fifty-two students, including seven couples and their nine children, along with five nannies. Over the next days and weeks, a sifting process will occur, whereby some of the initial candidates will be sent home. More on that later.

All present students were *selected* to attend this school: they did not volunteer. Two years earlier in meeting with the major "uncles" of this movement, I was told the original candidates would be the sons, daughters, nephews, and nieces of the overall leaders of the network countrywide. In response, I asked them about the concepts of nepotism and cronyism. Yes, they knew about such concepts. I then asked if they fully realized the danger of this assignment—that candidates may ultimately be imprisoned or killed for going as missionaries to Muslims. Yes, they knew that, too, but I apparently did not fully grasp their motivation.

These "uncles" wanted their own children to be sent first, because when their own kids were killed or imprisoned, everyone else in the network would know they were willing to sacrifice their own kids first. Thus, no other parent would have any excuse for not sending his or her own children next—to take the place of those imprisoned or killed. It was a humbling, teachable moment for me. Their motivation is so different from our Western, security-conscious, comfort-driven mindset. So, these candidates are going to the mission field because they were told to go.

FIRST WEEK OF CANDIDATE SCHOOL

Most large house church networks in China began in the late 1970s or early 1980s in smaller cities around the country and then gradually spread to every prefecture and province. They did not start in cities like Beijing or Shanghai. In China, a city under a million is considered rural. Thus, 80–85 percent of the large house church networks are comprised of people who grew up in rural counties throughout China. Candidates come to the urban centers of China to be trained and to gain anonymity amid the sprawling masses of humanity. The fifty-two candidates who are entering this first week of training have come from virtually every province and territory of China and are excited to see what God might do.

Living Arrangements

Everyone is anxious to see where he or she will be living for the next many months. Because our candidate class is so large, we occupy floors three through seven of one section of an apartment complex: one floor for desks, chairs, tables, and school activities; one floor for cooking, eating, cleaning, and fellowshipping; one floor for the families; and one floor each for the single women and single men.

One apartment bedroom has four bunk beds for eight girls, and one of the men's bedrooms contains three bunk beds for six men. No one has a dresser, closet, trunk, or personal space. Each person's possessions are neatly folded atop the foot of each bed. Some folks are lucky to have a second change of clothes. I never see any candidate wearing a second outfit during my days with them.

It is astounding how apartments are assembled and furnished. Three months before a candidate school starts, a lease is negotiated (and put in the name of a network leader) for each of the flats. Beds, desks, chairs, tables, furniture, lamps, cook pots, and utensils are purchased and stored. Then, over the next months, all that is needed for a school is slowly, quietly moved to the new school at night and assembled. It is an incredible accomplishment to move fifty-two new people into a neighborhood without any neighbors noticing.

Shopping, Cooking, and Rubbish Removal

Everyone takes turns doing all the necessary chores. Two men and two women go out each night to shop. It is not possible to have fifty-pound or hundred-pound bags of rice delivered to an apartment, as that would obviously attract a lot of attention. So a lot of people have to do a little bit of shopping all the time. Everyone, men included, takes turns cooking and cleaning up in the kitchen. A huge storage closet in the kitchen has cubby holes, like big mail box slots, to give all candidates individual storage space for their rice bowls and chopsticks. All rubbish and garbage is taken out each night by different people. It is really hard to hide the trash of fifty-two people every day! And the trash has to be stashed in different bins around the neighborhood. Staying invisible is our greatest chore.

Exams: Physical and Emotional

During the first week, everyone is given a physical examination by a Chinese medical doctor. The physician, a female in her mid fifties, is married to a well-known house church pastor, and both attend in order to provide physical, moral, and spiritual guidance to the candidates. Thirteen candidates (25 percent) test positive for hepatitis A—a dangerous predicament for so many residing in such a cramped living space. Our doctor must further evaluate each situation and recommend who will stay and who will have to go home.

Also, during the first week we administer to the candidates a Mandarin version of Dr. Muriel Elmer's Intercultural Assessment Inventory. This great predictor of success in living and working overseas was developed at Michigan State in the early 1980s and has proven to be quite accurate as a pre-field assessment tool. The highest score among the candidates is one hundred seventy eight, and the lowest score is one hundred six. Unfortunately, one of the married couples has a difference of sixty points in their scores, which ultimately leads to their dismissal from candidate school. The point spread is too great to risk thrusting them into an extreme Islamic situation in the future. Nobody wants one of our missionaries to break under the stress of a new and hostile culture.

THE ORDERED LEARNING EXPERIENCE

All candidates arrive at our "candidate school" already having had one to three years of Bible training at illegal underground training centers comprised of lower-level cadre leaders of the same house church network. This previous training—though not really "school" per se—had all the features of formal schooling: classes, teachers, desks, dorms, an admission process, lectures, homework, quizzes, exams, and graduation. Our present school is trying something different: to provide non-formal, participatory learning in a safe environment that stresses character development and skill acquisition over lecture content.

The Learning Center

One floor in our apartment complex is our Learning Center. All arise at five or five-thirty in the morning, go to the prayer room on that floor for personal and corporate worship, eat breakfast on the floor dedicated as the kitchen and dining room, and then congregate on the floor designated for their mission classes. There are no elevators between floors, so all must walk quietly, two-by-two, up and down the stairwell between floors. Such movement is always risky, but there is no alternative. They have two to three hours in the morning for classes (nine-thirty until noon) and two to three hours in the afternoon (two-thirty until five). Rather than sitting at desks in rows, we arrange the tables in our classroom in the shape of a large square. Everyone is able to see everyone else in this arrangement, and the room set-up creates an "open" feel.

Time With the Uncles

Most of the rural house church networks are organized similarly to the Learning Center. There are usually three uncles who lead their movement. Our group has about twenty-one thousand house churches, with roughly one hundred forty thousand leaders at various levels. One brother is the lead uncle, and two other men round out a holy triumvirate. These dear men have been elevated to such positions because they have spent the most time in prison. They are intelligent, crafty, clever, resourceful leaders but have only three to six grades of formal learning in government schools. Most have never attended high school.

These leaders are so busy, so hunted by the police, so stretched in every way, that they can only spend this first week with the candidates.

Then they are off on the run again. For the candidates, this is the first time they have ever met a leader of the movement, unless, of course, they are relatives. So they all enjoy this special time with the uncles: speeches, storytelling, dedicatory prayers, and an individual commissioning of each new missionary.

An Opportunity to Unload and Decompress

Near the beginning of the week, an entire day is given over to the candidates so that each man and woman can tell his or her story to the whole group. The testimonials are phenomenal. Many participants were orphaned as children, have had fathers or brothers put in prison for their faith in Jesus Christ, or were saved as a result of a miraculous healing or dream. Approximately 75 percent of the candidates break down in tears as they recount their stories. I am shocked at how transparent and non-defensive they are and how many of the men cry openly before others. "Saving face" has no place here.

These stories impress me regarding how much work will need to be done in the future to help the candidates become fully free in Christ. They have "stuffed" so much for so long. They are wounded, broken, precious believers who have long repressed raw emotions and are weary of conflict, pain, suspicion, and rejection.

Facilitation, Not Just Lectures

Since candidates are used to sitting in rows, taking notes, and listening to lectures, we introduce them to case studies from our educational toolbox. The response is immediate and spontaneous. They love having a case study at the start of a lesson to help them to grasp the issue being unpacked. A real-life case study gets them into a problem-solving mindset, into the Scriptures for perspective, and into animated discussion of the issue. They also enjoy having teachers who allow them to take an active role in class, meet in small groups, and work on projects. Men still sit on two sides of the square, and women on the other two sides, but they are excited to be learning together as one group.

THE TRAINING-IN-MINISTRY MODEL

These Chinese missionary candidates come into the program with a variety of ministry experiences. It is not completely unusual to have nineteen or twenty year olds who have already planted a number of house churches or who serve as lieutenants in their network, overseeing twenty-thousand house church members in their county or prefecture. Many unregistered house church leaders start out young, and the only thing they know is their movement's infrastructure. The last section of this case study presents a glimpse into the training-in-ministry model, something at which the Chinese church excels. Instead of training neophytes *for* ministry, these candidates are being trained *in* ministry, serving while they learn.

The Importance of the Ministry Environment

Some candidates, before coming to our candidate school, have spent time planting house churches among some of China's minority peoples. If candidates are going to succeed as cross-cultural workers, they need time outside their Han Chinese frame of reference. Although the Han are divided into sixteen different sub-groupings, they still comprise 92 percent of China's overall population. The remaining 8 percent of the population is divided among fifty-five distinct minority peoples, who further divide into at least four hundred ninety distinct ethno-linguistic groups. Even four hundred ninety is a low figure. For example, the Zhuang, China's largest minority group, are traditionally divided into Northern Zhuang and Southern Zhuang. But in actuality, linguists now say the Zhuang have at least nineteen distinct linguistic groups. An anecdote about Han house church leaders planting churches among a minority people in China will prove instructive at this point.

Members from our house church network traveled over five hundred kilometers from their home province to plant house churches among a minority people in South China. They wanted cross-cultural experience, but they also wanted to demonstrate Christ's love for this great, neglected minority people.

One day, three Han missionaries were beaten by the local government officials, expelled from the county, and told never to return. The response was immediate and explosive. The local people, who made up nearly one hundred percent of the county population, began burning down the county seat's administrative government buildings. The enraged locals threatened to burn them all down unless the officials immediately brought back to the county the same three Christian Han workers who had been expelled. Why? The Christians had ministered to the locals, taught them Mandarin, loved their kids, administered simple health care measures, and told them Bible stories.

It was said that in the three to four years that Christians were in the county, the locals felt more genuine good was done for them than all the centuries of Han governmental bureaucracy and domination. The Chinese government is notorious for neglecting minorities, denying them even the basics of education, health care, and protection. In a very startling reversal filled with shame and loss of face, officials allowed the three Han missionaries to return and continue their house church-planting ministry in a poor, downtrodden county. The lesson: to prepare workers for real foreign missions experience, candidates need genuine cross-cultural experience closer to home first. And such experience, in and of itself, can prove exceedingly fruitful.

Learning by Practicing in Real Life

Part of our candidates' training will involve practical internships overseen by experienced church-planting mentors. Since our candidates desire to work with Muslim people groups in Central Asia and the Middle East, their training path needs to go, at least in part, through Western China. Western China comprises perhaps one-third of the landmass of China. Except in large cities, few Han Chinese, relatively speaking, live here, and the vast majority of the population is Muslim.

Why go into Western China? Candidates need ministry experience among *Muslim* minority peoples, not just among traditional Buddhist minority peoples. And in cities like Kashgar (Kashi), which is not one of the locations of our internships, that is exactly the kind of exposure Christian workers get. Kashgar has a population of half a million, boasts 2,400 mosques, and lies almost on the Afghan border.

What does an internship look like? Instead of candidates living together in an apartment complex for the entire three years, for a period of time during everyone's training process, four men or four women or one family will live in a rented apartment in several cities in Western China. This will allow them to put into practice the cross-cultural and missiological training they receive. Periodically, mentors visit them in their apartment, spending days or several weeks with them, tutoring them, answering questions, and helping them to apply their studies. The rest of their time is dedicated to starting to learn a new language, making friends, and learning the culture.

Role of Spiritual Mentors and Coaches

What is the most important thing a mentor must do? The answer may be surprising. A mentor's biggest task is to provide these Han missionary candidates safe ministry platforms that allow them to live in areas that are foreign to them without raising too many suspicions with the local population about their presence there. This is not an easy task.

An ideal situation is to find a "mom and pop" business or shop run by a Han Chinese family—if possible, for a generation—that can be purchased reasonably and run by a *new Han family* (i.e., missionary candidates from Eastern China). One house church leader will make the running of that local business his sole focus, allowing candidates to work part-time in the business and part-time in learning Uighur (or whatever the local language), and building friendships in the neighborhood. The issue: candidates cannot be viewed with suspicion by the locals. If locals can see that new Han Chinese in the neighborhood are there because a local business was sold to a new family of outsiders, they have a familiar category for the new visitors. Then locals at least have a chance to meet the new outsiders and to find out how different (and wonderful) they are compared to all the Han they had known before. And in that brief transition, relationships are built, trust is established, and the gospel is incarnated.

Such a strategy does not work well in a large megacity like Urumqi, with four to five million. Even though the majority of the city is non-Han Chinese, there still is a large Han presence—maybe two million. So this strategy must be implemented in small cities throughout Western China, if candidates are to have a genuine cultural immersion experience. It cannot be an immersion experience if 40 percent of a city is transplanted Han. In fact, one house church leader, a missiologist for his house church movement, was able to plant a cell group church in a town of seventy thousand using candidates who took up temporary residence, helped run the business, and started churches which in time became linked to their national network.

As challenging as this undertaking is, it is only the next step in the long process for one to serve finally in Central Asia or the Middle East as a cross-cultural worker. Obtaining a passport, learning some English, receiving some offerings from underground cell groups, learning Arabic in Cairo, starting a business in Dubai or Algiers, and strengthening the growing movement of Muslim-background believers in the region—all these challenges, and many more, await these brave but still mono-cultural Han Chinese who are learning what it means to trust God day by day with the unknown. They believe that they are already a success because they have obeyed the Lord and their uncles. They will leave their future ministry up to God. He will continue to do miracles, open closed doors, and accomplish the impossible. They are content now to enjoy the journey. They are on their way.

Case Study 6

Growing an Evangelical Church in Southeast Asia[1]

IN 1997, A PARTNERSHIP began between my mission organization and Paul Benjamin, the founder and leader of the Transforming Grace Evangelical Church[2] in South Asia. The goal was to multiply churches among a Hindu minority scattered in isolated villages of this country, beginning in the northwest. The partnership wed my organization's Global Village Campaign (GVC) ministry and resources with Paul's passion, vision, and entrepreneurial gifts and leadership.

As the primary facilitator, called a GVC Shepherd-trainer, working with Transforming Grace, I made three to four visits a year to spend a few days to two weeks to advise, train, problem-solve, and hold Transforming Grace accountable to the partnership principles. When I began, Transforming Grace included only Paul and his wife, Rachael, located in the capital city, one paid evangelist whom they supported from Paul's wife's income with a Christian NGO, and twenty-nine small village churches in the far northwest. Paul was also in the midst of constructing a five-story building that would become Transforming Grace's national headquarters, home of a multifaceted Child Development Project, and his personal residence.

In March of 2009, Transforming Grace celebrated the planting of one thousand churches and a host of support ministries that included five children's homes, four regional training centers, a burgeoning micro-credit ministry, nearly one hundred village primary schools, several

1. Thanks go to my friend Jerry Hogshead (jhogshead@sbcglobal.net) for providing the information used in this case study. Jerry and his wife, Marilyn, served in the Philippines, and in training and coaching North Americans and Majority World missionaries before their current work of facilitating church-planting partnerships in South Asia.

2. For security reasons, the names of nationals, mission organizations, location, and the church have been changed.

income-generating secondary schools, a number of smaller projects, and periodic relief work. The following paragraphs attempt to capture some of the factors, pro and con, that impacted the growth of the church, focusing primarily on my role as facilitator.

THE PRIMARY PLAYERS

My organization, an evangelical faith mission based in the United States, focuses on reproducing Christ-centered churches among the nations. GVC serves as the primary church-planting ministry arm of my organization. GVC partners with national churches in other countries to plant new churches by combining funding, strategy, accountability, and oversight with the national church's vision, personnel, and experience.

Local evangelists, who usually work in teams, establish new churches through a program of extensive evangelism. When I began in 1997, teams were required to follow GVC guidelines, including submitting detailed monthly records of their activities to GVC headquarters.

Paul and Rachael grew up in Christian homes in adjacent villages north of the capital. Both of their parents were converts to Christianity from Hinduism. Paul and Rachael were good students and natural leaders. After high school they went on for advanced training, Paul in accounting and Rachael in public health.

Both also completed one or two years of Bible school. When I began, Paul had just resigned from his job as the leader of a small Christian media organization to devote all of his time to his growing ministry and vision.

As a mid-career missionary I was invited to coach the partnership in 1997. My prior experience included earning an MDiv from Fuller Seminary, with an emphasis in cross-cultural communication in 1978, helping direct the Perspectives on the World Christian Movement course from 1978 to 1981, pioneer church planting in the Philippines from 1982 to 1987, and training and coaching North American missionaries from 1989 on. My spiritual gifts fall in the area of exhortation, mercy, and wisdom.

COUNTRY, CONTEXT, AND PEOPLE

The context is South Asia. The country in focus has a large Muslim majority and a Hindu and tribal minority. The constitution guarantees freedom of religion. The people in focus—the Hindu minority—are scattered in small, often isolated villages. Most are daily laborers living in extreme poverty and subject to the whims of the majority landowners they work for.

While the country remains relatively stable, it is subject to frequent strikes and endemic corruption. In times of political instability, the army has taken control and suspended freedoms. Grass-roots evangelists would say their most difficult problem is the hostility of radical Muslims.

A CHRONOLOGY OF HIGHLIGHTS

The table below describes the yearly growth in terms of baptisms and church plants. While it is impossible to recall all the circumstances, events, and activities that unfolded over the eleven years of my involvement, the following are highlights of what took place over that time period.

TABLE 1: GROWING AN EVANGELICAL CHURCH IN SOUTHEAST ASIA: TIMELINE AND RESULTS

Year	Evangelists	Baptisms	Church Plants	Total Churches	Total Baptisms
1993–1996	1	1,421	29	29	1,421
1997	12	1,172	21	50	2,596
1998	40	1,574	36	86	4,170
1999	80	3,116	96	182	7,286
2000	80	5,566	65	247	12,852
2001	80	6,703	95	342	19,555
2002	80	3,551	90	432	23,106
2003	80	2,793	72	504	25,899
2004	80	4,284	90	594	30,183
2005	69	4,361	113	707	34,544
2006	69	7,139	159	866	41,683
2007	69	2,875	50	916	44,558
2008	69	5,299	89	1,005	49,857

1996

In 1996, my organization asked me to visit Paul for the purpose of making a final recommendation on beginning a GVC partnership. Another GVC Shepherd from Asia accompanied me, who (as it turned out) also had plans to visit one of his countrymen working in the capital.

When he found out that Paul's prearranged schedule did not leave much time for his visit, he proposed changing the schedule. Paul objected. Sensing a problem arising, I persuaded my companion that I could visit with Paul alone so that he could meet his friend. It seemed clear that if I did not intervene, the conflict could have escalated and put the partnership at risk.

Paul and I developed a quick friendship. I listened while he explained his ministry and vision, explained to him the way a GVC partnership works, and assessed the potential. I returned to my organization with a strong recommendation that GVC begin a partnership with Transforming Grace.

1997–1998

The partnership officially began in 1997 with GVC funding three teams of four local evangelists. Paul was salaried as the National GVC Coordinator and began recruiting evangelists through ads in local Christian magazines. By 1998, the number of teams grew to ten.

In the first year I made four visits to further explain the GVC strategy and administrative requirements to the teams. During those visits Paul gave me great freedom to teach the evangelists anything I thought relevant to their work. This turned out to be important because Paul had little knowledge of missiology or church-planting strategy. Paul's gifts were vision and entrepreneurial leadership.

I communicated with Paul in English but spoke to the evangelists through translators. While there was much I could endorse in the GVC strategy, my training and experience told me some things needed greater emphasis than were apparent in the guidelines. I was thankful I had the freedom to adapt and change where I thought necessary.

Two things not emphasized in the GVC literature that I began teaching early in the work were storytelling rather than preaching or handing out tracts, and finding "people of peace"[3] rather than witnessing

3. Luke 10:6

door-to-door. When more than twenty-seven hundred were baptized and fifty-seven churches organized within the first two years, it seemed apparent we were working among a responsive people.

1999–2000

The work continued to grow with ten more teams added in 1999. In 1999, 3,116 people were baptized and ninety-six new churches were planted. 5,566 more baptisms were added in 2000 along with sixty-five new churches.

Four things were readily becoming apparent. First, for the work to keep growing, the evangelists would have to start passing the baton— that is, to appoint and train local leaders. Unlike most other GVC fields, Transforming Grace had no formal theological training institutions.

Second, any pastoral or leadership training program would have to be on-the-job (apprenticeship) and contextualized to the low literacy rate and oral tradition of the responding population. As a result, I began to teach the need and biblical basis for appointing local leaders, regardless of their level of formal education.

Second Timothy 2:2 became a watchword and a constant theme. Somewhat to my surprise, although Paul was favorable to the idea, the evangelists were quite reluctant!

All of the evangelists were graduates of one of the country's several Bible schools or seminaries, and most had serious doubts that the local, uneducated people could properly lead. Nor were they interested in sharing the power and prestige that accompanied their position.

After much debate and prodding, I convinced them to test the idea by appointing provisional leaders in one region. I also proposed testing a proven pastoral training program called Train and Multiply (T&M).

Developed originally by George Patterson, one of the pioneers of Theological Education by Extension, T&M is an obedience-oriented, on-the-job, pastoral training program that combines regular meetings between more experienced workers and younger "Timothies," Bible lessons, and practical work. The curriculum includes sixty-four short, theological booklets based on pastoral activities. We translated a handful of the booklets, and I taught the leaders how to use them with the emerging local leaders.

Third, I reasoned that the pattern of the early church described in 1 Corinthians 14:26–33a would be more appropriate for village churches than the preaching, pastor-dominated model typically found in the West. Sadly, the latter model is often mimicked in much of the developing world.

As a result, I began to teach and advocate that the teams adopt the early church's more participative style. Additionally, I emphasized the early church's pattern of meeting in homes or simple meeting places rather than relying on the construction of special church buildings often beyond the means of the local churches to build.

And finally, I began to talk more and more about the need for Transforming Grace to become sustainable on its own resources. As the churches had multiplied and the number of teams grown, so had the need for additional layers of administration. Paul wanted to appoint several of the more mature leaders as full-time, paid trainers and make others paid area coordinators, while continuing to salary the same number of evangelists. All this would require increasing the amount of funding from GVC.

I spoke passionately and lobbied for increasing Transforming Grace's reliance on the tithes and offerings of the emerging churches, while holding the line or even reducing the size of the GVC contribution. Despite my efforts, I was unable to persuade either Paul or GVC leadership to this effect, and the size of the GVC contribution continued to grow.

2001–2002

The work continued to grow vigorously in the next two years. 10,254 more were baptized, and another 185 churches were planted. By now, the experiments with appointing local leaders and T&M had both proven successful. Local leaders were being appointed and trained on a regular basis, and the Transforming Grace workers were convinced that the strategy was effective.

As the work expanded both within and across the country's district boundaries, Paul found it necessary to break up the original teams of four into teams of two. Within a couple of years, all of the evangelists were working alone, and some had been appointed district coordinators.

T&M had by this time been purchased by Project World Reach (PWR), a training and resourcing group in Canada. At my recommendation, we secured the rights and worked with them to translate and use the material. Paul hired local translators to begin the task of translating the entire curriculum.

During this time I continued to emphasize Bible storying—evangelizing and teaching through biblical stories, often in chronological order, and in culturally appropriate ways—and facilitated the acquisition of various sets of Bible pictures for the evangelists to use. Paul and I spent much time during my visits traveling to see the teams in their locations. I usually taught something to the entire group of evangelists at least once during the year, and other times to smaller groups.

When area coordinators were appointed, I began to focus most of my attention on them, usually at the headquarters in the capital. By now the partnership was the most fruitful of all the GVC partnerships, and both my organization and GVC leadership were taking note in a big way.

2003–2006

Transforming Grace was now making as big an impact on my organization and GVC as my organization and GVC were making on Transforming Grace. Most of the other GVC partnerships were planting churches one-by-one and baptizing handfuls. Transforming Grace was planting hundreds of churches and baptizing thousands.

Most partnerships relied on the national church's formal theological training institutions and appointed a limited number of paid pastors. Transforming Grace used mentoring chains and appointed numerous local volunteer leaders with little education.

Paul and I received a lot of attention, and both of us took advantage of it. I lobbied the GVC International Director to follow more closely the principles of church planting seen in the early church and outlined in David Garrison's influential book, *Church Planting Movements*. I continued to press Paul to make self-reliance a more realistic goal, and to move away from unhealthy dependency.

I also suggested church-planting movements become the theme of a gathering of GVC Shepherds and National Coordinators, and made Garrison's book the centerpiece. My organization asked me to present a paper on avoiding unhealthy dependency at a similar gathering a couple of years later. The concepts began to seep more deeply into the warp and woof of GVC planning and thinking.

Within a few years, this led to major changes in the GVC strategy. Most of the teams in the various GVC partnerships would now be called Church Multiplication Teams and were expected to plant churches that plant churches. Most new churches would be expected to meet in homes or locally available and sustainable places. Leaders would be trained on-the-job with emphasis given to Bible storying. Transforming Grace's story played a major role in paving the way for these changes.

Paul used his entrepreneurial and business acumen to make money at home (he continued to give some time to business interests) and to raise funds abroad for Transforming Grace training centers, children's homes, micro-credit projects, and relief work. His work became a featured part of GVC's fund development efforts.

The GVC International Director brought Paul to the States to speak at fundraising events and linked him with interested donors. Paul and Rachael eventually sent their two boys to America for high school and college. This widened their network of contacts.

As donors and small foundations took note, funds were given and Transforming Grace's ministry continued to grow. The resources made it possible to build a large regional training center and children's home in the north and another in the northwest. Paul, often with his own funds, purchased land for small centers in the southwest and in other areas. Burdened that many of the Hindu minority children could not attend the government-run, Muslim-dominated schools, we began a Sponsor-a-School Project to fund small village schools.

Two activities took a great deal of my time during these years. I worked constantly with Paul, his director of training, and PWR to keep the translation of T&M on track. They completed Level 1 in late 2005, and coordinators were first trained with the Student Activity Guide early in 2006.

Secondly, I continued to teach and lobby the Transforming Grace leadership team, and to a lesser extent, the GVC administration, to do everything in their power to make financial self-reliance a realistic goal of the work. It was obvious that the tithes and offerings from the churches fell considerably short of being able to sustain Transforming Grace on their own. Although Paul agreed in principle that self-reliance was an important goal, I seemed unable to get him to produce a workable plan for moving the church in that direction.

I continued to advocate in a number of other areas as well: one, the use of Bible storying in all aspects of the work, including linking appropriate stories to each of the T&M booklets; two, encouraging extended family meetings in addition to the gathered church meetings; three, encouraging a more participative style for church meetings; and four, advocating an equal role for women in church leadership.

The impact of launching T&M throughout the work was dramatic. Putting simple theological booklets with South Asian graphics into the hands of local leaders resulted in tremendous empowerment. As regional and local T&M training multiplied, local leaders and believers began to take greater ownership of their churches.

Some potentially serious problems, however, also arose. Some of the trainers were using the T&M booklets in large groups rather than in the Paul–Timothy mentoring chains for which they were designed. They were also selecting the booklets in a somewhat arbitrary way, rather than basing selection on the current needs of the local church. I feared this might be the case because the evangelists were not familiar enough with the content of the booklets or the overall program. In hindsight, I also believe I failed to spend enough time teaching and modeling the way the program was meant to work.

I also felt certain that T&M, organized to address pastoral activities, would not prove adequate in and of itself to guide the teaching for the churches. Without greater familiarity with the Bible's unfolding story or a well-crafted Bible story curriculum for discipleship and overall ministry, the local leaders would end up teaching the booklets rather than what the local church needed most, the pure milk and solid meat of the Word.

I checked this out, and in many cases this was exactly what was happening. To their credit, those who were teaching the booklets had followed my urging to link each booklet with appropriate Bible stories. But we still lacked objective assessment to ascertain more clearly just what or how the leaders were teaching in the local churches, or to measure their effectiveness.

Other concerns included the diminishing rate of new church plants, especially among the second generation, although there were some wonderful exceptions. Though pressure to increase the GVC budget continued, Transforming Grace's budget actually began to come down slightly as a result of decreased GVC funds.

2007–2008

Other than the fact that GVC was forced to cut the budgets of most of the partnerships because of lower than expected income, we made little progress in reducing the size of Transforming Grace's dependence on GVC funds. I continued to press Paul and his staff to come up with an alternative solution. My main concern was not to end the partnership, but that the churches make steady progress toward financial sustainability.

Then, just prior to putting plans in place for a consultation between GVC and Transforming Grace on this issue, Paul proposed a solution during my November visit. If it succeeded, within three years the thousand churches spread over seventeen districts would be completely under first generation leadership and totally responsible for their own finances and administration.

Without spelling out all the details, the proposal included the following stipulations:

1. Every church would appoint and be led by unpaid boards of five.

2. The churches would be yoked in circuits of three and led by a circuit board composed of two members from each church and a circuit pastor appointed by the board.

3. All the circuits in each *thana* (like our counties) would be overseen by a *thana* board made up of the circuit pastors, the district pastor, a yet-to-be determined number of lay men and women, and a salaried *thana* pastor.

4. All *thana* associations in a district would associate together and be led by district boards composed of their *thana* pastors and a number of lay men and women elected from the district churches.

5. Each *thana* and each district would aim to be fully self-reliant with salaried workers and other expenses covered by tithes and offerings, micro-credit profits, and other income-generating businesses.

6. District boards would have the authority and responsibility to set budgets based on income and expenses.

7. Transforming Grace's national office would help meet the initial setup expenses and provide incentives for further development, such as raising funds for special projects, offering to match funds

raised locally, and so forth.

To date, some three hundred unpaid circuit pastors have been appointed, each overseeing three village congregations, with each congregation led by a team of local elders of its own. The jury is still out on how successful the plan will be in erasing the dependency, but thus far it has been a hopeful start.

LESSONS AND OBSERVATIONS

Most Enjoyable

I loved the opportunity to influence the work with good missiology and model a participative teaching style. I loved to challenge the workers to think biblically and strategically, and to see them grow and mature. I loved seeing the evangelism and church planting being complemented with programs for educational and economic empowerment, such as the children's homes, primary and secondary schools, micro-credit programs, cow projects, and more. I loved connecting receptive workers with ideas, people, and resources.

Most Difficult or Frustrating

Communication was a constant challenge. I did not speak Paul's language, and Paul's English was poor. Two of his leaders did speak some English, but the cultural and cognitive processing differences were still large. None of the coordinators or evangelists spoke English, so all teaching and discussion was through translation. To make matters worse, in the eleven years I have been involved, I have never felt that I have had a really good translator.

In the early years when I spent much of my time traveling with Paul, I had to be content with minimal interaction because of his limited English. I often arrived already depleted from the previous ministry in a neighboring country, something the hot and humid climate only exacerbated. On at least two occasions, I experienced minor emotional meltdowns.

Another frustration was my seeming inability to move the church away from its dependency on GVC funds and towards self-reliance.

I think my relationship with Paul and the leaders was generally good, but I am also certain that their dependence on GVC funding made it difficult for them to be completely honest and transparent. Many times I thought they were telling me what they thought I wanted to hear rather than what they really thought.

I was also frustrated that I was not more effective at helping develop the Bible storying curriculum I was convinced was necessary. I had too much other work and/or was not wise and creative enough to help them make it happen.

Most Important

The lasting impact of the work is yet to be determined. But in terms of what has been accomplished to date, several factors made my work as a facilitator successful: the context of a responsive people group; my people skills; sound missiological training and experience; persistence over the eleven years I have been involved; the prayers of God's people; the freedom I was given to influence the work as I felt led; and most of all, the unmerited favor of God to use me.

Biggest Fears

Three big fears haunt me. First, I fear that the church will fail to grow out of its dependency on foreign funding, whether from GVC or another sincere but naïve, and possibly even predatory, organization (looking to make a name for itself). Second, I fear that I will fail to help the ministry develop a comprehensive and effective leadership training program that fits its culture and context. And third, I fear that the forms that dominate the Western church (the sermon monologue, reliance on Western logic, discourse, linear outlines, and the prominence of a single leader) will dominate the local churches, just as it does in the West.

What I Would Do Differently

One of the things that I would do differently is to spend more time helping Paul develop a comprehensive and reproducible education and leadership development curriculum based primarily on the biblical narrative. I would also be more careful to collect and analyze grassroots data. Apart from that, it is very difficult to understand with real clarity what is actually happening and what needs to be changed, improved, and built upon.

Case Study 7

Facilitating Near-Culture Evangelism with Aid Sudan[1]

A S OUR RUGGED TOYOTA Land Cruiser bounced down the dirt path out of our southern Sudanese village that day in 2005, my racing mind was slowed only by the threatening flood of tears. I was consumed with emotion as I reflected on our calling to the Sudanese and what it was that had brought my wife and me to this small village in the bush of southern Sudan.

The journey had begun years ago with my first encounter with southern Sudanese in Egypt in 1998. The stories of those refugees captivated and overwhelmed me. I had grown up in Africa, but it was a different Africa than the one they knew. God began to speak deeply to me, and my calling and life direction has been with the southern Sudanese ever since.

January of 2002 found my wife, Shauna, and me landing on southern Sudanese soil for the first time. Our three weeks in that mud hut landscape confirmed the calling on our lives and deepened the burden in our hearts. We returned to the States, finished preparations, and in November of 2003, arrived to stay.

The first six months were amazing. We settled into our mud hut and became acquainted with the Jur people. We focused heavily on learning the tribal language and culture. It was exhilarating, and the newness of it all overshadowed the myriad of challenges inherent to living in a mud hut in the bush of southern Sudan.

The next six months were significantly more difficult. The Lord blessed our language learning, allowing us to reach fluency in the main

---

1. Peter Swann is Executive Director of Aid Sudan (www.aidsudan.org), an interdenominational nonprofit missionary organization working among southern Sudanese in the United States and in southern Sudan. Peter and his wife, Shauna, have two children and live in Houston, Texas.

tribal language and make final preparations for the formal launch of our ministry. However, the newness wore off quickly, and without it to combat the overwhelming challenges, life in the bush began to take its toll.

The next six months were incredibly challenging. From a ministry standpoint, we were thrilled. Shauna had begun to teach in the primary school and use her nursing skills in the local mud hut clinic. I took over the local oral Bible school, training Jur pastors in Chronological Bible Storying in the heart language.

With each Bible story, the group of pastors composed a song and made up a drama. I could not have been more convinced of the significance of what we were doing and the impact it would have. Yet in the midst of it all, we began to struggle.

The isolation was intense. While we had community with our dear local friends, they had no real concept of the Western world. There were no foreigners nearby, and our only contact with westerners was the brief security check by short-wave radio early each morning.

Diseases were common, including some that remained undiagnosed. We faced a raiding tribe. Once they came through when we had time to evacuate, and once we did not.

Pressures from the community were significant, including the constant appeals from officials and friends who simply hoped that we could help them alleviate some of their overwhelming suffering. Snakes and scorpions greeted us at every turn, as did countless other creatures.

And the living conditions were harsh, with temperatures up to 130 degrees, no running water, limited solar power, and bug-ridden beans and rice for lunch and dinner each day. In it all, Shauna and I sought to walk closely with the Lord and with each other, relying heavily on the prayers of the prayer partners with which God had richly blessed us. Yet against the incoming tidal wave of challenges, we began to crumble.

The last six months were brutal. We were deeply in love with the Jur people and burdened for a great movement of God among them. To that end we labored diligently each day. We believed in the significance of our ministry and its great potential. Our calling was firm, and it was with great resolve that we committed to stay there, no matter what the challenges.

But the toll was significant. Tears flowed constantly as we struggled just to make it through each day. We were later diagnosed with clinical depression, an almost mundane label for what racked us each moment.

In Nairobi, on a regularly scheduled time out of southern Sudan, a visit to the doctor resulted in grim news. He had discovered heart damage, telling me that my heart looked like that of a seventy year old. Continuing to live in the bush of southern Sudan, he told me, could kill me.

Shauna and I began to pray diligently, struggling to reconcile our deep calling to the Jur and to the southern Sudanese with such a strong warning to immediately vacate our home area. It soon became clear that we were indeed to leave.

And so it was on that day in 2005, I found myself on the jarring journey on the dirt road out of our village for the last time. I had flown in to pack up and say goodbye to our deeply concerned friends. They pleaded with me never to forget them. I wondered how in the world we ever could. And as I drove away, with men and women and children running through their gardens to wave goodbye, I could hardly see through the tears in my eyes.

My grief was intense, as was my bewilderment at what God was doing. I simply could not understand why we had to leave a people we loved so much and to whom we felt such a strong calling. The resulting question dominated my prayer time on that drive: "Why, God?" Over and over I entreated the Lord for an answer, begging Him for a glimmer of understanding.

THE MOSES PROJECT

Although I did not understand our situation, one thought resonated in my head as I bounced down the road. Perhaps Western missionaries were *not* the answer for long-term ministry, even if their methodology was contextual and effective.

Surveying the situation around us, we had realized early that Western missionaries did not last long in southern Sudan. There was no waiting list to come, and those who did arrive in the bush rarely stayed for two years.

The fact that we had made it for only two years deeply troubled us, sensing how little was accomplished in the bush. It was barely enough time to gain fluency in the language and become acquainted with the culture.

The challenge to remain long-term hits new missionaries as well as experienced ones, large organizations as well as small ones. Western missionaries generally struggle mightily in the bush of southern Sudan, making it for two years or less.

With that in mind, Shauna and I began to wonder about the possibility of sending indigenous personnel from the United States back to Sudan. It seemed that same-culture and near-culture missionaries could be so much more effective for long-term work.

Southern Sudanese returning to Sudan would already know the language and culture and would simply have to readjust to the living conditions. Ugandans and other near-culture peoples would only have to learn a similar language and culture and handle living conditions significantly closer to their way of life than to a Western way of life.

In time, God grew the seed he had planted. Shauna and I moved back to the States and joined Aid Sudan, a small ministry focused on impacting southern Sudanese refugees in the United States, and also ministering in southern Sudan. The US component was fairly established, but the options in southern Sudan remained wide open. I began to wonder if the seed was about to sprout.

As we looked toward the future of Aid Sudan's ministry, two key questions plagued us. First, how do we saturate southern Sudan with the gospel? And second, how do we saturate southern Sudan with missionaries? The answer to the first question was dependent on the answer to the second question. The answer to the second question was to launch the Moses and Philip Projects.

The Moses Project involves the training, sending, and supporting of southern Sudanese from the United States as they return to southern Sudan as missionaries to their own people. But some background is necessary.

During Sudan's tragic twenty-two-year civil war, two million were killed and five million were displaced. A significant percentage of those displaced eventually found their way to the United States.

By the time we formally began the Moses Project in 2007, most Sudanese had been in the States for five or ten years. In that time, the refugees had focused largely on obtaining as much education as possible and working toward US citizenship.

One key distinctive of these southern Sudanese refugees is that perhaps unlike many refugees, most Sudanese desperately want to return to their country. They live with a burden for their people and a calling to their land.

A Sudanese leader once said to me, "Peter, we are desperate to return to Sudan to help our people. We simply do not know how to get training or support. We are eager for your help." Confirmation of the leader's statement came with the inundation of interest shown with the announcement of the Moses Project.

We knew that the need was huge in southern Sudan and that the southern Sudanese in the United States felt a great responsibility to gain education and return to help their country. What we were to come to realize was that for a lot of Sudanese, this was the plan all along.

Before many Sudanese ever came to the States, they were challenged by elders in their communities to learn all they could in the United States so that they could return to help their people. It was for that reason that a church leader in Sudan's Bor area once told us, "This Moses Project was our idea long before it was your idea!"

As my friend David Humphrey assumed the directorship of the Moses Project, we began to sift through applications. We were looking for the best of the best. A burden to return to Sudan was not enough. In addition, a brand new program demanded high standards.

We found no example to follow and needed Sudanese who could help us tweak the model as it unfolded. We were also keen on finding missionaries who were very passionate believers, quick to learn, and emotionally strong. We knew many of these leaders would return to their homes in Sudan for the first time in twenty years and would relive the horrors of the war they had fled.

We had not set education requirements for the applicants as part of the profile, focusing more on humility, teachability, and commitment. In fact, we were significantly concerned about those who had received higher education in the States, worried that the Sudanese may struggle to separate the Western model from our contextualized approach in Sudan.

Reliable statistics do not exist on literacy rates across southern Sudan, but if using the definition of literacy as one who has obtained an eighth grade level of proficiency, it would probably be less than one percent. For this reason, we decided to use only an oral approach in ministry, focusing heavily on Chronological Bible Storying.

We took the story sets used in the Bible school among the Jur and customized them for a southern Sudanese worldview. This gave us a total of more than one hundred stories, stretching from Genesis to

Revelation. As Aid Sudan also focuses on the spread of the gospel and on community development, we additionally planned for training in our community development areas of health, education, and water.

We asked for a three-year commitment from the missionaries, with about half the time spent in the United States and about half the time in Sudan. Most of the time in the States focused on training and assisting us in raising prayer and financial support from churches.

The first stay in Sudan would be a short one, followed by increasingly longer stays. By the last year of the program, the missionaries would spend the vast majority of their time in Sudan.

We were especially concerned about applicants with families in the United States, but Sudanese elders in the United States strongly encouraged us not to worry. Sudanese are not at all like Americans, they explained. It would not be fair to keep someone from going by imposing a Western requirement.

After months of applications and interviews, David and I settled on three missionaries. Two were from the Dinka tribe and were former "Lost Boys," i.e., young boys who fled the war without parents. They had been in the States about five years.

Of those two, one was single and a recent graduate of a Bible college in Houston. The other was married, and his wife and young daughter lived in Arua, Uganda, near the Sudan border. Both were leaders in Houston's Sudanese Community Church and in their twenties.

The third missionary was from the Nuer tribe. He was in his late thirties, with a family. His wife and five children lived in Nebraska, and he had been in the States about ten years.

We felt confident in these three men, in terms of both their calling and their competency. We thought it was very significant that they represented the two largest tribes in southern Sudan, tribes that have a long and painful history of conflict. It seemed critical to us to bring the two tribes together in our first missionary class, modeling the unity we all have in Christ.

As the missionaries filed into our Houston office that first day in September, 2007, there was great rejoicing as the Moses Project was officially launched. We began the daily prayer time, and as the new missionaries prayed, my eyes filled with tears as they did that day on the drive out of the village. Yet this time, my "Why, God?" tears had turned to "Yes, God!" tears as I embraced the journey of the past two years and looked forward to what He had in store.

Although we were training Sudanese who had received some education in the States, we felt that they still maintained the bent toward orality that had dominated their childhood. In addition, we wanted to make sure they were trained in the same way in which they would train others.

So, from the first day, our Chronological Bible Storying training involved no pen or paper, with David simply sitting in a circle with the missionaries. The training was straightforward, yet intense, and although it started slow, the missionaries soon began to learn quite rapidly.

When the missionaries first arrived back on their home soil in December of 2007, it played out exactly as we had hoped. They disembarked the small Cessna airplane and began ministering in their language and their culture to their own people.

The impact was immediate and obvious! David and I had promoted the missionaries as experts, and from the outset, the local Dinka and Nuer church leaders soaked up the Chronological Bible Storying training.

During their first and second rotation, the missionaries focused on getting reacquainted with family and friends, surveying the area in the process. They conducted short-term training and oversaw some community development projects. All of that established credibility, paving the way for long-term training. The missionaries have now started their third rotation in Sudan.

Our main long-term goal for the Moses Project is to nurture the rapid expansion of the gospel through interdenominational pastor training. Instead of training the missionaries to plant new churches for some new denomination, we were burdened instead to have them work with churches of all denominations.

The oral Bible schools do a tremendous job in helping provide church leaders an "oral Bible" that they can then pass on to others. In addition, we seek to implement practices and patterns in the training that are key to church growth in southern Sudan. This ranges from the style and format of the training to the objective of seeing all church leaders in training start storying groups that can develop into new churches.

With over one year into the three-year program, we can say categorically that the Moses Project has had a powerful impact. Two of

226 THE FACILITATOR ERA

the three missionaries have recently begun leading long-term oral Bible schools in their home areas in southern Sudan.

The other missionary backed out of the program earlier this year, choosing instead to focus on some personal needs. While the Moses Project has contained a myriad of challenges, it has simultaneously yielded some tremendous rewards.

Included in the list of challenges is the simple fact that we are taking former refugees and training them to return to the place from which they once fled. It is a daunting challenge emotionally. Memories of the war haunt them, and many of their friends have died.

Another challenge pertains to being outside the country for so long. While they are fully accepted as one of their tribe, the outsider tag gives them much greater respect, but also opens the door for tremendous expectations. The missionaries generally return to the States each time with virtually nothing in hand, having given everything away.

There are also the challenges of the reduced salary and time away from family and friends. To their enormous credit, the missionaries each took a cut in pay in order to accept the Moses Project salary. However, they are always pulled by the temptation of returning to family and friends in the United States and the higher salary awaiting them there.

The issue of funding has perhaps been our greatest challenge. It is extremely expensive even just to pay salaries and fly the missionaries back and forth to the United States. While we have sought to reduce cost as much as possible, there is simply an inherent base cost that must be covered in order for the Moses Project to exist. The present budget allows for only two or three missionaries in the program at a time.

One other notable challenge has been the fact that the Sudanese work under us to impact their people. We were concerned about this, but the high mutual respect and cooperation with our missionaries has made it a very strong partnership. Cross-cultural communication has indeed been a challenge at times, with faulty assumptions and misguided expectations to work through on both sides, but we are all quickly becoming better communicators across the cultural lines.

In most conventional approaches, missionaries are trained by same-culture personnel and go overseas to minister cross-culturally. In the Moses Project, the training instead occurs cross-culturally, but the ministry is to same-culture peoples. This becomes a challenge in the training but a huge benefit in the ministry on the field.

It also sets up a middle step. In contrast to westerners who go straight to the bush to minister to those of a vastly different culture and setting, we train somewhat Americanized Sudanese who then minister to their own people. This model reduces inherent cross-cultural obstacles.

One tremendous strength of the Moses Project is that the missionaries provide great input and leadership, especially while they serve on the field. Given that we are charting a new path, we often find ourselves uncertain as to how best to proceed.

Our friendship and collaboration with the missionaries creates an atmosphere for them to offer much needed insights. Beyond that, we also seek to practice ultimate dependence on the Lord, praying together daily for his leadership and direction.

All this has nurtured a key discipleship component of the Moses Project. By default, the intense training means that we spend a lot of time with the missionaries, in a number of different settings. As we invest in our missionaries, they do the same with their own church leaders in Sudan. It is the Great Commission in action.

Another strength of the Moses Project is that it allows churches in America to adopt missionaries who are not American. The churches appreciate the opportunity to support the Moses Project missionaries and look forward to having them report back in person twice a year.

Other strengths of the Moses Project have been alluded to earlier. Indigenous personnel arrive on the "field" already knowing the language, the culture, the people, and the history of the place, far better than any foreigners ever could.

THE PHILIP PROJECT

Our goal remains to saturate southern Sudan with missionaries, but we know that with the Moses Project, we do not have the funding to be able to send out a mass of missionaries. Primarily for this reason, we began to look at neighboring African countries, intrigued by the possibility of sending near-culture missionaries.

While there is more of a gap to bridge in terms of language and culture, these near-culture missionaries could be trained, sent, and supported with far less cost and fewer logistical challenges. With this realization came the initiation of the Philip Project.

Although we hope the Philip Project may also spread to other neighboring countries, we began with Ugandan missionaries, as they have enjoyed a tremendous time of numerical growth. We received a very positive response from them.

It was our conviction from the beginning to ask the Ugandan churches to provide the salary support for their missionaries, so that Aid Sudan could cover other costs. We thought this may create some resistance to the program, but even across denominational lines, the response has been overwhelmingly positive.

This partnership allows for greater ownership of the program by the Ugandan churches, and from our perspective it provides increased capacity to send masses of missionaries. The Philip Project enables Aid Sudan to potentially fulfill its goal of saturating southern Sudan with missionaries.

Conceptually, the Philip Project was to have the same focus as the Moses Project, except that it would be a bit broader. Instead of sending out just one missionary to a location, the Philip Project involves a team approach.

We defined a team as a minimum of four missionaries. One will focus on pastor training, just like in the Moses Project. The other three will concentrate on community development in the areas of education, health, and water wells.

The Ugandan missionaries will follow a schedule similar to that of the Moses Project, with Aid Sudan personnel in Uganda's capital city of Kampala providing their training. In that missionaries will come from various locations within Uganda, Aid Sudan will attempt to find the best fit linguistically with tribes in southern Sudan. Some tribes in Uganda even have related tribes in Sudan with the same language.

As I write this in December of 2008, interviews of potential Philip Project missionaries are underway. We expect to launch the Philip Project formally within just a few months.

There are still plenty of questions on the table. Will the Ugandan churches indeed provide the necessary salary support? Will Ugandan missionaries step up en masse? Will the southern Sudanese respect the Ugandan missionaries sufficiently to receive a hearing? Based on research and personal observations, we anticipate positive answers to these questions and others, but much remains to be seen.

One key factor to note is that of all the foreign missionaries or aid workers in southern Sudan, the majority originate from East Africa. In other words, numerous Ugandans and Kenyans already work in southern Sudan. In addition, we know of a couple of expatriate missionary organizations already utilizing near-culture missionaries in some capacity. There is much hope that the Philip Project will indeed allow us to saturate southern Sudan with missionaries.

RADIO

Aid Sudan strives to spread the gospel through radio and the Moses and Philip Projects. Planning and fundraising began in early 2008 with installation of a base station in Kampala and satellite-fed repeater stations in key locations across southern Sudan planned for early 2009.

Programming includes Chronological Bible Storying and worship songs in the heart language of each targeted tribe, as well as community development. We believe that this programming received in huts in the heart language through solar-powered, hand-held radios is the prime way to nurture the saturation of the gospel across southern Sudan. Yet for this to become a reality, the missionaries must play a crucial role.

With the current Moses Project missionaries, whose two tribes collectively compose over half of southern Sudan's population, we have already begun recording stories and songs. Our greatest challenge lies in producing accurate programming in all the other tribal languages, which makes our Philip Project missionaries critical.

Philip Project missionaries will need not only to train in Chronological Bible Storying, but also to produce accurate recordings in the tribal language for radio use. This will not only facilitate church leadership training in a specific area through the mass distribution of hand-held, solar-powered radios, but also Aid Sudan's goal to saturate southern Sudan with missionaries and the gospel. Aid Sudan will raise funds for this endeavor.

Both projects are young, and there is still so much that remains unknown. We certainly do not have all the answers or know how it will all unfold. But this we do know. Just as Moses returned from the land of Midian to lead his people out of Egypt and Philip left for Samaria to minister there, same-culture missionaries from Sudan (residing in the United States) and near-culture missionaries from Uganda are eager to serve in southern Sudan.

We rejoice in this, grateful to God for calling them forth and convinced of the long-term impact they will have. May God indeed saturate southern Sudan with missionaries and the gospel, working there as only he can for his great glory!

Case Study 8

Whole-Life Transformation in Uganda[1]

JOHN KOTAKYI, A UGANDAN believer, was explaining to me how things were going in his village, where we had worked some fifteen years earlier. As he described improved health, agriculture practices, and discipleship, he said off-handedly, "And one day we noticed we had become a church." Such are the fluid movements between community development for the Kingdom, community life, and Body life in what we now call Discipling for Development (D for D).

BACKGROUND

In 1987, when a team of three American families—Tim and Barbie Stevenson, Dave and Nan Muhovich, Gary and Merri Lee Hipp—began working in Mbale, Uganda, with a vision for whole-life discipleship of whole communities, church planting per se was not a goal.

There had been over one hundred years of Christian influence in Uganda, and in Mbale District, churches were fairly evenly split between Catholic and Anglican (with a small number of Baptist and Pentecostal churches scattered around). The number of attendees with a personal relationship with Jesus was quite small. Our goal could more be seen as church revitalization through discipleship that included every part of individual and community life.

In 1987, the Mbale District, located in the Eastern Region and one of thirty-three districts in Uganda, was comprised of 560,000 people primarily from one people group—the Bamasaaba—with several dialects

1. Appreciation goes to my friend Dr. Gary Hipp (gary.hipp@navigators.org) for providing this case study. Gary, his wife Merri Lee, and two children served as missionaries for ten years in East Africa with Mission: Moving Mountains (M:MM) before moving back to the United States in 1995 to lead M:MM and travel as non-residential Discipling for Development mentors.

of the Lumasaaba language. English is the secondary language, although it is the official language of Uganda. Since 1987, the population and the numbers of villages and parishes have more than doubled.

Covering twenty-five hundred square kilometers, most of the district is five thousand feet above sea level with over half of the people living in the mountainous parts. Over 90 percent of the population is rural. Rainfall is adequate, and most of the people are self-sufficient in food crops. Coffee and cotton are the cash crops, while plantain, maize, and millet comprise the food staples. Beans, groundnuts, and vegetables are seasonally abundant.

MINISTRY APPROACH

From the beginning, the American team designed the ministry to be holistic (including all aspects of individual and community life), transformational (aimed at transformed hearts and worldview), and empowering (equipping local communities with the abilities to improve their lives and become what God has always intended).

The team embraced a definition of Discipleship for Development as a *process empowered by God*, in which the people of a *community grow* in their ability to solve their own problems and take control of their lives, resulting in growth of the *whole person* (physical, psychological, spiritual) and improvement of the various aspects of their community (health, agriculture, water, relationships, etc.). Through this process, the individuals and the community become *all that God intends them to be*.

With these outcomes in mind, the American team consisted of two people with medical backgrounds, two with theological backgrounds, one with an agricultural background, and one with an educational background. The nine initial Ugandan colleagues who joined them included those with pastoral backgrounds, educational backgrounds, medical backgrounds, agricultural training, and agricultural experience (all farmers in their own families). All team members were committed to whole-life discipleship with an intentional effort to balance the advancement of spiritual development with other aspects of community life.

Two decisions were made early on that have impacted the overall outcomes. First was the decision to equip equippers, in contrast to merely doing some good and seeing God's kingdom come into the few villages the westerners could work in over time. Second was the decision to establish a phase-out plan from the beginning. This set the scene for intensive discipling with the end in mind. This would include a specific time frame and indigenous workers who would carry on the work beyond the initial villages.

Part of the equipping process for all Western and Ugandan team members included limiting the initial work to three villages in order that the process of seeing a whole community being transformed could be refined before expansion. A transforming community would be one not only able to hear God's Word and His Spirit for life's questions, but also able to analyze, evaluate, and plan for the development of their own resources and for the removal of obstacles to the improvement of their lives.

In short, the goal was a community that was dependent on God, not outsiders (though outside consultants would be a part of their resource pool). This is the essence of what *empowerment* means in the D for D context.

The international team used adult nonformal methodologies of teaching, ones that drew on the experiences and knowledge that people had within themselves. This was the way in which the development-disciplers and community leaders were trained. They would develop their community members in a similar manner.

A TRANSFORMING COMMUNITY

After the international D for D team had prepared itself through training and refining their approach to communities, they spent time looking for the *right* communities in which to start. These would be communities that had shown initiative and desire to help themselves, were open to innovation and the Good News, were unified, and had trustworthy leaders.

Initial meetings with target groups of youth, women, and men (and eventually a committee of key leaders) facilitated discussions on issues of dependency versus community initiative, appreciating the resources and accomplishments the community already had in place, and exploring the obstacles to improving their lives and becoming all that God intends them to be.

Firmly embracing the desire to develop skills and knowledge rather than having things done for them, the villagers and key leaders categorized the strengths they could build on and the obstacles to improving community life (things like diarrhea, HIV, marital discord, envy, soil erosion, storage loss from pests, deforestation, alcoholism, low income and poor use of income, and poor access roads), and they prioritized the training that would bring the results they sought.

Because Uganda lives with a history of more than one hundred years of Christianity, communities in Mbale District were open to a truly integrated approach in which stories and life principles from scripture were integrated into the teaching of the development-disciplers as they worked with community leaders. That is not to say that everyone in these mostly nominally Christian communities wanted to hear *preaching*. However, the natural integration of the proclaimed Word of God into helping people develop their lives and communities (holistic ministry) is demonstrated in the life of Ishaya Lusambu from Yembe community. Here is his story.

At the start of the international D for D team ministry in his community, Ishaya Lusambu would avoid any person or place that was preaching or teaching about Jesus Christ. He did not attend church and would not come near a seminar, crusade, or Bible study. In fact, he now says he feared such events.

Because Ishaya was a farmer and saw the value in improving his agricultural techniques, he attended some meetings hosted by the Mission: Moving Mountains (M:MM) Uganda staff. He appreciated what he was learning and found himself attracted to the message about Jesus that was an integral part of learning how to be good stewards of what God has put in our hands.

In this process, he committed his life to Christ. Without the holistic approach he experienced, he says he would not have heard the gospel and committed his life to Christ. "And there are many people in our communities that are like me in that regard!"

Here's another example. Nathan Kutosi, one of M:MM Uganda's development-disciplers, recalls discipling John Kotakyi in those early years. John, like many villagers, struggled to make ends meet. To make a living, he sold charcoal (made by burning trees and putting the charcoal into bags). But due to heavy deforestation, local authorities had placed a ban on chopping down any more trees. Even so, John continued to make charcoal and soon found himself in trouble with the authorities.

When Nathan discovered the problem, he lamented, "I have spent much time discipling John but ignored helping him think through how he could provide for his family legally. This is my mistake as his discipler!"

Nathan vowed to be more balanced in discipling people in the future. He would include their economic, health, agricultural, and social concerns, along with helping them mature in Christ. It is a lesson and a principle that has driven the integrated and holistic nature of discipleship that M:MM Uganda staff practice.

CHURCHES FROM TRANSFORMED COMMUNITIES

An integral part of the D for D process is small group Bible study using Community Bible Lessons with a stimulating adult learning approach. Because of the communal nature of the holistic approach described here, these groups are interdenominational, often finding their way into the specific churches of the participating members. At one point, for instance, a community that was primarily from the Catholic Church moved their Bible Study into the Sunday morning worship service, adding it on to the end of their normal liturgy.

As mentioned earlier, the intent in this nominally Christian district was really aimed at revitalization and transformation of current churches in the process of seeing the whole communities transformed, not just church planting per se. However, Sam Soita, Executive Director of M:MM Uganda (trained as a church leader, pastor, and medical assistant), says at least twelve churches have spontaneously grown out of the D for D process. One influential leader, Mr. Mayeku, describes a typical example of those churches.

Mr. Mayeku is both a M:MM Uganda staff member and a community member in one of the areas where D for D has taken root. A member of a large Anglican church in Nabongo for most of his life, he and many of his neighbors found that it was too far for their wives and children to walk, especially through the mud of the rainy season.

Mr. Mayeku and his father decided to speak with many community leaders who had been active for seven years in D for D in Yembe. All agreed they should start a local church. An amazing thing happened. A community leader donated land, and many others began supplying cement and iron sheets, completing a building—foundation to roof—within one month!

In 1999, the Yembe Anglican Church was launched. D for D Community Bible Study leader, Ishaya Lusambu, became the pastor and has remained there preaching the Word until today. Initially, fewer than ten members were committed believers, but today almost thirty of the sixty adults who attend have trusted Christ and are part of whole-life discipling groups that were initiated in the D for D community program. Mr. Mayeku reports that every couple of months, at least two or three people commit their lives to Christ.

From its first Sunday, this daughter church has tithed generously and has faithfully contributed back to the mother church. Recently, the bishop of the northern Mbale diocese visited the church for the first time. He praised this community church for its vibrant growth, faithfulness in preaching the Word, and discipleship of its members physically and spiritually. His glowing affirmation confirms that the mother church now considers Yembe Anglican Church as an invaluable partner in the diocese.

Because the process is unequivocally inclusive of all members of the community, (whether Muslim, Catholic, Protestant, animist, etc.), working together in unity is both a requirement and a goal. This, in turn, creates a natural avenue for interdependence as community members engage in holistic development.

As an example of how automatic this approach has become, Nathan Kutosi, one of M:MM's development-disciplers was in his home area and offered to disciple some eight pastors from various denominations. They were eager for training that they saw as both spiritually edifying and relevant to their family and community concerns.

One requirement was made of them: they must disciple community members including people beyond their own congregations and denominations. Later, asked what the content of the discipleship included, Kutosi almost seemed insulted as he replied, "Health, agriculture, income generation, marriage, and our relationship with God. Did you think it would only be spiritual?"

PROGRESS TO DATE

The original team of Americans and Ugandans worked in three villages as they refined the D for D model, later expanding it to fourteen more villages in two separate areas of the district. The American team members phased out in 1992, and M:MM Uganda subsequently went through two significant board member changes and three changes in staff leadership.

Today, under the leadership of Executive Director of M:MM Uganda, Sam Soita, the Ugandans are currently working in 126 villages.

Additionally, several of their staff participate in the equipping of holistic practitioners (development-disciplers) throughout Africa, including Rwanda, Nigeria, Malawi, and Kenya.

As mentioned earlier, more than twelve churches have been established among the more mature project areas. These grew out of community Bible study groups in which an inductive, adult learner centered approach was used, an approach enthusiastically embraced by the majority of pre-literate community members. Through these Bible studies in each community, many people have become believers in Christ Jesus.

The Mbale District staff equipped D for D leaders within the community over a two-year process to lead the Bible Study groups that evolved into community churches. Sam reports that these churches "are a great unifying presence among all the churches in the community: the church has a wide vision (God's vision) for the communities. Where churches form, the church is seen as the light of the world for all the people and as a bridge to better living because of the whole life discipleship."

Walls that divide people have been torn down as a community begins to work together with God to solve its problems. Denominationalism is reduced, divorce rates have plummeted, and literacy rates have soared as parents send their children to school. In one community where at least 50 percent of the members were Muslim, almost all have become followers of Jesus because of the loving relationships community Christians have built with them through the D for D process.

When asked what that looks like in practice, Sam enthusiastically describes at length the inclusion of Muslim neighbors in that community in all social celebrations in which Christians are involved. Whether church weddings, community meetings, local feasts, health and agriculture training, even Muslim holidays, the community members *all* participate together, enjoying one another's presence.

In one example, Sam described Hamida Mwenyi as giving her life to Christ because of this outpouring of love. Today she is one of the most effective messengers of the gospel, having led not only her nominally Anglican husband, but also Muslims and non-Muslims, into authentic relationships with Jesus.

Local community health services have come into the communities through Community Health Workers (CHWs) and Traditional Birth Attendants (TBAs) who have been trained by D for D. As a result, families are becoming far healthier. No malnutrition has been cited in recent years. Infant mortality and morbidity rates have been significantly reduced, along with maternal mortality and morbidity.

Modern farming methods have been employed, resulting in greatly improved crop yields and increased income. The Mbale staff has found that people do not run short of food during hunger seasons. Many communities have seen an increase in reforestation as they have evaluated their environment.

Finally, Income Generating Activities (or IGAs, from trees, cows, goats, rabbits, poultry, beans, groundnuts, bananas, and cooperative loan schemes) have improved living standards. Sam even notes that they have seen a reduction in theft because "people are busy earning something for themselves."

In summary, the D for D process has resulted in community members depending on God—not other people—for their physical, economic, social, and spiritual needs. In each project, the Mbale development disciplers observe a "passion in the transformed individuals and communities to assist their neighbors to improve their lives as well." This is a testimony to the whole-life discipleship process that integrates transformation as a way of life.

OBSERVATIONS AND LESSONS LEARNED

As Sam and his colleagues reflect back on their ministry over the past twenty years, they remain enthusiastic that though it is a slow process, it is a sure process. In promoting dependency on God while seeking to develop their own resources and overcome the obstacles to improving their lives, it is clear that local community members must sense God's calling and become servant leaders to engage effectively in such transformation. The working of these principles eliminates discrimination, promotes unity and collaboration in and between communities, and reaches the whole community with the gospel message lived out and verbally proclaimed.

Teamwork, prayer, personal responsibility, and healthy family relationships all work together as both a model and an outcome in the communities that have seen transformation. They have tasted the fruit of their desire that "God's kingdom come, his will be done in their communities as it is in heaven." As one discipler has said, "When people taste hope, they will pursue it to its ultimate Source, the Maker of heaven and earth."

Case Study 9

Facilitating by Following in Papua New Guinea[1]

LATE ONE EVENING IN June of 2006, in the tropical lowlands of West New Britain, Papua New Guinea, four individuals sat on bamboo slat benches under the thatched-leaf roof of a stilt-style literacy house designated for teaching reading and writing to the residents of the Ata community of Sege. These four had stolen away from the busier center of Sege village life to converse in quiet, serious tones in the light of a smoky kerosene lamp dimly illuminating the woven bamboo floor under their feet.

Kaikou, an Ata elder serving in the church in Sege, was articulating various current concerns of the Ata church to New Tribes Mission (NTM) members Paul and Linda McIlwain. The couple had spent ten years in onsite church planting with the Ata and now consulted with the Ata regularly as friends and colleagues on an offsite basis.

Paul and Linda had learned the Ata language and taught the Scriptures in two different Ata villages, using the chronological teaching approach. They had also formalized an Ata alphabet, introduced reading and writing in Ata, discipled Ata Bible teachers, appointed Ata elders, and translated, along with Kaikou, the Ata New Testament.

Even in the initial Ata church plant and during their subsequent outreach, the McIlwains encouraged the growing believers to share responsibility actively in ministry tasks. The reality of this ministry participation was demonstrated in the way that the Ata continued to reach out enthusiastically to new communities themselves to plant churches, such that eventually ten Ata churches were established in villages scattered throughout the thirty-five-hundred-member people group in the mountains and lowlands of the Nakanai mountain range.

---

1. Thanks for the content of this case study go to Kaikou Maisu, Ata church elder, and Mike Griffis of New Tribes Mission.

The fourth member of the party was Mike Griffis, an NTM missionary who had previously worked for five years in pioneer church planting with an unreached people group in Venezuela. Mike and his wife, Michelle, were in the process of learning the culture and language of that particular people group when the Venezuelan president, Hugo Chavez, made unfounded accusations of NTM that led to his expelling all NTM missionaries from the remote ethnic group areas of Venezuela.

Due to Mike's current leadership and consulting roles with NTM, the McIlwains had invited him to Papua New Guinea to help with a Culture and Language Acquisition (CLA) workshop for PNG missionaries. They suggested that Mike might subsequently accompany them on a visit to the Ata churches following the workshop, where Paul planned to teach through the book of Philippians at the request of the church.

Mike and Michelle were on home assignment in the United States at the time, contemplating moving to another country where NTM worked due to the closed door in Venezuela, and had no intention of seriously considering PNG as an option. Nonetheless, Mike felt that a visit with Paul and Linda to the Ata area would be a great opportunity to interact with them and with the leaders of the Ata ethnic group church that had been functioning without onsite missionary presence for the past six years.

ATA PERSPECTIVE

Kaikou's concerns on that moonless June evening were not easy for him to express concisely. He labored to pull together several threads of extensive Ata leadership thinking and conversation that connected his own ten-plus years of church planting experience and observation of expatriate missionary work.

First was the challenge of the potential for more intentional partnership of the Ata church with NTM. The Ata had observed in recent years various expatriate teams beginning their church-planting work with what the Ata described as "weak foundations." Recent opportunities to interact with some very new expat teams had impressed the Ata with the thought that they may have insights that could be a help to the expats. But what shape might this kind of discipleship interaction take?

Second, the Lord had given the Ata the opportunity to extend outreach into a neighboring people group through bilingual believers who had intermarried with that group. Relying primarily on partially-developed chronological Bible lesson material from a previous missionary and on informal translations of chronological materials from Ata, the bilingual teachers had the privilege of seeing seven churches established in that second people group.

Bible teachers were trained and discipled by the bilingual Ata, and these teachers themselves participated in outreaches to others of their own communities. Literacy classes in that language were simultaneously initiated as well, such that many learned to read and write.

The Ata then began working with these new leaders to continue to develop more formalized Bible teaching materials in their language. But the procedure was a slow and difficult one, involving long, laborious hours of writing out new lessons by hand on a blackboard, then transferring those lessons to notebooks, and sending them away to be proofread and printed.

The Ata were dissatisfied with that less-than-efficient process, primarily due to the fact that they were unable to keep up with the demand of the hungry and growing churches. Also, the Ata were acutely aware of the importance of the written, translated scriptures, yet did not know how the written Word of God itself might be made available to this people group.

The third thread of Kaikou's concerns related to the potential for cross-cultural outreaches to the other people groups surrounding the Ata, where mature churches had not yet been established. As Kaikou later described, "So we leaders stopped and asked ourselves, if God's Word comes up on this kind of border, on the verge of jumping into another language, whose work is that? We asked that question, those of us who are Bible teachers and elders. That lingering question was whether this kind of work was in the hands of expatriate missionaries only, or the responsibility of the church as well."

PARTNERSHIP EXPLORATIONS

As his explanation of these three threads of concern wound down, Kaikou concluded with gentle questions to the missionaries: "What do you think of all this? How do you see us responding to the challenges we are facing?"

Mike remembers very vividly the beginnings of serious introspection at this point. Having grown up as a missionary kid in South America, Mike was familiar with numerous examples of pioneer church-planting works in CP-3 contexts—that is, where culture and language are very distant. But this encounter was reshaping his thinking, as Mike related in a letter to his wife:

> The Ata leaders impacted me as living a biblical worldview and an integrated Christian life. As much as I can tell, Christianity *is* life; life *is* ministry. Their testimony is impressive. Can tribal churches really be such a thing? What can we do to help the Ata with the vision *they* have? How can we facilitate the development of *their* potential to impact their region and beyond? How could we serve these servants? How could we learn from *their* experience and wisdom?

PROFILE OF A DISCIPLE

As the lamplight conversation continued, the four friends began to detail what shape this partnership between NTM and the Ata church might take. Kaikou clarified that while the church would be potentially interested in a direct partnership with an onsite expat family, their primary concern was the kind of interaction the family would have with them.

Would this family take the time as a learner and disciple of the church to become an insider, and offer assistance under the authority and leadership of the Ata church as a servant of the church, rather than seeking to fill a traditional missionary role? Could this family avoid the temptation of taking on a directing, patronizing role in church affairs? What discipleship track might be defined in order for this partnership integration to take place? How would that discipleship track mesh with their overriding concerns as a church and their concomitant, long-term ministry objectives?

As the four colleagues and several other Ata elders continued thinking about this issue over the next week, they worked to further define that possible discipleship track. The Ata were already implementing a training approach for Bible teachers and elders that included extensive participation in chronological Bible teaching and practical discipleship to ensure godly character, ministry faithfulness, and teaching consistency.

The Ata would apply this same system of training to an expat family desiring to be incorporated into ministry life with them. They would expect the expats to suspend any prejudicial views of the superiority of Western missiological expertise that might interfere with this integration into and understanding of Ata church life and ministry.

This expectation would help the Ata church corporately to understand the contrast of this type of expat role to that of more traditional missionaries. During the discipleship period, it would also enable the expat family to learn practically from culturally appropriate Ata experience in church planting, church leadership and function, discipleship, literacy, and Bible lesson development. All this would set the stage for a genuine partnership of interdependence.

Finally, even while this discipleship of the expat family was taking place, the expats and Ata could begin to evaluate the use of this same discipleship training as the foundation of an equipping track to prepare Ata families for future cross-cultural ministry. They could then determine how to blend additional cross-cultural training elements with this discipleship foundation. These could include, among others, a systematic means of uncovering and documenting important language, cultural, and worldview issues that should be highlighted and contrasted by the biblical theology approach of chronological teaching in the course of cross-cultural outreach.

CONCRETE DECISIONS

Through this time of interacting with the three missionaries to establish together the basis on which a healthy Ata partnership with NTM might emerge, and having expressed various concerns as well as potential opportunities, the Ata leaders determined to extend the invitation to Mike and Michelle to consider joining their ministry team. So different from what the couple had planned and trained for all of their missionary lives! They were, after all, pioneer missionaries working with a pioneer missionary agency, carrying the responsibility *themselves* of reaching the most unreached people groups in the world.

But as Mike rejoined his wife in the United States for the completion of their home assignment time, the Lord was challenging them both to evaluate their commitment to the potential of His church. Were they willing to serve the church in belief of that potential, no matter what the ethnic or cultural background? No matter what that meant for their personal roles or ministry expectations?

Mike was now in his last year of a masters program in sociolinguistics in Dallas, and he and Michelle recognized that the Lord had given them unique training and experience which could be a benefit to a relationship of interdependence with the Ata. They communicated about the ministry opportunity with their US support team and received a favorable response.

In August of 2006, two months after Mike's first PNG visit, the couple wrote to accept the Ata church partnership proposal. They arrived in PNG in the fall of 2007, and moved into the Ata village of Sege in the spring of 2008, eager to discover what the Lord had in store for them.

CLA: STARTING POINTS FOR THE ATA INITIATIVE

But an obvious question and anomaly was in the making. In order for this previously described discipleship process to begin, the couple would need first to learn the Ata culture and language, as Ata would be their common language of partnership. Of course Mike and Michelle had studied Tok Pidgin, the national language of PNG, and most of the Ata were conversant in Pidgin as well. But none of the partners were satisfied with Pidgin as their primary communicative medium. Their partnership objectives and underlying ministry values included the primacy of the mother tongue as the most effective medium for teaching God's Word.

What principles could the couple apply to their learning of Ata that would contribute to the discipleship foundation established by the Ata? What could they do that would concurrently benefit the developing cross-cultural perspective of the Ata church? Their partnership?

Over the course of several previous years, Mike had had opportunity to assist in workshop presentations of the new Culture and Language Acquisition program. This training focused on dovetailing the underlying set of principles for learning culture and language with the stated NTM goals for church maturity.

Providentially, Linda McIlwain had been instrumental in the development of the CLA materials and now served as the NTM International CLA Coordinator. This placed her in a good position to help Mike and Michelle adapt CLA to the Ata context.

Paul McIlwain, as the NTM International Church Planting Coordinator, had worked with others in the NTM Field Ministries Office (2007) to author the aforementioned NTM Mature Church Model. This document provided important reference points for the work and exit strategy of church planters by focusing on an incremental evaluation of church maturity in four major areas:

1. God's Word for the church,

2. the identity of the church,

3. the life of the church, and

4. discipleship in the church.

For each of the four areas, objectives were defined that would help consultants direct the attention of church planters toward a holistic evaluation of church maturity, and ultimately, the readiness of the church for extended missionary absence.

Mike had little doubt that the CLA principles themselves would serve the Ata church well and could contribute to an appropriate discipleship foundation, both for the Griffises' work and for future Ata cross-cultural work. Derived from NTM's global experience in culture and language acquisition research, the CLA principles pointed learners to relationship development through personal experience in the cultural context of the language they were acquiring.

The principles emphasized the priority of listening comprehension as an avenue for building effective communication skills. Finally, the CLA principles included a very careful evaluation process that culminated in the learner's in-depth investigation of abstract cultural issues based on deep relationships within the community. Such learners would be well-acculturated and could function in extended discourse with no patterns of error in basic language structures.

But some serious adjustments to the CLA approach would be required as well. Mike and Michelle realized, for example, that many of the technical and technological expectations that accompanied the CLA program were not that relevant or helpful to the Ata.

So the couple decided to maintain the underlying principles of CLA, but to focus their own methods of acquisition in such a way that their learning process could serve as a model of CLA that the Ata could emulate. They would eliminate acquisition and processing techniques that were highly computer, camera, printer, and office dependent. They would also adapt the number and complexity of acquisition techniques, as well as the process for evaluating learner progress to fit the Ata context.

Additionally, Mike and Michelle would attempt to show that an underlying common foundation of biblical understanding ultimately generates the principles of CLA. With this goal established, they, together with the mature Ata believers, would identify appropriate and creative CLA methods that consistently support those CLA principles.

The resulting CLA methods would allow for mature ethnic churches like the Ata to take up cross-cultural responsibility in a way that suits their cultural situation. And it would be based on the training foundation of their own extensive biblical understanding and church-planting experience, rather than on expat technical or technological expertise injected into the situation in more sterile or paternalistic fashion.

Furthermore, the couple desired to demonstrate that the CLA principles, or any other cross-cultural church planting principles for that matter, do not have to exist as "technical" equipping or facilitative appendages to institutionalized church or para-church structures. More ideally, they should be viewed as the outworking of a proper foundation of biblical teaching, discipleship, and church life already in place in the local church context.

With these goals in mind, Mike and Michelle began their Ata Culture and Language Acquisition. Both they and the McIlwains felt that their CLA process should be well-documented so that an Ata CLA Training Manual could be developed to assist in the later equipping of the Ata for cross-cultural outreach.

Also, this documentation would help the believers to experience and give regular input into the specific acquisition techniques that seemed appropriate for later use by the Ata. So as the couple started learning Ata, Mike began explaining the foundational principles of CLA to Kaikou and other church leaders as they applied them. Soon they developed an introduction in Ata of those key components, including the CLA Principles, the concept of cyclical learning as a practical framework for organizing learning activities, and an understanding of the system of proficiency levels for evaluating culture and language learning progress.

FUTURE CHALLENGES

As this NTM partnership with the Ata church continues forward, many questions still confront the team. For example, what about the possibility of the Ata having their own worksite where they might become computer literate in order to expedite the development of church-planting related materials? How would this be funded? What about the need for New Testament translation in future Ata cross-cultural projects? The translation of the Ata Old Testament? The Ata serving as consultants to NTM missionary teams? How might the Ata discipleship training foundation incorporate the equipping of mature believers for these tasks?

While the Ata, the McIlwains, and the Griffises face many yet un-answered questions such as these, all are encouraged with the growing conviction of the Ata church regarding their own potential and respon-sibility to handle, by God's grace, some tremendous challenges tradi-tionally viewed as beyond the "technical expertise" of tribal churches. Kaikou concludes the still-in-progress Ata CLA Manual introduction by saying,

> So we know that the work which is beginning amongst us today will serve us well in answering this question which we had ini-tially. Our question was that if the Word of God is going to jump to a new language area, is that the work of an expatriate mission-ary, or just whose work is it?
>
> But we now feel that the work that is beginning amongst us today will greatly help those who go and learn the languages of these other communities to take God's Word to them. Our living example of acquiring this knowledge demonstrates that there is no separation between the responsibility of expatriate missionar-ies and the work of the national church. The answer to the above question is clear.
>
> This living example of partnership will serve the national church well when it goes to new language groups. As we envision joining in their lives and learning their languages, this isn't some-thing for us to continue to question. And we aren't so concerned about the obstacles that we once thought were major hurtles.
>
> We now see that effective cross-cultural work will actually come through acquiring language and through building relation-ships with those of other languages. In this way we want to see followers of Christ truly prepared not only to communicate God's Word in the language of the host community, but also to apply that teaching correctly to their customs and traditional beliefs.

Case Study 10

Team Poland's Story of Short-Cycle Church Planting[1]

KIRK, THE TEAM'S LOGISTICS person, his wife, and two daughters arrived in Poland the last week of January 2004. A week later my family—Kenn, Doreen, and our two sons—arrived. Three singles (Cathleen, Estella, and Beth, whose name has been changed), along with a third family (Tim, Spring, and their son), arrived over the next month. My role was to lead the team.

All arrived well trained, armed with the Short-Cycle principles and eager to see what God would do. We had a clear idea of what we hoped to accomplish: plant a healthy, reproducing, truly Polish church in five years.

We also came with a deep understanding that we had absolutely no idea how to do that in Poznan, Poland. This dynamic tension between our humble recognition of personal inadequacy and our overwhelming confidence in God's ability would become a hallmark of the team. It also eventually became a principal part of Avant's core mindset definition.

The team entered Poland with a big advantage due to some divine serendipity that occurred during the site survey in 2003. The survey team came in contact with a local pastor through a seminary student studying about a mile from Avant's International Service Center in Kansas City.

That pastor had previously helped facilitate at least three new church plants in Poland and had a kingdom mindset. He offered to provide legal status for the team through his church, along with invit-

1. Appreciation for this case study goes to Poland team leader Kenn Oke (koke@avmi.org) and Scott Harris (sharris@avmi.org). Kenn, now Avant's Europe Regional Director, lives with his wife, Doreen, and their two sons in Spain, where they began ministry in 1996. They help facilitate the success of Avant missionaries and assist Word Zone from a distance. Scott and his wife, Jolyn, live in Kansas City, where he serves on Avant's Exec Team with responsibility for field ministries. They previously served over a decade with SIM in West Africa and in Charlotte, NC.

ing them to worship with his congregation during language study. As we met together one evening during the survey, he told me, "Come to my church and make friends while you study language. Then in a year, you can take those people and start your church. They aren't my people; they're God's."

As we geared up for arrival, the pastor put Kirk in contact with a real estate agent in his church who helped find excellent rentals for the team. Once we arrived, he and members of his church helped with getting utilities hooked up, submitting government paperwork, and many other details of beginning life in the country. Their assistance greatly reduced entry stress.

LANGUAGE

Another helpful factor as we entered Poland was that many Poles speak English. That, coupled with known local language-learning opportunities, allowed us to enter with only a few survival phrases of Polish.

After researching study possibilities, we decided to hire private language teachers rather than use the existing schools other missionaries had used. This allowed us to hire instructors whose teaching style fit our various learning styles, along with providing a much higher level of flexible timing than the institutional programs. It also proved a lower cost alternative.

In an attempt to recognize the varied public contact required by different team members' roles, we limited the training of our less publicly-involved members. That proved to be a mistake, creating additional stress for those people, who subsequently failed to develop a high level of comfort in the culture.

Conversely, with the relative prevalence of Anglophones in Poznan, we at times played our lack of fluency to advantage by pleading language inability, thus making it imperative very early on that the Poles translate our teaching and do much of the ministry themselves.

CULTURE

Within the first three months, the church asked us to consider heading up a long list of ministry opportunities. As we looked over the list, one of our working principles immediately came to mind: *restricted scope*. Many of these ministries could be done by local believers. Plus, we were not sure if any of them would lead to a reproducing church in five years, so we initially said no to all of them.

We eventually helped with a few as a means of getting a feel for what ministry in Poland looked and felt like, but we never led them. If we were going to figure out what would work, we needed some hands-on experience, which fit our primary goal for the first year: to be learners.

Throughout 2004, our team used many avenues to learn Polish culture. We turned the hands-on ministries in the church into research projects, evaluating our experiences and seeking to identify cultural clues.

We also seized the tactical advantage of our pastor friend's good name to quickly gain a hearing with, and transparency from, other pastors around the country. Some team members conducted surveys of local church members to discover what initially drew them into a Protestant church.

CONNECTING WITH THE MISSIONARY COMMUNITY

Team members befriended and interviewed missionaries from other organizations, along with taking part in many mission community activities. Our relationships with other missionaries were quite good.

However, coming in with a five-year goal and a radically different philosophy of ministry did present the potential for problems. We countered that potential by staying humble, taking time for relationships, and freely sharing our training and strategic tools with others.

Here are a few of the things we shared with them about Short-Cycle Church Planting, including some history. Avant Ministries,[2] formerly Gospel Missionary Union, emerged from the student missionary movement of the 1890s. It focused on church planting among the unreached of Morocco and Ecuador, but over time became involved in a broader spectrum of ministries.

In 2002, the International Board changed its governance model and appointed a new president, Dr. Paul Nyquist. The board adopted a new ends statement mandating a return to the group's pioneer church-planting roots and requiring results-based accountability.

Although the mission's new direction required a return to its roots, the radically changed world of the twenty-first century demanded new means to achieve the goal. Urbanization and globalization, along with

---

2. Avant Ministries website, http://AvantMinistries.org

relatively high levels of literacy and education, reach into virtually every country, presenting new avenues of opportunity to spread the gospel.

Socio-political unrest has rapidly become the norm, rendering the timeframes required by traditional methodologies unreasonable in many locations—especially those involving least-reached peoples. An emerging millennial generation eagerly desires to find causes worth investing in through a team effort. Avant was ready to change its church-planting model that formerly took some fifty years to plant a single church. Team Poland would be the first to implement Short-Cycle Church Planting.

Short-Cycle Church Planting has four main elements: the Faith Context, a High Performance Team, Five Operating Principles, and Phase II. They are supplemented by a metrics tool that provides strategic guidance in the process.

It all begins with God's power in what Avant calls the *Faith Context*. Four things contribute to this component. Avant begins with the power of the gospel from Romans 1:16, believing that the gospel message itself is powerful. Indeed, the message is central, while methods are just tools.

The *faith context* continues with a second piece dubbed *divine serendipity*. It is believed that God provides leverage in church-planting situations that aids the process—as he did, for example, with the altar to the unknown god in Athens (as recorded in Acts 17:22ff). It is the team's responsibility to recognize what God has provided and exploit the opportunities presented.

The third part is simply *God's ability*, as Paul eloquently described in Ephesians 3:20–21. He is indeed able to do the amazing. The final portion of the faith context is the *primacy of prayer*. Avant emphasizes to teams that prayer helps them connect to the power provided by the other three elements.

Having begun with God's power flowing through a team, the Short-Cycle philosophy recognizes Five Operating Principles:

1. *Simultaneous Activity* releases the team from a linear modus operandi by seeking both to accomplish multiple steps of the church-planting process concurrently and to achieve multiple results from a single activity. Examples include effects like promoting the authority of Scripture while evangelizing, or identifying and preparing potential leaders while discipling.

2. *High Trust,* the most important of the five principles, emphasizes

trust in teammates, the Holy Spirit, and national believers. It recognizes that those believers—having the same Holy Spirit that the team members do, having developed a high view of scriptural authority, and having been trained in hermeneutics and application—are capable of doing ministry and leading their church very early on.

3. *Overt Witness* recognizes the power of the gospel. The team will share the gospel early and often, while doing so appropriately within the cultural context. As new believers emerge, witness will quickly become their privilege and responsibility.

4. *Restricted Scope* is a powerful accelerator of the church-planting process and works strongly in conjunction with High Trust. Stated simply, "We will do only what only we can do." Therefore, if a national can do it, we will let her, even if team members can do it better.

5. *Tactical Advantage* seizes the leverage provided through divine serendipity, using the people, situations, and other opportunities God provides, many of which appeared quite outside of our strategies.

Once the church demonstrates a healthy maturity on the Avant Metrics, the team leaves and Phase II begins. Avant assigns a couple to remain in contact with the church, and the couple may be resident or distant. Their primary roles are to encourage, coach, and provide friendship as seen in the Apostle Paul's follow-up with churches. This phase lasts at least as long as the initial work of the team, hopefully resulting in a long-term relationship and perhaps partnership in new ventures of faith.

The Avant Metrics grow out of a progressive disaggregation of the five core values defining a healthy church in Avant's Global Ends Statement. These include the following five indicators of growth: believers being saved; believers being discipled towards maturity; believers not being dependent on mission or missionaries; interdependence and partnership with other churches; and missionaries being sent cross-culturally.

The five statements become thirteen biblically irreducible minimums, which are in turn expanded into thirty-five evaluative elements describing actual behaviors representing church health. Each evaluative element is rated on a one-to-ten continuum. The resulting numeric data is charted and used to guide team strategy so that they know ultimately when to leave.

THE RADAR CHART

The metrics found in the Radar Chart below are designed to focus the strategy in two ways. First, simply answering the questions on the Evaluative Elements will remind team members what is important. Second, the radar chart clearly shows what should be done next.

FIRST YEAR

As we reflect on that first year, two key events transpired that eventually impacted our ultimate ministry goal. Someone invited one of our team members, Estella, to join a gospel choir. This was not a planned strategic move on our part; rather, it was just a team member being herself and getting to know people.

The choir had fifty members in January 2004 with only three being believers. One of those was the choir's manager, Andrew, who had a deep desire to see the choir used as an evangelistic tool—another clear case of divine serendipity.

Through Estella's experience, we discovered that African American gospel music is *huge* in Poland. Meeting the demand for it ultimately provided an incredible tactical advantage for our team and the emerging church.

The relationship between Estella and Andrew that began in the choir led to the second event. With Estella's support and encouragement, Andrew started a Bible study for interested choir members in September. They met at Estella's flat and invited a local Baptist pastor to teach. They quickly discovered, however, that many of the predominantly Roman Catholic choir members would not come to a study led by a Protestant pastor.

The perceptive pastor immediately recognized the problem and left the group, allowing them to study the Bible on their own. Learning of Catholics' aversion to Protestant pastors provided a key insight for our future strategies.

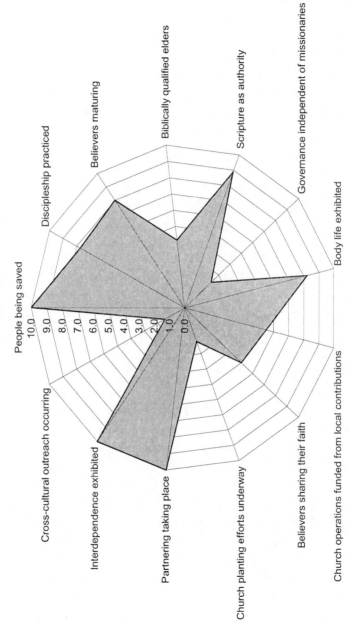

Team Poland Irreducibles

People being saved · Discipleship practiced · Believers maturing · Biblically qualified elders · Scripture as authority · Governance independent of missionaries · Body life exhibited · Church operations funded from local contributions · Believers sharing their faith · Church planting efforts underway · Partnering taking place · Interdependence exhibited · Cross-cultural outreach occurring

0.0 1.0 2.0 3.0 4.0 5.0 6.0 7.0 8.0 9.0 10.0

LEARNING THE TEAM

When we arrived in Poland, the only people who had clearly defined roles were Kirk, the administrator, and Doreen, the encourager/team-care person. Based on past ministry experience, I knew that both fit these roles well. I very quickly realized that Kirk was also an excellent strategic thinker, so I started leaning on him to play that role as well.

Ironically, past ministry experience for the rest of the team actually hindered the process of finding a role for them because they had not played to their strengths in previous ministries. For example, I had assumed that Tim would be a discipler because that was his role in Ecuador.

That is not his natural gifting, though, and it took time to determine how he could best contribute to our strategy. Once determined, I gave him projects that played to his strengths based on Gallup's Strengths Test. Tim set up a team language-study plan and partnered with Kirk to develop our supporter communication strategy.

The most helpful thing I did to define roles took place in months three and four. I had all team members individually write out what they thought their role on the team was supposed to be, and what they thought I expected from them. Most of them wrote volumes on both areas. As I sat down with each one to edit their lists, it helped them focus on what they were truly good at rather than their perception of "good missionary" activities. Then as I edited their expectation descriptions, it gave them permission to focus on the heart of their strengths.

The roles that emerged for the other team members had Dannel and Spring dedicating most of their time to being mothers, which is an acceptable and encouraged role in Avant. They also attended team meetings and had full voice in our deliberations. Beth's roles included teaching the MKs and helping document the team's activities. Cathleen became part of the strategic team and was involved in designing projects.

Some people's roles evolved during the cycle. Kirk, for example, ended up taking a lot of the organizational leadership responsibilities, calling meetings, keeping us focused on when we needed to re-work strategy, scheduling metrics evaluations. This happened as I became more hands-on in the church plant and dedicated more time there.

This evolution of roles for Kirk and me was never an official decision but a natural outcome of the way our team operated. Kirk saw a need and knew that he would not be stepping on my toes by taking on leadership responsibilities.

STRATEGIES

By the end of the research year, we had learned enough to test two projects. In March 2005, we organized a church-planting leadership training course. Five Polish believers attended whom we hoped to encourage to form and lead church-planting teams made up of local believers and some of our Avant missionaries. We expected them to lead the efforts from the beginning.

Also in March 2005, Andrew and Estella invited me to teach the Bible study they had started. By this point there were three more new believers in the choir, and they believed I could provide the needed teaching.

In that I wasn't seen as a Protestant pastor, the group agreed it would be okay. However, as our team discussed it, we saw that it could easily turn into "Kenn's Bible study," which, if it developed into a church, would be difficult to transfer back into Polish hands.

So instead of teaching, I took three believers from the choir, met with them privately and taught them the inductive Bible study method. I never attended their Wednesday night studies. We simply trusted that the Holy Spirit would use them to teach their peers. From March 2005 until the end of the year, they taught their own studies.

A few months later, I was invited by Andrew to attend the choir's weekend retreat. Andrew asked me to explain, from the Bible, the meaning of two new songs that the Poles were learning in English.

My team said when I described what happened that weekend to them I looked like I was in shock! I have never seen a group of people so attentive to biblical teaching or so hungry to understand the incredible words they were singing. At that point, the team decided Doreen and I should join Estella in the choir and focus the majority of our time developing that Bible study into a church.

In September, once again the Bible study group asked if I would come and teach them. They were finding the inductive method hit-and-miss; some weeks were great, and other times they were left with more questions than answers. Recognizing a bona fide need, but still having the earlier concerns, I agreed to lead them through the first eight chapters of Romans on Monday nights, while they continued leading their studies on Wednesday nights.

Meanwhile, our leadership training course had ended with one of the participants believing he should lead a church-planting team. In September 2005 we committed Cathleen, Dannel, and Kirk full-time to that Polish-led church-planting team called "Project New Creation."

By the end of 2005, the Bible study that emerged from the choir had become a tight-knit community. They realized that they had something good and decided it was time to become intentional about opening up the group to as many new people as possible.

A PROACTIVE CHOIR

The Gospel Joy Choir had an annual gospel music workshop that was open to the public, and the Bible study group decided to use it as their first outreach event. Prior to 2005, the gospel music workshop had primarily been a cultural event.

The organizers did not ignore the gospel, but it was not the focus— nor was there any follow-up for seekers. Participants came on Saturday morning, memorized in English ten gospel songs in three- and four-part harmony, had a final rehearsal on Sunday morning, and then performed a concert on Sunday night.

The energy of these weekends is impossible to explain in words. Participants regularly get so deeply involved intellectually and emotionally that it creates an amazing opportunity to share the gospel. The transformation of the workshop from a cultural event to an evangelistic tool involved three strategic pieces, each building on the previous one.

1. They asked me to explain the meanings of the songs to the workshop participants. I spoke five times on Saturday for ten to fifteen minutes. Using the words of the songs that they were learning, I gave a progressive gospel presentation.

2. Saturday night ended with a worship time in which a Polish believer invited people to make a decision.

3. On Sunday morning, the participants were invited to a twelve-week study of Ephesians, sponsored by the Bible study group that had now adopted the name Strefa Slowa or the Word Zone.

Fifty people attended the first Word Zone study of Ephesians. By the end of the twelve weeks, we had twenty-five people attending regularly. I wish that I could say that from this group we steadily grew, but the reality is that over the next months and through the summer, attendance dwindled to ten to twelve people—not much bigger than before the outreach.

TEAM TRANSITIONS

As Avant selected our team members, each was asked for a five-year commitment with the assumption that the entire team would remain intact for the full cycle. Reality proved somewhat different, as two members went home and one was added.

In May 2006, the need for one team member's strategic skills diminished radically as the team adopted a singular ministry focus, which I will detail below. With a growing number of teams training for Short-Cycle at the International Service Center and her teaching gifts, it made sense for the mission to reassign her to that broader role.

By July 2006, it became evident that another team member also needed to leave the team. She had struggled with cultural adaptation since our arrival, and her struggles persisted despite all efforts to help.

In that context, other issues developed. Chief among them was her inability to trust me as leader, accompanied by contentions that she was intentionally excluded from decisions. This continued in spite of the fact that our team did not operate as a democracy but relied on the strategic team members to set direction.

Eventually, the issue was adversely affecting our ability to function well. It also consumed the majority of my effort and emotional energy for the final six months she was part of the team.

Ultimately, I concluded it would be best for this member and the team for her to leave. Although I knew it would be very difficult for her and our families, I was convinced it was the right decision. It was also my most difficult decision of the entire cycle.

Brian, our team's only added member, first came to lead a gospel music workshop in December 2005 and then returned in May 2006. Seeing his passion for the lost and the chemistry demonstrated at the workshops, we asked him to join our team as a one-year mission specialist, which he did in November 2006. His presence enabled us to strategically maximize the tactical advantage provided by Gospel Joy Choir.

LOOMING FAILURE

Avant leadership gave our team the freedom to fail—and even encouraged us to push the envelope far enough that we did fail as a path to learning. As we understood more about Poland, we concluded we would rather fail than begin another typical Polish Evangelical church that effectively required people to leave their culture in order to be part of the church. By April 2007, it seemed we were about to fail.

As attendance at Word Zone dwindled, things in Project New Creation were also falling apart. The project team had been meeting and planning for months, but nothing was really happening. The Polish leader of the project was now concluding that he did not want to be part of a church plant. He had plans for doing some very good things, but when it became clear that they would not result in a church—our main focus—our three team members had to step out of the project: over a year of time and effort invested, and nothing to show for it.

We assessed the situation and concluded that even though Word Zone's numbers were dropping, the potential for this group to develop into a church was still there. In our tradition of giving descriptive names to our strategic periods, we dubbed the next period "Bet the Farm."

We decided that the entire team would focus on working to help Word Zone grow. That did not mean that we were all going to start attending Word Zone meetings! Much of what was happening at Word Zone was led by Poles. We were not going to step in and steal ministry opportunities from them. In fact, throughout the whole process, only three Avant missionaries attended Word Zone regularly. Some have never attended, and those who did not attend focused on improving the five Gospel Music workshops that Word Zone used as their outreach strategy.

TURNING POINTS

Since beginning the Ephesians study, I had done almost all of the teaching at Word Zone. When my family went on home assignment during the summer of 2006, the quality of the teaching suffered. Word Zone members said, "The next time Kenn goes away, it can't be like that!"

So in the fall of 2006, I changed my teaching style and made the study more interactive. As I taught the Bible, I also focused on teaching the interpretive process. I am happy to say that if you ask a Word Zone member what the three important questions are, s/he will say, "What did it mean to the original audience? What is the timeless principle? What does that mean to me?" If you ask what are the three key things to pay attention to when interpreting, s/he will say, "Context, context, and context."

In the midst of this learning, the group began demonstrating what were to become three core distinctives: living life together (fellowship), being active in ministry together, and equipping people so that they can feed themselves through scripture.

Then in October 2006, I realized that Word Zone had transformed from simply being a Bible study into being a church. Avant's baseline definition of a church is "a group of believers meeting together regularly, who recognize they are a local representation of the body of Christ and who are organized to carry out God's will." Further clarity is added with key word definitions:

- Believers—redeemed individuals.
- Group—an undefined number greater than three.
- Regularly—repetitive, at recurring intervals assumed to be at intervals of one month or less.
- Organized—intended as a statement of purpose, not form.

From the defining moment when Word Zone became a church, our team concentrated on helping them develop the full biblical character of a healthy church.

That same month, Word Zone organized a weekend retreat. We studied the parable of the talents, and nine leaders who were present concluded that Word Zone was the talent that God had given them to invest. Though the group was small, they committed themselves to investing what God had given them as a group and committed to organizing themselves so that they could carry out his will in the world.

Word Zone organized, financed, and chose the Bible study topics for the events following the gospel music workshops. All I had to do was show up and teach.

As new people joined in the Wednesday night meetings, the core group of Word Zone began seeing the need to do some of the teaching themselves. I taught them the basics of leading a Bible study, and by summer 2007, when I had to be in Canada for a few months, they led all the studies!

Under their teaching, Word Zone grew like never before! At times, forty people packed into the flat where we met. The balcony became an overflow area where seven or eight people would sit and listen through the open window to the study going on in the living room. We quickly realized that, while this worked during the summer, there would be no option of putting people on the balcony during the Polish winter! We either needed a bigger place to meet, or the group had to divide into two Word Zones. We opted for the latter.

In October 2007, Word Zone made its first attempt at reproduction. Each group had three trained teachers. One group continued to meet on Wednesday at the original location in the north end of Poznan, and the other on Thursdays at a new location in the southern part of the city.

We tried this for three months, and concluded it was not going to work. People were accustomed to meeting in the original location, and very few transitioned to the new one, even though many of them had to travel an extra twenty to thirty minutes to get to the northern location. We decided to regroup and find another way to reproduce.

Though the first attempt at reproduction failed, we learned a valuable lesson. The Polish leaders at Word Zone had always led very informally, making decisions through email or in ad hoc meetings without all leaders present. That failure helped them see the need for more intentionality in leadership. The group officially identified eight leaders, and a monthly leaders' meeting was initiated.

In January 2008, they set new goals for Word Zone: two strong Word Zone churches in Poznan by the end of the year and the seeds of new Word Zones established in other cities where gospel music workshops were held. They also decided to hire their first full-time staff member to help realize these goals. From that point, things began moving quickly, and the leaders handled some very difficult issues.

By April 2008, one of the eight leaders, who brought many new people to the group and who did an excellent job of keeping group members informed, also had recurring problems that hindered the body. Ultimately, the other seven leaders asked that person to resign from the leadership team and set up counseling sessions to help work through the problems. They did so, fearing that the person would spread rumors about poor treatment by the other leaders.

Their fears proved well founded as many seekers simply stopped coming. In my mind, this was a crucial test for church leadership, which they successfully passed when they made the right decision, even though it was not the easiest or the most popular.

During the spring and summer of 2008, something happened that I call "spontaneous combustion of new ministries." The leaders began to start new ministries, not as part of a plan for church development, but simply as a response to needs they saw. I think this demonstrated leaders naturally taking responsibility for the spiritual health of the church.

Then in October 2008, Andrew, probably the strongest organizational leader, saw all those ministries and concluded that leadership needed to develop a comprehensive strategy. At the final leadership meeting I attended, each leader was given responsibility for a ministry that fit his or her gifting. Each was also to be held accountable to show how that ministry either contributed to bringing people into Word Zone or moved them through the growth process. These actions created a viable framework for continued numeric and spiritual growth.

Also in October 2008, Word Zone became a missionary-free zone when the last of our team left Poznan and Doreen and I assumed Phase II responsibility at a distance. Though it has not reached full maturity at this point, lacking only in the metric for sending cross-cultural missionaries, we are confident that it will continue to grow under the Spirit-led Polish leaders.

The church began with mostly single twenty to thirty-five year olds. Now some have married and are starting families, creating the need for developing family-friendly ministries. Leadership assigned their staff worker the task of developing proposals to address this new situation.

REMINISCING

Going back to August 2008 at Avant's biennial Europe conference, we spent an evening rejoicing in what God did through Team Poland. It was a chance to reflect and for team members to share some of the human side of the Short-Cycle adventure of faith.

One of the toughest areas for most of the team involved their deliberate decision to limit participation in Word Zone to three team members. Dannel, who never attended, explained in tears how it felt to have her supportive parents visit and not be able to take them to Word Zone because of that decision.

Her husband, Kirk, who also refrained from attending, added another facet as he described a lunch meeting with one of the church's leaders during their last week in Poznan. At that time, the Polish leader thanked Kirk for his role, explaining that without his and other team members' involvement—even at a distance—Word Zone would not exist, and most of the members would still be lost.

Tim, the graphic artist/communicator, explained eloquently how God, through Team Poland's experience, taught him that a missionary was simply someone using their gifts cross-culturally for kingdom good. He had struggled in the past, believing that all missionaries should be like some of the pioneers in tribal areas—able to do everything from Scripture translation to building houses to serving as a pastor of the church plant.

Tim's amazing gifts empowered the outreach efforts through providing world-class publicity for the gospel music workshops. He also gave the team's communication pieces a level of excellence far above most missionary communications, helping to garner and maintain solid prayer support.

A TEAM LEADER'S FINAL THOUGHTS

During our early years in Poland, I continually challenged our team to take on more than we were able to do so we could give God a chance to show us what he is able to do. What we have seen in Word Zone could only be accomplished through God's power! It is an amazing privilege to have been part of it!

I'm certain that future Avant teams will have very different stories than ours in Poland. But as they trust God to do more than they are humanly capable of, they will see the church-planting cycle shortened and healthy reproducing churches established where they are most needed.

Case Study 11

Multiple Facilitative Church Planting in Kursk, Russia[1]

IN THE FOLLOWING PAGES, I share a modern story of multiple facilitative church planting, the fruit of a partnership between a Baptist church in Kursk, a regional capital in western Russia, and a North American missions agency. Not unlike the Ephesus–Asia Minor church-planting movement of yesteryear—where Paul's two-year-long daily intensive interaction with disciples of Jesus in a strategic urban center resulted in the evangelization of the entire province of Asia!—a Bible training program for followers of Jesus in a strategic regional capital became the centerpiece of this joint faith venture. The result? Between 1998 and 2005, this strategy gave birth to eight churches in Kursk and many others planted by graduates in other cities of the Russian Federation and Ukraine.

THE CHALLENGE

Despite the unprecedented investment of missionary resources in Russia since the early 1990s, North American missions agencies have experienced difficulty in planting truly indigenous churches. Churches that become missional communities in their own right, spontaneously giving birth to new churches and ministries counting solely on their own resources and leadership, do not come easily in this part of the world.

Jim McNeil, former pastor from Nebraska, and his wife, Lois, were recruited by the Evangelical Free Church Mission (EFCM, recently renamed ReachGlobal) in the mid–1990s to take on the task of founding a pastoral training ministry in Russia. This ministry would become

1. Thanks go to Ben Beckner for providing this case study. For seven years beginning in 2001, Ben was visiting professor of mission and church planting at Trinity Bible College in Kursk, Russia. Since 1984, he has served with ReachGlobal, the international mission of the Evangelical Free Church of America, as church planter and missions trainer and consultant in French-speaking Europe.

the equipping center and seedbed for an indigenous church-planting movement.

How would EFCM go about founding a training center in Russia that would not only respond to the need of training Russian pastors, evangelists and church planters, but also help foment and sustain an *indigenous* church-planting *movement*?

THE CONTEXT

Before looking at the actual facilitated church-planting movement, some contextual background will be helpful in order to appreciate the experience and its lessons.

The National Context

The transition from Marxist–Leninist communism towards Western style capitalism—even with heavy doses of *perestroika* and *glasnost*—has happened very slowly and only partially in provincial Kursk, as is the case in Russia as a whole with the exception of the largest metropolitan areas. The moderately successful capitalistic ventures and corresponding structures must regrettably function within a criminal state—that is, a state that governs not by the rule of law, but through criminal structures, powers, and personalities.

There is as of yet no independent judiciary in Russia and, therefore, no functioning justice system, which is essential to democracy and Western-style capitalism. Consequently many Kremlin observers believe Russia to be one election away from dictatorship and one step away from economic collapse. Kursk reflects in every point the ambiguity of this post-ideological national reality and dilemma.

To a large degree, Russians and Russian culture and society have been functioning in default modes, falling back on pre-communist imperialism and Russian Orthodox religious hegemony, as well as communist era institutions. Such institutions would include, among others, the Federal Security Service (FSB), the heir to the infamous state security apparatus, the KGB.

The Russian Orthodox Church, in symbiosis with the State, is on the ascendancy and exerts increasing influence simultaneously on the Russian people and on the power structures of society. After seventy years of humiliating subjection to communism, the Orthodox Church seems to be yielding to its old demons, attempting to hold the Russian people hostage by claiming exclusive religious, social, and political privilege in Russia as well as in the former Soviet republics. There are a few enlightened Orthodox figures, but too few to counter the rise of new forms of passive and active persecution of all other Christian confessions and non-Christian religions.

Protestants in Russia, referred to generically as Baptists, Pentecostals, or Lutherans, were unfairly ridiculed, maligned, and subjected to moral, psychological, and physical persecution by the Orthodox Church under the Tsars, then by the communist ideologues under Marxist–Leninism, and now once again by the Orthodox Church. There were, however, several decades under communism when the Protestants were actually given freedom to function and grow—but only as a scourge to the Orthodox Church!

Under communism, evangelicals were divided into two factions, which have yet to be reconciled: those churches that accepted registration with the authorities, and those that did not. The "unregistered churches" accuse the "registered churches" of collaboration and compromise and have remained even more isolated from Russian society than the registered churches, resembling to some degree the fundamentalists in North America in their "second degree" separationism.

Evangelicals historically have been kept out of the inner circles of influence in Russian society, such as the university and municipal, regional, and national governments. The relative isolation and sectarianism of Protestant churches are, therefore, quite understandable. The issue for Russian evangelicals today is how to find their way out from under the burden of their history, to be reconciled among themselves, and to take advantage of their new freedoms (while they last). They must take this opportunity not only to forge a more informed and positive image of themselves in Russian society, but also to take their rightful place in Russian culture and life.

The first wave (some might prefer the term *onslaught!*) of North American missionary activity in post-communist Russia in the early nineties was the largely parachurch-sponsored "Co-mission" initiative, spearheaded by Campus Crusade for Christ. Co-mission sought to take advantage of the newly opened doors to the West in order to blitz Russia with evangelism, mostly of the North American variety, and hired Russian believers and nonbelievers as translators. This form of mission, initially quite successful in winning converts, was bound to be short-lived.

The second wave of missions to Russia, this time responding to the requests of Russian church leaders, has sought to provide training for Russian evangelical leaders in church and society, founding Christian universities, seminaries, and Bible schools as well as launching training programs of all sorts.

The Local Context

Founded 950 years ago, the large city of Kursk in western Russia is remembered for the largest tank battle in history, the Battle of Kursk, which took place in 1943 and which many historians believe to have been the turning point of World War II. Historically, beginning with the Tsars but also up into the present time, the city of Kursk has been for the west of Russia what Siberia has been for the east—that is, a place of banishment for both criminals and political dissidents. Its numerous prisons and penitentiaries have given Kursk the reputation of a penal colony in the minds of Russians. Many neighborhoods in the city bear the names of infamous criminals from Russian history.

This city of five hundred thousand inhabitants is the regional capital of the Kursk *oblast*, or state. Kursk, with over fifty thousand students, is a university center for the *oblast*, the home to four major universities, including a nationally known medical and health care university. Kursk is also home to numerous factories and several military bases. Kursk was until recently under local communist government.

Economic development in Kursk, like most Russian cities out of the Western eye, has been painfully slow. Seventy years under the "regime of the lie" not only bankrupted the municipal infrastructure and its institutions, but also seriously damaged morale and the culture as a whole. Following the crash of the Ruble in the mid-nineties, the Kursk economy as a whole came to a grinding halt.

When the first missionaries arrived in Kursk in the mid-nineties, it seemed to them to be a city that had lost its soul: social conditions and health care were in shambles; industry and agriculture at a standstill. Alcoholism, hopelessness, apathy, bitterness, and pessimism were rampant, and still are. Those who were able moved to Moscow or emigrated; they still do. Kursk, neglected by prosperous, modern Moscow, was starving for contact with the outside world.

Although EFCM personnel were largely unaware of it before moving there, these social and historical factors converged to make Kursk a favorable environment for a facilitative church-planting movement.

EFCM PARTNERS WITH
GRACE BAPTIST CHURCH IN KURSK

EFCM entered Russia with the vision of establishing a flagship theological seminary in Moscow. Its purposes would be to train leadership for the Russian evangelical movement as a whole and to serve as a springboard for launching an Evangelical Free Church denomination in Russia. A church in Pennsylvania pledged over a million dollars to fund the initiative, christened "Trinity Equipping Center" (TEC).

A significant handicap for EFCM was that it opened its work with no Russian-speaking missionaries or personnel with experience in a Slavic, majority Orthodox, former communistic country. Moscow proved to be especially costly and hostile for foreigners. The absence of legal protection for foreign renters forced EFCM personnel to make frequent and destabilizing moves. Several failed and costly attempts at negotiating the purchase of real estate for TEC in Moscow, which is largely ruled by underworld mafia, served as a sobering introduction for EFCM personnel to cross-cultural missions in Russia.

In 1997, a new and oppressive Freedom of Religion law was passed by the Russian State Duma (the house of Parliament) and enforced in Moscow. The law required that all pastoral training institutions be affiliated with a religious organization with a minimum of fifteen years of legal existence in Russia. This threw EFCM into a crisis, as EFCM had no sponsoring Russian entity that predated the fall of communism.

Vitaly Petrov, a Russian evangelical, doctoral student at Trinity Evangelical Divinity School, and friend of EFCM, suggested that EFCM seek a partnership with Grace Baptist Church in Kursk, his native city and congregation. Grace Baptist Church is the sole Protestant church in Kursk to have survived Tsarist rule, the Bolshevik Revolution, and the ensuing seventy years of communist rule.

Founded at the end of the nineteenth century, Grace is in many ways the conservative, traditional, somewhat reactionary "old lady" of the Baptist churches, as well as the seat of the Baptist bishopric for the *oblast*. Soon after the collapse of communism, and with the help of foreign generosity, mostly from Germany, Grace built a large, classically-styled church structure that seats approximately five hundred worshippers. Grace is filled to capacity on most Sunday mornings, and is used throughout the week as a gathering place for evangelicals.

In addition to satisfying the fifteen-year existence requirement, Grace had opened a one-year Bible institute—Kursk Bible Institute—which it launched with the help of funds and visiting pastors from Germany. It included a classroom building and guest house for visiting professors.

Despite many cultural and some theological discrepancies between EFCM, the German KBI, and Grace, EFCM leadership made the difficult decision of abandoning, at least temporarily, its vision for pastoral training in Moscow and entered into a partnership with Grace Baptist Church in Kursk. Some perceived Kursk as a non-strategic city located in the backwaters of southwestern Russia. The goal would be to add two more years of training to the KBI program, thus providing a full three-year Bible college curriculum.

Jim and Lois McNeill arrived in Russia following many years of fruitful local church ministry in the North American Midwest. Lois, an RN by training, had been heavily involved in youth evangelism and evangelism training in the churches that Jim served. Jim had completed a Doctor of Ministry. Language learning was difficult, yet effective use of translators and personal language tutoring allowed them to become functional in Russian language and culture. They and their EFCM colleagues chose to live indigenously, which in Kursk meant living in very modest circumstances.

Jim, a man of confidence who embodied holy living, a sanctified sense of humor, and Christian scholarship, demonstrated competency in tailoring theological education to fit the needs for church planting in Russia. Lois gave herself to ensuring that the practice and not just the theory of evangelism be made and kept central to the college experience. In the process, she pioneered methods of evangelism in Kursk, as well as inspired, trained, and deployed many evangelists.

But perhaps the most important contribution that Jim and Lois would make to the success of the church-planting movement in Kursk was providing entrepreneurial focus on a goal bigger than themselves, one to which God was clearly calling them, albeit against established wisdom. The McNeills embodied the guiding motivation of founders, which corporate lifecycles expert Ichak Adizes says must be transcendental and move beyond the narrow limits of immediate gains. Their self-sacrificial love of the students, unwavering commitment to the vision of launching a church-planting movement, and confidence in God's provision for the college, provided a living model for staff and student body to emulate in their church-planting activities. Their courage in difficult circumstances has motivated a generation of young Russian believers to live their faith courageously and publicly.

But other players and factors would be more or less crucial to the success of facilitating a church-planting movement in Kursk. The McNeills came to Russia with significant and generous funding from a mission-minded church in Pennsylvania, which provided complete stipends for all students and salaries for all staff, something that only exceptional missionary contexts would provide (and even then only temporarily). The McNeills had the benefit of the spiritual, material, and moral support structure and supply line of their missions agency and supporting churches.

Painfully aware of their deficiencies, Jim and Lois surrounded themselves with a strong team of Russians and a few key missionaries. Of particular importance are the Petrov brothers, Igor and Vitaly, born and raised in the home of a devout Russian pastor, a bold preacher and evangelist who was often jailed and persecuted for his beliefs.

Both Igor and Vitaly came to faith in Christ at an early age, are involved in pastoral and evangelistic ministry, and have added postgraduate theological degrees to their ministry skills and experience. Both Igor and Vitaly lend credibility for the college vis-à-vis Russian evangelicals and municipal authorities, provide leadership for the college, model Christian ministry for the students, and devote many hours to guiding students through their research projects as well as mentoring them in their local ministries.

Missionary colleague Kevin DeVera, who managed the Christian service placements of the students, built many bridges between the students and the new church plants, spending countless hours coaching students. Kevin recruited a team of students and then facilitated their planting of the Immanuel Church through intensive coaching over several years. From its inception, Immanuel has been team-led and co-pastored by college students and graduates.

Key to the success of the college in its training of church workers and leaders was the example of a well-led, interdependent, multinational, and multi-generational leadership team which modeled healthy team dynamics and attitudes that should be operative in the local church environment. The leadership team invested itself in many activities, rooted in their commonly-held values and mission to facilitate a church planting movement:

1. annually recruiting a new body of students of various ages and backgrounds, whose common denominator was the desire to discover and develop spiritual gifts to serve the advancement of the kingdom of God in the Russian-speaking world;

2. providing conscientious teaching, training, and pastoral care for the students;

3. putting students and graduates to work in the planting and building up of new churches in Kursk;

4. training and creatively deploying students in evangelism and social involvement with chemical dependants, cancer victims, and prisoners; and

5. targeting a significant unreached people group, the Romas, for evangelism and church planting—a ministry that was at first strongly resisted by national leaders.

REFLECTIONS

As I returned annually during seven years to Trinity Bible College in Kursk as visiting professor of mission and church planting, I had the opportunity of observing the evolution of the city on the one hand, and on the other, the growth of the churches. It became clear that the churches are developing what the city desperately needs: community built on truth and gospel. Another outside observer of TEC and the movement to which it has given birth summarizes the TEC experience as a divinely orchestrated coalescence:

> TEC's brief history is an amazing example of God coalescing gifted and blessed people from Russia and the USA to implement his intention to bless all peoples on earth with the blessings of his grace, redemption, and restoration. TEC combines the lives of third generation Russian Christian servant leaders, a pastor from Nebraska, a wealthy US church, a US mission organization, and a nation in crisis.

In the midst of all the ambiguity of what is post-ideological Kursk and Russia, there is a steadily growing body of Christian youth and young adults, a new phenomenon in a region where it was prohibited under communism to teach religious faith of any kind to young people under age eighteen. This Christian youth culture, which is hopeful, sophisticated, and forward-looking, is developing in the context of a number of young church plants and ministries. If Grace Baptist Church remains in many ways the stable "old lady" of the Baptist churches, then her daughters are dynamic and creative, conceived and led by the new post-communist generation of youthful believers.

Weightier and longer-term issues must be addressed in the coming years. What role could and should the body of Christ in Kursk play in relation to the renewal of culture? How could and should the body of Christ outside of Kursk responsibly aid and encourage the churches in Kursk to engage the culture further in ways that were proscribed for the better part of the twentieth century?

At the end of his two years of intensive ministry, Paul confidently affirmed to the Christians in Rome: "There is no more place for me to work in these regions"![2] Paul had been actively engaged in a first-century form of "multiple facilitative church planting," of which the hallmark was the teaching and training of disciples in a strategic urban center, and then sending them to outlying areas for gospel proclamation, disciple-making, and church planting. Paul's method met with astounding success, giving birth to a Spirit-empowered and gospel-centered church-planting movement that proliferated long after his departure.

Increasing pressure exerted by Russian authorities on foreign missions agencies and NGOs has resulted in the recent departure of all missionaries from Kursk, as well as the closing down of the residential program of the college. One must not underestimate, however, the resilience and resourcefulness of Russian evangelicals, nor the power of the Word sown in human hearts!

In the absence of missionaries and with some continued subsidy, the Petrov brothers and their team in Kursk are remaking the college "in their own image," adapting its ministry to the new realities. The entire curriculum has been video-recorded and put on DVD, and augmented by classes from Trinity Evangelical Divinity School. The curriculum is being distributed throughout the Russian-speaking world, including ex-

2. Rom 15:23

patriate populations in the former Soviet Asian republics, Europe, North America, Israel, and China

I close with a question: Is it not true in the history of the church that every time she takes the pains to sow, plant, and reproduce, she rediscovers the fullness of her gospel, re-encounters the world for whom Christ died, and renews and rejuvenates herself?

A BRIEF CHRONOLOGY OF THE TBC CHURCH PLANTING MOVEMENT

Sept., 1998	EFCM enters into a partnership with Grace Baptist Church, opening the College with thirteen students
1998	The Light of the Gospel Church was half planted when the college opened. Sergey Popov, one of the first graduates, becomes pastor in April 1999, and has since utilized, supervised, and mentored many other College students, as have virtually all the pastors and church plants in Kursk.
1999	The Revival Church is launched in the Northwest region of Kursk where eighty thousand people live without a single church. Valerie Guterov, a graduate of the College, is church-planting pastor.
1999	St. Peter's Evangelical Christian Church is launched as an initiative of the Grace mother church. Yuri Momentov, an elder from Grace, serves as church-planting pastor.
2000	A fourth church plant, the New Testament Church, starts in the northeast of Kursk, a region with a population of fifty-five thousand and no evangelical church. Andre Zachenkov, also a graduate of the College, is church-planting pastor.

2001   EFCM, in agreement with Grace, begins a fifth church plant, the Immanuel Church, located near the city center and the universities, targeting the student population. Kevin DeVera, staff member of the college, is the facilitating church-planting pastor. Before Kevin's departure in 2007, a College student and eventual graduate becomes pastor.

2003   The sixth church plant among the deaf emerges from within the Grace church, where there has been a ministry to the deaf for a number of years.

2004/2005   Two church plants reaching the Gypsy population emerge. One is led by a team of graduates from the College and facilitated by Lois McNeill—who trains evangelists at the College—in a village twenty miles west of Kursk. The second Gypsy plant is launched by a Gypsy student at the college, a deacon in a Gypsy church in Ukraine who found members of his tribe living in Kursk.

Case Study 12

Biblical Leadership Training Coalition in the Former USSR[1]

THE WHEELS TOUCHED DOWN on the tarmac of the runway in Manila, and the plane came to a stop. As we descended the stairs and took our first steps on Philippine soil, the heat and humidity quickly overwhelmed us. My wife, Diane, our daughter Joy, and I had moved halfway around the world to reach unreached peoples, to plant and establish churches where there were none. Our hearts were bursting with zeal and excitement.

We had not been in the country ten minutes before I made my first cultural faux pas, shaming a poor Filipino woman. It would be the first of hundreds, perhaps thousands, to come during our fourteen years of ministry in these islands.

LEARNING BY DEFAULT

The next years were filled with extremely long, hot days spent learning two languages, continually wrestling with the task of trying to explain the deepest eternal truths with a kindergarten vocabulary. With a growing understanding of the language and culture, I set out to share the gospel with the lost world around me, only to discover that no one was really interested in what I had to say. Thus I learned my first lesson in evangelism: people don't care how much you know until they know how much you care.

1. Thanks for this case study go to my long-time friend Bryan Thomas (holisticlife-management@gmail.com). Bryan served with his wife, Diane, as a missionary for 28 years, first in the Philippines and then in Russia, Georgia, and Azerbaijan, planting churches, training nationals as church planters, and forming and leading the Biblical Leadership Training Coalition (BLTC). Presently he resides with his wife and children and grandchildren in Nashville, TN, where he operates his consulting firm, L–Evate, which specializes in organizational development and executive coaching. He also works in Northeast Planning Corporation as a financial advisor.

So my wife and I began to spend time developing friendships with those around us. In this process, we began to find that Filipino friendship was costly in terms of time and real commitment.

As our friendships began to deepen, these dear people whom we now loved began to open their hearts and homes for us to hold a Bible study. The study group grew as family members and friends were invited. And a growing number trusted Christ as their Savior. By the end of the first year we had twenty-five believers meeting together.

It was then that I realized that we had a church, and I wasn't quite sure what to do to take them to the next level. Even though I had been taught the phases of church planting, I had never experienced it. I wished I had someone to mentor me through this growth process.

Diane and I quickly learned that church planting and discipleship were very messy endeavors. There was open conflict between believers and families. Grudges, schisms, and gossip raised their ugly heads. Couples fought and needed counseling. Young unmarried girls found themselves pregnant. Believers struggled with addictions and other sins. Some lost their jobs or were too poor to support their families. All needed help and teaching.

In addition to all of these issues, as we walked through their lifecycle with them—birth, schooling, marriage, and death—we were confronted with their worldview and the subtleties of syncretism. Their deeply-held spiritual and animist cultural values and beliefs now mingled with their new-found faith.

We came to feel the cry of Paul's heart in Galatians 4:19: "My dear children, for whom I am again in the pains of childbirth until Christ is formed in you." It was becoming clear that this was going to be a long, complex, and sometimes painful road. We feared that this child could end up being severely handicapped or even die in the birthing process!

As we fellowshipped with other missionaries around the country, it became clear that they were experiencing the same types of struggles in their church plants. We were all foreigners, as well as amateurs, attempting a colossal task. We were desperately in need of ongoing training and coaching.

These struggles led me to look deeper into the life of Christ and at how he had trained his disciples. It became clear to me that Jesus lived three years with his disciples, pouring his life into them. He not only taught them how to live; he also showed them how to do it, modeling it for them.

I also studied the apostle Paul's method of church planting and discipleship. I saw in Acts 19 that Paul evangelized for three months and then discipled his believers for almost three years. The result of this commitment was dramatic multiplication of believers and churches throughout Asia Minor. Acts 10 became my favorite picture of the church-planting process from beginning to end. In this passage, during this three-year period, the believers were able to see first hand Paul's love, compassion, devotion, passion, diligence, integrity, and commitment both to God and to them. As Paul committed the church in Ephesus to the leaders he had developed there, he challenged them never to lose sight of the intrinsic value of every individual for whom Christ had given his life. He taught them day and night with tears. He showed them how to live, not only ministering but also working alongside them and sharing what he earned with them.

The depth of love and relationship between Paul and the believers struck me. I came to understand that in church planting, it was more important to focus on the *people* than on the *program*. Love and discipleship was spelled T–I–M–E. Just as Jesus and Paul walked with and faced daily issues of life with their disciples, I would commit to do the same to help bring these believers to maturity. There were no shortcuts.

As the church began to grow, I discerned that I needed to spend more of my time on the emerging leaders because the life of the church would be entrusted to them. Since Jesus taught and modeled servant leadership, I looked for those who had a servant's heart.

I took the leaders with me out to other villages and tribal areas to show them how to evangelize and teach others and then coached them through the process themselves in new church plants. As my wife and I watched these believers and churches grow, we marveled at the power of the Word of God and the Spirit of God to change lives.

At this point in the story, it became painfully evident to me that God was just as interested in building me as he was in building his church through me. I worked very consciously to plant a church that would include lower to upper classes. The mother church in Butuan City had now ordained five elders. It was self-supporting and was planting six daughter churches in the surrounding villages. This ministry became totally life consuming for me.

God in his sovereignty allowed our city to be taken over by rebels. The fall-out from the short war that followed resulted in about 40 percent of the church members (mainly upper class) leaving the city to move to safer cities or to move abroad. This deeply impacted the self-governing, self-supporting, and self-propagating capabilities of the church.

I soon found myself lying in a hospital bed with a stomach full of ulcers and a heart full of anger towards God for allowing "my church" to be destroyed. As I wrestled with God, he made it very clear to me from Matthew 16:19 that it was *his* church and *he* would be the one to build it!

I vowed to keep God always as my vision and never again to allow the ministry to take first place in my heart. I shared these struggles openly with the remaining leaders, and we together began the church rebuilding process, starting each day with two hours of prayer at dawn. We sought God and his heart, desiring to allow him to build the church as he saw fit. It was a very freeing and joyful experience.

In the past, I had taught and mentored the leaders on how to evangelize, disciple, preach and teach, do visitation, lead worship, and develop other ministries in the church. I focused on *doing*. Now, my own personal growth process prompted me to focus more on the *being* aspect of leadership. In searching through the scripture, I discovered over one hundred characteristics that should be in the life of a leader. I developed lessons to teach these characteristics with questions for the leaders to use to evaluate themselves in each of these areas.

The more I worked with the leaders, the more I understood that developing godly leadership was the most challenging and time-consuming aspect of establishing a church. I also discovered that it was the pivotal issue in church planting. If the church has effective leaders, the rest will follow. Without effective leaders, there is no one to follow.

The joy I experienced in seeing some strong leaders begin to be raised up in the church was short lived when these fellows could not get along with one another. Each had his own idea of where the church should go and how to get there. Teamwork and unity became an ellusive dream.

A closer look at the Gospels and Acts revealed that this trouble was par for the course. Godliness, sanctification, and character are chiseled out in the matrix of relationships and life circumstances.

TRAINING BY DESIGN

Throughout the first nine years of ministry on the island of Mindanao, I prayed for missionaries to come to reach the forty-five unreached people groups there. Few came and the attrition rate was very, very high. Gradually, God opened my eyes to see that he had already answered my prayers and that the laborers were to be raised up from the churches we had planted. My limited American worldview had kept me from seeing the answer right under my nose.

I shared this vision with the leaders of our church, and in a short time, there were a dozen young people committed to go to the unreached. I now was faced with the daunting task of training them as cross-cultural church planters.

I set about designing a training program and curriculum for these young people, fully cognizant of the inadequacies in the way I had conducted training. Although I had been taught well in a classroom setting, like most Americans, I had not had the opportunity to apply what I had learned about ministry and church planting with ongoing mentoring and coaching. Instead, like most missionaries, I had to plant a church without experience, in a difficult language and culture, with the book knowledge I had acquired, and with the power of the Holy Spirit. It just seemed to me that there must be a better training model.

With this in mind, I set up a teaching schedule that incorporated three days of in-class learning and three days of living and ministering in the villages, giving them the opportunity to apply what they had learned with real people. The leaders and I would travel around with them to these areas in order to mentor them through the process of church planting. Although this approach was still in a primitive stage, during the three years of training, our students were able to minister through the four stages of church planting found in Tom Steffen's *Passing the Baton: Church Planting That Empowers.*

During this three-year process, the students also spent six weeks each summer living in the tribe where they would eventually work, learning language and culture to help prepare them for their cross-cultural ministry. This time in the village also afforded them an opportunity to begin to get to know the principal gatekeepers in the area who would sponsor them to live there.

While the students were finishing up their last summer session in the tribe, they received copies of the New Testament translated into the

Sindangon Subanon language by our good friends with Wycliffe, Bob and Felicia Brichoux.

After graduating the first group of students and seeing them settled into their church-planting locations, we were forced to return to America for an extended two-year medical furlough due to my wife's serious health problems. At the end of this period, our agency asked us to help to pioneer their work in the newly opened former Soviet Union by applying the training principles we had developed in the Philippines.

For the duration of our first year of survival in Siberia, enduring the freezing weather and the rigors of learning a new language and culture, I experienced a deep sense of regret about not continuing the development of the model of training and what I had set out to do in the Philippines. God, however, made it clear that he was continuing his work there.

Our hearts were filled with joy to receive a letter with the picture of thirty new Sindangon Suban-on believers, the first church in the history of this tribe. Our graduates had developed chronological Bible teaching lessons from creation to Christ in the Suban-on language as we had done in Cebuano, and they had trained them with the training we had received from New Tribes Mission. Throughout the years, these church planters have had a focus on discipleship and leadership development that has resulted in the multiplication of churches and leaders in this tribal group.

After Diane and I spent the initial years in Russia learning the language and culture and developing a Russian language school for missionaries, I began to travel around the former Soviet Union to assess the needs, build relationships, and teach introductory seminars about church planting. I was overwhelmed by the staggering harsh reality that less than one half of one percent of the population of the country comprised the evangelical church in Russia.

Approximately 80 percent of the evangelical church was made up of women and elderly people, and many churches did not have pastors. The majority of the pastors had little theological training. The churches were very divided, and there was much legalism, little emphasis on grace, some syncretism, and suffering because of persecution or pressure from the government.

After living in Siberia for two years and serving with the Russian Baptist Church, we moved to Krasnodar, a strategic city to the Northern

Caucasus which is home of fifty different language groups, most without the scriptures in their languages or churches.

God provided me with a wonderful opportunity of partnering with Peter Dyneka's Russian Ministries to teach Russian church leaders. This afforded me additional exposure to the inner workings of the Russian churches that would equip me to better serve them in the future.

It soon became evident to me that the church-planting context in Russia varied greatly from that in the Philippines. I felt it was necessary for us to plant a church in Russia in order for me to be able to train Russians effectively in how to plant churches within their own culture.

Therefore, my wife and I partnered with another NTM couple, Klaus and Franzi Libuda, along with Russians Volodya and Lena Rajabov, and Vadim and Lilli Strong to plant a church in the Slavyanskaya Region of Krasnodar in 1997. The Church of the Open Door continues to grow under national leadership with cross-cultural church-planting out-reaches in the local area and the Muslim region of Daghestan bordering Chechnya.

Throughout our first five years of ministry in the former Soviet Union, we were repeatedly confronted with two pressing issues that burdened my soul. First and foremost, churches from the Arctic Region, Western and Central Russia, and the Caucasus regions, as well as the countries of Georgia, Azerbaijan, Ukraine, and Belarus, were pleading for us to train their people. Secondly, since the fall of Communism was relatively recent, many agencies had rushed into the country without long-term strategies for reaching the country. Foreign missionaries struggled greatly to master the Russian language and culture and to un-derstand the underlying cultural values and challenges of teaching the Word and planting churches in the Russian context.

THE GLORIOUS VISION

After much prayer and communication with some of these missions, we formed a Biblical Leadership Training Coalition (BLTC) with East West Ministries International (EWMI), New Tribes Mission (NTM), Peter Dyneka's Russian Ministries, TEAM, World Venture, Elmbrook Church (Wisconsin), and others. The vision of this organization was to train national leaders who would spearhead grace-oriented church-planting movements throughout the former Soviet Union.

We recruited potential leaders from western Russia (Bryansk), the Arctic (Salexard), the Caucasus region (Nalchik), Daghestan, and the country of Georgia. Later we began centers in Central Russia (Saratov) and Azerbaijan. Our objective was to give them a balanced training approach of knowing, being, and doing—or head, heart, and hands.

We challenged churches in the United States to adopt these strategic centers and partner with them. These churches not only provided financial support and prayer; they also sent teams from their churches to assist with building projects, Business as Mission, and special training needs.

Lessons learned from the Philippine training experience led me to develop the following strategy.

- The student body was divided into four church-planting teams with staff mentors over each team.

- Students would be taught in the classroom several hours per day.

- Students would meet daily in their groups to interact, to discuss how to apply these lessons, and to give feedback.

- Throughout the week, in afternoons and evenings, the students would be active in beginning church plants in their regions along with their teachers and mentors.

- The program would last for three years.

- Each quarter, the students would be sent back to their own regions to help teach extension seminars to trainees there. The goal was to produce a domino effect of multiplication: we would train in Krasnodar; in turn they would train those in their own regions; and their trainees would plant churches in those regions.

- After three years, the Krasnodar trainees would return to their regions to oversee the regional centers that had been established and would coordinate the church-planting movements in these regions.

Throughout the development of the BLTC, it really was not my desire to develop a residential training program. I knew it would be very expensive, and I did not want to pull the trainees from their local ministry and environment. However, it seemed clear that the best method for training leaders was Jesus's model, that of *tabernacling,* or living with the potential trainees in order to model life and mentor them in life and ministry.

It would have been ideal to send out church-planting mentors to each of these areas, but human resources were very limited and logistics more than difficult. The next best solution seemed to be the gathering of available church-planting mentors from the various missions into one location, and gathering the first wave of potential leaders into one location to begin the process.

THE MESSY REALITY

We began this glorious endeavor with the highest of hopes and dreams, but the often messy reality seemed to accost us at every turn. For starters, we had no building, no facility, no curriculum (in the Russian language), no finances for our budget. But we did have a president (yours truly) with the gift of faith who was willing to rush in where angels fear to tread!

The missions which formed the coalition were eager to allocate personnel to the BLTC but for the most part were unable to provide financial backing due to the needs of their own organizations. Financial backing was desperately needed since the former Soviet Union was close to bankrupt, the believers were living below the poverty level, and their churches were struggling to survive financially. Funds were needed for travel and student housing, translation of materials, the facility, and so forth. So, as the president, my task was to raise funds yearly for the BLTC budget—work which would require extensive travel and time away from home.

It soon became evident that although we had gathered some of the most experienced foreigners in Russia, many of the missionaries who were to be the church-planting mentors had insufficient church-planting experience. They were also unable to teach well the deep concepts in the lessons in the Russian language as they were still grappling to understand the Russian culture.

It had only been a short time since the Iron Curtain had fallen, so this was new territory for agencies. We were all starting from scratch. It was very difficult and very intense for all on many levels. I found that I had to expend more and more time and energy to keep up communication and work for unity with the mission coalition because each mission had its own ministry philosophy and expectations.

As if this was not enough pressure, we experienced opposition from the Orthodox churches in our areas and from the Russian government. Our visas were in constant jeopardy, and we had to find new ways to "legally" stay in the country when "religious visas" were outlawed.

Although we had taught seminars and done what pre-screening was possible with our trainees, we were beginning to see that they were much less prepared than we had anticipated for what we were attempting. Church planting is an extremely difficult work of relating with people, persuading, evangelizing, preaching, teaching, strategizing, planning, discipling, counseling, administrating, team building, leadership development, and ministering to people of all ages, with all of their baggage, needs, and expectations. Therefore, this training was intense, and they were to be involved in ministry while they were still struggling with knowing and understanding themselves and their God.

Years of communism had caused great damage to the Russian psyche, including the family structure and personal relationships. Many had not experienced a father's love or healthy family relationship.

Under communism it was dangerous and against the law to express an opposing opinion. The state made all decisions for life and work. These cultural values had become deeply imbedded in their hearts, so it was difficult for them to express how they felt or make plans and decisions for themselves. We were teaching them how to become leaders of others when they still needed to learn first how to lead themselves and their families.

Under communism it was common for homes and telephones to be bugged. Neighbors and even family members were taught to spy on and monitor one another. This led to a deep lack of trust, a high level of suspicion, and a wariness and watchfulness at an unconscious level. Vulnerability or openness was considered a great weakness and dangerous. Most had learned to bury their feelings deeply, so getting them to open their hearts and lives seemed like the impossible dream.

At the BLTC, we focused on teamwork and character development in a matrix of relationships, deep teaching, and application of the Word of God and church planting with mentors. During the first year, we taught them the Bible chronologically from Genesis through Christ, followed by the Epistles.

We taught them principles and practices of discipleship and the various stages of church planting. We helped them to work through much conflict in their team building relationships, and we sent them out to begin the first stages of church planting. For pre-evangelism, we encouraged them to begin to develop friendships with their neighbors.

As you may imagine, in some ways they were overwhelmed with the struggle to develop friendships with other trainees—much less to befriend suspicious strangers who were unbelievers. They did try to invite their neighbors into their homes, but they met with much rejection because it takes years to trust someone enough to develop a friendship in the Russian culture. We were beginning to fall behind in our goals and expectations, and I was feeling the pressure. It was over a year before we had one small home group started.

Due to these problems and the other noticeable character issues, we felt we needed to focus more on sanctification and the personal growth process. We were finding that many of the students had experienced deep and long-term emotional traumas that kept them closed and prevented them from making good progress in their growth and relationships.

We called in some counseling help, focused on healing emotional wounds, and tried to help them to deal with their marriage relationship problems and child-rearing issues. Principles of stewardship and servant leadership were like concepts from another planet or culture—so much so that in some cases, it was necessary to adopt new vocabulary words to express these new values.

As a result of the somewhat slow progress, we felt it would be better to extend the training to five years rather than three. They would leave Krasnodar at the original three-year mark, but we would continue to mentor them for two more years as they continued ministry in their regional centers. This would require more traveling and stress but was deemed necessary for the success of the training program and the growth process in their lives and ministries.

At the five-year mark, we needed much time to regroup and rewrite curriculum. The same was true for strategy and processes. Facilities in both Krasnodar and the regional centers required expansion.

We lost some of our BLTC staff due to the intense stress and pressure they had experienced during the three- to five-year period. We recruited new staff members, and I tried to focus on developing a national leadership team of mostly BLTC graduates to lead the BLTC. My intentions were good, but I was stretched too thin. I had neither enough time nor energy to accomplish all of my "good and worthy" goals. Of course, that didn't stop me from trying!

The BLTC ministry had achieved the following results by the beginning of 2006:

- a church-planting movement across the country of Georgia which encompassed twenty groups and church plants;

- a church-planting movement in the Arctic Region with twenty church plants mostly focused within the Nentsi and Khanti people groups;

- two church plants in Daghestan;

- an expanded training center in Nalchik focused on reaching eight Causcasus people groups;

- a new training initiative in Saratov (Central Russia);

- three church plants in Krasnodar;

- a new training initiative in Astrakhan (north of the Caspian Sea); and

- a new training initiative and church-planting partnership in Azerbaijan, reaching even into Iran.

The BLTC graduates who were now out in the fields were experiencing many difficulties in their ministries. They needed advice, encouragement, conflict resolution, and help with the many issues of church planting and leadership development.

I became even more stretched as I attempted to oversee the ten different regions of training that required almost constant travel and as I worked to develop the national team to lead the BLTC. I also flew over 150,000 miles per year in order to fundraise for these steadily growing endeavors and to meet with (and try to please) the board of the BLTC, the partnering churches, and the missions.

I was feeling overwhelmed with the enormity of the task, and it became obvious that I had tried to build too much too quickly. This caused much stress for my family, especially my wife, and for all the staff and board involved in the BLTC. I had been riding the crest of the wave, and in a short time I found myself being churned up in the vortex and then spit out on the shore, desperately in need of resuscitation. In this process, I had become too much of the BLTC and the BLTC had become too much of me. God did not want me to go on in this way.

In all the lessons I had endeavored to pass on to the trainees at the BLTC, the most important to me was that God had created us for himself, and more than anything else, he desired our hearts. I taught them that God would spare no expense to get every part of our hearts. Unfortunately, in the end, I became one of the most vivid examples of this very important truth. I personally imploded, failed greatly, and crashed and burned both spiritually and emotionally.

One of our deeply-held values at BLTC was the reality of the grace of God in contrast to the law of legalism. We had endeavored to inculcate this knowledge and the practice of God's grace into the life of our trainees. We hoped that this would result in the multiplication of the needed grace-oriented churches being planted in and through their ministries.

Back in America, as I struggled to pick up the pieces of my life and reconcile with my family, I received word from many BLTC grads. This was an amazing example to me as well as an outpouring of God's grace and love. They expressed a desire for me to come and be restored among them. They extended their forgiveness!

I smiled at the dawning reality that they had understood the message of God's grace better than I had. I bowed my head in humble thankfulness to God that he had accomplished this in their lives. All was certainly not lost due to God's amazing grace.

EPILOGUE

As a result of the loss of staff and revenue, the BLTC is evolving into a more decentralized training effort out in the regional centers, while the Krasnodar center serves as a resource hub for the regional center and other churches throughout Russia. This actually was our original intention, and God has ways of using even our failures for his purposes. I am learning that he is greater than all our sin and inadequacies. He is God and he will build his church in spite of us. EWMI spearheads this partnership with Chuck Schwartz as the BLTC president.

Case Study 13

Business as Mission in Russia[1]

WHAT A WASTE OF time, I thought! Herding cattle for Jesus? How could these people possibly think that they were missionaries? They were spending all of their time feeding cows, doing accounting work, and teaching farming techniques!

It was 1979, and my husband and I were embarking on a career as full-time missionaries after spending three and one-half years in training with New Tribes Mission (NTM). I was totally convinced that social work or business involvement of any type was not really missionary work. I believed that authentic missionaries ministered by teaching and living the Word of God. They did pre-evangelism and evangelism and church planting. They learned the language, and then they translated the Word of God into tribal languages.

I wanted to live the biblical injunction, "Do the work of him who sent me. Night is coming!"[2] There was not a moment to spare, no minutes to waste on peripheral doings—I wanted to be about God's work. I was convinced this was closest to his heart. Of course, I felt that these were the *proper* biblical responses to Jesus' call that we go into the world and make disciples of all nations.

---

1. Thanks for this case study go to my longtime friend Diane Thomas, DThomas@ eastwest.org. Diane served with her husband as an overseas missionary for twenty-eight years. She is now a part-time missionary with EWMI, where she serves as a language/ culture consultant and helps with women's ministry and business with the Business as Missions arm of EWMI. She is also an English proficiency tester with the American Council for the Teaching of Foreign Languages, and the owner and designer of www. bybella.com, a small business that sells handcrafted jewelry made by women who are being empowered in Russia, Georgia, and the Philippines. She is also a wife, mother, and grandmother of four.

2. John 9:4

TO THE PHILIPPINES

Obviously, I was just a young know-it-all missionary who needed to learn many lessons, be taken down a few notches, and walk through some real mission experiences to really begin to know anything at all!

So, that is what my husband, Bryan, and I did. We went to the Philippines in January of 1979, studied Tagalog, the national language, and then the Cebuano language of Mindanao, and promptly began the task of planting a church in Mindanao.

Since Bryan and I were both linguists, we also became involved in writing a language course to help other missionaries learn the Cebuano language. We felt strongly that a deep knowledge of the language and culture were essential to effective ministry, and we continue to hold that view until today.

Bryan turned this job of administrating and running the language school over to me as he focused on church planting. The language school became a little business to administrate as I hired and trained Filipino teachers and charged students for our services. The teachers were able to make a good salary.

As I worked with the Filipino teachers daily and we became close friends, God gave me an invaluable window into the Filipino culture. I learned the culture of the Filipino working world as we worked together and also about how to manage and lead the "Filipino" way as I struggled to train and motivate the teachers and to keep everything running smoothly.

I found that their values and motivation for work and the working environment were very, very different from my own American cultural values. Unbeknownst to me, I was getting an "insider" view as we lived and worked together.

We were also thrilled to see the Word of God at work as Filipinos came to Christ and a little church soon formed. As the church grew, we were greatly hampered by the poverty of the new believers as they struggled to support themselves and their own missionary and church-planting efforts. They didn't have the personal resources that we in the West have, so even supporting their own pastor was difficult.

Most of the believers in our little congregation lived at poverty level and couldn't afford to send their children to school or buy them shoes, much less avail themselves of medical care for their families. The weekly church offerings were barely enough to pay for the rent of the building and the utilities, so supporting a pastor became a long-term goal.

Of course, we (missionaries) lived a lifestyle that was much more comfortable than theirs because of our support from the States. This in itself was extremely difficult for us, and we struggled with the contrast in our living styles and how to *help* the struggling church and the impoverished believers. Frankly, at times we just gave gifts of money and medicine and clothing to help people because we couldn't live with ourselves.

On the other hand, we were schooled in missionary training that a church must be self-governing, self-supporting, and self-propagating, and we were *religious* in this belief. We didn't want to create a dependence on us or funds from the West. We so wanted this to be a truly indigenous church.

We felt so strongly about this that we went so far as to reject the offer of a church in Texas to fund a church building for our struggling believers. We were honestly afraid of making them dependent, of being criticized by other missionaries and our mission organization, and we worried that this would keep the church from becoming self-supporting. We were convinced that we should just wait until the Filipino church could afford to buy property and build a building to meet in.

We also were locked into our American way of conducting church and missions to some extent. Our model avowed that the church would grow large enough to support the pastor or elders, and the missions program. What became obvious, however, is that none of our home US churches, some of which were quite large, were able to *completely* support their own missionaries.

Instead, all of the missionaries that we knew were being supported by a *group* of churches and personal supporters in order to facilitate their missionary work. The financial support was then funneled through a mission organization. This was a model that we could not replicate in one or two generations in the Philippines.

All we had to work with was a small church plant and a church full of believers who lived in poverty. Hmm. . . . Planting a successful church was more complex than we had imagined.

Add to the poverty issue the complexity of training and turning over the leadership to the local pastors, and you have just moved into the *for experts only* level in this game. We were the pioneers who had done the pre-evangelism, and evangelism, and church planting, and leadership development, and now our job was simply to pass this job over to the local leaders. It may sound easy and elemental, but in practice this proved to be one of the most difficult areas of our mission work.

Turning over a church required that we train and develop the upcoming leaders in all areas of pastoral and leadership development, and help them walk through the church-planting process themselves. We believed wholeheartedly in discipleship on a daily basis and practiced this life principle.

But it soon became evident that some formal training was needed in order for these leaders to know the Word in depth and to be fully trained in the knowledge and practice areas of leadership, training, missions, and church-planting principles. Add to that the need for these local leaders to command the same respect that we as the educated, wealthy, pioneer church planters had, and you are faced with a monumental task.

What sounded basic and elemental on paper became a huge and at times seemingly un-scalable mountain with rocky cliffs and deep dangerous precipices that can cause some ultimately to give up the fight. For that reason, I believe too many missionaries are unable to work themselves out of a job—a goal which we proclaim in our PowerPoint presentations to be our mission.

As time passed, my husband, Bryan, began to feel the need to do something to help the church and believers financially, or it seemed they would never become self-supporting. Having a heart of mercy and feeling the pressure to do something to help with the poverty of our believers, and in the interest of church growth, my husband became convinced that he should begin a social project. This would provide employment for the believers so that they could support themselves and their church.

Although I wanted the believers to be able to support themselves, I was still sure that becoming involved in social work was not the job of the missionary. Bryan and I disagreed on this point, and I knew that we were walking into something we knew absolutely nothing about.

Something significant to note is that most missionaries do not have business experience or business training. Bryan was a prime example of this—someone who had the spiritual gifts of mercy and faith and giving—bless his heart! Are you beginning to get the picture about our social project?

To Bryan's credit, he did the research and came up with what sounded like a fantastic eco-project plan that included raising chickens, goats, turkeys, tilapia fish in a fish pond, with snails and ducks to provide feed, as well as planting castor beans for castor oil. He consulted with the International Mission Board (IMB) mission and attended their seminars with some of the believers before beginning this endeavor.

The project included building some buildings, and since the project required investment funds, we contacted the church who had originally offered to build the church building and asked them if they would allow us to use the funds for the social project instead. The motto here is the Chinese proverb, "Give a man a fish and he will eat for a day; teach him how to fish and he will eat for a lifetime!" So much more cost effective!

The project was going to provide income-producing jobs for the believers so that they could support their own church and ministry! What could be better? This was the perfect plan! Didn't Jesus command us to help the poor?

The scriptures referring to the poor could not be ignored and all of a sudden, they became very real to us. Didn't one church help another in the Epistles? This is exactly what was happening: the Western church was helping the Eastern church. The Bible in action! We began to get excited about all of the possibilities.

So began the run of the two-year project that culminated in the death of a water buffalo who was worked to death, and the concurrent deaths of some 3000 chickens due to unrefrigerated vaccines in a tropical country, and a host of other problems. Following this debacle was the sale of my personal jewelry and the Thomas family eating fish and rice for months to pay back some of the outstanding debt. What had happened?

Somehow we were unable to get the believers to be on board and feel ownership of the project, and that led to the eventual failure of this work. In retrospect, I recall that the workers always referred to it as "Bryan's Project"! There seemed to be a lack of diligence in work and an attitude of *expectation and entitlement* from the workers.

These were the very same workers who always looked to *us* to fix any problem that came up. It seemed that our responsibility was to take care of them and to take care of the whole project and to pay them *well*. I surmise that they just wanted to be a part of the project and be told what to do but not take any personal responsibility. That would be too overwhelming, and they felt unqualified for that.

A photo of the head of the water buffalo is a perfect ending to the project story. Squatting next to the head is our neighbor's son and our two daughters. They had no idea about what was going on, and truthfully neither did we. It is late and they should have been in bed, but Mom and Dad and the project workers were in the house cutting up the meat and putting it in the large chest freezer on our porch. At least the meat from our exhausted, dead water buffalo could be salvaged and sold in the market the next morning to recoup some of its value.

My daughter recently came upon this photo in our family album and asked me what happened that night, as her children wanted to know about this grisly picture. I looked at the picture and thought, "Oh, how a picture speaks a thousand words!" My ensuing explanation made about as much sense to her as it did to me.

Following the failure of our social project, I was even more firmly convinced that missionaries had no business being about the world's work. We should focus on the ministry of the Word of God exclusively. However, I was very cognizant of the fact that God wanted us to care about the poor and help in some way, but it just wasn't clear how.

It tugged at my heart, and yet it was easiest to just give money away, to be quite honest. That involved the least amount of effort. So, I tried to find ways to help by giving and buying and providing for services for those whom I felt God was leading me to help. It was messy and difficult to know what to do and how to do it, but I asked God to give me wisdom.

Bryan felt terrible about the failure of the project and didn't understand why God didn't somehow bless it, since it was for his children. It was quite a life trauma for him, but he moved on and focused on another difficult issue. This essential and important task was training the believers as leaders and teachers. And so, he began a training school within our local church.

TO RUSSIA

After our fourteen years in the Philippines, God led us to begin a work in Russia. Bryan began the Biblical Leadership Training Center (BLTC, described in the preceding case study), a training center that grew into a group of centers where leaders were trained and churches were being planted.

I focused on starting and running a Russian language school that we opened so that missionaries from all agencies could come to us and study the difficult Russian language. I spent four years with my Russian teachers writing the Russian program that is still in use today in Krasnodar, Russia. Again I hired and trained teachers, and our teachers were able to earn a good salary and support themselves.

We were again working with people who were poor and on the average were receiving monthly salaries of $100–$300 monthly. Poverty was again an issue in all of the church plants.

We were now working with East West Ministries International (EWMI), an agency that was beginning to get involved in programs that started businesses to help address poverty. I was frankly hoping not to get involved in any of this because I saw it as a difficult issue that would ultimately end in failure.

My husband again became convinced that God wanted the BLTC training centers to help holistically by helping to provide businesses for the believers. He worked with some organizations that provided training and capital, and frankly, until this day, I have not seen much success with these ventures. The efforts continue but it is uncharted territory, pioneer work, and I believe that it is difficult for pastors to be involved in business unless they are naturally business minded.

Some of the leaders in our mission mentioned that I should possibly get involved with business as mission (BAM), since I had begun a thriving business that was making money! I was shocked to hear this, and they pointed out to me that the language school was making a profit.

I realized that in the twelve years of its existence, it had made a profit and provided jobs for seven teachers and the director, as well as some capital to purchase an office. I did have the spiritual gift of administration and was pretty good with numbers, but I was terrified of having anything to do with business—it was too much of a risk!

I have always enjoyed handcrafts and had begun designing some jewelry and phone accessories for my daughters and their friends as a hobby. A friend and mentor of mine, Jill Briscoe, international author and speaker and Executive Editor of the magazine *Just Between Us*, saw what I was doing with materials from the Philippines and Russia. She told me that I should use the jewelry as a business to help the Filipino and Russian women who were in ministry and struggling financially. She said this to me as we were teaching the Word together in Siberia.

I was shocked to hear that Jill was a natural entrepreneur as she told me about the businesses she had helped start in her ministry. In spite of my surprise, and while I was mulling over the possibilities, God opened a new door of thinking in my mind and heart. For you see, to me, Jill was the epitome of a *missionary* and *biblical* teacher, and here she was telling me to help start businesses for women! This was way outside of my comfort zone and beyond anything I could have imagined, yet God was urging me to do something.

It scared me to death, and yet I felt that God was in it and for it. In Luke I read how it was women who were helping to support Jesus and his disciples with profit from their businesses.

> After this, Jesus traveled about from one town and village to an-other, proclaiming the good news of the kingdom of God. The Twelve were with him, and also some women who had been cured of evil spirits and diseases: Mary (called Magdalene) from whom seven demons had come out; Joanna the wife of Cuza, the manager of Herod's household; Susanna; and many others. *These women were helping to support them out of their own means.* [3]

I thought about that woman above all others in Proverbs 31 who considers a field and buys it. I realized that in the real world, women have to work and support themselves and their families, *and* that they could also help to support God's ministry. These women whom I was training would never have the same opportunity to raise support as I did in order to facilitate fulltime ministry.

This was an American model based on a strong middle class that could not and perhaps should not be replicated throughout the world. The example in Luke was a workable biblical model, and admittedly it was something I had never really considered before. I prayed about the possibilities, consulted with mentors and friends, and began the process. It has not been easy, but it has been fulfilling.

To be honest, I still haven't jumped in with both feet. I have raised some funds from selling the jewelry I have made and have collected enough funds to provide the startup materials for twelve women in Russia, Georgia, and the Philippines to start out in the jewelry business. I didn't give them a loan but instead provided them with the necessary

3. Luke 8:1–3, italics added

instruments, materials, and training to make the jewelry and begin their businesses. I have trained them in how to do it and most have been able to supplement their incomes and help provide for the ministry through their efforts.

I have a webpage (www.bybella.com) and am a legal business. I am also working on a marketing plan—which, for me, is the most difficult area. Anyone who has built a business from scratch knows that it isn't easy and requires diligence, organization, perseverance, knowledge of business practices, marketing skills, and loads of sheer grit and the ability to take risks. That would be faith!

The truth is that most missionaries are not trained at all in business nor have the personality type or specific skills necessary. The challenges of mixing business with missions are gargantuan. I believe that we need training and practice and a whole new paradigm of what missions is all about if we intend to get involved in this way.

At the foundational level, it still takes knowledge of the language and culture to even attempt to be involved in BAM. Without a deep understanding of the host culture's worldview and values, including business and family values, BAM ventures will stand a high risk of failure. BAM is surely not something that we should enter into with glib confidence that we can succeed. I believe that what is needed is a different perspective and a change in our thinking, along with a reordering of priorities, mission practice, procedure, and protocol.

It would also be very helpful for American missionaries and missions to work harder to better understand their own cultural values and practices and how they impact mission work. I feel that too much of what passes as mission work is the translation of American books into another language and trying to implement American spiritual programs that work in America into another cultural system. I don't believe that this necessarily works, and I fear that it will be something that we do in BAM, as well.

I would like to sound the warning bell and strongly suggest that missionaries and the agencies they represent do more study and investigation of the host culture in all of our cross-cultural ministry ventures— whether it is church planting, training, or business. The results of these studies should highly impact the form and practice of our ministry or business reaching across the culture. It will take more time and resources and may slow down the work, but I believe it will prove to be well worth the effort in terms of results. By the way, Americans highly value *results!*

As I mentioned earlier regarding BAM, I haven't yet jumped in with both feet but am testing the water with my big toe. For launching the jewelry business with the twelve women in Russia, Georgia, and the Philippines so that they can support their ministries, my agency (EWMI) is standing behind me. Also supportive are the two directors of our fledgling endeavor, who are considering giving me a loan of $25,000–$50,000 to begin the jewelry business as a BAM project. Den Roosien, one of the directors, says this about BAM:

> EWMI is committed to the concept of BAM, which can have several labels, from Kingdom business to tentmaking to micro-lending. We are excited about BAM because it can accomplish so many of the purposes and opportunities of missions today, whether abroad or stateside. For me it is wrapped up in a "label" used in a 2007 article in *Christianity Today*, "The Mission of Business." Business can be the platform or vehicle for missionaries to be able to do ministry and to create opportunities for nationals to be self-supportive, thus reducing dependency on the West. After retiring from Microsoft in 2005 to become the COO of EWMI, I can't think of anything more important for me to be doing than to use the business experience and skills God allowed me to gain to move our mission and ministry in the direction of "The Mission of Business."

Gene Short adds:

> I retired from a career in management consulting where I was involved in performance improvement of companies in various industries. A friend suggested that I contact EWMI. Hearing my background, EWMI asked me to develop some sustainable platforms for both nationals and expats that supported church planting. I was excited because I had started businesses and had international business experience.
>
> In Central Asia we have helped over twenty nationals with financing, and starting and operating small businesses to sustain them and support their ministry activities. In the process, we have discovered the critical part that mentoring plays in the success of these entrepreneurs. Experienced businessmen can provide important counsel essential to self-sustainable church-planting efforts.

I truly am convinced at this point that BAM is valuable, necessary, and fulfilling as missionary and ministry work. Why do I not just jump in and move ahead with everyone's blessing? The honest truth is that I am absolutely terrified!

I know that it won't be easy and that over half of start-up businesses fail within the first year, even when people with business degrees begin them. I know that there are risks in any market and risks in investing in people who also may fail. As the Filipino translation of the American idiom states, "Been there, been that!"

I know that most businesses take at least three years to become profitable. I've heard that most founders of a new business work 60–80 hour weeks in their first years of business. I know that I will have to train women to manage their own businesses. Turning over the leadership and management of these businesses will be a huge endeavor.

I don't have any formal business training, although I do have a head for numbers and some natural business talent. I am scared to death that I will fail, the businesses will fail, and I won't be able to pay back the loans. This is another lifetime of work, and there is *high risk* involved. There are dangers and hazards I don't even know about yet, and I am a grandmother, for goodness sakes!

But even as I write this, I know that God is moving in my heart and that he cares about these women because he cares about the poor. I know that he urges us to give and to help and to care. I know that he gives us gifts that differ and that he wants us to step up in faith and allow him to do his good work through us. I know that He has given me gifts and resources and put me in special places for his unique purposes. I know that he is in the process of building a team that I can work with to forge ahead.

I know that BAM can have a huge impact on the world as lives are touched with the gospel, the principles and precepts of God's Word, and as believers live these out in the real business world. I know that God says that people must work in order to eat and that working with God's values is a part of mission. I believe that BAM is something that God wants me to be involved in, and I am cautiously moving ahead, holding tightly to his hand and seeking to follow his leading.

Case Study 14

Short-Term Missions in Peru[1]

M ISSIONARIES FROM THE CHRISTIAN and Missionary Alliance
(C&MA) founded The Church of the Constitutional Provide of
Callao, Peru, in 1981. This large church, made up of the lower and lower-
middle classes, was a direct result of the Lima Meets God movement
(*Lima al Encuentro con Dios*) that began in 1973.

Prior to the mid–1970s, Protestant churches in Lima were few,
small, and composed of lower class members who worshiped on side
streets in small, often rented, buildings. In 1973, through the guiding
efforts of the C&MA, the Protestants began a joint campaign that emphasized evangelism and discipleship. This was a first.

Some wider currents that made the campaign possible were the
generous philanthropy of R. G. LeTourneau, who had provided funds
to purchase highly visible properties in prominent parts of Lima and
to construct large church buildings, following the Catholic model.
Argentinean pastors with accents and identities that associated them
with the middle and upper classes were brought in. One result of the
Lima campaign was the founding of a number of large C&MA churches
meeting in central areas of the city. Size varied from several hundred
to several thousand. One of those churches was the C&MA Church of
Callao.

Prior to 1985, expatriate missionaries played a role in starting a little
over one third of the churches planted in Lima. In the last decade, they
helped found only 15 percent of the churches planted. Today, several
thousand Protestant churches pepper the landscape of Lima. Seminaries

1. The materials for the case study derive from three sources detailed in the bibliography: Robert J. Priest's "'Linking Social Capital' Through STM Partnerships"; Joaquin
Alegre Villón's "Short-Term Missions: Experiences and Perspectives from Callao, Peru";
and Grace Church's "2008 Peru Report."

and Bible Institutes provide theological education for several hundred Peruvian students in Lima. Around 75 percent of the congregants identify themselves as Pentecostals or neo-Pentecostals. Peru is the ninth most populous country in the world with around eight million people.

THE ROLE OF EXPATRIATES CHANGES FOREVER

This campaign, which resulted in a movement that is currently composed of some sixty churches, would change the role of expatriate missionaries forever in Lima. The C&MA career missionaries are now all gone, as the agency no longer considers Peru a mission field. Most other career missionaries have also left.

Those career missionaries who remain find themselves mostly involved in connecting Peruvian churches with short-term mission (STM) groups. These individuals play a major role in reconnecting the severed ties with resource-rich churches from around the world.

Every summer, short-termers from every denominational flavor and from numerous countries flood Lima's Jorge Chavez International Airport with small (five or six members) to large groups (several hundred). They come for multiple purposes: evangelism, cooking classes, orphanages, medical aid, tennis, English teaching, outreach to street children, surfing, business, providing wheelchairs for handicapped people, sky diving, soccer, and construction.

Almost 60 percent of the Protestant churches in Lima host these groups each year. And they deeply appreciate these collaborative efforts that provide not only a bridge for people of different ethnicities and nationalities, but also an opportunity to reconnect old relationships.

PARTNERSHIP FORGED

One of the partnerships that came out of the movement was between Grace Church of Eden Prairie, Minnesota, of Baptist origins, and the C&MA Church of Callao. Grace Church began sending small groups of STM with emphasis on construction in 1989. In more recent years, Grace Church, a megachurch, has sent larger groups focusing on evangelism and discipleship. Two examples follow.

In 2005, 198 short-termers set out for Peru to work side-by-side with five- to six-hundred Peruvians from the Church of Callao. Planning for the trip began a year in advance. Joaquin Villión, senior pastor of the

C&MA Church of Callao, made a trip to Grace Church in Minnesota to encourage participation in the partnership.

The Callao Church named the upcoming event the "Callao Festival 2005." This was to fit in with the church's larger goal to make disciples and found churches. They called this the "200/23 Vision"—two hundred thousand decisions of faith, and two hundred churches, in the next twenty years until the year 2023. Their motto was to populate the heavens and depopulate hell.

The Callao Church planned to accomplish this goal through various types of evangelism, including use of the arts: puppets, magic, dance, drama, and so forth. If everything went as they hoped, evangelism would take place in public institutions and places, such as prisons, jails, hospitals, orphanages, parks, plazas, and on the streets. Church workers would travel to rural communities as well as into the city. Compassion ministries would include a free medical campaign.

Who could make this all happen? Certainly not the Callao Church alone. This need for partnership was where Grace Church from Eden Prairie joined them.

A little background may help explain why the partnership made sense. First, if Peruvian evangelicals knock on Catholic doors, they are usually turned away due to pressure from the local priest. But if a gringo is standing by their side, they get not only an open door, but coffee and a hearing for the gospel as well.

Second, gringo participation opens doors to more than just homes. It also opens doors to high schools, universities, English language schools, hospitals, orphanages, and jails. Peruvians working with short-termers often refer to them as bait (*carnada*) or as hooks (*anzuelos*) to pull people in. Gringos open otherwise closed doors to Peruvian evangelicals.

Third, a natural outreach venue already existed. Peru celebrates its independence from Spain annually in July with several days of festivity, including a circus, culminating with the hoisting of the national flag and a speech by the President, given from the palace. Grace Church was excited to provide short-termers and supplies for the circus component of the event—clowns, puppeteers, jugglers, magicians—all infused with an evangelistic message shared through the Peruvian hosts.

The Callao Church knew that all kinds of preparations would have to be in place to handle the arrival, stay, and departure of 198 short-termers: lodging, meals, transportation, communication, interpreters (at least seventy of them), statisticians, security guards, materials for counseling and advertising, scheduling, training, and prayer. This preparation required a tremendous amount of time, personnel, and prayer.

Both churches committed to pray for the event. A prayer chain was established that ran twenty-four hours a day for thirty-three days.

The churches had to decide who would pay for what. They agreed that Grace Church would be responsible for their food and lodging, and that the Callao Church would cover lunch. As it turned out, Grace Church paid for lunch and gave a small donation to fund the interpreters, rental of communication equipment, and counseling and training materials. The Callao Church also picked up the cost for the reception, signs, training, cleaning, sound equipment for open-air events, and appreciation gifts for each Grace Church participant. The total cost of the trip for Grace Church came to four hundred thousand US dollars.

CALLAO FESTIVAL 2005

From Monday, July 25, through Friday, July 29, participants from both churches started around 9:00 a.m. each day and finished (although it rarely happened as planned) at 9:00 p.m. During the mornings, multiple teams saturated the city and outlying areas, visiting prisons and hospitals, and holding open-air evangelism forums in parks and plazas.

In the afternoons, special events were held featuring the Flom family, well-known stage magicians, and Justin Kelm, a World Champion unicyclist. Personal evangelism accompanied each event.

In the evenings, various events were offered at the Church of Callao, which seats eight hundred. These included the Jesus film, a concert for youth, and numerous presentations of the Grace Circus for different ages. After every presentation, more than two hundred people filled out decision cards for Christ.

Some mayors in the rural areas opened their towns to the teams, attended events, and were witnessed to by the Peruvian missionaries, who provided spiritual counsel. The mayors were particularly thankful for the medical services—dentists, medical doctors, eye doctors—which meant that a long trip to Lima for the same services was no longer necessary.

A Christian parade that made its way four blocks to downtown Callao climaxed the week's activities. The mayor attended, and the police provided an escort for the parade.

Children decorated their bikes. A trailer transported the musicians and singers who led in worship. Other cars followed. Flags of different nations were waved. Posters proclaiming Christ as the Good Shepherd, the Prince of Peace, and the Light of the World were carried. A visible and verbal proclamation greatly impacted the city that day. The final tally for the decisions of faith over the five days came to 5,294.

On Saturday the Church of Callao held a farewell party for the Grace Church participants. It had been a long, tiring week, and some of the Grace Church team members had become sick. But they had given it all they had. Each gringo received a silver pin with flags from each country and a piece of a gratitude cake, the idea for which had come from Leviticus 7:12.

The next afternoon six hundred new believers from the Festival met at the church. Another twenty-six made decisions for Christ that night.

Between three- to four-hundred of the young believers stayed with the church, resulting in the start of a fourth worship service. A month later, the Church of Callao rented a building and planted a daughter church for another group.

Several days after the festival, the mayor invited the church's leadership to participate in the celebration of Callao's anniversary. There he presented them with two medals of honor for their service to the city.

For many of those from Grace Church, this was their first visit to Peru. For some it was the first time to share their faith. As the week progressed, so did their ability and passion to share Christ. The participants were also exposed to the harsh realities of life and the deep spiritual hunger in Callao.

Working one week with people of a different culture and language also brought its challenges. When problems arose, both groups were committed to addressing them immediately, and they did. Grace Church expressed a desire to partner in this manner every three years, and many participants began looking forward to the Callao Festival of 2008.

CALLAO FESTIVAL 2008

In the summer of 2008, 268 short-termers from Grace Church, a few coming from other sister churches, again headed for Peru to work should-to-shoulder (*hombro a hombro*) with the Church of Callao. The teams that set out to declare and demonstrate the gospel included those focused on children's, women's, student, prayer, and evangelism ministries, as well as medical workers, unicyclists, circus staff, and adult choir members.

One member of a team, a grandmother over seventy years old, took her two granddaughters to experience evangelism in a poor country. As before, thirty-three days of prayer around the clock by both churches laid the foundation for the festival.

Once all the teams were on the ground, a large parade of over eight hundred people kicked off the Festival of Callao. Unicyclists, clowns, jugglers, illusionists, signers, soccer players, band members, choir members, flag bearers, dancers, evangelists, medical personnel, and bucket brigadiers paraded down the busiest streets of Callao, passing out invitations to the week's events.

During the week, teams of Americans and Peruvians fanned out across the city and rural areas to ten to fifteen different venues daily: city parks, hospitals, outpost clinics, prisons, orphanages, slums, and many other places. Soccer teams played, got beat, and witnessed using the evangelism bracelet. Evangelists preached. Cardiologists placed thirty-two pacemakers. Surgeons conducted over twenty surgeries, including plastic surgery to remove tumors. Several hundred people saw dentists. Some two hundred were fit with eyeglasses, and over two thousand received primary care in multiple outpost clinics. Peruvian medical students accompanied the medical team to gain invaluable experience and to serve as translators. And they heard the gospel, as did some other four thousand people.

Each evening brought the Callao and Grace teams together at the Coliseum, where pastor Dave Gibson of Grace Church preached to around four thousand each evening. Over twenty-four thousand heard the gospel during those evening programs. The Callao church leaders estimated that by the end of the week some fifty thousand people had heard the gospel, with 6,047 indicating first-time decisions for Christ. The bait and hooks had worked.

Lives of participants from Grace Church were also transformed. They learned to get out of their comfort zones, depend on him, experience God's great love for all peoples, and see the necessity to give more for missions. As one returnee confessed, "Prior to this trip my extent of supporting missions was giving financially every once in a while. I'm ashamed to say I just didn't care very much. You never would have heard the words come out of my mouth: 'I strongly desire to give my life to full-time mission work.'"[2]

Another said, "One [interpreter] pushed me to lead my first person to Christ, a woman named Luz. All I needed was that little push. From that point of the trip on, it was non-stop sharing the Gospel and leading people to Christ, to the point where we would simply run out of time at the venues. . . . I am now praying about pursuing full-time mission work for the rest of my life. I can now say, 'With all my heart, I desire to give my life to full-time mission work.'"[3]

Although one festival in Peru came to an end and short-termers returned home to the United States, the Holy Spirit has continued to work in the lives of those who went and those who are preparing for participation in the next festival.

2. Participants' comments available at Grace Church website, Missions and Outreach, Missions Trips, http://atgrace.com/uploads/missions/Peru_trip_report.pdf

3. Ibid.

Case Study 15

Youth English Camps in Ukraine[1]

FIFTY YOUTH WORKERS FILLED the small chapel. Mike and I listened to the words of the American speaker as our new Ukrainian friends listened intently to the translation: "Are you willing to stand in the gap? Are you willing to answer the call? David went forward with his little tools, and God used them to conquer a giant. Will you use your little tools in any way God chooses? Are you willing to give everything you are and have to Christ? Are you looking at sinners as God does? Does your heart burn with passion for their souls? Are you willing to stand in the gap for them?"

These were words from a veteran American youth pastor speaking to a group of youth leaders at a camp in Ukraine. Mike and I were sitting among them that day in April, 2001. We had come to Ukraine on a "vision trip" with Youth Ministry International, feeling certain that God was calling us to be full-time missionaries to this country and people. For fifteen years since his graduation from Bible college, Mike had been involved in youth ministry. For six of those years, he had been a chaplain, teacher, and development coordinator at a Christian boarding high school. The final six years had been spent building a youth ministry in our church in South Dakota. Now God was leading him to combine these experiences to develop a program for teaching youth ministry to youth leaders in Ukraine.

Mike had become acquainted with our mission, Youth Ministry International (YMI), through a click of the mouse on the internet when

1. Thanks go to Judy Manna for writing this case study. She and her husband, Mike, have served with Youth Ministry International in Kiev, Ukraine, for eight years. They have three biological children, Mandie, Luke, and Samantha, and have adopted their youngest daughter, Katya, from Ukraine. Judy is a homemaker and loves being a wife and mother. She also enjoys her support ministry of hosting Mike's students and different church activities in their home. She may be contacted at judy.manna@yahoo.com.

he was looking for a group who could facilitate an overseas missions trip for our youth group in South Dakota. We had a group of student leaders in our youth ministry who had proven themselves faithful in ministering to their own peers. Mike thought it would be good to expand their horizons and give them a cross-cultural ministry experience.

YMI agreed to take our group of eleven to Ukraine. Our young people combined with a Ukrainian youth group, planned a program, and together did street ministry in Sumy, Ukraine. Through songs and skits, they shared the gospel of Christ. While on that trip, Mike saw a need for the development of youth ministry in Ukraine. He felt compelled to come back. Since YMI had led our trip to Ukraine, Mike contacted them to ask if they could use us full-time in Ukraine. Randy Smith replied immediately. He had been praying for a full-time missionary for Ukraine—one who was a veteran youth pastor.

YMI is a small mission with a clear focus. Our mission was born as a result of our president, Randy Smith, an American Student Ministries pastor, taking his youth on overseas evangelistic missions trips, mainly to Mexico, Brazil, Kenya, and Ukraine. Randy and his teams challenged pastors and church leaders in these countries to train up and disciple a generation of youth in their churches who would be equipped to reach their peers for Christ. Randy and his colleagues began teaching youth ministry seminars in these countries, but the nationals wanted more. "You can't just teach us for two weeks and leave! We need more training."

Therefore, Randy Smith founded YMI to meet the need for formal theological training in youth ministry. He discovered that 97 percent of the world's formally trained youth pastors are ministering in the United States to only 3 percent of the world's youth population. Randy responded to the need. From the beginning, his goal was not to do youth ministry in these countries directly. Instead, he wanted to facilitate a youth ministry training movement. First, he wanted to deepen the level of training for youth workers around the world, i.e., to raise a youth worker to the level of a theologically trained youth pastor. His ultimate desire, however, was to give nationals an education that would enable them to train their own youth pastors. In other words, he wanted to "train the trainers" for youth ministry in countries around the world. When YMI is invited, they bring a four-year bachelor's or master's degree of youth ministry into a key seminary in that country.

FINDING GOD'S DIRECTION

This is how it came about that on April 6, 2001, Mike and I were sitting in that small chapel in central Ukraine among fifty youth workers, listening to the words, "Are you willing to stand in the gap? Are you willing to answer the call?" Throughout the days of the youth ministry conference, we'd had a chance to get to know some of the youth pastors. We were impressed. The sincerity of their love for Christ, their commitment to ministry, their love and joy deeply impacted us. But it also made us feel unworthy and created doubt about the validity of coming to Ukraine.

I wrote this entry in my journal,

> I can see the *why* behind the sincerity. If you choose full-time ministry in Ukraine, you choose a life of faith because there will probably be no financial compensation for your time. I had heard this before; now I am seeing it with my own eyes.
>
> The last couple days, I have been realizing the financial sacrifice these youth leaders have made just to be here at this conference. This is Mike's first time to teach with an interpreter. It is hard. He has to be so basic, and he does not get to flesh out what he is teaching and speak freely. They cannot discuss things and ask questions back and forth. Is his teaching relevant enough to warrant their sacrifice in being here at this conference?
>
> Look at these young men! Their faith is so strong! What do we have to offer them? What can we teach them? Did we really hear your call, Lord? We were so sure of Your leading. Did we make it all up? Do You still want us to come, God?

I continued writing in my journal:

> I don't know if I have what it takes to face needy people, needy youth pastors, hopelessness, homeless children, orphans. My heart is killing me, Lord! I don't want to face their pain. It is too hard! I find myself wishing that I could go back home and stick my head in the sand, forget about the needs, forget the faces of these youth pastors who are giving ALL to the Lord, forget their needs. . . .

Then it seemed as if God was speaking His reassurance to my heart: "Judy, for what purpose do you think I've given Mike his administrative gifts?" Suddenly, I got a clear picture of Mike's job as a youth pastor, of what he does all the time. He takes big tasks and breaks them down into doable pieces. He delegates many of these pieces to his students and includes them in ministry. Mike is an organizer.

Later, after a talk with Mike, I finished my journal entry with these words:

> Mike, too, was struggling with doubt. He brightened when I shared this bit of encouragement with him. This is a way he *knows* he can be used here. He *knows* he can help youth pastors organize themselves, delegate, and train leaders under themselves, so that they can be multiplied. We prayed together and renewed our commitment of moving to Ukraine to be used however God wants to use us.

FORMAL YOUTH MINISTRY TRAINING BEGINS IN KIEV

In June of 2002, Mike and I moved to Ukraine with our three school-aged children. We studied Russian for two years. During the first year of language school, Mike implemented the youth ministry major at Kiev Theological Seminary. Two translators began the work of translating into Russian the courses and reading material. The second year, Mike started teaching the courses with a translator.

The first year of students were residential and remained that way throughout their four years of study at the seminary. They lived at or traveled to the seminary every day for classes. Mike moved to a modular format when he saw the benefits of teaching young men and women who are already involved in various youth ministries. Since they cannot leave their ministries to go to seminary full-time, they come for two weeks of classes, four to six times a year.

The classes are not just theory to these students. They are highly relevant. The modular students, who come from all over Ukraine as well as a few from Belarus and Russia, soak up the teaching like sponges. They talk openly together, share their struggles, ideas, and victories. Together, they are like iron sharpening iron. The students take their theology, Bible, and other required courses from different professors at the seminary. Mike and an ABWE (Association of Baptists for World Evangelism) missionary, Mike Gustafson, teach only the youth ministry courses. After two weeks of classes, the students return home and are able immediately to put into practice the teaching they have gained. It is a wonderful system of education.

Mike has developed a close relationship with the church planting professor at the seminary, a missionary with IMB (International Mission Board) named Joel Ragains. Both Mike and Joel see the potential of Joel's church planting students pairing up with Mike's youth ministry students to plant churches. Mike and Joel now teach their introductory courses (Youth Ministry 101 and Church Planting 101) to each other's students to open their students' eyes to the potential of working together.

UNDERSTANDING THE CULTURE

Ukrainians are a highly superstitious people. For example, one must not whistle inside a building or shake hands with someone over the threshold of a door, as either will bring bad luck. It is a good idea to put out chocolate for the *domovoi* (house spirit), which every family has, because it is important to keep the spirit happy; otherwise, the house spirit may do nasty things like make pipes leak or cause things to break in the house. Most villages in Ukraine have a *babka*, a Ukrainian folk healer who concocts potions and chants to heal the sick. Ukraine is a country that is in tune with—yet needs direction in discerning—the spiritual world.

In an Orthodox church, one may enter, purchase a candle, and say a prayer to icons of Mary, Jesus, and many of the saints. Purchasing candles is considered giving in the Orthodox Church. Meditating and praying to icons is how one improves fellowship with Christ and the saints. If the church is in session, a priest chants and sings and waves incense. Religious ritual abounds: kissing of holy instruments, genuflecting, crossing oneself, and so forth. People may pay a fee to have the priest pray for them or to bless their food or their well. Many villages do not have a church, not even an Orthodox church. Even the poorest village homes, however, have an icon corner where pictures of Jesus, Mary, and one or more saints have been hung among decorative, handmade scarves. The main purpose of the icons is to ward off and protect the inhabitants of the home from evil spirits.

After three years of living in Ukraine, our family took in an eight-year-old girl from an orphanage. Katya was a social orphan, as are the majority of children who live in orphanages in Ukraine. These children find themselves in orphanages because of poverty, neglect, alcoholic parents, parents in prison, and so forth.

We received permission from her mother for Katya to live with us instead of in the orphanage, and we have maintained relationship with Katya's family. Not only has God given us a new daughter (the end of a five-year process culminated in her adoption on June 22, 2010), but he has also used contact with Katya's family to help us understand what life is like for many people who live in the villages of Ukraine.

Katya's father is presumed dead, and her mother is an alcoholic. Katya and each of her four older siblings have a different father. Katya can name off at least ten men with whom her mother has lived. Her older sister, who was actually a mother figure for Katya, has now begun repeating this cycle. She has lived with at least four men in the last five years. She is now twenty-two years old and has a child from her first "husband" to care for, but with very little opportunity for paid work in her village. While gardening provides a main source of food in a village, having a man is still a matter of survival for women with children.

Ukraine is a rapidly developing country with great diversity in financial status. In the cities, huge, glitzy malls, grocery stores, and building supply stores have gone up everywhere, yet an abundance of kiosks and outdoor markets remain. Jobs are available, with the average wage in Kiev being around three US dollars per hour. The upper class, 10 percent of the population, make 40 percent of the revenue. The streets are filled with sleek, shiny BMWs, Mercedes, and Audis.

In the villages, however, it is a very different story. With limited opportunity to secure earned income, poverty is not uncommon. Horse-drawn carts, hand-drawn wells, and outhouses are considered normal. While most houses are connected to electricity, residents use it sparingly or have had it cut off, as happened to Katya's mother. She had a single light bulb dangling in the center of their one room *hata* (hut), but her electricity had been shut off by the power company. One must have money to pay for electricity.

Some still heat their homes and cook with fire in a brick or clay oven, called a *petchka*. In villages, people's main source of food is from their gardens. Even in cities, many families have access to *dachas* (country homes or huts) where they garden on weekends. Produce from gardens and forests is canned or stored in root cellars. Extra produce and flowers are planted to sell on sidewalks or roadsides as a means of making money. They also make their own alcohol, especially strong wine and vodka, from forest fruit and potatoes. They seem to have an unlimited supply.

Poverty in both the urban and rural contexts helps breed a spirit of discouragement and hopelessness. To cope with the pain, many turn to alcohol, substance abuse, and sex. For the great majority of teenagers growing up in Ukraine, drinking and partaking in sexual freedom is what they do for fun, having complete access to these cheap forms of entertainment. This reality, in varying degrees, provides a picture of the home life that makes up approximately 50 percent of the campers who attend our English camps.

ENGLISH CAMPS

Mike is always praying for ways in which he can help his students develop their ministries. A few American churches have sent student teams to us on missions trips. We have found that the ministry of English camps is a very effective way to use the teams. American teens have a valuable commodity to offer: their language. Ukrainian youth and college students jump at the chance to improve their English. One of the best ways they can do this is to have practice with native speakers. Mike's youth ministry students help to plan and organize the camps, secure the facilities, work out the budget, food, meetings, and program. Four or five of them from different areas around Ukraine bring kids from their youth ministries or communities, making sure that half of them are non-Christians. These youth leaders also serve as the counselors at camp.

As the week goes on and English classes are taught by the American team, strong relationships are built. Love transcends language barriers. During the morning and evening group sessions, songs are sung, skits and testimonies are shared, and God's Word is explained. Ukrainian youth are surrounded by people who love Jesus. The atmosphere at camp is often a complete contrast to the atmosphere they live in at home or experience in their school. The aroma of Christ given off by Christians draws the non-Christian campers to the Lord.

> But thanks be to God, who always leads us in triumphal procession in Christ and through us spreads everywhere the fragrance of the knowledge of him. For we are to God the aroma of Christ among those who are being saved and those who are perishing.[2]

2. 2 Cor 2:14–15

After coming to Christ, for the most part, the new Christians take a strong stand against their roots. In Christ, they want no part of consuming alcohol, except for communion. Friends hang out in groups, and relationships are often developed within the company of these groups until the couple is declared publicly before the church. This declaration is equivalent to engagement. At this point, it is acceptable for the couple to go on dates and walks alone, to hold hands in public, to be considered a couple, and to discover if they are compatible for marriage.

In each English camp in which we have been involved, at least half of the non-Christian campers have surrendered their lives to Christ by the end of the week. For most of them, the commitment has been real and life changing. We have heard from several campers that upon returning home, their friends have rejected them and no longer want to spend time with them because they are completely changed. They have nothing in common anymore. Very often, the church becomes their source of social life.

One of the important things to note is that in our English camps, the campers have come with Mike's students. Therefore, when they go home, they can immediately enter a healthy youth ministry with a theologically-trained youth pastor. They have already established a relationship with that youth pastor because he was their camp counselor for the week. They also have friends in the youth group from camp. We have enjoyed hearing ongoing reports of these new believers as Mike's students have come to the seminary for classes. Most of the campers attend church and youth group, and grow in the Lord. We rejoice when we hear of their decisions to be baptized in order to make public their commitment to Christ.

What about the American teens? What affect has all of this had on their lives? We have heard report after report from young people who have returned home with lives permanently changed. The promises and truths of God's Word have come alive to them as they have witnessed their campers surrender their lives to Christ. The impact of this ministry has been long lasting. After our last camp, a Facebook group was set up to facilitate ongoing relationship between the American and Ukrainian teams and campers. American teens have written to tell us that the experience of seeing their campers come to the Lord has helped them to share their faith more boldly with their peers. Several of these teens are seriously praying about going into full-time ministry. Incidentally, three of the four teenage boys who came with Mike on his first trip to Ukraine in 2000 have grown up and chosen careers in full-time ministry. The fourth is a teacher in a public school, living his life for Christ and impacting young people every day.

FINDING A CHURCH HOME

One of the greatest difficulties for our family in Ukraine was finding a church home. We attended four different churches during our first five years in Ukraine, one of them for three and a half years. We never felt like we belonged. For the first few years, we barely understood the words of the sermons, and fellowship after the church service was minimal. We did not have enough language to support a conversation, though we had a goal to visit with at least two Ukrainians each Sunday. People seemed content to nod a hello, ask us how we were, and politely move on. Our children wondered why we even went. For a year, we attended a church that provided translation in English over headphones, but it was a very large church, and we knew we would never be able to establish close relationships with Ukrainian friends there.

During our fifth year, Mike's assistant at the seminary, Natasha Bochko, invited us to visit her church. She and her husband, Sergey, who translates for the church planting professor at the seminary, had been involved in planting a two-year-old church. At that time, they had about twenty-five in attendance. Sergey is the pastor. On the first Sunday we attended, our oldest daughter flew back to the States to attend college. We had said our goodbyes to her at the airport that morning before we went to church. My heart was breaking. During the worship service, the words of the songs touched my spirit and made me cry. There was an older woman standing beside me. She saw my tears and took me into her arms. She let me cry on her shoulder. She did not even know me. We had found our church home—Open Hearts Church. The name fit.

That summer, Open Hearts did an English camp. They partnered with a church in the States who sent a team of teenagers and adults to teach English. Our family was invited to teach, as well. Twenty-five Ukrainian university students attended, half of them non-Christians. Mike and I had the privilege of teaching an intermediate class of seven. Two of them did not know the Lord. Since the Ukrainians in our church led all of the activities and the morning and evening camp sessions, Mike and I were able to focus on teaching English and getting to know our students. Any time we mentioned Christ, we saw walls rise up in the eyes of our two students who did not know Him. Thankfully, camp lasts for an entire week. As relationships deepened among the campers and leaders, the barriers were breached. The walls began to come down.

On one of the last nights of camp, an invitation was given for these university students to surrender their lives to Christ. Six of them responded. The two in our class were not among them. The campers who lived in Kiev were invited to come to Open Hearts Church on Sunday after camp. The relationships that had been built were so strong that *all* of the university students from Kiev came to church that Sunday. Our church had an immediate growth spurt of seekers and brand new believers!

One of Mike's students had been chosen to be the youth leader in our church. Before camp, he had a group of only two or three. After camp, he had a group of twelve to lead. Our church leadership did an excellent job of discipleship. They taught new believers' Bible studies during the week, and Sergey continued to teach on Sundays in a way that the new believers could understand. The last student from Mike's and my group finally repented. We had noticed that for several Sundays, this young woman, Yulia, was in tears by the end of the service. The struggle that was going on within her was so obvious. I believe she understood that giving her life to Christ meant giving up her old lifestyle. Finally, she surrendered. Yulia entrusted her life to Christ.

What a joy to see the transformation of this young woman! Her guarded, rather cool eyes now sparkle with happiness and radiate the love of Christ. Yulia and all of the new students from camp two years ago are thriving, growing believers. They are actively involved in our church and were completely involved in the leadership of the English camp this summer. In fact, Yulia recently told me that next year, for the 2011 English camp, they would like Pastor Sergey and Natasha to come to camp only to participate and build relationships. Sergey and Natasha work so hard in the organizing and the leadership of these camps that they become exhausted. Our young people want to do more to relieve them of the burden of leadership.

Our family has greatly enjoyed the ministry of our church. We have a large apartment and have hosted some Bible studies and English classes, women's fellowships, and so forth. We are not the leaders; we just get to love on people and feed them! We do teach English for a quarter, two or three times a year. It is a help to our church and especially draws non-Christians. Sometimes new people come to our English classes and leave before church, but sometimes after relationships are formed, they stay.

LOOKING AHEAD

As for our future here in Ukraine, Mike is in the process of transitioning leadership to his Ukrainian students. One of them, Vasya Ostriy, has earned his master's degree and is teaching three of the twelve youth ministry courses for Mike at Kiev Theological Seminary (KTS) on his own credentials. Vasya also started a youth ministry degree at a Bible college in western Ukraine and is teaching the courses there. Mike is using several of his bachelor's degree graduates to co-teach courses at the seminary. In the 2010–2011 school year, 50 percent of the youth ministry courses at KTS will be taught by our graduates.

Mike has recently accepted the position of vice president of our mission, YMI. His responsibilities are shifting. The youth ministry major has been asked for and implemented in seminaries or Bible colleges in several more countries. Mike will be making visits to Nepal, Greece, and Malaysia this year as an adjunct professor. YMI prefers teaching the courses at a master's level, because then the graduates can immediately implement a bachelor's degree without the need for American professors. In Cuba, YMI taught the courses only at the master's level to thirteen students who already had their bachelor's degrees in theology. In addition, each one of them had ten years of experience in youth ministry. They graduated in the spring of 2009. The courses are now completely taught in four different Bible colleges by these Cuban professors. Graduates from our Malaysia program will soon be starting youth ministry training centers in nearby limited access countries, as well.

We are finding that church planters and established churches all over the world are asking for trained youth culture specialists to assist their teams in reaching the current generation. As we facilitate seminaries to begin master's and bachelor's degree programs in youth ministry, we help meet church planting needs.

Mike and I may have answered the call to missions thinking that we would stand in the gap by *doing* missions, but God's intent has always been that we serve as facilitators. Facilitating has taken many different forms in our ministry: partnering with an indigenous seminary to start a youth ministry bachelor's degree; helping American short-term teams to minister with Ukrainian churches using English camps as a tool; introducing youth ministry specialists to church planters to develop a student church-planting team; assisting a local church through building relationships in English clubs but leaving the seed-sowing and discipleship to the local church; encouraging youth ministry graduates to train other youth leaders in their regions; and setting up national youth ministry professors to teach at seminaries and Bible Institutes and to train the trainers. God has used the small tools in our hands to multiply in ways that we never envisioned.

Case Study 16

Bible Translation in Southeast Asia[1]

WHEN I JOINED THE Summer Institute of Linguistics (SIL), part-nership was a radical new idea in Bible translation. There were only a few Bible translation teams who were considered to be facilitating community-owned projects. Even so, when another young, single woman and I decided that we would like to be assigned on a translation project together, we both preferred to have the role of facilitator for a group of Christian believers who desired to translate the scriptures into their language.

We wanted to enable others to do the work that God had called them to. So we began to pray for the group that God had prepared for us and was now preparing us to go to. Little did we know how God would answer those prayers.

In order to explain my role as a facilitator, I will first describe how my role in the Galat[2] translation project changed from leader to facilitator with the formation of the Galat translation committee. I then describe the expansion of the role of the translation committee into other areas of ministry and how they were able to organize the resources of the Galat churches to implement those ministries. And finally, I conclude by summarizing the partnership between the Galat translation committee and me as the facilitator.

1. Thanks for this case study go to Sue Russell. Dr. Russell worked in S. E. Asia for fifteen years. Presently she teaches anthropology and early Christian history at Biola University. She holds master's degrees in Intercultural Studies, Christian History, Divinity, and Theology. She holds a PhD in Linguistics and a Doctor of Missiology, and she is completing her third doctorate in Early Christian History at UCLA.

2. All names and places have been changed.

FROM LEADER TO FACILITATOR

When my colleague and I arrived in S. E. Asia, one of the senior members of the SIL branch outlined the immediate needs for translation. The Galat community caught our attention. About half of the forty thousand Galat had converted to Christianity about forty years previously with several churches in three of the four Galat districts. Missionaries had started translation twice before, but both times were asked to leave the country before the translation was completed. Now forty years later, the Galat church asked for an SIL team to assist them in completing a translation of the whole Bible.

After a year of language and culture learning, my colleague began to make preparations to return to the United States to get married. During that time, an outside agency decided that they wanted to sponsor the translation project in Galat on the condition that SIL would supervise the project.

SIL asked me to supervise the project as well as select and train the Galat translators. I selected one translator who had attended a statewide translation seminar. The church recommended another. Two years after arriving in S. E. Asia, I began supervising the Galat translation program.

One of the steps in the sponsoring agency's procedure is to have a committee of readers who edit the work of the translators. Typically these readers are trained in translation principles before editing selections of the translation.

When I went to the Galat churches in search of pastors and other lay leaders to be readers, there was little interest in the translation project. After several months of prayer and searching, I was about to give up on having a committee of Galat men and women to participate in the project.

It was at that time that the Lord brought to mind Sammy Empat, who had participated in one of the state-wide translation training courses. I had not had contact with him for over two years, so I was not sure if he would even be interested in helping with the project.

After getting directions to his house, I drove to his village wondering how I would explain the project to him. To my surprise, when I arrived at the village, he greeted me and then began to explain how I should form a Galat translation committee that would oversee the translation project. He wanted to ensure that the translation would be completed this time and even volunteered to write to all of the pastors and arrange for them to meet to form the committee.

During the first meeting, I explained to the committee that we should hold a translation principle course in order to train them all to be readers. In a typical translation project, the translation committee of readers works under the supervision of the translation team, myself, and the two translators.

For the first Galat translation principles course, I arranged funding and made all the arrangements for the course, including food, housing, transportation, and the course material. At the end of the week-long translation course, I handed out portions of the translated Galat scripture to each of the fifteen readers to edit and return at our next meeting, which was scheduled for four months later.

Four months later I drove out to Sammy's village to discuss the agenda for the next Galat translation committee meeting and the dates and place for the next training workshop. When I arrived I discovered that the translation committee had already met without me and had decided to hold the translation training course and checking meeting during school vacation.

Additionally, they had made arrangements to hold the meetings at one of the churches in the area rather than at a conference facility as I had planned on doing. The dates that they decided to hold the meetings were also in conflict with other mandatory meetings I had to attend in the city.

I asked Sammy to change the meeting dates so that I would be able to attend, and we drove to the village to change the meeting times with the pastor of the local church. However, as soon as we spoke to the pastor, the Lord convicted me that this was not my decision to make.

I apologized to Sammy, and we rescheduled the meetings to the original dates. We decided I would train one of the translators to teach the translations principles course, and I would arrive one week late.

The following month as I was driving to the second week of the translation checking session, I wondered how the committee was doing. When I arrived, I discovered to my amazement there were about fifty people in the village center checking translation and about thirty people in the church completing the last of the translation principles lectures. The following day, they joined the fifty who were already participating in the translation process. But the Galat committee had planned far more than I could imagine for the two-week checking session.

On the day of my arrival, I became ill and was confined to bed in the pastor's house for the rest of the checking session. However, each night at around eight o'clock, I heard singing coming from the church. Then there was a sermon followed by more singing. Finally, at around four o'clock in the morning, the church service ended. This went on every night, and I began to wonder what was going on. This was not part of the original plan.

Finally, the last night of the translation checking session, I was well enough to get up and sit in the back of the church and watch the events of the revival meeting unfold. At the end of the meeting, the pastor of the church got up and thanked the committee for coming because they were the answer to his prayer.

What I did not know is that Sammy had visited the church on the Sunday before the translation checking session. It was then he discovered that the community of faith was a "sick church." Only the older people attended; the younger people had walked away from the Lord.

Sammy decided that when the committee came, they would hold revival meetings. So from eight o'clock in the morning until four o'clock in the afternoon, they checked translation. Then from about eight in the evening until four in the morning, they held revival meetings. As every member in the congregation got up to shake hands with the members of the committee, I realized that this is what God intended for this translation project: Galat helping Galat.

It was this realization that changed my relationship with the Galat translation committee. I moved from thinking that I was the leader, to the realization that I was the facilitator. However, it was also this realization that made the project a community-owned project.

The Galat translation committee harnessed the resources and personnel of the Galat churches to do far more collectively than individual village churches could do on their own. As the facilitator, my role was to help the Galat coordinate these activities and to find outside resources as necessary to facilitate their vision for their people. The following section discusses the various ways in which this occurred.

MINISTRY OF THE GALAT TRANSLATION COMMITTEE

The Galat translation committee not only oversaw the translation of the Galat Bible, but additionally initiated the creation of a new Galat song-book and recordings, evangelism into unreached Galat areas, and the teaching of literacy classes. Each of these projects could not have been accomplished without the leadership of the committee to coordinate the efforts of the majority of Galat churches, or without the help of an outside facilitator to provide expertise, develop materials, and find outside funding when necessary.

Translation

One of the major roles of the Galat translation committee was the supervision of the Galat translators. The salaries for the two translators were paid by the outside sponsoring agency, yet I had the responsibility to supervise their work. However, I had no real authority over them since their salaries came from another source. Additionally, I could not control the quality of the translation.

When the Galat translation committee was formed, they began to supervise the translators. Since they were church leaders, they were able to use cultural sanctions to encourage the Galat translators to perform, both in quality and quantity of translation. The translators were no longer under my supervision but rather under the entire Galat church.

A visible difference in this arrangement came with the location of the translators. Originally the translators lived in their home villages, but because the Galat wanted a more visible presence and a more closely supervised project, they moved the translators to a central location and built a translation office.

The married translator lived in the village where the office was located, but the single translator lived in a room at the office. I moved to the village where the office was located so that I could more effectively help with exegetical checks. My role was much easier because I no longer was directly responsible for the translators, but I could concentrate on helping the translators with the exegetical process and editing.

Another change that occurred when the Galat committee took leadership of the project was in the translation checking process. The traditional method used by the sponsoring agency was to hire individual readers to read the translation as it was finished. I soon discovered that when I did this, the readers did not complete their assigned portion of the scripture.

When the Galat committee took over the supervision of the translation project, they were able to harness the resources and personnel of all of the Galat churches. By using a church for the checking session, the translation process became visible and open to the whole Galat community.

The church that hosted the event was able to call upon the resources of the other churches in the district to provide the food necessary to feed the hundred or more participants who attended the checking sessions. Furthermore, the Galat committee called upon the personnel from each of the churches, asking for at least fifteen people from each of the four church districts to participate in the checking.

By holding the checking sessions during school vacation, the committee was able to tap into the most educated portion of the Galat community, the school teachers. Additionally, anyone who wanted to check translation could do so after attending the translation principles course that was always held the first week of the checking session. This allowed more Galats to participate.

During the checking session, the chairman divided the people into groups. Anyone who had attended the translation principles course could participate in the checking. However, I noticed that the chairman placed in each group one of the more educated and trained members of the committee. The rest of the group was usually made up of a balance of men and women, old and young, and people from both dialect groups.

Although people checked the material as a consensus process, the leader of the group generally had final say over the edits. This assured that the checking quality was consistent. Generally, at one of these two-week periods, the Galat could check about 25 percent of the New Testament. My role was to have enough scripture ready for the checking by the readers.

The other benefit of the translation checking sessions is that they gathered the major leaders from the Galat churches and used their collective talent to hold revival meetings during the two-week sessions. The revival meetings resulted in many Galat repenting, burning their magic paraphernalia, and being baptized.

Music

The Galat translation workshops also allowed Galat from different churches to share songs that they had created. This led to a request for the creation of a new Galat songbook. I told the committee that I myself did not have time to create the songbook but that I would be glad to train a Galat to input the songs into the computer.

The committee provided two Galat high-school students. I provided the computer that they could use to input and format the songbook and provided the training. They asked some of the musically inclined at one of the two-week checking sessions to compile a songbook as well as to create the artwork for the cover. I then found funding to print the first edition. During the two weeks, the Galat also recorded the songs on cassette tapes. These were then distributed to the churches so that the congregations could learn the new songs.

Bible Training

The committee decided that they wanted to provide Bible courses for the participants who attended the translation checking sessions. I asked the pastor of my church in the city if he would be willing to do exegetical teaching through a New Testament book during the two-week checking session. We choose a book that had already been checked and was ready for distribution.

I found funding to print five hundred copies and took them to the translation workshop. Each participant was given a free copy and permitted to buy additional copies to take back to his/her church. The pastor taught exegetically through the book during the checking session.

As a result, Galat pastors had the scripture in Galat and the exegesis of that book to take back to their churches. One of the most rewarding experiences was returning to my village and hearing the pastor preaching out the Galat scriptures using his notes from the Bible training the committee had provided.

Literacy

The illiteracy rate among Galat women was about 50 percent, so literacy material development was one of my main priorities. I worked with others to develop and test a primer, readers, and a teacher's manual and then found funding to print fifty sets of material, one set for about each of the Galat churches. I needed to train Galat teachers because I could not teach literacy classes in the fifty Galat villages that needed them. However, every time I mentioned the need to train literacy teachers, the translation committee had other priorities and did not seem interested in the literacy project.

Two years after completing the literacy material, I was discussing with Sammy his plans to distribute and sell the nearly completed Galat New Testament. He off-handedly made a comment that the committee needed to do more evangelism so that there would be additional readers of the New Testament. Seeing my opportunity, I interjected, "But what about all the people who can't read? They won't buy a New Testament."

He looked at me for a moment and said, "You better do something about that." So I explained that I had material ready but needed people to train to teach the material. He immediately wrote letters to all the churches and requested that they send their "literacy teacher" to the next translation checking session.

Four months later, I trained fifty literacy teachers. I gave them the materials to hold literacy classes in their respective villages. After two years of preparation, the Galat literacy program was launched. The accountability and follow-up were done by the pastor of the church and the Galat committee.

Evangelism

One of the steps in the Bible translation process is to take the translated material and test it with people who have not been involved in the translation process. In this checking, scripture portions are read to people, often non-Christians, who are then asked questions to determine that the translation is clear and that there are no unintended ambiguities or wrong meanings.

I could not do this part of the checking because of the sensitive nature of the country in which I worked. Nor could I get the Galat committee to understand the importance of this process. However, I kept it on the translation progress board, and as we continued to make progress in other areas of translation and checking, this column became increasingly noticeable because of the lack of progress in it.

One day as I was in the translation office drinking coffee with Sammy, he looked up at the board and said, "What was that reader checking again?"

So I explained the process of reading the scripture to those who had not heard it before and then asking questions to make sure it was understandable. Suddenly he got it. "What a great way to do evangelism! We can't go up to an older man and preach to him, but we can ask him if the translation is good Galat!"

Two weeks later, I came back to the translation office, and Sammy introduced me to two young pastors, "These are your readers. Now teach them." I was taken aback a bit, but Sammy went on to explain that these two men would take the translation out to an unreached area of fourteen Galat villages and go to one village every day in order to read the portions of scripture that were ready for checking.

The committee had already found a place for them to stay and funding for their salaries. They asked me to find funding for their boat and engine, which I was able to do, as well as funds for a two-year supply of gas.

For the next two years, the two readers went around to the fourteen villages. These villages were considered some of the most "closed" Galat villages. They had a reputation for having the greatest knowledge of magic, and most evangelists were not even allowed up into the longhouses. But because the two men asked if they could read some material that had been translated into Galat, they were allowed into the longhouse and even invited back.

After two years of reading, asking questions, and continuing a dialogue about the scriptures, the translation chairman told the readers, "OK they're ready." One Christmas day, people were invited to become followers of Jesus, and three hundred accepted that invitation and were baptized. Seven churches were established, and additional personnel were sent to pastor these people.

REFLECTIONS

When I started working among the Galat, I had prayed that I would be a facilitator of a community-owned project. At the time I had no idea what that meant or what it would eventually look like. To truly be a facilitator, I had to let go of the decision-making power over the project and listen to the dreams and priorities of the Galat. I had to learn to do things their way and learn the roles where they needed my expertise and my access to resources.

The process of learning to be partners on a truly equal footing meant that the decisions were jointly made, and I had to put what I thought were priorities on a back burner and work with the Galat on their priorities. What was interesting is that the Galats eventually owned those priorities, such as literacy and readers, and facilitated their completion in a way that I could not have imagined.

The Galat translation project and committee provided a centralized organization where the fifty to sixty churches could combine their resources to do things that individual churches lacked the personnel and resources to do. Their combined resources provided the housing, food, and personnel to check the Galat translation for two weeks, twice a year, for five years.

In return, the Galat committee returned to the church two weeks of worship services in which they could hear pastors from other villages, learn new songs, and plan joint ministry ventures. They received a two-week Bible exegesis course. And perhaps most of all, they got to see God's Spirit move among their people and bring revival to the Galat churches. Because the checking sessions were rotated among the four Galat districts, every church benefited from the checking sessions. Every church was able to participate in the translation process.

The Galat committee itself organized the resources for the checking sessions, as well as the daily operations for the translation project, such as supervising, feeding, and housing of full-time personnel. They also found other personnel as needed, such as a secretary, computer formatter for the songbook, the readers, and the checkers. They provided the cultural expertise to organize and facilitate the participation of the Galat churches in the translation project and other Galat-wide ministries such as music, evangelism, Bible courses, and literacy.

My role as facilitator was to find funding for capital projects, such as a translation office, a boat for transportation and printing materials, a songbook, literacy books, and individual New Testament books for testing and distribution. I also provided the necessary expertise in the translation process and organization, the development of literacy materials, and computer training. I provided the Galat with access to outside experts, such as the pastor who provided the Biblical teaching, as well as coordinating the translation project with the outside sponsoring agency.

As I have reflected on the Galat translation project, I have wondered just how much difference it made for me as an outside facilitator to be a part of the project. I do not think it was so much what I did, but my willingness to come alongside Galat leaders, hear their vision and their heart for their people, and work in such a way that the translation project became a way to organize the Galat churches into a common vision.

It was not always easy; sometimes I did not understand their priorities. I sometimes wondered if what I thought were priorities, such as literacy, would ever be completed. But the answer to my question came as the photo-ready Galat New Testament came off the printer and one of the translators picked up a page and said with tears in his eyes, "With this we can harvest." This is what God had intended: Galat helping Galat. I am so thankful that I got to be a part.

PART THREE

Facilitation as Praxis

Week 8

So What Did You Learn from the Case Studies?

"CAN'T BELIEVE THAT OUR time together is almost over," sighed Bev as she poured steaming coffee into three mugs. "These sessions have been tremendously insightful and helpful, Dr. Nobley."

"For sure," chimed in Bill with a broad smile, "even if sometimes a little intimidating."

"Well, here's what we did with the case studies," continued Bev. "Very interesting reading, I must say! When we got home, we read through all sixteen of them—which is a lot of reading!—and sorted them into geographical and topic areas: Training, BAM, STM, English, and Bible Translation. We then identified—"

"Not without some argument," interjected Bill.

"—some of the take-aways from each," resumed Bev. She handed Dr. Nobley a printout entitled, "Facilitation Case Study Take-Aways."

The professor took the paper and began reading, stopping periodically to sip some coffee and snack on some old cookies left over from last week. Bill and Bev watched over his shoulder.

FACILITATION CASE STUDY TAKE-AWAYS

Training

"We began with training since that aspect had the largest number of case studies," Bill explained. "In this grouping of cases, training was a central feature of the facilitative work that North American missionaries were doing. We've listed what each case taught us about training."

Case Study 1: The Amazon and Lowland Tribal Empowerment Coalition

Multiple expatriate groups set aside their differences to partner together with tribal churches in the Amazon to reach the unreached in that expansive area by addressing both life and livelihood issues.

- Consider restrategizing—but not necessarily retooling.
- Aim for interdependence, which trumps both dependency and independence.
- Offer both life and livelihood.
- Plant healthy, reproducing churches.
- Create sustainable financial resources.
- Don't just do something; teach someone what you do.

Case Study 2: Ibero–America's COMIBAM International

Expatriates from Worldview Resource Group work hard to build an effective partnership with the top trainers in COMIBAM to help improve training for Latin Americans serving around the world.

- God orchestrated the Global South mission enterprise.
- Strategic partnerships are divinely appointed.
- Learning together should precede working together.
- Working together demands self-critique.
- Effective partnerships move beyond the task to well-maintained relationships.

Case Study 3: Training Latin Americans for Missions Among Muslims

Don and Angie Finley partner with other expatriates and Brazilians for over a decade to help prepare Latin Americans for holistic ministry among Muslims in the Mediterranean area, as well as other unreached peoples around the globe. The training focuses on the integration of theology, missiology, character, and practice.

- Home churches vet their candidates; parents OK their children's training.
- Adequate training in theology and missiology is foundational.

- Training should focus on academic learning, practical experience, and spiritual formation.

- Teamwork includes veteran mentor oversight all along the journey.

- A radically incarnational approach to missions opens doors to ministry on a deep level.

- Christians and Muslims can relate to one another in mutual trust and friendship.

Case Study 4: Facilitative Church Planting in Japan

Mike Wilson calls for new thinking and practice to reach the Japanese, who have been slow to respond to Christ. He seeks church multiplication through in-depth relationships and supernaturally-empowered evangelism.

- God gives tremendous influence to expatriates who submit themselves to local leadership.

- God draws people to himself through the active love of his people in community.

- Supernaturally-empowered relational evangelism is very effective discipleship.

- Job descriptions should remain fluid.

- The goal is not evangelism or discipleship, but church multiplication.

- Newly developing churches can inspire the birthing parent church.

Case Study 5: A Chinese Missionary Training Center to Reach Muslims

Monroe Brewer continues to make forays into China to teach in clandestine schools set up to train highly vetted Chinese believers to become effective church planters in areas of the world where bi-vocationalism and persecution are the norm.

- Persecution builds character but can leave deep wounds.

- "Be as shrewd as snakes and as innocent as doves."[1]
- Female trainers are necessary and welcome.
- Students don't volunteer for service; rather, they are selected by those who know them best.
- Trainers include expatriates and locals.
- Team should identify God's global plan (Muslims in Middle East) and tackle it incrementally.

Case Study 6: Growing an Evangelical Church in Southeast Asia

Jerry Hogshead documents successful, long-term, holistic, church-planting movements that evolved through partnerships in Southeast Asia—partnerships that emphasized missiology-based training. These partnerships came, however, with a high price tag for both Jerry and the locals.

- Sound missiology should drive the training, strategy, and curricula.
- God uses less-than-ideal strategies.
- Facilitators who invest years of time and energy have the opportunity to see long-lasting results.
- When workers do not know the language, communication remains a constant challenge.
- Facilitators are not exempt from emotional breakdowns.

Case Study 7: Facilitating Near-Culture Evangelism with Aid Sudan

When health problems arise, God redirects Peter and Shauna Swann from a church-planting ministry in the Sudan back to the United States, where they start missions agencies that train, fund, and send Sudanese believers and others back to their home countries as church planters.

- God turns so-called catastrophes into new kingdom adventures.
- Near-culture missionaries are an extremely valuable resource.
- Indigenous personnel require cross-cultural training.
- Not all hopeful candidates will make it.
- Radio complements boots on the ground.

1. Matt 10:16

Whole-Life Transformation

Case Study 8: Whole-Life Transformation in Uganda

An expatriate team enters Uganda, where nominal Christianity prevails. Through a whole-life approach, they and trained national partners challenge communities to break down the religious and ethnic barriers for the good of the community. Many find Christ in the process, and churches are born. Transformation and revitalization take place.

- Address needs perceived by the nationals (Scratch where they itch!).
- Require community members to branch out beyond their religions or denominations.
- The holistic nature of the Good News does not have to compromise spiritual results.
- National leaders pass on the gospel (content & methodology) in much the same way as they receive it.
- Kingdom citizens live holistically.

Case Study 9: Facilitating by Following in Papua New Guinea

Through an unexpected turn of events, Mike and Michelle Griffis find themselves moving from Venezuela to Papua New Guinea to assist the Ata church in culture and language acquisition so that the Ata can become effective cross-cultural church planters. The Griffises model a learner role by following Ata leadership.

- Expatriates have as much to learn as to offer.
- Technical expertise is most effective when relationships exist.
- Belief is essential that national local churches can fulfill Acts 1:8.
- Partnerships take time to form.
- A biblical foundation is fundamental.

Case Study 10: Team Poland's Story of Short-Cycle Church Planting

Team Poland's goal was to plant a church within five years, changing the culture of the mission agency. God serendipitously brought people into their path all along the journey, paving the way through multiple partnerships for this goal to become a reality—but not without a cost to the team.

- Discover what the host culture appreciates and start there.
- Find sponsors (pastors) because they provide credibility and open doors.
- Have an exit strategy.
- Place team members in their strength areas.
- Accept the fact that some team members may leave.
- Evaluate constantly.

Case Study 11: Multiple Facilitative Church Planting in Kursk, Russia

A North American missions agency partners with a Baptist church in western Russia. The partnership births eight churches in the area and produces many graduates throughout the Russian Federation and Ukraine.

- History impacts the present, so know it well.
- Partnerships are sometimes forced to form.
- A great benefit is a local church willing to give of itself and its members.
- Also of great benefit are visionary leaders and enthusiastic trainers devoted to mentoring and training students.
- Training should wed commitment to theological education and in-service ministry.
- Training and deploying kingdom-minded graduates is the goal.
- CPMs have a strong possibility of continuing in unchurched or under-churched urban settings.

Case Study 12: Biblical Leadership Training Coalition in the Former USSR

Bryan Thomas chronicles the highlights and lowlights of the messy nature of facilitating church-planting movements in the Philippines and the Former Soviet Union. A driven, gifted organizer and fundraiser eventually finds himself stretched too thin.

- The past impacts the present; know the history well.

- People care more about how you treat them than about how much you know.

- Learning is lifelong.

- Church planters need competence and careful training in three areas: knowing (cognitive), being (affective), and doing (behavioral).

- Trusting Jesus to build his church is the way to avoid crashing and burning.

- Grace is caught more than taught.

Bill and Bev noticed Dr. Nobley nodding, smiling, and rubbing his earlobe as he turned the pages. Bill gave Bev an encouraging thumbs-up behind the professor's back. Bev cleared her throat.

"These next sections include only one case study each," she explained, "even though there's a lot of overlap among all the case studies. The ones we present here are those that best illustrate the challenges and opportunities that come with business, short-terming, English teaching, and Bible translation."

Business as Mission

Case Study 13: Business as Mission in Russia

Diane Thomas documents her growing understanding of BAM possibilities in relation to making indigenous ministries sustainable economically.

- Do your homework! Know business, the host culture and language, and your own culture.

- Create a business that is eventually owned and operated by locals.

- Build a capable network for sales and distribution.

- Provide the locals with training in business, leadership, Bible, work, and life.

- Be flexible and adaptable, but work smart.

- Seek wealth, not riches.

Short-Term Missions

Case Study 14: Short-Term Missions in Peru

The facilitator role replaces the pioneer role in Peru, paving the way for long-term partnerships between the Peruvian churches and North American churches, and resulting in church growth and new churches being planted annually.

- On-site missionary roles change over time from pioneer to facilitator.
- Resource-rich countries travel to the less wealthy, making large-scale events possible.
- Outsiders use their social capital (bait) to open closed doors to insiders.
- Medical services open closed doors.
- Long-term commitment to annual festivals leads to long-term relationships that lead to new churches.
- Symbols (like a pin with two flags) celebrate and solidify a unified partnership.
- Short-termers are challenged and changed.

English Camps

Case Study 15: Youth English Camps in Ukraine

Judy Manna provides a glimpse of Ukrainian youth culture, the implementation of English camps to meet some of their needs, and the church growth and new churches that result from this facilitative effort.

- God's call to missions may be a call to administer and facilitate ministry rather than to be directly involved in local ministry.
- Youth ministry, STMs, English camps, and church planting mix well.
- Exit strategies should include methods to train the trainers.
- Trained national youth pastors are a vital component to church-planting teams who are reaching the current generation.

- Formal youth ministry training at the seminary level can create a nationwide youth ministry training movement.

Bible Translation

Case Study 16: Bible Translation in Southeast Asia

Sue Russell relates her involvement in facilitating Bible translation and literacy in Southeast Asia, describing some of the many twists, turns, and teachable moments in this new adventure.

- Roles change from leader to facilitator.
- Facilitators may create momentum in which they have little further input.
- Changes and challenges are to be expected.
- Facilitation aids in the development of new leaders.
- Each partner has blind spots.
- Centralization allows for maximized use of resources.
- Fundraising for capital projects is necessary.
- Facilitators must show a willingness to hear the locals' vision and to wait patiently.

✵ ✵ ✵

"With these take-aways, you've created a great thematic summary of each case," commended Dr. Nobley. "Very well done."

Bill and Bev, pleased with their effort, contentedly took a cookie.

"Well, where should we go from here?" asked the professor. "You've summarized and considered themes, and now we should synthesize. As you reflect back on the take-aways, what stands out to you and why? What are the best practices? Let's compile a list of best practices in relation to facilitation."

"Great idea," responded Bill through a mouthful of cookie crumbs. "Bev, would you please take notes for your PowerPoint presentation?"

"Will do," responded Bev, holding up a finger while she swallowed. "And I'll begin with the first best practice: Recognize that God orchestrates changes within global missions. The center of missions has constantly changed over time. It did not stay long in Jerusalem or Antioch. Paul's letter to the Romans seems to be asking the Gentile and Jewish believers to get over their differences and unite so that they can start a new missions center in Rome, the heart of the empire, to reach Spain.

"It's no surprise to God that the center of Christianity has now shifted from the north and west to the south and east. We must never forget that it's God's game, not ours. It is we who must learn to adjust to the game plan he orchestrates."

"Philip Yancey has a theory on that point," noted the professor, "and it is this: 'God goes where he's wanted.'[2] I think Yancey just may be on to something."

"So do I," agreed Bev. "A second best practice would be to expect divine encounters. The case studies were replete with examples of how God orchestrated events positively—like in the Amazon, COMIBAM, Mediterranean, and Ukraine case studies, using even dreams. There were also plenty of examples of God allowing events to unfold negatively, as he did in the Sudan case study. He does this to connect people and begin new kingdom adventures. Facilitators should be constantly alert for such changes, and expect divine encounters.

"I'm on a roll, Bill. Can I do one more before you add yours to the list?" Bev laughed.

"Feel free," agreed Bill.

"Thanks," replied Bev. "The third best practice would center on relationships. On the human side, relationships determine to a great extent the outcomes. Facilitators excel when they listen, when they follow, and when they serve—*not* when they lead. The Bible translation case study demonstrates this principle, as do the COMIBAM, STM, BAM, Papua New Guinea, Uganda, and some other case studies."

"Something I came across the other day fits in well here," noted Dr. Nobley. "Mark Goulston wrote a book entitled *Just Listen,* in which he argues that to truly win and influence people, one must be more interested in listening than impressing.[3] He goes on to level this charge: 'These days, we don't relate—we transact.'[4] Ouch! That hurts, but it's so true.

2. Yancey, "God at Large," 136.

3. Goulston, *Just Listen,* 57.

4. Ibid., 156.

"Transacting will get any facilitator into trouble anywhere in the world, but especially in relationally-oriented societies. Building deep relationships will do just the opposite. And that's why Bob Strauss uses email and Skype, mentioned in the COMIBAM case study, to keep in constant touch, and why the team spends time with Dr. Gava's family in Argentina before and after the planned event. Who knows what facilitators will be using in the future to keep in contact?"

"I would add one more caveat," insisted Bev. "Relationships are a two-way street. Working together demands the self-critique of all parties. For example, the ethnocentrism of the north is just as wrong as push-back from the south. The Ugandans who reached beyond their religions and denominations serve as a great model for everyone to follow."

"I agree. And now it's my turn," said Bill. "I'll add two more best practices because they are kind of related. The first is the implementation of an exit strategy. Bev and I had a little disagreement on this one, but here goes.

"It always amazes me how few pioneer church planters, much less facilitators, give attention to an exit strategy. The Bible translation case study shows that an exit strategy was unplanned but that the translator discovered the beauty of it over time. The Ukraine case study seems much the same. The Poland case study, however, demonstrates a planned exit strategy from the beginning through the use of their short-cycle CP model. I think that one of the most important questions that facilitators should ask themselves is *how far can I realistically take this group?* Wise facilitators will know the answer to this question and plan an exit strategy accordingly. Task, context, and competency should determine each timeframe on-site."

"What was your contention, Bev?" inquired the professor.

"It seems to me," said Bev as she thoughtfully twisted her ponytail, "that an exit strategy is very different for a pioneer church planter than for a facilitator. Once churches continue to multiply, it's time for the pioneer church planter to move on. Yes, determining that point in time is a little more messy than translating X number of verses to complete a translation project. Nevertheless, when the Bible is translated, the translator is done, and it's time to leave. In contrast, it seems that facilitators—especially those involved in training—could continue to do this training and facilitating indefinitely. I mean, for example, does the owner of a BAM project always have to turn it over to the locals? I don't know. It's all just a little confusing to me."

"Be assured that you are not the only one confused on this topic," began Dr. Nobley. "If we can keep focused on the pilgrim nature of our life and ministry, I think that will help. Two of the major assumptions behind exit strategy are that we are finite, which includes our time in ministry, and that we should be training others to replace us. This type of thinking is kind of a 2 Timothy 2:2 thing. Trained people become key to transitions. Facilitator trainers, for example, especially those who are no longer involved in the practical side of ministry, can fast become obsolete. I think Bill's question is a great one that everyone involved in ministry at home or abroad should ask."

"That helps," replied Bev, "even without specific answers to my questions. Thanks, Dr. Nobley."

"I like your answer, Dr. Nobley," said Bill, pleased. "Here's my second best practice: CP-1 and CP-2 will be implemented more often than CP-3. Let me unpack this.

"CP-3 is complex, as we saw—much more so than CP-1 or CP-2. Ask those short-termers who went to Peru. But for their Peruvian partners, CP-1 and CP-2 are not that complex and, therefore, become their focus. The same dynamic is found in the case studies from Sudan, Uganda, Russia, former USSR, and the Amazon.

"The case studies from Ukraine and Japan seem to focus exclusively on CP-1. Some, however, do include CP-3: the Chinese, COMIBAM, and the Latinos working in the Mediterranean. How facilitators train should take into consideration the cultural complexity implications for all three levels of church planting, and they should know their limitations."

"Here's the sixth best practice," said Bev. "Avoid burnout by trusting Jesus to build his church. Burnout does not automatically bypass facilitators just because they may be spiritual giants, intellectuals, great orators, go-to statisticians, or excellent trainers. As the facilitation ministry grows, the advice given to Moses from his father-in-law, Jethro, seems appropriate. Jethro basically told Moses that what he was doing was not good, that the work was too heavy, and that he would soon wear himself out. So, he should find capable people and train them to do what he was doing.[5] In other words, share the load and help out only on the tough issues. Not only would Moses save his own life by dispersing power, but he

5. Exod 18:13–23

would develop new leaders in the process. The Messiah complex driven by the alpha personality, time-orientation, insecurity, or whatever, must be placed on the cross."

"The next best practice that I would add," offered Bill, "is that long-term impact requires long-term participation. The case studies that represent years of facilitation demonstrate significant growth and depth, albeit not always fast growth. That doesn't mean that they are not without challenges, but that the movements are alive and kicking. The case studies that come to mind that represent this best practice include both Southeast Asia case studies, Sudan, Uganda, Mediterranean, Japan, Ukraine, Russia, and the Former Soviet Union.

"Say what you will, but I think that there is something to say for long-term partnerships. And I like the way the Peruvians celebrated their lengthy, unified partnership with the Americans by giving them a pin with the symbol of both countries' flags. Symbols and rituals should play important roles in partnerships."

"Something just hit me," said Bev. "Most of those involved in long-term facilitation seem to give special attention to culture and language acquisition. Even the Poland five-year short-cycle model gave attention to these. One's language and culture is one's identification. Not to learn these is not to respect another's identity. Even in Manila, where a lot of English is spoken, I would not want to be without the capability of speaking Tagalog. Otherwise, I would feel that the locals were for sure talking about me. And I would never really know what was going on. I think the facilitator in the Southeast Asian training case study wishes he would have learned the language. And the couple working in Ukraine seem to wish that they knew more than Russian.

"I have another best practice. Facilitators see transformation holistically. I really like the 'life and livelihood' concept developed in the Amazon case study. It was so good to see the different skills and giftings come together to work for a single purpose. They really didn't have to add to their ministry focus; they just needed to have a mindset to work with others who already had the other components. That's the body of Christ in action.

"The medical services provided by expatriate teams in Peru did much to open closed doors and hearts. The whole-life transformation model used in Uganda did the same. Demonstrating the compassion of Christ through deeds often provides opportunity for the Word to be heard.

"Since social needs in Japan were different than those in the strained physical conditions of the Amazon or Peru, the facilitator in Japan provided marriage and family counseling, prayer for healing, and encouragement for those experiencing mental conditions. We often forget that people experience other needs than just social ones—and that prayer and the use of healing and miraculous spiritual gifts are other worthy, scriptural means of meeting them. And don't forget the English camps—that is, the bait—in Ukraine."

"Here's another possible best practice," suggested Bill. "Facilitate sustainable human and economic resources. Sometimes a one-time financial gift is what's needed, such as a boat and gas for the indigenous Bible translation team. At other times, however, sustainable funding will be needed, such as the chiropractic center in Argentina."

"After our discussion of BAM a few weeks ago," noted Bev, "it was good to read the Russian case study of Bybella, the handmade jewelry business. I loved watching Diane work through all her hang-ups about starting a business. There are a lot of locals who have benefited from her journey who will never know the internal and external discussions and debates—battles if you will—that took place before Bybella became a reality. I applaud her emphasis on building wealth rather than riches. And I loved her humility and persistence."

"And don't forget," reminded Bill, "that other facilitators were considering BAM in their ministries. I would not be surprised to hear someday of the use of BAM in the Southeast Asian training case study as well as in China and the Amazon. The era of Great Commission companies is here, making economic sustainability possible. Without BAM, the facilitator will be required to raise funds for capital projects through other means, as the Bible translator did. And I don't think such assistance automatically translates into dependency. This to me can be interdependence at its best.

"And human resources must also be sustainable. This means we don't just train any warm body. Remember the Mediterranean and China case studies? No volunteers. Those who knew the candidates best did the selection. And our training must move beyond the cognitive to include the practical. Education and in-service ministry should be wed, as in the Ukraine and Mediterranean case studies. Candidates should be carefully trained and observed in three areas: knowing (cognitive), being (affective), and doing (behavioral). For those involved in CP-2 and CP-3, cross-cultural training is a must. Missiology is a must. We should not assume that the locals can work effectively cross-culturally without good missiological training any more than we ourselves can. All of this training makes deploying capable kingdom-minded personnel possible, as we read about in the Mediterranean and Southeast Asian training case studies. Even so, not all our hopefuls will make it. Some may even leave to set up competitive organizations."

"Here's another best practice," said Bev. "I think that sound missiology should drive all the training, strategy, and curricula. Please don't misunderstand me, I'm assuming a strong Bible foundation is in place, like what we saw in the Mediterranean, Papua New Guinea, and Russian case studies. But we need missiology—Christian history, social sciences, theology, and strategy—to help us discern how our own culture influences Bible interpretation and Christian practice.[6] Those we train should require nothing less. If expatriates have as much to learn as to offer, would not this also be true of the indigenous workers?

"I would also be quick to say that God is able to use less than ideal strategies, as we saw in the Southeast Asia training case study. And he uses less than ideal people, as all of the case study facilitators would no doubt admit. Even so, that should not minimize the emphasis facilitators give to missiology. Stewardship demands that facilitators attempt to get a good return on their talents,[7] or in this case, on their training, strategies, curricula, and yes, businesses.

"Oh, one more addition. Can't let this one slip by," Bev said. "We should not underestimate the ability of women to teach Bible and missiology, like in the China case study, or English, as in Ukraine. Both genders, expats and locals, all combined, make for a powerful facilitative team."

"Here is my favorite best practice," began Bill. "Focus on holistic church multiplication. This has to be—"

"Oh, wait! There's a question that I've always wanted to ask," interrupted Bev as she motioned to Bill to stop. Bill rolled his eyes bemusedly. "I understand the differences between the pioneer and facilitator roles.

---

6. See Steffen, "Missiology's Journey for Acceptance," 131–153.

7. Matt 25:14–30

But why are facilitators really needed? Doesn't the need for facilitators imply that the pioneers failed to do their job?"

"You want to answer that, Dr. Nobley?" asked Bill, looking for a quick escape.

"Another great question," began the professor. "We should have kept track of all our questions over the weeks. That would make a great list. Anyway, back to your perceptive question, one not often asked— and much less often given serious reflection.

"In some cases the pioneers *did* fail. Some stopped with evangelism. Some stopped with discipleship. Some stopped with leadership development. Some stopped with a single church. Some focused solely on the spiritual. Driving some of this practice was an eschatology that argued for the immanent return of Jesus Christ; therefore, the reasoning went, get the good news out there to as many people as possible as fast as possible. The result? Lots of undiscipled disciples. In far too many cases, Christianity became a mile wide but only a half-inch deep, as the Uganda case illustrates.

"Some focused solely on the material and/or social. Some failed to pass the baton in any area of ministry. Because these pioneers, for some reason, failed to see that the goal was holistic church multiplication—as you remind us, Bill—the need to reproduce and to minister to the whole person was either not communicated to the new followers of Christ, or communicated very poorly.

"But we can't stop with the pioneers. In some cases, the locals didn't hear what was taught, or didn't catch what was practiced, or did catch it but dropped it. Still in other settings, the locals did not want to hear of it, much less practice it.

"And please don't misunderstand me: all this is certainly not to overlook the undisputable successes of many pioneers. But whatever happened, whether success or something short of it, follow-up facilitation is in order, now with much more specialization. If equated to the New Testament practice, this would be like the teams that followed up the initial church plants of Paul and others. Timothy and Titus, who had been with Paul for some fifteen years, would serve as good examples. Remember Paul's instructions to Titus? He desired that Titus ' . . . might straighten out what was left unfinished and appoint elders in every town.'[8]

8. Titus 1:5

"But the facilitators we're talking about are more than this. Today's facilitators assume that the pioneer work where they seek to serve is well-along, or even complete. They assume that some level of pastoral leadership already exists. They then go to these places to build upon what was previously done, and they even make corrections where necessary. And all of this may be done with the discipled and/or the undiscipled. I should also add that the mere status of some expats could open closed ministry doors for the locals, as in the Peruvian case study," Dr. Nobley concluded. "Hope this is helpful."

"It is," responded Bill. Bev agreed by nodding her head as she typed on her laptop.

"I'll now return to my last best practice," Bill asserted, clearing his throat and casting a wary glance at Bev, "which, as I was saying earlier, is a focus on holistic church multiplication. Notice I didn't say just social ministry, or just church multiplication, but *holistic church multiplication*. Facilitators promote transformational training that helps produce new communities of worshippers capable of reproducing themselves. There's ongoing discipleship, and there's ongoing social transformation. It's not just a movement. It's a holistic, transformational movement. I think next week Dr. Nobley is going to tell us why he still teaches pioneer church planting so maybe we'll get more specifics then.

"Anyway, as I noted earlier, the movements will most likely take place in CP-1 and CP-2 environments. Some of these CPMs, or HCPMs—*h* standing for *holistic*—will be enhanced by technology, such as radio, to complement boots on the ground, as we saw in the Sudan case study. As mobile cell phones replace laptops, new avenues will emerge in the Global South to facilitate CPMs. Sadly, the accessibility of these technological advances on both sides of the ocean will make it possible for affluent America to mass-communicate in nanoseconds totally non-contextualized curricula, sermons, models, strategies, textbooks, and so forth—and to create the illusion of intimacy. But speed and cheapness should become no substitute for localized or glocalized witness. Receptor, beware! That's why constant evaluation by the team is necessary, as demonstrated in the Poland and Mediterranean case studies," he concluded. Bev and Dr. Nobley nodded in agreement.

"Oh, one other thing that often gets overlooked," Bill remembered. "The HCPMs that result will do much to inspire and motivate the birthing parent church, not to mention the facilitators."

"I totally agree," affirmed Bev, typing. "I'm glad I finally gave you room to talk! Anyone have other best practices to add?"

"Well, I do have two," said the professor. "But that will give us thirteen, rather than an even dozen."

"That's fine," said Bev. "We'll go for a baker's dozen."

"OK, here's goes," began the professor. "I'll try to keep it moving. Our time is just about up, and I have a date with my wife this evening.

"The twelfth best practice is that facilitators recognize that those they train may be persecuted—or even become martyrs. I think of the Sudanese returning to their home country and those serving in Southeast Asia. The Chinese also come to mind: What might happen to many of those men and women who are being clandestinely trained? Even so, they consider it an honor to suffer for Christ or to have family members do the same. The cross costs. Persecution and martyrdom are part of that cost.

"These Christian workers must be 'as shrewd as snakes and as innocent as doves.'[9] Some Christian workers may purposefully put themselves into situations that are sure to generate persecution, which they see as a badge of spirituality. Others don't seek out persecution; yet they still experience it. The first may demonstrate self- or family-aggrandizement, while the latter demonstrate the true cost of the cross.

"Pulse-pounding persecution does several things that should not be minimized or glamorized. Having your house stoned or set on fire takes an emotional toll. So does being taken to court on trumped-up charges—or being tortured or jailed, or having your children get beat up at the local school.

"First, persecution builds deep Christian character and a willingness to suffer as Jesus suffered. This suffering fires evangelism, making witnesses fearless and tireless in the face of tyranny. Persecution helps drive proclamation because the witnesses see suffering as partnership with the Christ of the cross. Like Jesus, they know that they are victims of injustice, yet they also know the power of the resurrection and the power of the Truth they tell.

"Second, persecution can leave deep wounds. Loved ones are killed or maimed for life. Family members are jailed for years, resulting in separation from family and creating financial hardships. Children grow up fearful and insecure. Facilitators responsible for member care

9. Matt 10:16

for those serving in areas of persecution should not overlook or minimize this aspect of training. Trainees should constantly be reminded of the faithfulness exhibited by the tested ancients who suffered for their beliefs and actions, as noted in Hebrews eleven. There's some character theology for you. Strangely, at least to me, the teachings of suffering and joy are conjoined twins in Scripture. Facilitators should remind trainees of this dualism through character theology that weds suffering and joy.

"The baker's dozen best practice is this: facilitators don't try to stereotype what form facilitation should take. If the case studies teach us only one thing, it is that God uses a variety of facilitation models and strategies in the Fourth Era to expand his kingdom. And we only looked at sixteen cases! Some promote holism. Some promote culture and language acquisition. Some reject volunteerism. Some rely on short-termers, and others promote long-term relationships. Some use chronological Bible stories for evangelism and discipleship, and some use English camps. Some promote ongoing evaluation, some connect to agencies, and some connect to educational institutions. Some promote BAM. Some promote female trainers. Some promote technology, and others promote missiology. Some emphasize exit strategy. Some urge CP-3 work. And on and on we could go!" Dr. Nobley exhaled, shaking his head and pretending to run out of breath. "But you get the point.

"Our God is a very creative God! That means there is no one size that fits all. Or three or six sizes, for that matter. Wise facilitators will seek God's wisdom to know the type of facilitation necessary for a specific context and time. And we will need new creative combinations that have yet to exist. So be creative!"

✻ ✻ ✻

"Well, that does it for the moment," concluded the professor with a clap. He turned in his swivel chair and began gathering his things. "Recognizing that we're working off of a limited number of case studies, Bev," he said over his shoulder, "could you read us what you've compiled on best practices for facilitators?"

Bev read the following:

Best Practices of Successful Facilitators

1. Recognize that God orchestrates the changes in global missions.

2. Expect divine encounters.

3. Know that relationships greatly determine outcomes.

4. Implement an exit strategy.

5. Work in CP-1 and CP-2 more often than CP-3.

6. Avoid burnout by trusting Jesus to build his church.

7. Accept that long-term impact requires long-term participation.

8. See transformation holistically.

9. Facilitate sustainable human and economic resources.

10. Make sure sound missiology drives the training, strategy, and curricula.

11. Focus on holistic church multiplication.

12. Recognize the reality of persecution and martyrdom.

13. Guard against stereotyping the form facilitation should take.

"Not too shabby if I do say so myself!" exclaimed a proud professor. "You two are to be commended for all your hard work. See you next week, when we'll discuss an important question. If I believe so strongly in facilitation, then why do I still teach pioneer church multiplication? You may be in for a few surprises."

Dr. Nobley had already stuffed his laptop and a stack of papers into his computer bag. He hurriedly swept cookie crumbs off the desk with his hand and nearly stumbled over a chair on his way to the door. "OK," he beamed, with a wink and a wave, "I'm off to meet my wife! Take care."

WEEK 9

So Why Do You Still Teach Pioneer Church Multiplication?

"**W**E REALLY ENJOYED EXAMINING the sixteen case studies with you last week, Dr. Nobley," said Bev. "The cases gave us a glimpse of what God is doing today in the Fourth Era all over the world, and last week's review helped us to pull out some meaningful lessons."

"I'm glad to hear that, Bev," Dr. Nobley said. "I thought that the discussion would be helpful. For seven weeks, we had considered the historical and theoretical underpinnings of the facilitator era. Then through the case studies, you got a feel for facilitation in practice. Last week, I thought it was time for you to delve into praxis—to bring study and experience, or theory and practice, together so that each informs the other."

"Making a list of the take-aways from the case studies really helped me," Bill said, "and I noticed several consistent themes. Relationships determine outcomes, to a great extent. Facilitators need to be good listeners, have a lot of patience, and be willing to undergo constant role changes. Things are always changing—"

"And I was amazed at the variety of venues and styles for facilitation out there," Bev interjected enthusiastically before stopping short. "Oops. I'm afraid I interrupted you again."

"No problem, dear. I'm used to it," Bill chuckled, motioning for her to continue.

"I noticed the innumerable shapes facilitation can take. The case studies showed facilitators working in rural and urban settings. Some were experienced missionaries and others were total newcomers. Some facilitators parachuted in. Others were semi-permanent or permanent. Some learned the language, and some didn't—and seemed always to be wondering what was going on. Several facilitators used story to communicate the gospel. Some were holistic, and others focused exclusively on the spiritual side. Endless possibilities!"

"So what are we discussing today, Dr. Nobley?" Bill asked.

The professor, with his usual cheerful hospitality, poured three cups of steaming coffee.

✳   ✳   ✳

"I know you two have been wondering why I would still be teaching a course on pioneer church multiplication if I really believed in my own theory about the Fourth Era," he smiled. "So that's our topic for this week.

"Be alert to the fact that out in the missions world, you may hear some pretty harsh slams against pioneering. You may hear someone say something like, 'Pioneer church planting is passé, just a thing of the past.' Or here's a stronger one that I actually read the other day: 'The day of the white man going and starting churches among nationals is over.'[1] That's pretty strong, but the author went even further: 'Equipping nationals who are less expensive, just as smart, and already know the language and culture just makes sense. Their effectiveness will always outstrip a westerner. That isn't an insult to us as much as it exposes the fact that we aren't being smart about how we strategize.'[2]

"Why is it that mission agencies focusing primarily on pioneer church planting—like New Tribes, SIM, and World Team—suddenly lack clarity about their role? They want to continue sending their personnel into unreached groups, but the fact is that a strong national church now exists. As I mentioned in one of our weeks together, Jenkins affirms that pioneers have been successful in seeing national churches emerge, mature, and take up the challenge of making disciples.[3] So some ask, 'Why continue sending people overseas to pioneer if they're not needed?' All this sound familiar to your situation?"

"Sure does," nodded Bill with a sigh. "As we said before, we feel called to pioneer a cross-cultural CPM. And you just described some of the opposition that we're facing. We know there are still thousands of unreached people groups who need a CPM. We continue to pray for

1. Roberts, *Transformation*, 164.

2. Ibid., 166.

3. Jenkins, *Next Christendom*.

insight to know what to do. So, Dr. Nobley," Bill continued cautiously, "do you think that the harsh-sounding statements you mentioned really get at important truths? Or do they reflect the wrong questions?"

Dr. Nobley thought for a moment, choosing his words carefully. "I think you may be sensing that reality is a little bit of both, Bill," he said seriously. "I certainly don't want to argue about the success of missions over the first three eras, even with all the associated flaws. The success of pioneer missions is a reality, thank God. But it is also true that a lot more remains to be done.

"Regarding the quotation about white men—which, by the way, does not seem to apply to white women—you have to ask, *are the Great Commission, Great Commandment, and cultural mandate complete for certain ethnicities?* I think we know the answer to that question. *No!* So there's the first reason that I still teach a course on pioneer church multiplication: the Great Commission and Great Commandment remain for every generation and for each ethnicity.

"Pioneer church planting is not dead, nor should it be for any ethnicity. Paul sets the agenda for every generation when he states, 'It has always been my ambition to preach the gospel where Christ was not known, so that I would not be building on someone else's foundation.'[4]

"There's so much truth in Paul's larger quotation, but let's unpack it to get at some common misconceptions. One of the questions that we could ask about Paul's statement is, who is most effective at starting a CPM in any culture? The answer is obvious: those of the *same* culture. This rationale drives a common assumption reflected in the quote I just read you about the white man: that nationals alone—and not western-ers—should become the next generation of pioneer church planters. This idea makes sense, but we must dig deeper. Do you remember our discussion of CP-1, CP-2, and CP-3?"

"We do," said Bev as she twisted her ponytail.

"It's certainly true that evangelizing across cultures is complex," continued Dr. Nobley, "whether you're working in CP-2, near-cultural church planting, or in CP-3, cross-cultural church planting. How well you two know that! You probably also know through hard experience that the layers of complexity are often entirely overlooked by everyone involved, including teams, agencies, and supporting churches. Who can

4. Rom 15:20

most effectively start a CPM among those of a *similar* culture? Or of a *distant* culture?

"History gives us a hint. It has always been dicey for Caucasians to try to reach First Nations peoples because of past broken treaties and other breaches of trust. Mongolians receive a much more open response. In contrast, Caucasians can expect a warm reception when they work among Micronesians, who believe cargo cult myths that a white person will bring the keys to unleash material goods.

"But we can't settle for a simplistic answer. Even though it can be more complex to evangelize across cultures than within one's own culture, we—like Paul—have to make sure the gospel gets out there. Have you considered that not every people group can reach all the subcultures within itself—and much less all the near neighbors of a different culture? Some, like Iranians who escaped to the United States, do not wish to be reached by Iranians because of fear of who they are and what connections they may have back in Iran that could harm family members there. It will take outsiders to reach some of these people groups. That insight was the big bomb that Ralph Winter dropped at the first Lausanne Congress on World Evangelization in 1974.[5] Remember E-1, E-2, and E-3, the three degrees of cultural distance that Winter identified as being important considerations in evangelism? Winter was right then and he still is. And that's the second reason I still teach pioneer church multiplication. We must strategize wisely. And wise strategy means considering much more than skin color. *Every* group of Christians who wish to become co-laborers with God in starting a CPM must make the effort to do the job effectively, according to what the cultural context demands."

"A question for you," asserted Bev. "Do you discuss CPMs when you teach about pioneering?"

"Of course I do," responded Dr. Nobley, "and the reasons are numerous and varied. I touched on some of them in one of our times together, if I remember correctly. Let me give you a few of the more salient ones even if I do a little repetition from previous weeks," the professor said. "Would one of you mind listing the reasons for teaching the pioneering course on the whiteboard as we work through them?"

5. Winter, "Highest Priority."

"I'll do it," answered Bev as she searched for a marker.

"CPMs become the ultimate vision statement for church planters in that they help define the final goal: a movement. That's another reason I teach the course. The goal is to see not just an individual, not just a family, but multiple families—hopefully following the natural bridges of God that include extended families—all following Christ so that a movement evolves and continues to expand. The big question will be whether it can multiply outside of the initial culture. Can the movement cross cultural boundaries?

"We now must ask, what kind of movement should result? One common value you will hear today is the desire for a *sustainable* movement. This value raises another question: sustainable in what areas? If sustainable refers to just keeping the movement going, I would have some deep reservations. Keeping a movement going that includes mostly those who have experienced deep worldview transformation is one thing. Keeping a movement going without such transformation is a totally different matter. That's why I prefer to speak of *authentic* CPMs rather than merely sustainable ones.

"Part of an authentic CPM for me includes obedience to the Great Commandment. While this factor may slow down the rapidity of a movement, it says to all within hearing that Christianity is *a total way of life* that addresses *all* areas of life—the physical, emotional, intellectual, social, material, and spiritual—a message that really matters to those cultures that socialize their peoples to think holistically. Service ministries should accompany spiritual ministries. Even some BAM projects may be required. Transformational missiology should accompany frontier missiology.

"I disagree with CPM expert David Garrison that, 'slow sowing and slow harvesting communicate to the hearer that the message isn't urgent so why bother responding to it?'[6] Sounds too Western to me! People who make group decisions require adequate time to sort out the implications of such decisions, especially those associated with religion. Would you switch religions after hearing a few presentations on Buddhism, even by a persuasive advocate? That's a rhetorical question, of course. We must *make haste slowly* so that an *authentic* movement results, not just a sustainable movement.

6. Garrison, *Church Planting Movements,* 244.

"A few weeks back, we discussed the role of narrative in facilitating a CPM. Cross-cultural evangelism is much more complex and time-consuming than most people recognize. Our goals as church planters are to keep the gospel message pure, to make it contextually understandable, to challenge the existing worldview's misplaced allegiance, and to make the message reproducible by those who embrace it so that an authentic movement can take place.

"Our presentation of the gospel, for the most part, should not begin in the New Testament. This means that we need to present some Old Testament characters and events so that the Jesus story makes sense. The inclusion of Old Testament characters is foundational to interpreting the Jesus story and instrumental in the deep-level transformation of one's worldview. Notice that the time it takes to present the story, from creation to Christ, provides opportunity for hearers to sort out the significance of the story for themselves. The spider, or the central character, and the web, or the big picture, are both necessary for worldview transformation. How the evangelism goes determines to a large extent how the movement will go. It's that central!

"I think I said this before, but it bears repeating. If you mess up the message, you mess up the movement. That's why it's so important that those who present the gospel know how the host audience will interpret each component of the gospel: the Bible, God, Satan, Jesus, the Holy Spirit, sin, repentance, the free gift, faith, heaven, hell, and others. Knowing the correlations between gospel components and culture will help the communicator avoid the trip wires of culture. A simple team exercise in identifying how the host culture will respond to each element can help identify the bridges and barriers in communicating the good news. Few have taken the time to do it.

"Let me now review a few books that deal with CPMs," said the professor as he headed for a stack of books lying on the dark mahogany table. "Of course, terminology has changed over the many years this topic has been discussed, as you will see. In *Church and People in New Guinea*, George Vicedom tells the intriguing story of a CPM initiated by Christian Keysser which took place at Mount Hagen from 1900 through 1960. By 1960 the movement consisted of some two-hundred thousand baptized Papuans, among whom were twelve hundred national evangelists.

In *Christian Mass Movements in India,* J. Waskom Pickett, who lived from 1890 to 1981, documented a CPM in southern India. After learning of Pickett's work, Donald McGavran recruited Pickett to come up to the north and document a CPM taking place there. This endeavor resulted in McGavran's *Church Growth and Group Conversions,* which was first published in 1936 and then reprinted in 1973. All of this background helped lead McGavran to define *pante ta ethne,* or 'the nations,' in Matthew 28:19 as people groups. His pragmatic thinking went something like this. Evangelize *people groups* so that you get *people movements* that result in *homogeneous unit churches,* or *people group churches.*

"Alan Tippett followed with *People Movements in Southern Polynesia* in 1971. In the meantime, Winter helped popularize McGavran's people group concept by identifying the remaining number of unreached people groups, or UPGs, and providing the means to reach them for Christ through training, publications, societies, the Perspectives course, William Carey Library, and a host of other offerings at the US Center for World Mission. Winter continued this work up until his passing in 2009."

"Here's something I've always wondered about," said Bill, "What factors demonstrate that a movement is sustainable? How many generations are needed to prove that a sustainable movement is in place?"

"More great questions," responded the Dr. Nobley. "They point to at least two aspects of a CPM: leadership development and exit strategy. Let me break this down, beginning with McGavran.

"McGavran had a big heart for evangelism. In fact, his last book, *Effective Evangelism,* dealt with the topic. He was so concerned about evangelism that he gave little time to leadership development. It's not that he didn't recognize that leadership development was important; rather, he wanted more and more people to be able to hear the gospel, so that's where he focused. This narrow focus broadened over time, of course, but I say this to make a point. Evangelism without leadership development will kill a movement in a hurry, making it unsustainable. Leadership development is central to the sustainability of any movement.

"Now back to your question about how many generations. Craig Ott and Gene Wilson claim that it takes four generations to demonstrate a sustainable movement:

- Generation 1: Outside apostles start a church.

- Generation 2: Apostles work alongside locals, and locals take the lead.

- Generation 3: New leaders learn from their peers, and missionaries observe, intervening only when asked.

- Generation 4: Missionaries release local leaders to continue multiplication.[7]

"With my phase-out-oriented exit strategy in mind, I would probably settle for passing the final baton to local leaders in Generation 3. Of course, I'd pass other batons sooner for various aspects of ministry. After the final handover in Generation 3, I'd continue an itinerant ministry as needed. The key thing I'd keep in mind before passing batons would be to make sure that there is local leadership in place that is capable in character, commitment, competency, chemistry, and multiplication.

"Part of that competency would include the ability to communicate Bible stories accurately, contextually, and challengingly, so that the gospel is guarded and genuine worldview transformation can result, making an authentic movement possible. For some groups, competency would include the ability to work with missiological astuteness in cross-cultural contexts, whether CP-2 or CP-3. The fact that a well-thought-out exit strategy is central to any CPM gives you another reason I still teach the pioneering course."

✵   ✵   ✵

"Got it," said Bev. "One of the things I noticed when we categorized the books on church planting was that few of them even mentioned curriculum development, except for those that focused exclusively on the topic. Do you include curriculum development in your course?"

"I certainly do," answered Dr. Nobley. "And here's why. George Patterson and Dick Scoggins argue that telling Bible stories enables a movement to spread,[8] and I would add that character theology does, too. A curriculum helps a movement not only to stay on the move, but also to remain authentic. How? Well, it doesn't change. The printed word now in frozen format helps ensure that orally-presented Bible materi-

---

7. Ott and Wilson, *Global Church Planting,* 86.

8. Patterson and Scoggins, *Church Multiplication Guide,* 53.

als remain anchored to the written Bible. This safeguard becomes more necessary as time passes.

"Paul Gupta, president of Hindustan Bible Institute—I think you re-viewed his book back in Week 1—noted that when students went out to plant churches cross-culturally, the experience was 'far more challenging than anyone imagined.'[9] There are several reasons for this difficulty—history, worldview, decision-making patterns, pedagogical preferences, leadership styles, followership styles, economics, politics, and others—but I want to focus on just one: CP models and strategies. Here's another reason I teach the course. Because of all the cultural diversity out there, there's no universal CP model or strategy."

"It seems," began Bill, "that people tend to romanticize certain CP models and usually have some Scripture to support their claim. What tends to happen, then, is that they force the model into a different con-text and then wonder what went wrong. There are a lot of models out there today. How can we know which to use where?"

"Let me see if I can at least begin to answer your question," said Dr. Nobley. "For sure, a plethora of models exists out there, as your review of the literature demonstrated in the first week. And all models make various claims, some of which are utopian. One thing that often gets overlooked, however, is that they all have a history. More on that later.

"By *models* I mean some kind of construct, structure, framework, or grid that is designed to accomplish a specific goal. *Strategies*, on the other hand, refer to action plans that help convert models into ac-complishments. The former answers the *what* question, and the latter answers the *how* question. Even so, both are interrelated and cannot function appropriately without the other.

"Let me build on the four roles I identified back in Week 2: pioneers (whom some call apostles), founder–pastors, renewers, and facilitators. Which models and strategies work best in the context of each of these roles? Think about it. For example, which models and strategies work best in a pioneer context? Which may be better for a facilitator context? Roles and contexts, rather than personal preference, should influence the type of CP models and strategies chosen.

9. Gupta and Lingenfelter, *Breaking Tradition*, 57.

Four Types of CP Models

Bible Studies	Training	Service	Networks
House Churches	Short Cycle	PEACE Plan	DAWN
Chronological Approach	Vocational	Health Care	Saturation CPing
Alpha Course	Seminaries	English Camps	Multi-congregational
Virtual	Seminars	BAM	Multi-ethnic

"We can become more specific. To help corral the plethora of CP models out there, I created four categories to identify the main ones," continued Dr. Nobley as he headed to the whiteboard. "These include Bible Studies, Training, Service, and Networks. Here are a few models that would fit under each category. You'll notice that overlap is certainly possible.

"Probably the majority of CPMs get started through a Bible study of some sort—some of which include divine encounters and supernatural manifestations. Many house churches have emerged, as have some virtual churches, through this method. Chronological Bible Storying has swept the world in multiple versions, one of which we saw in the Aid Sudan case study by Peter Swann. The Alpha course has helped lead many to Christ, some entering exiting churches and others entering new churches.

"The Training and Service categories that I've written on the whiteboard serve as holistic approaches to ministry. The Short Cycle case study from Poland we reviewed began with a gospel music choir, which led to seminars on the meanings of the songs being sung, which led to Bible studies, which led to the birth of a new church! Once Russia opened, Koreans rushed in to start many seminaries to train local Christians to go out and plant churches. The Assemblies of God are big on starting Bible schools.

"Ben Beckner's case study about Trinity Bible College in Kursk, Russia, would also fall into this camp, as does Monroe Brewer's case study on the Chinese missionary training. The Moses Project and the Philip Project noted in Peter Swann's case study could fit here as well. Many have used vocational schools that teach students everything from how to cut logs to how to use complicated computer programs to how to find Christ and become part of a new faith movement.

"Others use sports, from coaching to clubs, from soccer to softball, as a means to start CPMs. Still others become involved in HIV/AIDS or human trafficking, as in the PEACE Plan, or English camps in Ukraine, or community development, or dentistry. A training or service strategy for sparking a CPM could even include a Great Commission company, as we saw in Diane Thomas's case study on handcrafted jewelry and in Steve Saint's ITec company, which manufactures and sells RV–10 airplanes and which was mentioned in the Jackson case study. Bible translation and literacy could also fall under either of these as demonstrated in Sue Russell's case study in Southeast Asia.

"The final major category, Networking, includes models that network or partner multiple groups to accomplish a specific goal. The groups' affiliation with one another may be long term, short term, or somewhere in between. In the first week, when you reviewed the literature, we saw this type of model in the DAWN movement, Saturation Church Planting, the multi-congregational model, and the multi-ethnic model. Our case studies that also highlight this type of model include Bryan Thomas's Biblical Leadership Training Coalition, Robert Strauss's COMIBAM, Jay Jackson's ALTECO, my STMs in Peru, and Mike Wilson's Asian Access.

"Many other models could be added under each of the four categories, but I'll leave that up to you. One thing we should be quick to learn, however, is that there is no silver bullet in this complex world. We must learn to match the model to the moment and to select effective strategies to accomplish it."

"Something that I have continually wondered about is whether church planters should use only one model for a movement," inquired Bev. "And how are you defining a generation? Twenty years?"

"More excellent questions," responded Dr. Nobley as he refilled everyone's coffee cups. "I think we may need multiple models and strategies for one CPM. Remember, if you're reaching out two to four generations, things will change—and I'm not talking about time here but about different groups of people, such as generations, sub-cultures, or ethnic groups. Times will change, and people will change. Therefore, models and strategies must change. We may even need multiple models within the first generation, depending on the various subgroups that comprise it.

"Here's another aside," the professor said, a wry smile crossing his face. "I'm convinced that not all of the necessary models are already out there. As Picasso once said, 'Good artists copy; great artists steal.'[10] So become great model artists. Get creative. Steal a lot—that is, be on the alert for the good ideas of others!—and, of course, give credit where credit is due. Creativity is far too often sacrificed on the altar of conformity. God is very creative, so we must be, too, if we are to be effective co-laborers in churching this world with authentic CPMs.

"But we can become more specific yet, going beyond the four types of models," said the professor as he handed charts to the couple.

"I've given you a handout based on three pages from Tom Steffen's church-planting book, *Passing the Baton*. I've known Tom since the day I was born. I've adapted his original work slightly, but we know each other so well that I'm sure he won't mind," Dr. Nobley said with a giggle and a wag of his head. "Because of the plethora of models out there, Steffen created a model to critique models. His critiquing tool considers a model's comprehensiveness as well as its effectiveness.[11] If you want to know how good a model is for your needs, test it with this tool.

"Look at the first page, 'Evaluating a Model's Comprehensiveness,'" directed Dr. Nobley. "You'll see that Steffen recommends five categories of questions that any team should ask about the model that they are considering."[12]

10. Brainy Quote website, "Pablo Picasso," example 10, http://www.brainyquote.com/quotes/authors/p/pablo_picasso.html

11. Steffen, *Passing the Baton*, 83–85.

12. Ibid., adapted from figure, 83.

Is it Biblical?

- Covers entire Word (OT/NT)
- Depends on Holy Spirit
- Encourages prayer
- Presents accurate gospel

Is it Incarnational?

- Enables language acquisition
- Enables culture acquisition
- Fosters healthy relationship within the team
- Fosters healthy team relationship with host community

Is it Holistic?

- Addresses felt needs
- Addresses spiritual needs

Is it Empowering?

- Plans and accepts role changes for church planters
- Plans and accepts role changes for nationals
- Nurtures long-term vision
- Maintains phase-out orientation

Is it Reproducible?

- Develops local community
- Promotes evangelism to, among, and by nationals
- Disciples new believers faithfully and develops national disciplers
- Trains leadership
- Builds organizational structure within new church
- Implements multiplication strategy within new church
- Remains economically feasible

"Helpful questions, wouldn't you agree?" the professor asked. "This part of Steffen's critiquing tool considers how much of the Bible a particular model covers. For example, does it cover just the New Testament or parts of both Testaments? It also investigates the incarnational demands of the model and how holistic it is. Finally, it investigates the extent to which the model empowers the local leadership and followership, and whether locals will be able to reproduce it, i.e., to keep the movement going generationally.

"As to *effectiveness,* Steffen's critiquing model requires that teams think through the reasoning behind the model. He instructs teams to analyze—and to write out their findings about—these six topics:[13]

- History
- Key Features
- Assumptions
- Strengths
- Weaknesses
- Adaptability

"First, Steffen says to consider the *history* of the model. Why? Because many times, you'll find that a new model is a reaction to a former model. For example, Venn and Anderson's three-self model was a reaction to dependency models. McIlwain's Chronological Bible Teaching model was a reaction to models that failed to provide sufficient Old Testament foundation for the gospel—quick-draw evangelism, if you will. Steffen's phase-out oriented exit strategy[14] was a reaction to all those models out there that unintentionally or intentionally overlooked the eventual need to leave. If you don't understand this background for the model you are considering, you may overlook a model's best insights or its blind spots.

"The next two components, *key features* and *assumptions,* are closely related. I guess—and don't you ever tell anyone I said this because it sounds ridiculously simple—that if you were able to identify accurately just the assumptions of a model, you'd almost have all you need for your critique. You'd almost instantly be able to isolate the theories that drive it and to identify its strengths and weaknesses.

"Since both of you are familiar with Steffen's *Passing the Baton,* what would you consider to be some of the assumptions that drive his five-stage model?"

13. Ibid., adapted from figure, 85.
14. Steffen, *Passing the Baton.*

Taking two dry-erase markers from the table, Bev and Bill began to write. In just a few minutes, they showed Dr. Nobley their list:

Steffen's Assumptions

—Evaluating a model takes a team

—Models should be holistic

—Solid relationships are necessary among teammates and with nationals

—Holy Spirit can develop *all* his people

—All followers of Christ should be empowered

—Mistakes are a given

—Leadership is stewardship, not ownership

—Empowering others multiplies power

—Role changes are necessary for expatriates and nationals

—Cross-cultural ministry is pilgrim in nature

—Interdependent movement is the goal

"You nailed the assumptions!" exclaimed an elated professor. "Assumptions are in reality the theories behind the model. And each assumption will have at least one rival theory. That's why it's so important to know the historical context from which the model originated. And that's why *every* model has a shelf life.

"Steffen's last component considers adaptability, or how well the model fits the moment in a specific context. This is where cultural re-

Steffen's Model Analysis, Part A	Score 1-10
Model Comprehensiveness	
Biblical? Does it cover both Old and New Testaments and present an accurate gospel?	
Incarnational? Does it enable the team to serve the nationals with the self-sacrificing love of Jesus?	
Holistic? Does it address physical, social, and spiritual needs?	
Empowering to Nationals? Does it include a timeline for handing authority over to national believers, and does it have an exit strategy?	
Reproducible? Is it designed to multiply new believers, leaders, and churches?	
TOTAL (50 possible)	

Steffen's Model Analysis, Part B

Model Effectiveness	Score 1-10
History receives no score, but team should a) understand the needs that produced the model and b) consider its unique insights, possible overreactions, or blind spots.	
Key Features	
Implementing this model is realistic and doable (logistics, finances, personnel, materials, timing, etc.).	
Assumptions	
Team agrees with the identified assumptions behind the model and knows how to handle/answer rival assumptions.	
Strengths	
Both benefits of implementation and advantages of this model over others are very compelling.	
Weaknesses	
Weaknesses are few, or team has a plan for managing them.	
Adaptability	
Team has thoroughly studied the cultural fit of the model.	
TOTAL (50 possible)	
TOTAL of A and B (100 possible)	

search is required. While we don't have time to go into depth on this now, Winston Churchill's questions surrounding the fall of Singapore to Japan during World War II are helpful in relation to model selection: 'Why didn't I know? Why wasn't I told? Why didn't I ask? Why didn't I tell what I knew?'[15]

"You could score each of the components if you want. While this activity is somewhat subjective, it does make for a great team exercise. Any score below eighty, look out. I like to say, 'Be sure of the before-math or you will surely face the aftermath!'

"Wow," Bev marveled. "I wonder what our team would have scored before we embarked on our work in the Philippines."

"I was just thinking the same thing myself," Bill mused. "Probably not too high, I'm sorry to say."

"But next time, we'll have a tool to help us think through the process of choosing a model," said Bev.

✳   ✳   ✳

"Could we talk a little more about facilitators for a minute?" requested Bill. "We've seen some of these so-called 'facilitators' come over to the Philippines and work with Filipino Christian leaders. As we listened, it became apparent that some were speaking cognitively with little or no pioneer church-planting experience, while others spoke out of deep understanding of the literature, the topic, and practical know-how. My question is this. Can someone really be a facilitator before being a pioneer church planter?"

"You two are on a roll today with astute questions," responded the professor. "I love it. Bill, you have placed your finger on one of the main reasons I teach the course. Ah, where do I start? Let's start with what makes a good facilitator.

"What we've discussed so far is definitely important, and that's why it's included in the course. But the background experience of the facilitator ranks high on the list. Can someone facilitate without first having gained experience in pioneer church planting? For sure, some are trying. But they don't seem to last long. Their listeners—the nationals—know that they will soon be out there doing pioneer church planting themselves, so they want to learn more than the facilitator can teach! And

---

15. Allinson, *Global Disasters*, 11–12.

that's another reason I teach the pioneering course: so that facilitators learn something about it. The reality is that nationals pioneer CPMs! If the facilitator has neither experience nor knowledge in pioneer church planting, it becomes very difficult to teach nationals how to do it.

"So yes, Bill, the facilitator must know, have experienced, and have the ability to teach what it takes to pioneer a cross-cultural CPM. To be a good facilitator requires that someone be a good pioneer church planter. Let me go further. Pioneer church planters can become facilitators, but facilitators without some pioneer church-planting experience should not apply. There's another one for your list, Bev."

"Got it," responded Bev.

"Did you notice what I just said? That the facilitator should have some cross-cultural church planting experience?" inquired the professor as he intently searched the eyes of both Bill and Bev.

"I heard it, but I'm not sure I understand all the implications," responded Bill.

"The reason I included *cross-cultural*," continued the professor, "is that such a perspective helps challenge the idea that the models for CPMs, evangelism, discipleship, community development, business, doxology, and so forth, that are used back home will work over there as well. When you consider all aspects of church planting from a cross-cultural perspective, it's like looking into a big mirror. The reflection challenges you to reconsider the validity of everything you do. And that's healthy!

"As we saw in Week 4, one of the major differences between the pioneer and the facilitator is the incarnational role. Pioneers have to be there on the ground for an extended period of time to see a CPM take off. That time spent with the nationals offers tremendous opportunities to learn the culture and language, critically contextualize the gospel, model Christianity, and immediately mentor and network potential and seasoned leaders. It is in this context, where lives touch lives, that deep relationships emerge. Things get talked about in homes and on journeys, just as described in Deuteronomy 6:7. Casual friends are casual friends. Close friends become family. We're now on our third cup of tea; we're no longer strangers or friends, but family.

"Those facilitators who parachute in will have little time to develop the level of relationships earned and enjoyed by pioneers. They will have little time to model what it takes to forge such deep relationships and start a CPM. Little if any modeling will be possible. And modeling is something of great significance to those who come out of an apprenticeship background—and to others as well. As Albert Schweitzer points out, 'Example is not the main thing in influencing others. It is the only thing.'[16] Semi-permanent and permanent facilitators, of course, would have much more opportunity to accomplish all of these."

"I guess I would summarize it this way," interjected Bill. "It takes some time, practical experience, and the ability to teach to make a credible facilitator. A facilitator has to know cross-cultural pioneer church planting because the people they teach must know it to be effective pioneer church planters."

"You caught it," smiled the professor, pleased. "And that means that facilitators will have to get pioneer church-planting experience somewhere, and hopefully it will be cross-cultural. We now have plenty of facilitators with pioneer backgrounds. A new generation of facilitators should come in no different.

✳   ✳   ✳

"The reason that ranks highest on the list for why I still teach the pioneering course is that the job of discipling the world is not yet done. Three statistics should suffice. There are close to three million unevangelized people residing in what some missiologists call World A, places where people have 'not yet heard of Christ, Christianity, or the Gospel' *at all*.[17] The Joshua Project has identified 6,838 unreached or least-reached people groups in the world, many of whom reside in the 10/40 window. That's 2.7 billion people—with a *b!*—or over 40 percent of the world's population.[18] It will take pioneers from every ethnicity to reach these people. Some of those pioneers will come from the West.

"But how does reaching them work out in practice? Remember our discussion on dependency, independence, and interdependence?" asked Dr. Nobley.

"We do," said Bev.

"Most likely, a lot of pioneer church planting by westerners will be accomplished through multiethnic teams in the Fourth Era. Some westerners gifted through the Holy Spirit will and should lead these teams.

16. Quotations Page website, "Classic Quotes," Albert Schweitzer quotation no. 34600, http://www.quotationspage.com/quote/34600.html

17. Gordon-Conwell Theological Seminary, "World A," para. 1.

18. Joshua Project, "Great Commission Statistics," Global.

Others will do it on totally Western teams. Still others, like a friend of mine in China, will spend eight years in pioneer church planting so that he can become what he felt he was really gifted to do: facilitate. However it gets accomplished, we should rejoice that more of the unreached will now have opportunity to respond to the good news. There's no room for tribalism, nationalism, or competiveness. Pioneer church planting is part of the residue from the first three eras that bleeds over heavily into the Fourth Era. Western participation will be part of that residue, however implemented. And you two will be part of that army," Dr. Nobley said, nodding at Bill and Bev.

"OK, Bev," he said, standing and collecting the coffee cups. "Review for us what you've got."

Bev read the following.

Why Teach Pioneer Church Multiplication?

1. The Great Commission & the Great Commandment remain for every generation & ethnicity.

2. Not every people group can reach all subcultures within itself or all near neighbors of a different culture.

3. We must be able to define an authentic CPM.

4. A well thought out exit strategy is necessary.

5. A well thought out curriculum is necessary.

6. There's no universal CP model or strategy.

7. Nationals pioneer new CPMs.

8. Facilitation requires pioneer experience.

9. The large number of unevangelized and unengaged people groups demands a response.

"Excellent," concluded Dr. Nobley. "Can't wait for the new semester to begin so that I can teach the course on Pioneer Church Multiplication and help prepare a new generation for the Fourth Era, pioneers and facilitators alike. See you next week."

Week 10

So Now What?

"**O**H, NO!" SIGHED BILL as he read a text message from Dr. Nobley. "He's been called out of the country for several weeks to do some emergency consulting, and he's leaving tomorrow! We're not going to be able to meet with him again before we take off on our own travels. This is *déjà vu*, like what happened to us the first week."

"Well, things worked out pretty well then," consoled Bev, "and they'll work out fine this time, too . . . except that Dr. Nobley won't be able to see the PowerPoint I made for last week." Bev and Bill sat in silence, disappointment on their faces. Bev began to twirl her ponytail as she stared into the distance.

"Oh, well," she sighed. "Maybe we should take what's left of this week to reflect back on our nine weeks together to see what we've learned—or maybe more appropriately, what we've unlearned. We could write up our thoughts, along with a big thank you, and email them to him. How does that sound?"

"That's why I married you, Hon," said Bill. "That's a great idea. Let's get started right now."

Dear Dr. Nobley,

While we regret that we will not be able to meet next week, we want to thank you for the nine weeks that we were able to get together. Our times have been instructive, challenging, and encouraging. Our paradigms have shifted. We think that we have gained some valuable insights regarding our future ministry, as we'll expand below. So please accept our heartfelt thanks. We know you're a very busy person and that you're in constant demand. When you return from your trip, you'll find Starbucks and Borders gift cards in your mailbox—just small tokens of our deep appreciation. Enjoy.

Well, what did we learn along the way? Here are a few of the main things in relation to North American missions. It's a laundry list for sure, but we tried to keep it concise to save you some time. If you need more clarification on any of these, just let us know.

- We're in the Fourth Era.
- Rick Warren leads the Fourth Era.
- Facilitators will play the dominant role in the Fourth Era.
- The Fourth Era requires North American and indigenous pioneers.
- It's important to distinguish between the roles and profiles of pioneers and facilitators.
- The Fourth Era includes long-termers and short-termers.
- The Fourth Era includes all age groups and both genders.
- Some efforts, like holistic church planting, continue through all eras but in different packaging.
- Pioneer predecessors were not perfect; nor are present-day facilitators.
- Facilitators should have cross-cultural church-planting experience.
- Pioneers and facilitators should have an exit strategy.
- Learn to "live loved" so that you can genuinely serve others.[1]
- Be a lifelong learner.
- Shared power results in multiplied power.
- Every model and strategy has a shelf life.
- Mixed ethnicities, in contrast to a people group, will require glocal theologies, models, strategies, and curricula.
- Build interdependent partnerships.
- Nationals tend to focus on CP-1 and C-P2.
- Define the "unreached" to include CP-3.
- Distinguish the CP complexity level to avoid oversimplification.

1. Young, *The Shack*, 177.

- Nationals involved in CP-2 and CP-3 require cross-cultural training.
- Capitalize on cyberspace, but know its limitations.
- Money matters in missions.
- BAM will play a major role in the Fourth Era.
- Rival stories help supplant engrained worldviews.
- Make haste slowly.
- Primacy should give way to ultimacy.
- Don't minimize member care for nationals who face persecution.
- Lay people bring professionalism as well as amateurization.
- Short-termers can open closed doors for locals.
- Require appropriate training for all short-termers.
- Short-termers should respect long-termers.
- Measure the results by what happens in the host culture, not by how many short-termers go.
- The 10/40 window, where the major-religious blocks reside, requires North American pioneer CPers.
- Westerners should play a facilitative role in revitalization where nominalism prevails.

So what does good stewardship demand of North Americans serving in the Fourth Era?

- Books and blogs on facilitative church multiplication
- Formal and non-formal courses on facilitative church multiplication
- Formal and non-formal courses on pioneer church multiplication
- Formal and non-formal courses on folklore
- Formal and non-formal courses on macro- and micro enterprise

Well, there you have it. We hope we've been good students ☺. We think you should write a book on facilitative church multiplication, Dr. Nobley. Feel free to use that last phrase in your title.

Let us give you a brief update on our thinking concerning our future ministry. Throughout our time together and while reading the case studies, we've come to believe that we should go back to the Philippines as facilitators, identify some key Filipino church planters from the training program we would facilitate, and invite them to join us as teammates to reach an unreached people group—possibly outside the Philippines. Not only would we be involved in pioneer church multiplication, but we would also be gaining new insights that we could eventually use as facilitators should God lead us back into this role. Kind of a cycle! Pioneer to facilitator, back to pioneer, and then facilitator again. And we haven't written off the possibility of using BAM in some capacity. We plan to Skype our old teammate Jun shortly and discuss this idea with him.

Any last advice for us, Dr. Nobley?

Regards,
Bill and Bev

Dear Bill and Bev,

Thank you for your generous gifts and your email. I read it with great enthusiasm. You *are* excellent students! I gave you both an A. I thank God for your lives and for what you've done in the Philippines, and I look forward to seeing how God will lead you in the future. I have great confidence in you and in the God we serve.

I'm reminded of a quotation from Valdir Steuernagel, a theologian with World Vision, who puts his finger on some of the issues that cause difficulty for North American facilitators attempting to minister cross-culturally in the Fourth Era:

> Not that long ago, as missions historian Andrew Walls points out, every missionary was a white, blue-eyed person. When they came to the table, they brought tremendous gifts. North Americans came out of an experience of church growth. You had experienced revival in your own country. You brought optimism: "We can do it." The church growth movement and the unreached peoples movement intensified that. "How many unreached peoples do we have? Let's map it out. A.D. 2000. Let's do it; let's do it now. Yes we can."
>
> It wasn't only theory; it was also experience. You came to the table with a lot of positive stories and ministry experiences that

you could share. Pentecostalism! Azusa Street. World Vision. Campus Crusade. Youth for Christ. Billy Graham. You could sit at the table and say, "Here it is; you do this, this, and this. You can follow the process. We know how to do it."[2]

But Steuernagel goes on to say that things have changed drastically in world missions in the last two to three decades, especially because of the rise of the Global South. Many North American Christian workers now find themselves—whether because of the successes or failures of previous pioneer church planters, or because nationals didn't catch the Great Commission for one reason or another—taking up a facilitator role. This role requires a different skill set and different spiritual giftings from those of pioneers, as we discussed in week 4. It requires not only cross-cultural pioneer church-planting experience, but also a learner attitude. Metaphorically, Edith Wharton captures the major distinction between pioneers and facilitators: "There are two ways of spreading light—to be the candle or the mirror that reflects it."[3]

Check out this statement by Aderemi Tesilimi Lawanson, a guest speaker whom I recently invited to one of my classes. He's a Nigerian who goes by Remi. I'm paraphrasing:

> Come serve with us. See what God is doing in the Global South. Take time to caution and correct us. Find those working in the Global South who are credible: there's lots of competition and pettiness out there. Give space to our slowness. Call the national workers *missionaries*. Please don't start an extension of your US agency in our country; it will kill the indigenous movement. We can't compete with you economically. Both partners must always keep the main thing the main thing—reaching the world.

Now there's some sound advice for *any* Fourth Era cross-cultural facilitator!

During our nine weeks together, I've tried to consider holistic church multiplication primarily from a North American perspective, recognizing that the North and South are tightly interlaced in the global missions enterprise. In that there's a lot of confusion out there—some claiming the superiority or the singularity of the facilitative role and others using the pioneer and facilitative roles interchangeably—I wanted to

2. Steuernagel interviewed in Stafford, "More Partners at the Table," 42.

3. Wharton, "Vesalius in Zante," 631.

see if some distinctions could be identified for their uses in the Third and Fourth Eras. So for these nine weeks, I've tried to step back, take a more global look, and ask the preliminary questions surrounding background and application differences for each of the two roles.

Gazing ahead into the foggy future, what we now need are some in-depth studies on the different types of facilitation being used in the Fourth Era. Yes, we do need a book entitled *Facilitative Church Multiplication*. Some of those case studies that you read should also become books. And we should consider how new technology will influence facilitation positively and negatively, as well as how different generations and genders respond to the facilitator role. We need major contributions on how to challenge existing syncretism, legalism, nominalism, and denominationalism. We need a beefy bibliography on facilitation from a missiological perspective. We need to look ahead and consider how a graying world will impact facilitation. And we must explore how pioneer-focused mission agencies will adapt to Fourth Era facilitation.

To answer your question about writing a book on facilitation, I'm anxiously awaiting your contribution to the missions literature, and I'll be glad to write kudos on the back cover for you. Don't forget to include all those great PowerPoint presentations, Bev, especially the little guy with the parachute. And by the way, I really missed not being able to see your latest creation. In the meantime, hopefully I've given you permission to participate in God's mission in whatever capacity he calls you— as pioneers, as facilitators, or maybe as both!

In this post–North-American-missions world, we've moved from the Third Era to the Fourth era. McGavran and Townsend have passed the baton to at least Warren. We've moved beyond the pioneer role to the facilitator role. Even so, the facilitative role should not be seen as a substitute for expatriate pioneer church planting, but rather as a supplement to further the kingdom of God. The pioneer role is part of the residue that was present in the First Era, has continued through the Second and Third Eras, and now carries on into the Fourth Era. And that's why I continue to teach a course on cross-cultural pioneer church multiplication. If we only produce facilitators without holistic field experience, they cannot speak out of the wisdom of ministry successes and failures, and the cognitive replaces practice. This shallow perspective limits the effectiveness of the facilitator, and it eventually becomes a dead-end road for both the facilitator and those they attempt to influence.

The Fourth Era redefines Western missions. In trying to be a catalyst for change, I may be in error on some of my conclusions. That's OK. Time will correct the incorrect and add new and needed insights. But I can say this categorically: correct realignment should be based on correct understanding of the current global changes within missions. I hope that in the process of realignment—especially among the megachurches, who will play a major role through short-termers and hopefully someday through long-termers—the North will

- become a lifelong learner,

- do her homework from a solid missiological perspective,

- avoid working from a guilt complex tied to the colonial era,

- respect the past and present efforts of assemblies, agencies, and academies,

- learn how to reconnect God's story to ministry,

- birth numerous profitable and job-producing Great Commission companies, and

- pass the baton often.

Wouldn't that be business as unusual?

Oh, I almost forgot. Bev, you also asked if I have any "last advice" for you. Here's what comes to mind. Make sure that the gospel continues to amaze you. Always stay long enough with the locals to drink three cups of tea. Research how your own generation could blow it. And keep in touch.

Blessings,
Dr. Nobley

Dear Dr. Nobley,

We will definitely keep you posted. You've moved us far beyond pioneer church multiplication into a whole new era: the facilitator era. Now, *that* would be a great title for your book! Keep us in your prayers.

With great appreciation,
Bill and Bev

Bibliography

Adamson, Andrew, director. *The Chronicles of Narnia: The Lion, the Witch, and the Wardrobe.* Motion picture based on book series by C. S. Lewis. Burbank, CA: Buena Vista Home Entertainment, 2005.

Adizes, Ichak. *Corporate Lifecycles: How and Why Corporations Grow and Die and What to Do About It.* Englewood Cliffs, NJ: Prentice Hall, 1998.

Allen, Roland. *Missionary Methods, St. Paul's or Ours?* Grand Rapids, MI: William B. Eerdmans, 1962.

The Alliance for Saturation Church Planting. *The Omega Course: Practical Church Planter Training.* South Holland, IL: The Bible League, 1999.

Allinson, Robert E. *Global Disasters: Inquiries into Management Ethics.* New York: Prentice Hall, 1993.

Anderson, Darrell. "Define Your Terms" *Simple Liberty* personal website. No date. Online: http://simpleliberty.nfshost.com/main/define_your_terms.htm

Apeh, John E. *Social Structure and Church Planting.* Shippensburg, PA: Destiny Image, 1989.

Appleby, Jerry. *The Church Is in a Stew: Developing Multicongregational Churches.* Kansas City, MO: Beacon Hill, 1990.

Banks, Robert. *Paul's Idea of Community: The Early House Churches in Their Historical Setting.* Grand Rapids, MI: William B. Eerdmans, 1980.

Banks, Robert, and Julia Banks. *The Church Comes Home: A New Base for Community and Mission.* Peabody, MA: Hendrickson, 1998.

Barclay, William. *The Acts of the Apostles.* Edinburgh: Saint Andrew Press, 1973.

Barnett, Thomas P. M. *Great Powers: America and the World After Bush.* New York: Putnam Adult, 2009.

Becker, Paul, and Mark Williams. *The Dynamic Daughter Church Planting Handbook.* Oceanside, CA: Dynamic Church Planting International, 2006.

Birkey, Del. *The House Church: A Model for Renewing the Church.* Scottsdale, PA: Herald, 1988.

Bolman, Lee G., and Terrence E. Deal. *Reframing Organizations: Artistry, Choice, and Leadership.* San Francisco: Jossey-Bass, 1997.

Bonk, Jonathan J. *Missions and Money: Affluence as a Missionary Problem.* Maryknoll, NY: Orbis, 2007.

Boomershine, Thomas E. *Story Journey: An Invitation to the Gospel as Storytelling.* Nashville, TN: Abingdon, 1988.

Bosch, David J. *Transforming Mission: Paradigm Shifts in Theology of Mission.* Maryknoll, NY: Orbis, 1991.

Boyd, David. *You Don't Have to Cross the Ocean to Reach the World: The Power of Local Cross-Cultural Ministry.* Grand Rapids, MI: Chosen Books, 2008.

Brock, Charles. *Indigenous Church Planting: A Practical Journey.* Neosho, MO: Church Growth International, 1990.

Brother Andrew. *God's Smuggler.* With John Sherrill and Elizabeth Sherrill. Grand Rapids, MI: Chosen Books, 2001.

Bruner, Jerome. *The Culture of Education.* Cambridge, MA: Harvard University Press, 1996.

Butler, Phill. *Well Connected: Releasing Power and Restoring Hope.* Waynesboro, GA: Authentic Media, 2006.

Carr, Edward Hallet. *What Is History? The George Macaulay Trevelyan Lectures Delivered at the University of Cambridge January–March* 1961. New York: Random House, 1961.

Chaney, Charles L. *Church Planting at the End of the Twentieth Century.* Carol Stream, IL: Tyndale House, 1993.

Cho, Paul Yonggi. *Successful Home Cell Groups.* Plainfield, NJ: Logos International, 1977.

Collier, Paul. *The Bottom Billion: Why the Poorest Countries Are Failing and What Can Be Done About It?* New York: Oxford University Press, 2008.

Conn, Harvie, M., ed. *Planting and Growing Urban Churches: From Dream to Reality.* Grand Rapids, MI: Baker Book House, 1996.

Corbett, Steve, and Brian Fikkert. *When Helping Hurts: How to Alleviate Poverty Without Hurting the Poor and Yourself.* Chicago, IL: Moody, 2009.

Crossman, Meg, ed. *Pathways to Global Understanding.* Seattle, WA: YWAM Publishing, 2007.

———. *Pathlight: Toward Global Awareness.* Seattle, WA: YWAM Publishing, 2008.

Danker, William, J. *Profit for the Lord: Economic Activities in Moravian Mission and the Basel Mission Trading Company.* Eugene, OR: Wipf & Stock, 2003.

DeYmaz, Mark. *Building a Healthy Multi-Ethnic Church: Mandate, Commitments, and Practices of a Diverse Congregation.* San Francisco: Jossey-Bass, 2007.

Dorr, Darrell. "The P.E.A.C.E. Plan: Are You Ready for Purpose Driven Mission?" *Mission Frontiers* 27, no. 3 (2005) 16–19.

Dylhoff, Joel. "Gen X." *Evangelical Missions Quarterly* 39, no. 4 (2003) 446–450.

Eldred, Kenneth. *God Is at Work: Transforming People and Nations Through Business.* Ventura, CA: Regal Books, 2005.

Encountering the World of Islam [organization website]. Online: http://www .encounteringislam.org/.

Evans, A. Steven. "Matters of the Heart: Orality, Story, and Cultural Transformation: The Critical Role of Storytelling in Affecting Worldview," *Missiology: An International Review* 38, no. 2 (2010) 185–199.

Fackre, Gabriel. "Narrative Theology: An Overview." *Interpretation* 37, no. 4 (1983) 340–353.

Fitch, David E. *The Great Giveaway: Reclaiming the Mission of the Church from Big Business, Parachurch Organizations, Psychotherapy, Consumer Capitalism, and Other Modern Maladies.* Grand Rapids, MI: Baker Books, 2005.

Ford, Leighton. *Transforming Leadership: Jesus' Way of Creating Vision, Shaping Values, and Empowering Change.* Downers Grove, IL: InterVarsity, 1993.

Friedman, Thomas L. *Hot, Flat, and Crowded: Why We Need a Green Revolution—And How It Can Renew America.* New York: Farrar, Straus, and Giroux, 2008.

———. "(No) Drill, Baby Drill." *New York Times,* April 11, 2009. Online: http://www .nytimes.com/2009/04/12/opinion/12friedman.html.

Fuder, John, and Noel Castellanos. *A Heart for the Community: New Models for Urban and Suburban Ministry.* Chicago, IL: Moody, 2009.

Galli, Mark. "Glocal Church Ministry." *Christianity Today* 51, no. 7 (2007) 42–46.

Garrison, David. *Church Planting Movements: How God Is Redeeming a Lost World.* Midlothian, VA: WIGTake Resources, 2004.

Gibbs, Eddie. *ChurchNext: Quantum Changes in How We Do Ministry.* Downers Grove, IL: InterVarsity Press, 2000.

Gordon-Conwell Theological Seminary. "World A." Online: http://ockenga .gordonconwell.edu/ockenga/globalchristianity/worlda.php.

Goulston, Mark. *Just Listen: Discover the Secret of Getting Through to Absolutely Anyone.* New York: AMACOM, 2009.

Grace Church. "2008 Peru Report." 2008. Online: http://atgrace.com/uploads/missions/ Peru_trip_report.pdf

Granberg, Hakan. *Church Planting Commitment: New Church Development in Hong Kong During the Run-Up to 1997.* Turku, Finland: Abo Akademi University Press, 2000.

Greenway, Roger S. *Discipling the City: A Comprehensive Approach to Urban Mission.* Grand Rapids, MI: Baker Book House, 1979.

———. *Cities: Missions' New Frontiers.* Grand Rapids, MI: Baker Book House, 2000.

Gregg, Viv. *Cry of the Urban Poor.* Monrovia, CA: MARC, 1992.

Grudem, Wayne. *Systematic Theology: An Introduction to Biblical Doctrine.* Grand Rapids, MI: Zondervan, 1994.

Gupta, Paul R., and Sherwood G. Lingenfelter. *Breaking Tradition to Accomplish Vision: Training Leaders for a Church-Planting Movement: A Case from India.* Winona Lake, IN: BMH Books, 2006.

Guthrie, Stan. *Missions in the Third Millennium: 21 Key Trends for the 21st Century.* Waynesboro, GA: Paternoster, 2000.

Hastings, Adrian. "The Clash of Nationalism and Universalism within Twentieth-Century Missionary Christianity." In *Missions, Nationalism, and the End of Empire,* edited by Brian Staney, 15–33. Grand Rapids, MI: William B. Eerdmans, 2003.

Hay, Alexander Rattray. *The New Testament Order for Church and Missionary.* Temperley, Argentina: New Testament Missionary Union, 1947.

Hesselgrave, David J. *Planting Churches Cross-Culturally: North America and Beyond.* Grand Rapids, MI: Baker Book House, 2000.

Hiebert, Paul G. "Critical Contextualization." *Missiology: An International Review* 12 (July 1987) 287–96.

———. "Anthropology, Missions, and Epistemological Shifts." In *Paradigm Shifts in Christian Witness: Insights from Anthropology, Communication, and Spiritual Power,* edited by Charles Van Engen, et al., 13–22. Maryknoll, NY: Orbis, 2008a.

———. *Transforming Worldviews: An Anthropological Understanding of How People Change,* Grand Rapids, MI: Baker Academic, 2008b.

———. *The Gospel in Human Contexts: Anthropological Explorations for Contemporary Missions.* Grand Rapids, MI: Baker Academic, 2009.

Hiebert, Paul G., and Eloise Hiebert Meneses. *Incarnational Ministry: Planting Churches in Band, Tribal, Peasant, and Urban Societies.* Grand Rapids, MI: Baker, 1995.

Hinton, Keith. *Growing Churches Singapore Style: Ministry in an Urban Context.* Robesonia, PA: OMF, 1988.

Hipp, Gary T. *Community Development and Discipleship: The Wedding of the Great Commandment and the Great Commission.* Burnsville, MN: Mission: Moving Mountains, 1991.

Hirsch, Alan. *The Forgotten Ways: Reactivating the Missional Church.* Grand Rapids, MI: Brazos, 2007.

Hodges, Melvin L. *The Indigenous Church.* Springfield, MO: Evangelical Publishing House, 1953.

Holy Bible, New International Version. Translated by the International Bible Society. Grand Rapids, MI: Zondervan, 1973.

Hooper, John. (2005, February 23). "Heart of Christianity Shifts from Europe—to Timbuktu." *The Guardian.* Online: http://www.guardian.co.uk/world/2005/feb/23/religion.uk1

Hozell, Francis C. *Church Planting in the African-American Context.* Grand Rapids, MI: Zondervan, 1999.

International Mission Board. "Chronological Bible Storying." On South America Region Resource Site website. Online: www.wsaresourcesite.org/Topics/storying.htm

Jenkins, Philip. *The Next Christendom: The Coming of Global Christianity.* New York: Oxford University Press, 2002.

Johnson, Alan R. *Apostolic Function in 21st Century Missions.* Pasadena, CA: William Carey Library, 2009.

Johnson, Todd. "World Christian Trends and Strategic Issues." Unpublished paper presented at meeting of the Evangelical Missiological Society Southwest Region at Biola University, La Mirada, CA, April 15, 2008.

Joshua Project. "Great Commission Statistics." No date. Online: http://www.joshuaproject.net/great-commission-statistics.php.

Koller, Charles W. *Sermons Preached Without Notes.* Grand Rapids, MI: Baker Book House, 1964.

Kouzes, James, and Barry Z. Posner. *A Leader's Legacy.* San Francisco: Jossey-Bass, 2006.

Lai, Patrick. *Tentmaking: Business as Missions.* Waynesboro, GA: Authentic Media, 2005.

Larkins, William J., Jr. *Acts.* Downers Grove, IL: InterVarsity, 1995.

Lingenfelter, Sherwood. *Transforming Culture: A Challenge for Christian Mission.* Grand Rapids, MI: Baker Academic, 1992.

Livingston, Greg. *Planting Churches in Muslim Cities: A Team Approach.* Grand Rapids, MI: Baker Academic, 1993.

Loewen, Jacob A. "Bible Stories: Message and Matrix." *Practical Anthropology* 11, no. 2 (1964) 49–54. Reprinted in *Culture and Human Values: Christian Intervention in Anthropological Perspective,* 370–376. Pasadena, CA: William Carey Library, 1975. Page references are to 1964 edition.

———. *Culture and Human Values: Christian Intervention in Anthropological Perspective.* Pasadena, CA: William Carey Library, 1975.

Logan, Robert E. *Beyond Church Growth: Action Plans for Developing A Dynamic Church.* Old Tappan, NJ: Fleming H. Revell Company, 1989.

Logan, Robert E., and Neil Cole. *Beyond Church Planting: Pathways for Emerging Churches.* St. Charles, IL: Churchsmart Resources, 2005.

Losch, Richard R. *All the People in the Bible: An A–Z Guide to Saints, Scoundrels, and Other Characters in Scripture.* Grand Rapids, MI: Eerdmans Publishing Company, 2008.

Love, Rick. *Muslims, Magic, and the Kingdom of God: Church Planting Among Folk Muslims.* Pasadena, CA: William Carey Library, 2003.

Lukasse, Johan. *Churches with Roots: Planting Churches in Post-Christian Europe.* Eastbourne, East Sussex, UK: Monarch, 1992.

Mackey, John. "Conscious Capitalism: Creating a New Paradigm for Business." Online: http://www.flowidealism.org/2007/Downloads/Conscious-Capitalism_JM.pdf

Malaquias, Assis. "Diamonds Are a Guerrilla's Best Friend: The Impact of Illicit Wealth on Insurgency Strategy." *Third World Quarterly* 22, no. 3 (2001) 311–325.

Malphurs, Aubrey. *Planting Growing Churches for the 21st Century: A Comprehensive Guide for New Churches and Those Desiring Renewal.* Grand Rapids, MI: Baker Books, 2004.

Maxwell, Joe. "The Mission of Business: Companies Around the World are Mixing Profits with Gospel Ministry." *Christianity Today* 51, no. 11 (2007) 24–28.

Mayers, Marvin K. *Christianity Confronts Culture: A Strategy for Crosscultural Evangelism.* Grand Rapids, MI: Zondervan, 1987.

McGavran, Donald A. *Understanding Church Growth.* Grand Rapids, MI: William B. Eerdmans, 1970.

———. *Church Growth and Group Conversion.* Pasadena, CA: William Carey Library, 1973.

———. *Understanding Church Growth.* Grand Rapids, MI: William B. Eerdmans, 1980.

———. *Effective Evangelism: A Theological Mandate.* Phillipsburg, NJ: Presbyterian and Reformed Publishing, 1988.

———. *The Satnami Story: The Thrilling Drama of Religious Change.* Pasadena, CA: William Carey Library, 1990.

———. *Bridges of God: A Study in the Strategy of Missions.* Eugene, OR: Wipf & Stock Publishers, 2005.

McIlwain, Trevor. *The Chronological Approach to Evangelism and Church Planting.* Sanford, FL: New Tribes Mission, 1985.

McIlwain, Trevor. *The Chronological Approach to Evangelism and Church Planting.* With Ruth Brendle. Sanford, FL: New Tribes Mission, 1981.

McIlwain, Trevor, and Nancy Everson. *Building on Firm Foundations: Guidelines for Evangelism and Teaching Believers,* Vol. 1. Sanford, FL: New Tribes Mission, 1987.

———. *Firm Foundations: Creation to Christ.* Sanford, FL: New Tribes Mission, Inc., 1991.

McKnight, Scot. "The 8 Marks of a Robust Gospel." *Christianity Today* 53, no. 3 (2008) 36–39.

Michell, Brian John. "The Role of Missionary Partnerships and Closure in Indigenous Church Development: A Malaysian Case Study." DMiss diss., Asia Graduate School of Theology, 2004.

Miller, David. "Scripture and the *Wall Street Journal.*" *Christianity Today* 51, no. 11 (2007) 33.

Moll, Rob. "Missions Incredible." *Christianity Today* 50, no. 3 (2006) 28–34.

Moltmann, Jurgen. *The Trinity and Kingdom.* London: SCM, 1981.

Montgomery, Jim. *DAWN 2000: 7 Million Churches To Go*. Pasadena, CA: William Carey Library, 1989.

Moreau, Scott A. "Short-Term Missions in the Context of Missions Inc." In *Effective Engagement in Short-Term Missions: Doing It Right*, edited by Robert J. Priest, 1–33. Pasadena, CA: William Carey Library, 2008.

Morgan, Timothy C. "After the Aloha Shirts." *Christianity Today* 52, no. 10 (2008) 42–45.

Mortenson, Greg, and David Oliver Relin. *Three Cups of Tea: One Man's Journey to Promote Peace . . . One School at a Time*. New York: Penguin, 2007.

Murphy, Mary. "Bring Hope to a Ravaged Nation." *Purpose Driven Connection* 1, no. 1 (2009) 42–47, 50–51, 55–56.

Myers, Bryant L. *Walking with the Poor: Principles and Practices of Transformational Development*. Maryknoll, NY: Orbis, 1999.

Naja, Ben. *Releasing the Workers of the Eleventh Hour: The Global South and the Task Remaining*. Pasadena, CA: William Carey Library, 2007.

Neely, Alan. "Missiology." In *Evangelical Dictionary of World Missions*, edited by A. Scott Moreau, 633–35. Grand Rapids, MI: Baker Books, 2000.

Neighbour, Ralph, Jr., and Lorna Jenkins, eds. *Where Do We Go from Here? A Guidebook for the Cell Group Church*. Houston, TX: Touch Publications, Inc., 1990.

Nevius, John. *Planting and Development of Missionary Churches*. Philadelphia: Reformed and Presbyterian Publishers, 1958.

Newbigin, Lesslie. *Foolishness to the Greeks: The Gospel and Western Culture*. Grand Rapids, MI: William B. Eerdmans, 1986.

Noll, Mark A. *The New Shape of World Christianity: How American Experience Reflects Global Faith*. Downers Grove, IL: InterVarsity, 2009.

Nyquist, J. Paul. *There Is No Time*. Portage, MI: Fidlar Doubleday, 2006.

Ortiz, Manuel. *One New People: Models for Developing a Multiethnic Church*. Downers Grove, IL: InterVarsity Press, 1996.

Ott, Craig, and Gene Wilson. *Global Church Planting: Biblical Principles and Best Practices for Multiplication*. Grand Rapids, MI: Baker Academic, 2011.

Packer, James I. "The Christian's Purpose in Business." In *Biblical Principles & Business, Vol. 3: The Practice*. Christians in the Market Place Series, edited by Richard C. Chewning. Colorado Springs: NavPress, (1990) 16–25.

Palmer, Parker J. *The Courage to Teach: Exploring the Inner Landscape of a Teacher's Life*. San Francisco: Jossey-Bass, 1998.

Patterson, George, and Richard Scoggins. *Church Multiplication Guide: Helping Churches to Reproduce Locally and Abroad*. Pasadena, CA: William Carey Library, 1993.

Payne, J. D. *Missional House Churches*. Waynesboro, GA: Paternoster Press, 2008.

———. *Discovering Church Planting: An Introduction to the Whats, Whys, and Hows of Global Church Planting*. Colorado Springs, CO: Paternoster, 2009.

Perspectives on the World Christian Movement [organization website]. Online: http://www.perspectives.org/site/pp.aspx?c=eqLLIoOFKrF&b=2806295

Pickett, Waskom J. *Christian Mass Movements in India*. New York: Abingdon, 1933.

Post, Ted, director. *Magnum Force*. Motion picture. Burbank, CA: Warner Bros., 1973.

Prahalad, C. K. *Bottom of the Pyramid: Eradicating Poverty Through Profits*. Upper Saddle River, NJ: Wharton School Publishing, 2006.

Priest, Robert J. "'Linking Social Capital' Through STM Partnerships." *Journal of Latin American Theology: Christian Reflections from the Latino South* 2, no. 2 (2007) 175–189.

Priest, Robert J., ed. *Effective Engagement in Short-Term Missions: Doing It Right!* Pasadena, CA: William Carey Library, 2008.

Rapaille, Clotaire. *The Culture Code: An Ingenious Way to Understand Why People Around the World Live and Buy as They Do*. New York: Doubleday Broadway, 2006.

Reymond, Robert L. *Paul, Missionary Theologian: A Survey of His Missionary Labours and Theology*. Rossshire, UK: Christian Focus Publications, 2000.

Richardson, Don. *Peace Child*. Ventura, CA: Regal Books, 1975.

Rickett, Daniel. *Building Strategic Relationships: A Practical Guide to Partnering with Non-Western Missions*. STEM Press, 2008.

Ridderbos, Herman N. *Paul: An Outline of His Theology*. Grand Rapids, MI: William B. Eerdmans, 1975.

Robert, Dana Lee. *Christian Mission: How Christianity Became a World Religion*. Chichester, UK: Wiley-Blackwell, 2009.

Roberts, Bob, Jr. *Transformation: How Glocal Churches Transform Live and the World*. Grand Rapids, MI: Zondervan Publishing, 2006.

———. *Glocalization: How Followers of Jesus Engage A Flat World*. Grand Rapids, MI: Zondervan, 2007.

———. *The Multiplying Church: The New Math for Starting New Churches*. Grand Rapids, MI: Zondervan, 2008.

Romo, Oscar I. *American Mosaic Church Planting in Ethnic America*. Nashville, TN: Broadman, 1993.

Rundle, Steve, and Tom Steffen. *Great Commission Companies: The Emerging Role of Business in Missions*. Downers Grove, IL: InterVarsity, 2003.

Russell, Walter B., III. "An Alternative Suggestion for the Purpose of Romans." *Bibliotheca Sacra* 145, no. 578 (1988) 174–184.

Saint, Steve. *The Great Omission. Fulfilling Christ's Commission Completely*. Seattle, WA: YWAM, 2001.

Sanneh, Lamin. *Disciples of All Nations: Pillars of World Christianity*. New York: Oxford University Press, 2008.

Saturation Church Planting International. "SCPI Mission and Vision." Online: http://www.scpi.org/scpi-mission-and-vision

Sayers, Dorothy. *Creed or Chaos*. New York: Harcourt, Brace, and Co., 1949. Chap 1. Online: http://www.gutenberg.ca/ebooks/sayers-greatest/sayers-greatest-00-h .html#ch01greatest.

Scherer, James A. *Missionary Go Home!* Englewood Cliffs, NJ: Prentice-Hall, 1964.

Schnabel, Eckhard J. *Paul the Missionary: Realities, Strategies, and Methods*. Downers Grove, IL: InterVarsity, 2008.

Schwarz, Christian A. *Natural Church Development: A Guide to Eight Essential Qualities of Healthy Churches*. Carol Stream, IL: ChurchSmart Resources, 1996.

Schwartz, Glenn. *When Charity Destroys Dignity: Overcoming Unhealthy Dependency in the Christian Movement*, Bloomington, IN: AuthorHouse, 2007.

Shaw, Susan M. *Storytelling in Religious Education*. Birmingham, AL: Religious Education Press, 1999.

Shenk, David W., and Ervin R. Stutzman. *Creating Communities of the Kingdom: New Testament Models of Church Planting*. Scottdale, PA: Herald Press, 1988.

Silvoso, Ed. *That None Should Perish: How to Reach Entire Cities for Christ Through Prayer Evangelism.* Ventura, CA: Regal, 1994.

Simpson, Wolfgang. *Houses That Change the World.* Waynesboro, GA: Authentic Media, 2001.

Sinclair, Daniel. *A Vision of the Possible: Pioneer Church Planting in Teams.* Waynesboro, GA: Authentic Media, 2006.

Slack, James B., and J. O. Terry. *Chronological Bible Storying: A Methodology for Presenting the Gospel to Oral Communicators.* New Orleans: International Mission Board of the Southern Baptist Convention, 1998.

Smith, John [pseud.]. "MBB Church, Inc. in Bangladesh: Overcoming the Destructive Effects of Naïve Western Funding." No date. Online: http://www.hopec.org/board/board_2/read_f.php?board_code=hopeccol&num=44&page=2&list_num=6

Stafford, Tim. "More Partners at the Table." *Christianity Today* 54, no.1 (January 2010) 40–43.

"Status of Global Mission, 2010, in Context of 20th and 21st Centuries." *International Bulletin of Missionary Research,* 34, no. 1 (2010) 36.

Steffen, Tom A. "Don't Show the Jesus Film." *Evangelical Missions Quarterly* 29, no. 3 (1993) 272–275.

———. *Passing the Baton: Church Planting That Empowers.* 2nd ed. La Habra, CA: Center for Organization & Ministry Development, 1997.

———. "Flawed Evangelism and Church Planting." *Evangelical Missions Quarterly* 34, no. 4 (1998a) 428–435.

———. "Foundational Roles of Symbol and Narrative in the (Re)construction of Reality and Relationships." *Missiology: An International Review* 26 no., 4 (1998b) 477–494.

———. "Caring for GenXers." In *Caring for the Harvest Force in the 21st Century,* edited by Tom A. Steffen and F. Douglas Pennoyer, 213–230. EMS Series no. 9. Pasadena, CA: William Carey Library, 2001.

———. "Missiology's Journey for Acceptance in the Educational World." *Missiology: An International Review* 31, no. 2 (2003) 131–153.

———. *Reconnecting God's Story to Ministry: Crosscultural Storytelling at Home and Abroad.* Rev. ed. Waynesboro, GA: Authentic Media, 2005.

———. "Making God the Hero-King of the Great Commission Company." *Mission Frontiers* 29, no. 6. (2007) 14–16.

———. "Pedagogical Conversions: From Propositions to Story and Symbol." *Missiology: An International Review* 38, no. 2 (2010) 141–159.

Steffen, Tom, and Michael Barnett, eds. *Business as Mission: From Impoverishment to Empowerment.* Pasadena, CA: William Carey Library, 2006.

Steffen, Tom, and Lois McKinney Douglas. *Encountering Missionary Life and Times: Preparing for Intercultural Ministry.* Grand Rapids, MI: Baker Academic, 2008.

Steffen, Tom A., and J. O. Terry. "The Sweeping Story of Scripture Taught Through Time." *Missiology: An International Review* 35, no. 3 (2007) 315–335.

Stetzer, Ed. *Planting Missional Churches: Planting a Church That's Biblically Sound and Reaching People in Culture.* Nashville, TN: Broadman & Holman Academic, 2006.

———. "The Gospel, the Kingdom, and Evangelicalism: Younger Evangelicals Consider the Balance of Presence and Proclamation." A paper presented at the American Society for Church Growth, Biola University, La Mirada, CA, November 14, 2008.

Stetzer, Ed, and David Putman. *Breaking the Missional Code. Your Church Can Become a Missionary in Your Community.* Nashville, TN: Broadman & Holman Academic, 2006.

Strauss, Robert, and Tom Steffen. "Change the Worldview . . . Change the World." *Evangelical Missions Quarterly* 45, no. 4 (2009) 458–464.

Swartley, Keith E., ed. *Encountering the World of Islam.* Waynesboro, GA: Authentic Media, 2005.

Thumma, Scott, and Warren Bird. "Not Who You Think They Are: A Profile of the People Who Attend America's Megachurches." Released June 9, 2009. Online: http://hirr. hartsem.edu/megachurch_attender_report.htm

Thumma, Scott, and Dave Travis. *Beyond Megachurch Myths: What We Can Learn from America's Largest Churches.* San Francisco: Jossey-Bass, 2007.

Timmis, Stephen, ed. *Multiplying Churches: Reaching Today's Communities Through Church Planting.* Hearn, Rossshire, UK: Christian Focus Publications, 2000.

Tippett, Alan R. *People Movements in Southern Polynesia.* Chicago, IL: Moody Press, 1971.

Vanhoozer, Kevin J. *The Drama of Doctrine: A Canonical Linguistic Approach to Christian Theology.* Louisville, KY: Westminster John Knox Press, 2005.

Vicedom, George F. *Church and People in New Guinea.* World Christian Handbooks, no. 38. London: United Society for Christian Literature, 1961.

Villón, Joaquin Alegre. "Short-Term Missions: Experiences and Perspectives from Callao, Peru." *Journal of Latin American Theology: Christian Reflections from the Latino South* 2, no. 2 (2007) 119–138.

Wagner, Peter C. *Church Planting for a Greater Harvest: A Comprehensive Guide.* Ventura, CA: Regal Books, 1990.

———. *The Healthy Church: Avoiding and Curing the Nine Diseases That Can Afflict Any Church.* Ventura, CA: Regal Books, 1996.

Warneck, Johannes G. *The Living Christ and Dying Heathenism: The Experiences of a Missionary in Animistic Heathendom.* Grand Rapids, MI: Baker Book House, 1954.

Warren, Rick. *The Purpose Driven Church: Growth Without Compromising Your Message and Mission.* Grand Rapids, MI: Zondervan, 1995.

Warren, Rick, and Kay Warren. "Peace Plan." *Online Newsroom* website. Online: www .rickwarrennews.com/peace_plan.htm

Weber, Hans Ruedi. *Communicating the Gospel to Illiterates.* London: SCM Press, 1957.

———. *Power: Focus for a Biblical Theology.* Geneva: WCC Publications, 1981.

Wells, David F. *No Place for Truth or Whatever Happened to Evangelical Theology?* Grand Rapids, MI: William B. Eerdmans, 1993.

Wharton, Edith. "Vesalius in Zante (1564)." *North American Review* 175, no. 552 (1902) 625–631.

Wilkinson, Bruce. *The Dream Giver.* Portland, OR: Multnomah, 2003.

———. *The Prayer of Jabez: Breaking Through to the Blessed Life.* Portland, OR: Multnomah, 2005.

Wilson, J. Christy. *Today's Tentmakers: Self-Support: An Alternative Model for Worldwide Witness.* Eugene, OR: Wipf & Stock, 2002.

Wilson, Sarah Hinlicky. "Blessed Are the Barren." *Christianity Today* 51, no. 12 (2007) 22–28.

Winter, Ralph D. "The Highest Priority: Cross-Cultural Evangelism." Paper originally presented at 1974 Lausanne Congress on World Evangelization, Switzerland. First printed in *Let the Earth Hear His Voice: International Congress on World Evangelization*, edited by J. D. Douglas, 213–225. Minneapolis, MN: World Wide Publications, 1975. Online: http://www.lausanne.org/documents/lau1docs/0226.pdf

———. "The Gravest Danger: The Re-Amateurization of Mission." *Missions Frontiers* 18, no. 2 (1996a) 5.

———. "The Re-Amateurization of Missions." *Occasional Bulletin of the Evangelical Missiological Society* (Spring 1996b). Online: http://www.missiology.org/EMS/bulletins/winter.htm

———. "Four Men, Three Eras, Two Transitions: Modern Missions." In *Perspectives on the World Christian Movement: A Reader*, 3rd ed., edited by Ralph D. Winter and Steven C. Hawthorne, 253–261. Pasadena, CA: William Carey Library, 1999.

Winter, Ralph D., and Steve Hawthorne, eds. *Perspectives on the World Christian Movement*. Pasadena, CA: William Carey Library, 2009.

Wright, Christopher J. H. *The Mission of God: Unlocking the Bible's Grand Narrative*. Downers Grove, IL: InterVarsity, 2006.

Wright, N. T. *The New Testament and the People of God*. Minneapolis, MN: Augsburg Fortress, 1992.

Wuthnow, Robert. *Boundless Faith: The Global Outreach of American Churches*. Berkeley, CA: University of California Press, 2009.

Yamamori, Tetsunao. *God's New Envoys: A Bold Strategy for Penetrating Closed Countries*. Portland, OR: Multnomah, 1987.

Yamamori, Tetsunao, and Kenneth A. Eldred, eds, *On Kingdom Business: Transforming Missions Through Entrepreneurial Strategies*, Wheaton, IL: Crossway, 2003.

Yancey, Philip. "God at Large." *Christianity Today* 45, no 2 (2001) 136.

Young, William P. *The Shack*. Newbury Park, CA: Windblown Media, 2007.

Zakaria, Fareed. *The Post-American World*. New York: W.W. Norton and Company, 2008.

Zogby, John. *The Way We'll Be: The Zogby Report on the Transformation of the American Dream*. New York: Random House, 2008.

Contributors

Ben Beckner served for seven years as visiting professor of mission and church planting at Trinity Bible College in Kursk, Russia. Since 1984, he has served with ReachGlobal as church planter, missions trainer, and consultant in French-speaking Europe. Ben has a DMin from Gordon-Conwell Theological Seminary.

Dr. Monroe Brewer serves as International Director for the Center for Church Based Training in Richardson, Texas. He is also on staff with CrossGlobal Link, located in Wheaton, Illinois. Monroe earned a DMiss from the Cook School of Intercultural Studies at Biola University.

Dr. Don Finley and his wife, Angie, are missionaries with Converge Worldwide/Baptist General Conference and have served twenty-two years in Brazil and Central Asia. Don earned his PhD in Intercultural Studies from the E. Stanley Jones School of World Mission and Evangelism at Asbury Theological Seminary.

Mike Griffis, a career missionary with New Tribes Mission, is presently serving in West New Britain, Papua New Guinea. Mike has an MA in Language Development (sociolinguistics concentration) from SIL's Graduate Institute of Applied Linguistics in Dallas.

Scott Harris and his family served for over a decade with SIM in West Africa and in Charlotte, North Carolina. He currently works in Kansas City, Missouri, on Avant's Executive Team and holds responsibility for field ministries.

Dr. Gary Hipp, MD, and his family served as missionaries for ten years in East Africa with Mission: Moving Mountains (M:MM). They moved back to the United States in 1995 to lead M:MM and to travel as non-residential Discipling for Development mentors.

Jerry Hogshead and his wife, Marilyn, currently facilitate church-planting partnerships in South Asia. They formerly served with their children in the Philippines and in the training and coaching of missionaries from North America and the Majority World. Jerry has an MDiv from Fuller Theological Seminary.

Jay Jackson, a long-time friend of the author, is presently the CEO of Alteco (Amazon and Lowland Tribal Empowerment Coalition), whose mission is "to strengthen the church where the church is, [and] to send the church where the church is not."

Kaikou Maisu is an elder in the Ata church in Sege, located in the tropical lowlands of West New Britain, Papua New Guinea.

Judy Manna and her husband, Mike, have served with Youth Ministry International in Kiev, Ukraine, for eight years. Judy is a homemaker and loves being a mother of four and a support to her husband, often hosting students and holding church activities in their home.

Kenn Oke currently serves as Avant's Europe Regional Director and lives with his family in Spain, where they began facilitative ministry among missionaries in 1996.

Dr. A. Sue Russell served in S. E. Asia for fifteen years. Presently she teaches anthropology and early Christian history at Biola University. She holds master's degrees in Intercultural Studies, Christian History, Divinity, and Theology. She earned a PhD in Linguistics and a Doctorate in Missiology, and she is completing a doctorate in Early Christian History at UCLA.

Dr. Robert Strauss is President and CEO of Worldview Resource Group in Colorado Springs, Colorado. Bob earned his DMiss from the Cook School of Intercultural Studies at Biola University.

Peter Swann is Executive Director of Aid Sudan, an interdenominational nonprofit missionary organization working among southern Sudanese in the United States and in southern Sudan. Peter and his wife, Shauna, have two children and live in Houston, Texas. Peter is presently completing a doctorate in intercultural studies at Fuller Theological Seminary.

Bryan Thomas and his family served as missionaries for twenty-eight years in the Philippines, Russia, and Central Asia. Presently he works in financial advising and operates his Nashville-based consulting firm, L-Evate, which specializes in organizational development and executive coaching.

Diane Thomas served overseas with her family for twenty-eight years. She now consults through East West Ministries International in language/culture acquisition, women's ministry, and business as mission. A grandmother of four, Diane also manages her own online business, www.bybella.com.

Dr. Mike Wilson and his wife, Mary Jo, have been serving as missionaries in facilitative church development in Tokyo and Okinawa for nearly fifteen years. Mike earned his DMiss from the Cook School of Intercultural Studies at Biola University.

Dr. Sherwood G. Lingenfelter (PhD, University of Pittsburgh) is provost and senior vice president at Fuller Theological Seminary. He is the author of *Transforming Culture, Agents of Transformation, Ministering Cross-Culturally* (with Marvin K. Mayers), and *Teaching Cross-Culturally* (with Judith E. Lingenfelter), as well as several volumes on anthropology.

Dr. Tom Steffen and his family served with New Tribes Mission for twenty years, fifteen of which were in the Philippines, planting churches among the Ifugao and consulting for the agency. He is Professor of Intercultural Studies and directs the Doctor of Missiology program in the Cook School of Intercultural Studies at Biola University in La Mirada, California. His books include *Encountering Missionary Life and Work* (with Lois McKinney Douglas), *Great Commission Companies: The Emerging Role of Business in Missions* (with Steve Rundle), *Passing the Baton: Church Planting That Empowers,* and *Reconnecting God's Story to Ministry: Crosscultural Storytelling at Home and Abroad.*

Index